It's All About Islam

Yahiya Emerick

Level 8

© Copyright 2014 Noorart Inc.

All rights reserved. No part of this book may be reproduced or transmitted in any form, or by any means, electronic or mechanical, including photocopying and recording, or by any information storage retrieval system, without permission in writing from the publisher.

First printing: August 2014

Published and distributed by:

E-mail: *info@noorart.com*
www.noorart.com

Printed in USA
ISBN: 9781933269153

In the Name of Allah, The Most Gracious,
The Most Merciful

Author:
    Yahiya Emerick

Chief Editor:
    Noor Saadeh

Religious Content Editor:
    Sheikh Amin Amer, PhD

Content Editors:
    Shaza Khan, PhD
    Farheen Khan

Language Editors:
    Kara Brunson
    Carole Strum

Production Manager:
    Ammar Saadeh

Designers:
    Mohammad A.Shream
    Wafa'a Abu-Hilaleh

A Note from Noorart

Noorart is dedicated to providing quality educational materials for Muslim and Arab youth throughout the world. The Noorart Islamic Studies Curriculum offers a comprehensive middle-school curriculum that promotes student reflection, critical thinking and action-oriented behavior, through the use of spiral methodology— that is, building upon key topics and concepts in greater detail each successive year. Additionally, new material is introduced in developmentally-appropriate increments. Students build upon their prior knowledge, while cultivating a deeper understanding in a logical and progressive format.

Each textbook in the Noorart Islamic Studies Curriculum is comprised of lessons; beginning with a thoughtful statement or question designed to foster reflection, students build upon their Muslim identity and beliefs about Islam, Allah ﷻ and the lives of the prophets. The accessible language used throughout helps students take ownership of the Islamic beliefs, practices and information presented in the textbook. The chapters conclude with review questions that encourage students to reflect on and discuss the meanings of Qur'anic ayaat, ahadith and Islamic teachings. Textbooks also feature a glossary of vocabulary words with age-appropriate definitions as well an index for easy reference.

Using the latest method of textbook development, this edition has undergone intense scrutiny and review. It has been tested to ensure that the vocabulary and sentence structure are best suited for the targeted grade level. Additionally, an interdisciplinary approach towards teaching Islamic beliefs and history is cultivated through the content of this textbook. A new attractive feature offers updated, color images. An extensive listing of enrichment materials can be found in the latter pages of the book, to assist educators and provide instruction for students wishing to further explore topics of interest.

Additionally, this textbook has been examined by religious scholars to authenticate all Islamic information presented herein. While many areas of study include legitimate differences of opinion, this book has presented Islamic material in accordance with the majority opinion of religious scholars. Noorart, however, trusts that students are capable of exploring differences of opinion in the religious material presented in this book. Teachers are encouraged to engage students in projects and discussions that cultivate an appreciation for these differences. By following this approach, we pray that respect and tolerance for differences in opinions and schools of thought will be fostered among our students.

We believe that teachers and students are best suited to offer suggestions on how to improve future editions of these textbooks. Your comments and feedback will be welcomed at *textbookfeedback@noorart.com* and will guide us in our textbook development.

Author's Foreword

All praise is due to the One Who created humans with a will to survive and a mind to understand. We are the creatures who agreed to accept the responsibility of consciousness and self-awareness. Allah, the Exalted, did not force us to be self-aware. Indeed, He offered this blessing and responsibility to the rest of creation first, but there were rightly afraid of the consequences and burden. This mighty responsibility rests upon our shoulders.

Our task in life is clear: surrender our wills to the perfect will of Allah and then deal morally with our fellow man. In order to facilitate our understanding and choice of this way of life, Allah has revealed His guidance to humans throughout time. The only one message that remains preserved in its original form is the Holy Qur'an.

Islam is the last installment of Allah's codified guidance. There will be no new prophets or faiths to come. The Blessed Prophet Muhammad assured us of that. Allah has said, *"This day I have perfected your way of life for you and completed My favor upon you. I have chosen Islam (surrender to My will) as your way of life." (Qur'an 5:3)* This is the way we must follow ourselves and teach our children.

Having worked in Islamic schools for several years, I noticed the need for a new approach in teaching Islamic studies and studying the Qur'an. American-born and those children raised in the West respond to new and different methods of teaching as opposed to the more traditional methods found in many Muslim societies. Modern society encourages children to demand relevance, seek logic and question all as they learn in a language and style both stimulating and enjoyable.

Islam has attracted millions throughout the previous centuries for precisely these characteristics of questioning, reflection and its dominant call for logic and consonance. Recently this spirit of inquiry in the Muslim world has given way to dogmatism and close-mindedness, and a lack of stimulating dialogue and tolerance. The time for reawakening has come!

If our children associate Islam with ignorance, intolerance and backwardness, then we will have failed to keep Islam alive and vibrant within those generations who follow us. If children know and rightly understand the message of Islam, then they will be filled with an enthusiastic zeal to live by and to promote the *deen*. In addition, they will be encouraged to utilize all the technological advantages the modern world has to offer to make the deen of Allah prominent in the world, *insha'Allah*. The key is to instill in their hearts the truth of the Qur'an and, the message and relevance of Islam in their lives and their environment as they develop sincerity of *emaan* and *taqwa*.

We hope and pray for the mercy and reward of our Lord to aid us in this endeavor. May He grant us the best in this short life and in the next according to His mercy and compassion. May He protect us from the punishment of the grave and the trials of the Day of Judgment.
"Oh Allah, increase me in knowledge." Ameen.

Yahiya Emerick

How to Use This Book

It's All About Islam is a three-part series designed for the middle-school grades 6-8. Each successive book presents a continuation of the themes presented here. All textbooks contain an overview of the basic belief system of Islam, Islamic history and culture, geography, Muslim achievements and the Muslim experience in the West today. There are two ways to use this book.

Method One
The teacher introduces the topic with a story, lesson, question or example. These are provided on the first page of every lesson. The students write one- or two-sentence answers in their notebooks. Next, the students take turns reading the lesson aloud. The teacher should pause periodically to write notes on the board which the students should copy, then resume by adding supplementary information or ask and answer students' questions and concerns. This procedure should take about half an hour per lesson. Then, for the last 15 minutes of class, the students can work independently on the review questions at the end of each lesson.

Method Two
The teacher introduces the topic of the day with a story or example. Then he or she can develop the whole content of the lesson, adding information as desired. Here, the teacher acts as guide and moderator, being careful to allow students plenty of opportunity to interact and comment, rather than merely continuing to lecture. The book can be referenced as needed. Then the lesson in the textbook can be assigned as class work or homework. The students read the lesson on their own in class and answer the questions. This method is effective for the prepared and knowledgeable teacher.

Whichever method is followed, after the completion of a unit, the students should spend one class period working on the unit review exercise found at the end of each unit. This acts as a test review and the teacher can follow the students' progress and help them. In the following class, the teacher should give the test. It is recommended that the teacher review each lesson before beginning the class so to more effectively answer whatever questions that may arise.

There is no answer key provided for the teacher. The teacher should be familiar with the material and correcting the assignments should pose no problems. This also acts as a constant refresher for the teacher.

Each of the units covers different themes. Activities are preceded by a heading at the top of each page. The title contained therein offers an adequate explanation of what skill or issue the lesson will explore. Under the heading there will be a reading selection or explanation of the topic, followed by Review Exercise.

The teacher is advised to have multiple copies of the Qur'an in the class for demonstration, access and supplementary material for the students. This is in keeping with our goal of acquainting the students with the Qur'an and how to search it for reference.

Tips for Teachers

The Noorart Islamic Studies Curriculum aims to increase the students' knowledge and application of Islamic beliefs and practices. It is part of a multi-faceted approach, including textbook, enrichment literature and extension activities that together make Islam accessible, understandable and applicable to students' lives. The way in which the curriculum comes alive, however, is through the teacher's implementation, which can occur in several different ways. The following tips for teachers can improve the overall impact of the curriculum. These tips draw upon the latest educational research and practices, which have been proven to enhance learning outcomes.

- **Access Prior Knowledge:**
    - New material is built upon what students have already learned or experienced and each student comes to class with different prior knowledge of the topic presented.
    - In order to understand what your students already know about the topic, different graphic organizers can be used, such as a **KWL Chart.** The **KWL Chart** encourages students to list what they **K**now, **W**ant to Know and what they have **L**earned. The first two columns, **K**now and **W**ant to Know, can be filled prior to the lesson, whereas the **L**earned column can be completed after the lesson is taught.
    - A concept map can be created in small groups to connect the upcoming lesson to prior knowledge that they believe is related to the topic. The teacher should walk around the classroom to facilitate and guide students to make more connections as they create these concept maps. The concept map can be revisited after the lesson is taught to build upon their prior knowledge and form new understanding of the material.

- **Differentiate Instruction:**
    - In an effort to maximize learning outcomes for every student, the teacher may create opportunities for providing students with background information and enrichment materials as needed. Various modes of teaching the subject matter should be used, including written, audio-visual and performance-based. Whole class, group and individual learning opportunities should also be employed.
    - For students who lack background information on upcoming lessons or topics of study, provide opportunities to learn about the topic by integrating background information about the lesson in daily classroom routines.
    - For students who have already learned the content and need more challenging material, encourage them to look up the ayaat and ahadith that are referenced in the lesson. Ask questions that encourage them to apply the lessons to their life and promote higher-order thinking.
    - At the end of each unit, encourage all students to choose a book from the list of enrichment literature and create a book report to share with peers. The book report can be a traditional written report, or it can be more creative, such as an artistic depiction or video report.

- **Build a Resource-Rich Classroom:**
    - Have copies of the Qur'an in the class for demonstration, access and supplementary material for the students.
    - Identify websites that allow students or the teacher to search for relevant *ahadith*, in order to learn more about the Prophet's ﷺ example and teachings in relation to the topic.
    - *Hadith* compilations are another resource, in place of websites, that can be used to learn more about a topic.

- **Culturally Relevant Pedagogy:**
    - Encourage students to apply the lessons to their daily life by using language, examples and thought-provoking questions that relate to the students' concerns and culture. For example, ask: "How would you feel if you were in their shoes?" Or "How does this lesson help you deal with a personal issue you are facing?"
    - Get to know what your students like and dislike in terms of technology or popular culture in order to guide them towards things that are Islamically acceptable and preferred.
    - Ask students to make connections between the lesson and their lives in whole group, small group and individual exercises. Teachers may direct students, for example, to "Work together with two other students to summarize the main points from this lesson. Then, come up with three ways you can apply these lessons to your lives."

- **Use Authentic Assessment:**
    - Authentic assessments are distinguished from traditional assessment methods because they encourage students to:
        1) Perform a task.
        2) Focus on real life.
        3) Construct or apply something.
        4) Structure their project.
        5) Use direct evidence.

    - In addition to the unit review, develop assessments that are personally meaningful to the student, center on real life problems and develop daily life skills, such as community service projects, science or history exhibits, role plays, or mini-business ventures.

- **Use Rubrics to Assess Student Understanding:**
    - Use rubrics, which are criteria-based grading tools, to understand what students have learned from the lesson. Rubrics are shared with students before the assignment is given, so that they are fully aware of the criteria that will be used to assess their work. Then, when students submit their work, they are graded based on the detailed criteria listed in the rubric.

Dr. Shaza Khan

Tips for Readers

1. The most useful translations used in this book are ranked as follows:

   1. *The Noble Qur'an* by Mufti Taqi Usmani
   2. *The Meaning of the Holy Qur'an in Today's English* by Yahiya Emerick
   3. *The Noble Qur'an* by Dr. Muhsin Khan & Taqi-Ud-Din Hilali
   4. *The Noble Qur'an* by Abdalhaqq and Aisha Bewley
   5. *The Holy Qur'an* by 'Abdallah Yusuf 'Ali

2. Selections from the Qur'an and hadith have been presented in a specific font and style for easy recognition:

   - **Qur'an:**

   Truly the way of life that Allah accepts is Islam. Surat Al 'Imran (The Family of 'Imran) 3:19

   - **Hadith:**
   Abu Huraira narrated that the Blessed Prophet said, "Every child is born following their Fitrah (i.e. they are a natural Muslim). It is the parents who make them a Jew, Christian or Zoroastrian (ancient Persian religion)." (Al Bukhari & Muslim)

   عَنْ أَبِي هُرَيْرَةَ ، أَنَّ رَسُولَ اللهِ ﷺ : «كُلُّ مَوْلُودٍ يُولَدُ عَلَى الْفِطْرَةِ، فَأَبَوَاهُ يُهَوِّدَانِهِ أَوْ يُنَصِّرَانِهِ أَوْ يُمَجِّسَانِهِ»
   رَوَاهُ الْبُخَارِيُّ وَمُسْلِمٌ

3. Glorifications used in this book:

   - (Arabic: عز و جل ﷻ, 'azza wa jal). "Glorified and Sublime be He." This phrase usually appears after the name of Allah in Islamic texts. Saying this phrase is seen as an act of reverence and devotion towards Allah among Muslims. It can also be translated in English as: "Mighty and Majestic be He" or "May His Majesty be Exalted."
   - (Arabic: صلى الله عليه وسلم ﷺ, salla Allahu 'alay-he wa-sallam). "Peace and blessings of Allah be upon him." This expression follows specifically after uttering the name of Prophet Muhammad, although the phrase "May Allah bless him and grant him peace" may also be used.
   - (Arabic: عليه السلام ﷺ, 'alayhi as-salam). "Peace be upon him." Muslims say this phrase after uttering or hearing the name of any of the prophets.
   - (Arabic: رضي الله عنه ﷺ Radhiallahu 'anhu). "May Allah be pleased with him." This phrase is usually uttered after a Companion's name. There are grammatical variations used after the names of female Companions or when more than one person is mentioned at the same time. For females, it is (Arabic: رضي الله عنها ﷺ Radhiallahu 'anha) and for more than one person, it is (Arabic: رضي الله عنهم ﷺ Radhiallahu 'anhum).

Contents

Lesson	**Unit 1: Qur'anic Research Skills**	
1	How Do I Study Islam?	15
	Skill Builder	
2	What is a Translation?	20
3	What is Transliteration?	23
4	How Do I Use the Qur'an?	25
	Review Exercise	

Lesson	**Unit 2: Understanding the Qur'an**	
5	How Was the Qur'an Revealed?	33
6	How Was the Qur'an Recorded?	36
7	The Qur'an Never Changes	39
8	The Book of Miracles	43
9	The Qur'an and Science	47
	Review Exercise	

Lesson	**Unit 3: What Is Islam?**	
10	What Is Islam All About?	58
11	Who Is a Muslim?	67
12	Why Some Don't Believe	72
	Review Exercise	

Lesson	**Unit 4: The Islamic View of Creation**	
13	The Creation of the Universe	79
14	Islam and Evolution	86
15	The Origin of Humans	91
16	Why Am I Here?	102
	Review Exercise	

Lesson	**Unit 5: Tales of Ancient Days**	
17	Who Were Adam ﷺ & Hawwa?	112
18	Nuh ﷺ and the Great Flood	116
19	Hud ﷺ: The Ancient Prophet	122
	Skill Builder	
20	The Quest of Ibrahim ﷺ	130
21	The Three Unknown Prophets	139
22	The Story of Yusuf ﷺ	142
	Review Exercise	

Lesson	**Unit 6: Bani Isra'il**	
23	From the Nile River to the Desert	154
24	Prophet Musa ﷺ the Leader	160
25	The Wanderers	166
26	Sulayman ﷺ and Balqees	174
27	Master of the Two Horns	180
	Review Exercise	

Lesson	Unit 7: The Legacy of Prophet 'Isa ﷺ	
28	The Family of 'Imran	186
29	The Struggle of Maryam ﷺ	191
30	The Message of the Injeel	195
31	The Sleepers of the Cave	204
	Review Exercise	

Lesson	Unit 8: Biographies of Companions	
32	Who Was Um Salamah ﷺ?	212
33	Mu'ath bin Jabal ﷺ	216
34	The Kitten Man ﷺ	221
35	Fatimah ﷺ, Jewel of Islam	224
36	Salman Al Faresi ﷺ	228
37	Julaybib ﷺ, the Unlikely Hero	232
38	Abu Dharr Al Ghifari ﷺ	235
39	Asma' ﷺ bint Abu Bakr	239
40	Other Sahaba ﷺ of Note	243
	Review Exercise	

Lesson	Unit 9: Timeless Teachings: Fiqh and Shari'ah	
41	Fiqh for Life: Islamic Law	249
42	What Are 'Schools of Thought'?	253
43	What Is Halal & Haram Food?	259
44	Muslims & Making Money	263
45	Who Makes the Best Friend?	267
46	How Is a Marriage Contract Made?	270
	Review Exercise	

Lesson	**Unit 10: Islam in Society**	
47	Building Islamic Character: The Essentials	277
48	The Muslim Family	281
49	Islamic Society: Ideals and Realities	286
50	An Islamic State: The Past and the Future	292
	Skill Builder	
	Review Exercise	

References Section 303

UNIT 1
Qur'anic Research Skills

1 How Do I Study Islam?

 **WHAT TO LEARN**

In order for something to be a complete way of life, what must it include?

 VOCABULARY

Islam   Allah   Sunnah
Muslim   Qur'an

 THINK ABOUT IT

What is the best way to learn about Islam?

The Arabic Roots of Islam

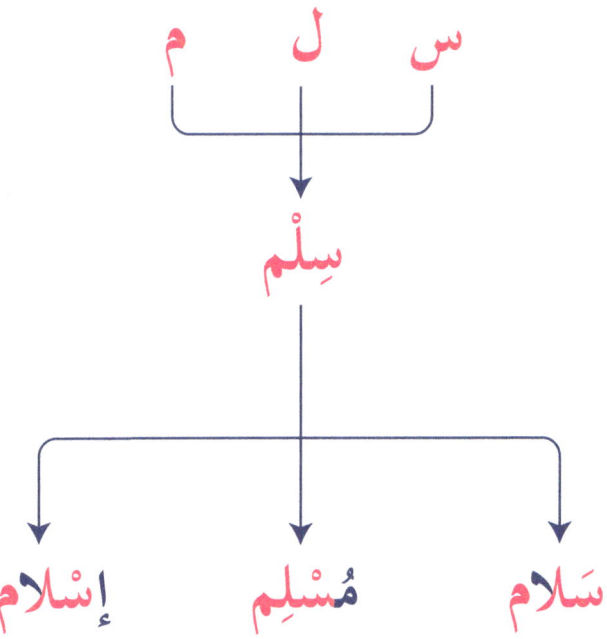

A. What Is Islam?

Islam is the way of life that is followed by approximately one billion people around the world. Muslims, or people who follow the Islamic way of life, comprise the majority population in over 50 countries. In addition, the global Muslim population is rapidly increasing every year. In the United States, for example, Islam is considered the fastest growing religion in the country.

The word **Islam** إسْلام comes from the Arabic word that means peace and surrender. The full religious definition implies that when you submit your life to God, you can find peace in your soul. Living Islam helps you learn to be patient when you face tests and trials in your life. The word **Muslim** مُسْلِم means a person who submits to God by following the guidance of the Qur'an and the Sunnah of Prophet Muhammad ﷺ, thereby finding inner peace.

Many of the spiritual traditions in the world are just philosophies. Islam, however, is a complete way of life that fulfills our physical, spiritual, emotional and psychological needs. The goal of Islam is more than praying five times a day. Islam helps people live in harmony with nature and with the society around them. Additionally, Islam provides a blueprint and a set of principles for how to turn societies into God-oriented communities; this sets Islam apart from all other faith traditions.

The basis of Islam is the belief in a Creator, or God, known as **Allah** الله in the Arabic language. The name Allah literally means 'the God.' Allah is not a God distinct from that of Judeo-Christian tradition. Even Arabic-speaking Christians use the name Allah when they refer to God. In fact, the name Allah is directly related to the ancient Hebrew term for God, *Eloh*. Both languages (Arabic and Hebrew) are Semitic and spring from the same ancient roots. Muslims who speak English will use both terms, God and Allah, when they talk about their faith, but most prefer to use the name Allah.

15

B. What Is Our Purpose?

Billions of years ago, Allah caused the Universe to come into existence. He created natural laws and ordered every particle to move in accordance with His will. Therefore, the actions of atoms and other matter were determined by Allah rather than by some random occurrence.

On some planets, Allah allowed living organisms to develop. For example, Earth supports a highly complex ecosystem of plants and animals. After untold years later, Allah created human beings. They would be unlike any other creatures before them, as they were given the ability to choose their actions.

Everything Allah created functions according to its instincts and natural tendencies. Humans, however, are allowed to make their own decisions about how to live their lives. With this privilege, however, would come great responsibility.

Allah created a Universe free of disorder and chaos. As human societies developed, people could choose whether to use their sophisticated thinking skills for good or to misuse their intelligence and abilities by creating chaos and disorder all around them.

The way of life that Allah wants humans to choose is the one in which we use our intellect and emotions in the pursuit of the higher truth of Allah's Universe. There must be no giving in to anger, hatred, violence and greed. All of these emotions are to be controlled, lest we become similar to or worse than the animals.

And Allah created the heavens and earth in truth and so that every soul may be recompensed for what it has earned, and they will not be wronged. Surat Al Jatheyah (The Crouching) 45: 22

﴿وَخَلَقَ ٱللَّهُ ٱلسَّمَٰوَٰتِ وَٱلْأَرْضَ بِٱلْحَقِّ وَلِتُجْزَىٰ كُلُّ نَفْسٍۭ بِمَا كَسَبَتْ وَهُمْ لَا يُظْلَمُونَ﴾ سُورَةُ الجَاثِيَة 45: 22

To aid us in this quest, Allah chose prophets and communicated messages to them. They were like lighthouses in a storm, calling people to salvation in a troubled world. Sometimes Allah would send a message to a prophet that He wanted to survive for later generations to understand and practice. Yet all too often, people allowed themselves to be tempted by their desires, resulting in war, hatred and chaos on Earth.

Instead, those who follow Allah's guidance are promised a reward in the next life. Those who deny this truth will receive a punishment for turning their backs on God's message. They reject not only Allah's prophets but also human nature, which prompts them to be good.

They prefer to cover themselves in shame and evil. When the Universe comes to an end, and Allah collapses all matter back into its origins, all humans will be assembled together on the Day of Judgement to be judged for their actions. Of course, human beings are not perfect, and they never will be. Allah knows what He created; so for those who have sincerity and faith, Allah promises to forgive their sins and encompass them in His Mercy.

Allah made us, and He knows best how we can be good to others and protected from our inner weaknesses. Those people who recognize this truth and wish only to serve Allah are the ones who try their best to live their lives in accordance with the laws He revealed.

Previous prophets were sent to people throughout the world at different points in history. They include Ibrahim (Abraham), Musa (Moses), Salih and 'Isa (Jesus), to name a few; may Allah be pleased with them all. The last message that Allah sent to humanity was given to Muhammad, who was born in Arabia in the year 570 CE. (40:78)

This final message is in the form of the **Qur'an** قُرْآن **The Reading**. It is a book that elevates a person's mind and spirit to a higher level—a stage from which they can escape the hold of their animal instincts to stand up for what is right and to forbid what is wrong.

Allah said, *This Qur'an guides (people) to what is right and gives good news to the believers, who do good deeds, that they will have a splendid reward.* Surat Al Isra' (The Night Journey) 17: 9

﴿ إِنَّ هَٰذَا ٱلْقُرْءَانَ يَهْدِى لِلَّتِى هِىَ أَقْوَمُ وَيُبَشِّرُ ٱلْمُؤْمِنِينَ ٱلَّذِينَ يَعْمَلُونَ ٱلصَّٰلِحَٰتِ أَنَّ لَهُمْ أَجْرًا كَبِيرًا ﴾ سُورَةُ الإِسْرَاء 17:9

The person whose goal in life is serving his Creator will come to understand that the Islamic way is also the natural way.

C. How Do I Study Islam?

To study Islam, one must begin with the Qur'an and refer to it at every stage. Only then can a true understanding of Islam and our ultimate destiny be achieved.

Today, many Muslims have become disconnected from the message of the Qur'an and have not applied its lessons as they should. One reason for a weakened commitment to faith is due to materialism. This has transformed many societies around the world into wasteful consumer cultures.

The Muslim civilization went from being the most advanced in the world to becoming among the least advanced, within only the past few hundred years. What is encouraging, though, is that this trend can be reversed. In fact, Allah has promised in the Qur'an that those who uphold its message will be successful, both in this world and in the next!

Islam is the way of life that Allah established from the very beginning of time. If you examine the teachings of Islam, you realize that it is the same way of life that has been taught by all the prophets and wise people throughout history. This lifestyle has been given various names and has included different rituals according to the customs of the people to whom it was revealed. However, the core teachings of God's true prophets were always the same: submit to the universal teachings of God and do what is approved as right and good.

If we want to improve the condition of Muslims, and even those who are not yet Muslim, then we must reconnect with the message of the Qur'an. Only the Qur'an has survived to this day, unchanged as a guide for people as they journey through this brief stage of life. Allah said, *We (Allah) have made this Qur'an easy to remember. Is there anyone who would receive a reminder?* Surat Al Qamar (The Moon) 54: 40

﴿ وَلَقَدْ يَسَّرْنَا ٱلْقُرْءَانَ لِلذِّكْرِ فَهَلْ مِن مُّدَّكِرٍ ﴾ سُورَةُ القَمَر 54:40

The Qur'an is the source of guidance; the life of the prophet who bore it, Muhammad, is our example of how to put it into practice. The example of Prophet Muhammad, including everything about how he lived his life, is referred to as the **Sunnah** سُنَّة. This textbook uses both the Qur'an and the Sunnah as the primary sources for understanding Islam. If you learn how to understand the Qur'an and Sunnah, and live by what they mean, you can become a living example of the Qur'an.

In the exercises that follow, you will be asked to research the Qur'an for specific information and then to make sense of it for yourself. By doing so, you will reach a deeper understanding of Islam and be able to practice this way of life accordingly. May your study be fruitful and may you find your sense of purpose in this life. Ameen (Let it be so.).

IT'S ALL ABOUT ISLAM

What Others Say about the Qur'an

"Whenever I hear the Qur'an being chanted, it is as though I am listening to music... It is like the beating of my heart." *A.J. Arberry*

"...I read it (the Qur'an) cover to cover in two days. It was poetry to me." *Jacqualine Cosens*

"The most beautiful experience was reading the Qur'an...I read it and shed a million tears." *Mariola L. Szczesny*

Questions to Answer

1. Although Islam can be described as a 'religion,' what is a more suitable way to describe it?
2. What is the full definition of the word 'Muslim'?
3. What do humans possess that no other creatures have?
4. How does Allah ﷻ help humans distinguish right from wrong?
5. What is the Qur'an?

Define: Islam, Sunnah, Allah ﷻ.

Reflect: How can the whole Universe be described as Muslim? Observe the behavior of three things in nature that can support this statement.

Act: Consider the different activities you do throughout the day and write down how you feel doing each. At the end of the day, choose one activity that brought you the most peace and develop a plan for how you can implement that activity into your life everyday or for how you can do more of those activities throughout the day.

How Do I Find That Ayah?

How would you find an ayah, or verse, about a certain subject in the Qur'an? Flipping through the pages of the entire book would be time-consuming. It would be more efficient to look at the table of contents found at the front of the Qur'an or the index found at the back. The Qur'an is comprised of suwar and ayaat. So, for example, 4:64 would indicate the fourth chapter or surat An-Nisa, the Women, verse or ayah 64.

The table of contents lists the suwar or chapters that comprise the Qur'an. Alternatively, the index lists topics alphabetically and the specific ayaat that mention them. The most complete indexes of English meaning are found in editions by:

The Meaning of the Holy Qur'an by 'Abdallah Yusuf 'Ali
The Noble Qur'an by 'Abdalhaqq and Aisha Bewley
The Meaning of the Qur'an by Abul 'Ala Maududi
The Message of the Qur'an by Muhammad Asad
The Gracious Qur'an (the Parallel Edition: English and Arabic side-by-side) by Ahmad Zaki Hammad
The Glorious Qur'an by Adbul Majid Daryabadi
Interpretation of the Meaning of the Noble Qur'an by Darrussalam
The Qur'an by Oxford University Press

Today, online sites abound with easy search engines that use English meanings or even transliterated Arabic words to search with. Examples are: www.searchtruth.com, www.islamicity.com, www.quranexplorer.com and corpus.quran.com.

IQ Builders:

Build your 'Islamic Quotient (IQ) through Qur'anic research.

Use your Qur'an's index and table of contents to answer the following questions:

1. What is the surat number for the chapter named *Al Hijr*?
2. What are the Arabic and English names of Surat 20?
3. Name two suwar in which we read about Prophet Sulayman ﷺ.
4. Which surat comes before surat Al Hadid (The Iron)? Which surat comes after it?
5. How many references in the index are there for the name 'Hud'?
6. What is the Arabic name for the surat that is translated as 'The Women'?
7. What surat first mentions the Ka'bah?
8. What is the last surat that mentions Prophet Shu'aib ﷺ?
9. How many ayaat are there in surat Al Ma'idah (The Table)?
10. How many ayaat are there in Surat 103?
11. Write down the translation of the last ayah of surat Al Hashr.

19

2 What is a Translation?

 WHAT TO LEARN

How do people communicate with each other when they don't speak the same language?

 VOCABULARY

Arabic language   Ayaat
Mus-haf   Al hamdulillah

 **THINK ABOUT IT**

What are the authentic and original sources of Islam?

A. Why Was the Arabic Language Chosen for Revelation?

If a person doesn't know the **Arabic language** اللُّغَةُ العَرَبِيَّة, or knows only a little, then a translation of the Qur'an is necessary to understand what Allah is saying to us.

"Why Arabic?" you might ask. An obvious reason that the Qur'an is in the Arabic language is that Allah revealed it to an Arab prophet and to an Arabic-speaking people.

We have sent it down, as an Arabic Qur'an, so that you may understand. Surat Yusuf 12: 2

﴿ إِنَّا أَنزَلْنَٰهُ قُرْءَٰنًا عَرَبِيًّا لَّعَلَّكُمْ تَعْقِلُونَ ﴾ سورة يوسف 2:12

Arabic was also the most advanced and sophisticated language when the Qur'an was revealed, and it remains even today a very specific and comprehensive language to explain its very weighty concepts. Due to the breadth and depth of the Arabic language, the chapters and verses offer great drama and poetic and lyrical beauty, designed to catch and hold the readers' hearts and minds.

The mission of Prophet Muhammad led many Arabs to accept Islam. Due to their strategic location in the Middle East (the crossroads of the world), they were in a position to spread the message of Islam to millions of Romans, Asians, East Indians, Africans and others who then accepted the message of Islam.

B. Preserving the Arabic Qur'an

The Arabs carried Islam with them in their expansion beyond Arabia. Although both the mighty Persians and the Byzantine Romans repeatedly attacked the new Islamic state, the Muslims were able to successfully drive back the armies of both empires.

The Muslims gained many new territories, yet they never forced anyone to accept Islam. Fortunately, scholars now recognize that the stories of Muslims forcing conversion is a myth. The fact is that for at least 200 years, Muslims comprised only one-fourth of the population of the Islamic Empire. People living in Muslim-controlled areas were allowed to freely practice their own religions.

> **Compare these two translations of the same chapter in the Qur'an:**
>
> - 'Abdallah Yusuf 'Ali translation: To you have We granted the Fount (of Abundance). Therefore to your Lord turn in Prayer and Sacrifice. For he who hates you, he will be cut off (from future Hope). 108: 1-3
> - Pickthall translation: Lo! We have given thee Abundance; So pray unto thy Lord and sacrifice. Lo! It is thy insulter (and not thou) who is without posterity. 108: 1-3
>
> **List of Translated Editions of the Qur'an**
>
> - Marmaduke Pickthall, *The Meaning of the Glorious Qur'an*, 1930.
> - 'Abdallah Yusuf 'Ali, *The Meaning of the Holy Qur'an*, 1934.
> - Muhammad Asad, *The Message of The Qur'an*, 1980.
> - Zafar Ishaq Ansari, *Towards Understanding the Qur'an*, 1988.
> - T. B. Irving, *Noble Qur'an: Arabic Text & English Translation*, 1991.
> - AbdalHaqq & Aisha B., *The Noble Qur'an: A New Rendering of its Meaning in English*, 1999.
> - Dr. Muhammad Muhsin Khan and Dr. M. Taqi-ud-Din Al-Hilali, *The Noble Qur'an*, 1999.
> - Justice Mufti Taqi Usmani, *Translation of Qur'an*, 2008.

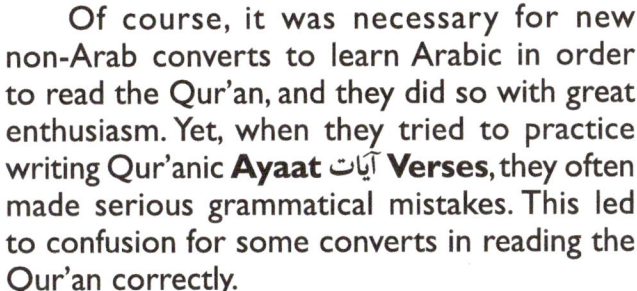

Of course, it was necessary for new non-Arab converts to learn Arabic in order to read the Qur'an, and they did so with great enthusiasm. Yet, when they tried to practice writing Qur'anic **Ayaat** آيات **Verses**, they often made serious grammatical mistakes. This led to confusion for some converts in reading the Qur'an correctly.

On the advice of a concerned native Arab Muslim who had witnessed this problem in Iraq and Syria, the third Muslim ruler, 'Uthman ﷺ, decided to take action. If he didn't, he feared that Muslims would fall into the same trap as those of previous generations. Namely, he did not want Muslims to lose their Holy Book through misunderstandings or misinterpretations.

The first thing he did was put the Prophet's ﷺ chief secretary, Zayd bin Thabit ﷺ, in charge of a team of Qur'anic experts. He then ordered that the original written copy of the Qur'an be used as the guide to prepare copies for distribution. This original copy was prepared in the time of Abu Bakr ﷺ, the first Muslim ruler. Zayd's ﷺ team borrowed the original Qur'an from Hafsah ﷺ, the daughter of 'Umar bin Al Khattab ﷺ, also a widow of Prophet Muhammad ﷺ to whom the Qur'an had been entrusted. By the time the team finished checking and copying their work, they had produced seven copies of the Qur'an that faithfully represented the original.

'Uthman ﷺ sent one of each of these copies to every major Muslim city in the empire, from which the local people could make more copies. Thus, the Qur'an would be available for all with no doubt about its authenticity. Of the original copies made during the reign of 'Uthman ﷺ, two copies still exist today—more than 1,400 years later.

In our own times, not everyone has access to a teacher of Arabic, so translations of the **Mus-haf** مُصْحَف **Bound Volume of the Quran** are often used. Even though translations are helpful for understanding the meaning of the Qur'an, it must be stressed that a translation of the Qur'an can never be as good as the original Arabic text. Translations are only a learning tool, as there is no perfect translation from one language to another.

C. The Only Unchanged Revelation

Allah ﷻ promised to protect and preserve His Book, and we should seek to learn it in its

original language so that we can understand it directly. **Al hamdulillah** الحَمْدُ لله **Praise be to Allah**, there are millions of Arabic copies of the Qur'an all over the world, and all of them have exactly the same text. No other religious tradition can make this claim.

Indeed, it is We who sent down the Qur'an and indeed, We will be its guardian. Surat Al Hijr (The Rocky Tract) 15:9

Other religious traditions have incomplete compilations of their holy books, many of which have been altered in successive translations. The original books were lost a long time ago. Since then, many additions, changes and deletions have occurred. For example, there are numerous versions of the Holy Bible, with significant differences among them. Thanks to the dedication of early Muslims, the Holy Qur'an was preserved in its original form, ensuring that such variations do not occur.

1. Why did people begin to read the Qur'an with grammatical mistakes?
2. How was this issue resolved?
3. What did Allah promise He would do with the Qur'an?
4. Who had the original copy of the Qur'an?

Define: Mus-haf, Ayaat.
Reflect: How were other religious books altered over the years? How can we be sure that the Qur'an won't also change?
Act: Memorize some of the most repeated Arabic words that appear in the Qur'an. Find out which words are mentioned the most by asking a teacher or researching them online.
IQ Builder:
1. What was one reason Allah chose to give His Message in Arabic, according to the Qur'an in 41:44?
2. What does Allah tell us in the Qur'an in 4:82?

3 What is Transliteration?

 WHAT TO LEARN

Have you ever written a word from another language using the letters from your own language?

 VOCABULARY

Surat   Dua'
Transliteration

 THINK ABOUT IT

How can a transliteration help you to learn?

A. How Do I Read Other Languages?

As non-Arabic speakers it may be difficult to pronounce some of the Arabic letters as you try to learn a **Surat** سُورَة **Chapter** from the Qur'an. Maybe you don't know how to read Arabic, so you may not yet know how to join the letters together, or perhaps you have forgotten how a letter sounds.

Until you can learn to read the Arabic language correctly and with ease, this problem can be solved with a useful tool called **Transliteration** التَّرجَمَةُ الصَّوتِيَّة.

Transliteration* means taking a word written using one alphabet and writing it in another. For example, take the word for house in Arabic, بَيْت. If you are unable to pronounce

Bismi Al-Lahi Ar-Rahmani Ar-Rahim.
Qul Huwa Al-Lahu Ahad.
Allahu As-samad.
Lam Yalid Wa Lam Yulad.
Walam Yakun Lahu Kufuan Ahad.

Surat Al Ikhlaas (The Sincerity) 112: 1-4 in Transliteration

بِسْمِ اللَّهِ الرَّحْمَٰنِ الرَّحِيمِ
﴿ قُلْ هُوَ اللَّهُ أَحَدٌ ﴾ ﴿ اللَّهُ الصَّمَدُ ﴾ ﴿ لَمْ يَلِدْ
وَلَمْ يُولَدْ ﴾ ﴿ وَلَمْ يَكُن لَّهُ كُفُوًا أَحَدٌ ﴾

سُورَةُ الإخلاص 112: 1 – 4

how it is written in the Arabic characters, you can use transliteration. The three letters used in Arabic are ت, ي, ب, and it is pronounced **Bayt**. So even if you don't read Arabic well yet, you can use the transliteration of words to help you pronounce just about anything.

Many volumes of the Qur'an offer the transliteration of the suwar so that those unfamiliar with the Arabic language can learn them easily. In this way, you can then offer your daily prayers in Arabic. These volumes also show the transliteration of dua'. A **Dua'** دُعاء is a request we make of Allah ﷻ. There are many dua' within the Qur'an and also those that Prophet Muhammad ﷺ advised us to recite for specific needs and occasions.

View the transliteration of surat Al Ikhlaas (The Sincerity, chapter 112) and compare it to the Arabic text. Try pronouncing the Arabic words using the English transliteration provided.

Transliterated copies of the Qur'an contain both the Arabic text and the transliteration, side-by-side. These books often include the English meaning as well.

---

* We have declined to add the Roman transliteration for any ayaat and ahadith in our textbook. Currently there is not a consistent method to demonstrate the many Arabic letters and sounds not present in the English language. Rather than pick and choose from the various styles, we have simply presented the Arabic fus-ha of all ayaat and ahadith, coupled with their English meaning. Additionally an audio version (MP3) is available at www.noorarat.com to listen to all the Arabic phrases and words written in the book. A wealth of websites are available online for students to hear the Qur'anic ayaat mentioned in the book (quran.com, quranexplorer.com/Quran, quran.muslim-web.com, mushafqatar.com). For Islamic words and phrases that are used regularly, we added the transliteration for them.

23

Our goal, however, must always be to learn to read and pronounce the Arabic language of the Qur'an to the best of our ability. As beginners, we can rely for a short time on transliterations to help us make the transition. There are many hadith that cite the rewards for those who even just try to read the original text.

B. What Is a Roman Transliteration?

The technical term for a transliteration into English is 'Roman transliteration'. This is a reference to the use of the Latin alphabet used by the Romans, which forms the basis of the English language.

There are many rules for transliteration between languages. For example, the sounds in the Chinese language for 'j' are often transliterated as 'zh' in English because the Chinese 'j' also has some of the 'zh' sound in it. Arabic, too, must be transliterated in a certain way because its sounds are slightly different from English sounds. For example, ق, ض, غ and ح are not found in English. You may see these letters transliterated as 'q', 'dh', 'gh' and 'kha', respectively.

Surat Al-Bayyinah (The Clear Proof) - Verse/Ayah 4

وَمَا تَفَرَّقَ ٱلَّذِينَ أُوتُوا۟ ٱلْكِتَٰبَ إِلَّا مِنۢ بَعْدِ مَا جَآءَتْهُمُ ٱلْبَيِّنَةُ ۝

4- Nor did those who were given the Scripture become divided until after there had come to them clear evidence.

4- Wama tafarraqa allatheena ootooalkitaba illa min baAAdi ma jaat-humualbayyina

1. How is a transliteration different from a translation?
2. How is learning with a transliteration helpful?
3. What is one rule of Arabic transliteration?

Define: Surat, Transliteration.
Reflect: Is a transliteration equal to the original Arabic writing? Why or why not?
Act: If you can pronounce Arabic text, write a simple transliteration for Surat 97.
IQ Builder: Write a summary of the meaning of Surat 97 in your own words.

4 How Do I Use the Qur'an?

 **WHAT TO LEARN**

You would never throw away the directions to something if you needed them to make that thing work. So too does the Qur'an have directions for us to use so that we can gain the maximum benefit of its wisdom for our lives.

 VOCABULARY

Etiquette   Ghusl   Tadabbur
Tilawah

 **THINK ABOUT IT**

How do I use the Qur'an properly and respectfully?

A. The Qur'an: Treat It with Respect

Now proof has come to you from your Lord. If anyone cares to see, it will be for (the good) of his own soul. If anyone would be blind, it will be for (the bad) of his own soul. *Surat Al An'aam (The Cattle) 6:104*

    The proof Allah speaks about is the Qur'an and all the miraculous statements within it. Allah informs us that we can either open our eyes to the truth or be blind to it.

    The Qur'an is not like any other book; therefore, it must be treated and used in a certain manner. To benefit from the Qur'an, it must be approached with a certain reverence and respect.

    If an employer or professor let you borrow a book for a report, you wouldn't treat it care-lessly. Why should the Qur'an be treated that way? It is, after all, the instruction manual from Allah on how to live the best life and to prepare our souls for the life to come.

    To proceed, then, we must become aware of the **Etiquette** آداب for using the Qur'an. It's not hard to learn, and if you feel in your heart that the Qur'an is a special book, then you will naturally treat it with respect.

25

Selected Sayings Regarding the Qur'an

1. 'Umar bin Al Khattab reported that the Messenger of Allah said, "Allah will raise some people up with this book (those who follow it) and bring down others (those who ignore it)." (Muslim)

قَالَ عُمَرَ بْنُ الْخَطَّابِ ﷺ: أَمَا إِنَّ نَبِيَّكُمْ ﷺ، قَدْ قَالَ: «إِنَّ اللهَ يَرْفَعُ بِهَذَا الْكِتَابِ أَقْوَامًا وَيَضَعُ بِهِ آخَرِينَ». رَوَاهُ مُسْلِمٌ

2. Abu Musa reported that the Messenger of Allah said, "The example of the believer who reads the Qur'an is like that of a citrus fruit whose smell is nice and taste is good. The example of the believer who does not read the Qur'an is like that of a fresh date which has no scent but whose taste is still sweet. The example of the hypocrite who does not read the Qur'an is like that of a basil leaf which has no smell and whose taste is bitter. The example of the hypocrite who reads the Qur'an is like that of a fragrant flower which has a nice smell but whose taste is terrible." (Al Bukhari & Muslim)

عَنْ أَبِي مُوسَى الْأَشْعَرِيِّ ﷺ، قَالَ: قَالَ رَسُولُ اللهِ ﷺ: «مَثَلُ الْمُؤْمِنِ الَّذِي يَقْرَأُ الْقُرْآنَ كَمَثَلِ الْأُتْرُجَّةِ؛ رِيحُهَا طَيِّبٌ وَطَعْمُهَا طَيِّبٌ، وَمَثَلُ الْمُؤْمِنِ الَّذِي لَا يَقْرَأُ الْقُرْآنَ؛ كَمَثَلِ التَّمْرَةِ لَا رِيحَ لَهَا وَطَعْمُهَا حُلْوٌ، وَمَثَلُ الْمُنَافِقِ الَّذِي يَقْرَأُ الْقُرْآنَ مَثَلُ الرَّيْحَانَةِ؛ رِيحُهَا طَيِّبٌ وَطَعْمُهَا مُرٌّ، وَمَثَلُ الْمُنَافِقِ الَّذِي لَا يَقْرَأُ الْقُرْآنَ كَمَثَلِ الْحَنْظَلَةِ لَيْسَ لَهَا رِيحٌ وَطَعْمُهَا مُرٌّ». رَوَاهُ الْبُخَارِيُّ وَمُسْلِمٌ

3. 'Aishah reported that the Messenger of Allah said, "A person who has expert knowledge of the Qur'an will be with the honorable writers (angels), and the one who reads the Qur'an and struggles with it in difficulty will get twice the reward." (Al Bukhari & Muslim)

عَنْ عَائِشَةَ ﷺ، قَالَتْ: قَالَ رَسُولُ اللهِ ﷺ: «الْمَاهِرُ بِالْقُرْآنِ مَعَ السَّفَرَةِ الْكِرَامِ الْبَرَرَةِ، وَالَّذِي يَقْرَأُ الْقُرْآنَ وَيَتَتَعْتَعُ فِيهِ وَهُوَ عَلَيْهِ شَاقٌّ لَهُ أَجْرَانِ». رَوَاهُ الْبُخَارِيُّ وَمُسْلِمٌ

4. The Messenger of Allah once said, "There is no envy (allowed in Islam) except for two cases: a person to whom Allah has given knowledge of the Qur'an and who lives by it through the night and day and a person to whom Allah has given wealth and who spends from it (in the Cause of Allah) through the night and day." (Al Bukhari & Muslim)

عَنِ النَّبِيِّ ﷺ، قَالَ: «لَا حَسَدَ إِلَّا فِي اثْنَيْنِ: رَجُلٌ آتَاهُ اللهُ الْكِتَابَ فَهُوَ يَقُومُ بِهِ آنَاءَ اللَّيْلِ وَآنَاءَ النَّهَارِ، وَرَجُلٌ آتَاهُ اللهُ مَالًا فَهُوَ يَتَصَدَّقُ بِهِ آنَاءَ اللَّيْلِ وَآنَاءَ النَّهَارِ». رَوَاهُ الْبُخَارِيُّ وَمُسْلِمٌ

5. 'Uthman narrated that the Prophet said, "The best among you (Muslims) are those who learn the Qur'an and teach it." (Al Bukhari)

عَنْ عُثْمَانَ ﷺ، عَنِ النَّبِيِّ ﷺ، قَالَ: «خَيْرُكُمْ مَنْ تَعَلَّمَ الْقُرْآنَ وَعَلَّمَهُ». رَوَاهُ الْبُخَارِيُّ

Manners When Reading the Qur'an

Internal
1. You should recognize that you are holding Allah's ﷻ words in your hands and have a humble heart. (7:204)
2. Whenever a description of Judgement Day or Hellfire is mentioned, you should recognize the importance of that real event. (16:107)
3. You should pay attention to understanding the meaning of the text since Allah ﷻ encourages us to ponder the meaning of the Qur'an. (47:24)
4. After reading the Qur'an, you should reflect on the lessons learned. It is reported that the Blessed Prophet ﷺ once remarked that a person's reward is increased if they understand the meaning of what they are doing. The word **Tadabbur** تَدَبُّر means **to Reflect Upon Something**.

External
1. If you are in a state of major impurity and need **Ghusl** غُسْل, which is **a Purifying Bath**, then you must take one before reading the Qur'an. (56:79)
2. Muslims are permitted to read and teach the Qur'an without wudu', although it is preferred to be in the state of ablution. When one is teaching and reading from the Mus-haf, which is the physical, actual Qur'an in book form, then wudu' is compulsory.
3. You are recommended to face the direction of Makkah when reading.
4. You should not eat or drink while reading the Qur'an.
5. If the Arabic text is being read out loud, called **Tilawah** تِلاوَة, you should try to pronounce it as correctly as you can. Don't be afraid to read it, even if you can't yet recite it well. The Blessed Prophet ﷺ said the person who recites the Qur'an with difficulty receives twice the reward of a person who says it without difficulty, because of the greater effort.
6. Before reciting, you should say, أَعُوذُ بِاللهِ مِنَ الشَّيْطَانِ الرَّجِيمِ. This means "I seek Allah's ﷻ protection from the rejected Satan."
7. After seeking protection from, Shaytan you are highly recommended to recite بِسْمِ اللهِ الرَّحْمَنِ الرَّحِيمِ "In the Name of Allah, The Most Gracious, The Most Merciful" except at the beginning of surat At-Tawbah (The Repentance), chapter 9.
8. After the reading is finished, you can say, صَدَقَ اللهُ العَظِيمُ. This means, "Allah ﷻ the Exalted, has spoken the truth."
9. The best time to read the Qur'an is after the early morning salah. (17:78)
10. Keep the Qur'an in a respectful place, but do not leave it merely as a decoration in your home that will go unused.

IT'S ALL ABOUT ISLAM

1. List three internal and three external etiquettes that we should apply when reading the Qur'an.
2. According to the hadith narrated by 'Aishah, what reward do people receive for trying to recite the Qur'an properly, even if it is challenging for them?
3. What is the best time to read the Qur'an?

Define: Etiquette, Tilawah, Tadabbur.

Reflect: The Blessed Prophet once remarked, "Whoever has nothing of the Qur'an in their heart is like a ruined house." (At-Tirmidhi)

قَالَ رَسُولُ اللهِ ﷺ : ((إِنَّ الَّذِي لَيْسَ فِي جَوْفِهِ شَيْءٌ مِنَ الْقُرْآنِ كَالْبَيْتِ الْخَرِبِ)). رَوَاهُ التِّرْمَذِيُّ

What do you think he meant by this statement?

Act: The Blessed Prophet once said, "The best among you are those who learn the Qur'an and teach it to others." (Al Bukhari)

قَالَ رَسُولُ اللهِ ﷺ : ((خَيْرُكُمْ مَنْ تَعَلَّمَ الْقُرْآنَ وَعَلَّمَهُ)). رَوَاهُ الْبُخَارِيُّ

Choose one ayaat that you have learned the meaning of and share your reflections on it with your parents, siblings or friends.

IQ Builders:

1. What is Allah telling us about the Qur'an in verses (17:81-82)?
2. How should a person feel while reading the Qur'an, according to (7:204-206)?

Personal Responsibility and its Consequences

Surat Al Muddaththir (The Cloaked One) سُورَةُ المُدَّثِّر

In the Name of Allah, The Most Gracious, The Most Merciful

O you who covers himself (Muhammad), don't lay there, wrapped up under your blanket! Get out of bed and warn your people! Glorify your Lord and keep your clothes clean and pure and stay far away from the idols. Don't confer favor to acquire more. For your Lord's sake, keep struggling onward. A mighty horn blast will blow (when the world finally comes to its end). That Day will be a difficult one (full of fear and stress). It certainly won't be easy for the disbelievers (people who hid the truth).

Leave me alone (to deal) with the one whom I created lonely and gave him extensive wealth and sons present before (his) eyes! I even made living in the world smooth and easy for him! Yet he was greedy and wanted Me to give more and more. No way! He was stubborn about Our signs! I will soon bring a load of trouble on him! He thought and he plotted against Me so ruin to him! Oh, how he schemed! Yes! Ruin to him! Oh, how he planned! He looked around and saw all the proof in the world about God but then frowned and scowled. He turned away in arrogance and said, "This (Qur'an) is nothing more than ancient magic. This is nothing but the word of a mortal man!" We'll soon throw him into Saqar (the Hellfire)! And how can you understand what Saqar (Hellfire) really is? It doesn't let anything survive nor does it leave anything alone! It darkens and warps people's skins! Watching over it are nineteen angels.

We put angels as guards in charge of the Fire and chose their exact number only as a test for the faithless so that the recipients of earlier revelation (the Jews and Christians) can know for sure, so that the believers can increase their faith and also so that no doubts can remain with the recipients of earlier revelation and the believers. Those who have twisted hearts and are the faithless will say, "What does God mean by this number?" This is how God leaves to wander whoever He wants and how He guides whoever He wants. No one can know the forces of the Lord except Him, and this message is nothing more than a warning to all people. No way! By the moon (as it arises) and the night as it closes and by the dawn as it shines ever and ever brighter, this (Qur'an) is only one of the tremendous signs and a warning to humanity, to any one of you who chooses to press forward on the path to heaven or to follow behind and fall into ruin. Every soul will be held as collateral for its actions, all except the Companions of the Right. They will rest in beautiful gardens, asking (each other how anyone could have refused to enter Paradise. Then they will be allowed to ask) the sinners far below them, "What led you to Hell?" The sinners will answer, "We weren't the kind of people who prayed or fed the poor. Instead, we used to gossip with useless people and we denied the Day of Judgement all the way up until the Promised Day came upon us."

(On that Day), no one's words will help them get out of trouble. So what's the matter with them that they turn away from being reminded, as if they were scared donkeys running from a lion? To be sure, every one of them wants to be given unrolled scrolls of revelation tailored just for them! But no way! They aren't afraid of the next life. But this is a reminder nonetheless! Anyone who wants to be reminded will remember it! But no one will remember it except as God wills. He is the Lord of Goodness and the Lord of Forgiveness.

Surat Al Muddaththir (The Cloaked One) 74:1-56

بِسْمِ اللَّهِ الرَّحْمَٰنِ الرَّحِيمِ

﴿يَا أَيُّهَا الْمُدَّثِّرُ ۝ قُمْ فَأَنذِرْ ۝ وَرَبَّكَ فَكَبِّرْ ۝ وَثِيَابَكَ فَطَهِّرْ ۝ وَالرُّجْزَ فَاهْجُرْ ۝ وَلَا تَمْنُن تَسْتَكْثِرُ ۝ وَلِرَبِّكَ فَاصْبِرْ ۝ فَإِذَا نُقِرَ فِي النَّاقُورِ ۝ فَذَٰلِكَ يَوْمَئِذٍ يَوْمٌ عَسِيرٌ ۝ عَلَى الْكَافِرِينَ غَيْرُ يَسِيرٍ ۝ ذَرْنِي وَمَنْ خَلَقْتُ وَحِيدًا ۝ وَجَعَلْتُ لَهُ مَالًا مَّمْدُودًا ۝ وَبَنِينَ شُهُودًا ۝ وَمَهَّدتُّ لَهُ تَمْهِيدًا ۝ ثُمَّ يَطْمَعُ أَنْ أَزِيدَ ۝ كَلَّا ۖ إِنَّهُ كَانَ لِآيَاتِنَا عَنِيدًا ۝ سَأُرْهِقُهُ صَعُودًا ۝ إِنَّهُ فَكَّرَ وَقَدَّرَ ۝ فَقُتِلَ كَيْفَ قَدَّرَ ۝ ثُمَّ قُتِلَ كَيْفَ قَدَّرَ ۝ ثُمَّ نَظَرَ ۝ ثُمَّ عَبَسَ وَبَسَرَ ۝ ثُمَّ أَدْبَرَ وَاسْتَكْبَرَ ۝ فَقَالَ إِنْ هَٰذَا إِلَّا سِحْرٌ يُؤْثَرُ ۝ إِنْ هَٰذَا إِلَّا قَوْلُ الْبَشَرِ ۝ سَأُصْلِيهِ سَقَرَ ۝ وَمَا أَدْرَاكَ مَا سَقَرُ ۝ لَا تُبْقِي وَلَا تَذَرُ ۝ لَوَّاحَةٌ لِّلْبَشَرِ ۝ عَلَيْهَا تِسْعَةَ عَشَرَ ۝ وَمَا جَعَلْنَا أَصْحَابَ النَّارِ إِلَّا مَلَائِكَةً ۖ وَمَا جَعَلْنَا عِدَّتَهُمْ إِلَّا فِتْنَةً لِّلَّذِينَ كَفَرُوا لِيَسْتَيْقِنَ الَّذِينَ أُوتُوا الْكِتَابَ وَيَزْدَادَ الَّذِينَ آمَنُوا إِيمَانًا ۙ وَلَا يَرْتَابَ الَّذِينَ أُوتُوا الْكِتَابَ وَالْمُؤْمِنُونَ ۙ وَلِيَقُولَ الَّذِينَ فِي قُلُوبِهِم مَّرَضٌ وَالْكَافِرُونَ مَاذَا أَرَادَ اللَّهُ بِهَٰذَا مَثَلًا ۚ كَذَٰلِكَ يُضِلُّ اللَّهُ مَن يَشَاءُ وَيَهْدِي مَن يَشَاءُ ۚ وَمَا يَعْلَمُ جُنُودَ رَبِّكَ إِلَّا هُوَ ۚ وَمَا هِيَ إِلَّا ذِكْرَىٰ لِلْبَشَرِ ۝ كَلَّا وَالْقَمَرِ ۝ وَاللَّيْلِ إِذْ أَدْبَرَ ۝ وَالصُّبْحِ إِذَا أَسْفَرَ ۝ إِنَّهَا لَإِحْدَى الْكُبَرِ ۝ نَذِيرًا لِّلْبَشَرِ ۝ لِمَن شَاءَ مِنكُمْ أَن يَتَقَدَّمَ أَوْ يَتَأَخَّرَ ۝ كُلُّ نَفْسٍ بِمَا كَسَبَتْ رَهِينَةٌ ۝ إِلَّا أَصْحَابَ الْيَمِينِ ۝ فِي جَنَّاتٍ يَتَسَاءَلُونَ ۝ عَنِ الْمُجْرِمِينَ ۝ مَا سَلَكَكُمْ فِي سَقَرَ ۝ قَالُوا لَمْ نَكُ مِنَ الْمُصَلِّينَ ۝ وَلَمْ نَكُ نُطْعِمُ الْمِسْكِينَ ۝ وَكُنَّا نَخُوضُ مَعَ الْخَائِضِينَ ۝ وَكُنَّا نُكَذِّبُ بِيَوْمِ الدِّينِ ۝ حَتَّىٰ أَتَانَا الْيَقِينُ ۝ فَمَا تَنفَعُهُمْ شَفَاعَةُ الشَّافِعِينَ ۝ فَمَا لَهُمْ عَنِ التَّذْكِرَةِ مُعْرِضِينَ ۝ كَأَنَّهُمْ حُمُرٌ مُّسْتَنفِرَةٌ ۝ فَرَّتْ مِن قَسْوَرَةٍ ۝ بَلْ يُرِيدُ كُلُّ امْرِئٍ مِّنْهُمْ أَن يُؤْتَىٰ صُحُفًا مُّنَشَّرَةً ۝ كَلَّا ۖ بَل لَّا يَخَافُونَ الْآخِرَةَ ۝ كَلَّا إِنَّهُ تَذْكِرَةٌ ۝ فَمَن شَاءَ ذَكَرَهُ ۝ وَمَا يَذْكُرُونَ إِلَّا أَن يَشَاءَ اللَّهُ ۚ هُوَ أَهْلُ التَّقْوَىٰ وَأَهْلُ الْمَغْفِرَةِ ۝﴾

سورة المدثر 74: 1-56

1. Based on what you read above, what is the primary objective of Islam?
2. Describe three activities, based on this surat, that can lead a person to ruin in the next life.

Unit 01 — Review Exercise

VOCABULARY REVIEW

On a separate sheet of paper, write the definition of each word below.

1. Muslim
2. Allah ﷻ
3. Islam
4. Qur'an
5. Ayaat
6. Arabic
7. Transliteration
8. Sunnah
9. Translation
10. Mus-haf
11. Dua'
12. Etiquette
13. Tilawah
14. Tadabbur

REMEMBERING WHAT YOU READ

On a separate sheet of paper, answer the following questions. Use complete sentences in your answers.

1. Why are translations of books sometimes needed?
2. What was the miracle that Allah ﷻ gave to Prophet Muhammad ﷺ?
3. Why did 'Uthman ؓ, the third Muslim ruler, have to prepare an official copy of the Qur'an?
4. List three manners we should follow when reading the Qur'an.
5. Why is it important to know that the Qur'an has never been changed or rewritten, unlike other scriptures?
6. What main choice did Allah ﷻ give to humans?
7. How does the Qur'an and its teachings shape our lives? List three ways.

THINKING TO LEARN

On a separate sheet of paper, answer the questions below. Use complete sentences.

1. How has Allah ﷻ tried to help humans choose their paths wisely?
2. How would you describe Islam to a non-Muslim?
3. What is the difference between a translation and a transliteration?
4. What is tadabbur and why is it important when reading the Qur'an?

UNIT 2
Understanding the Qur'an

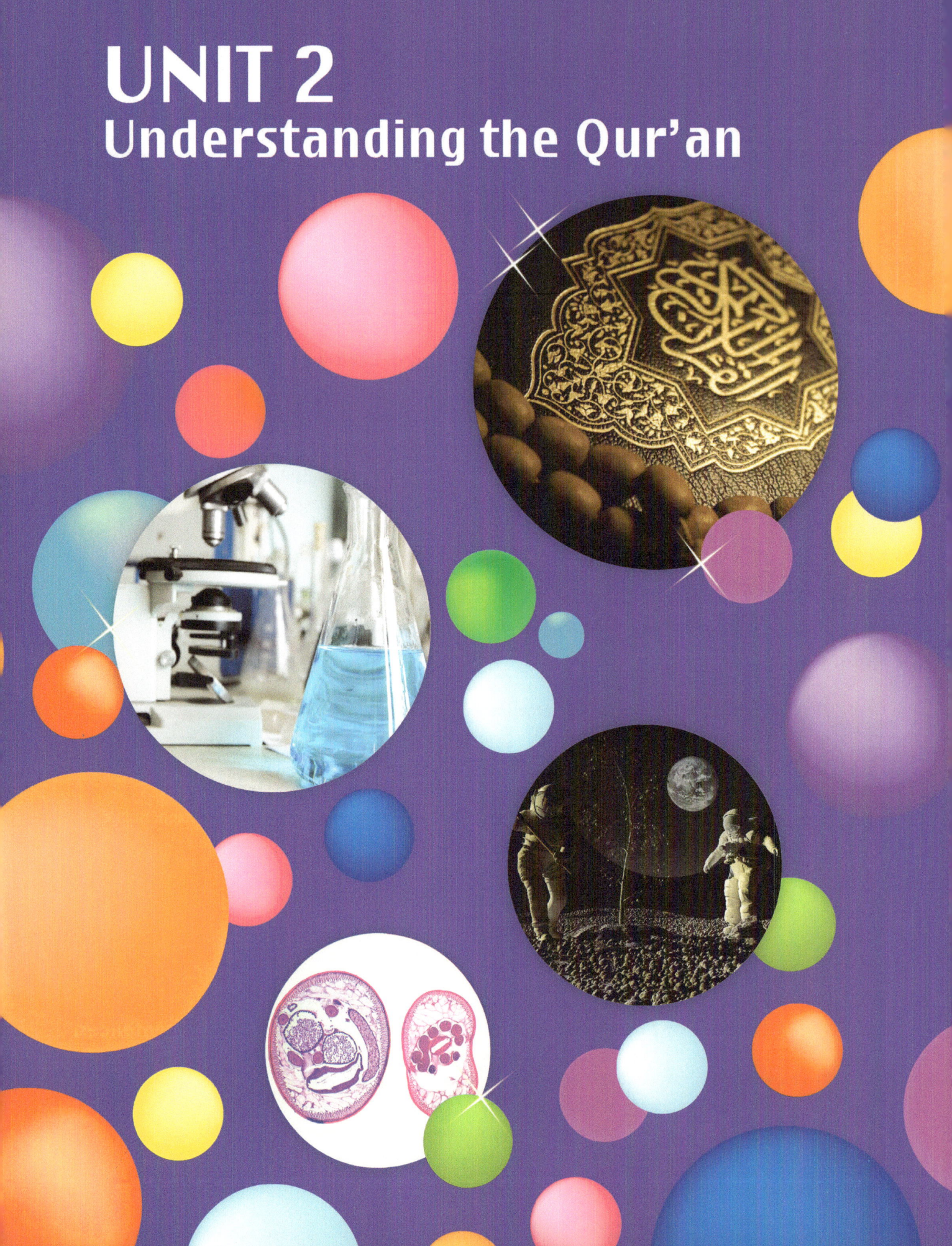

5. How Was the Qur'an Revealed?

 WHAT TO LEARN

The Qur'an was revealed to a man who could neither read nor write. Why might this be significant?

 VOCABULARY

Angel Jibreel ﷺ   Revelation

THINK ABOUT IT

How did the Qur'an become known to people?

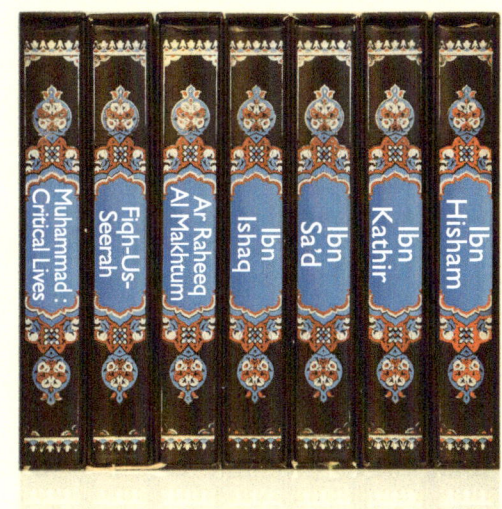

History books about the Blessed Prophet ﷺ are called books of seerah. Below are the names of the most important history books about the Blessed Prophet ﷺ.

A. Who Received the Revelation of the Qur'an?

The Holy Qur'an is Allah's ﷻ final message to this world. It was revealed between the years 610 CE and 632 CE to a person who lived in Arabia. The one who received this Book of Light was Muhammad ﷺ, the son of 'Abdallah and Aminah. Muhammad ﷺ was known for honesty and wisdom, a reputation that later earned him the respect of even his enemies. Allah ﷻ chose Muhammad ﷺ to be His last prophet for all of humanity.

Although at times it seemed Muhammad's ﷺ mission was doomed to fail because of the overwhelming odds against him, Allah ﷻ protected him and granted him the final victory.

Today, Muslims love and respect Prophet Muhammad ﷺ and ask Allah ﷻ to send peace upon his soul countless times every day.

Whenever we hear or read his name, we should say, either silently or aloud, **Peace and Blessings of Allah be upon him** صَلَّى اللهُ عَلَيْهِ وَسَلَّم, which will be notated like this: ﷺ.

To understand the Blessed Prophet's ﷺ mission is to understand the purpose of life for every human being. To learn about his noble and honorable example is to come to love him more than any other human being who ever lived.

B. One Night, Alone in the Dark...

"Iqra! Read!" commanded a voice out of nowhere.

The sudden appearance of a creature of light startled Muhammad ﷺ out of his deep sleep. He had come to this lonely mountain cave to think about the meaning of his life. Suddenly, he was faced with something so fantastic that he could hardly move or breathe. He was frozen in place. "I can't read," he muttered to the strange presence that seemed to encircle him.

33

IT'S ALL ABOUT ISLAM

The Angel then embraced Muhammad's ﷺ body and almost squeezed all the breath out of him, commanding him to read. Muhammad ﷺ protested again, so the Angel repeated the strange embrace a third time. He commanded once more, "Read!" Muhammad ﷺ cried out, "What should I read?"

Then, the Angel began to recite, Read in the Name of your Lord Who created humans from a clinging (embryo). Read, for your Lord is Generous. He is the One Who taught people with the pen, taught them things they didn't know before. Surat Al 'Alaq (The Clot) 96:1-5

﴿اقْرَأْ بِاسْمِ رَبِّكَ الَّذِي خَلَقَ﴾﴿خَلَقَ الْإِنسَانَ مِنْ عَلَقٍ﴾﴿اقْرَأْ وَرَبُّكَ الْأَكْرَمُ﴾﴿الَّذِي عَلَّمَ بِالْقَلَمِ﴾﴿عَلَّمَ الْإِنسَانَ مَا لَمْ يَعْلَمْ﴾

سُورَةُ العَلَقِ 96: 1–5

Muhammad ﷺ rushed out of the cave, flustered and frightened. He ran back down the mountain as fast as he could. All he wanted to do was to get home, to escape this strange sensation that he didn't understand.

Then, as he paused for breath, he looked up at the horizon and saw the Angel who confronted him in the cave in his actual form. Muhammad ﷺ turned around, and again the Angel was there, larger than the mountains and staring at him, saying his name was **Jibreel** ﷺ جِبْرِيل. Overwhelmed, Muhammad ﷺ ran back to his home in Makkah without looking back.

When he burst through the front door of his house, he fell into the arms of his beloved wife, Khadijah ﷺ. As he shook with fear, she held her husband tightly and wondered frantically what was happening.

"Cover me! Cover me!" he cried. So Khadijah ﷺ took him to their room and covered him with a sheet. She watched over him the whole night, sometimes holding his hands, other times wiping his moistened brow. What could have happened? What could she do? She would know soon.

O you, enveloped in a mantle, Stand up and warn, And pronounce the greatness of your Lord, And purify your clothes, And keep away from filth, And do not do a favour (to anyone merely) to seek more (in return). And for the sake of your Lord, observe patience. Surat Al Muddaththir (The Cloaked One) 74: 1-7

﴿يَا أَيُّهَا الْمُدَّثِّرُ﴾﴿قُمْ فَأَنذِرْ﴾﴿وَرَبَّكَ فَكَبِّرْ﴾﴿وَثِيَابَكَ فَطَهِّرْ﴾﴿وَالرُّجْزَ فَاهْجُرْ﴾﴿وَلَا تَمْنُن تَسْتَكْثِرُ﴾﴿وَلِرَبِّكَ فَاصْبِرْ﴾

سُورَةُ المُدَّثِّرِ 74: 1–7

Later that night, Muhammad ﷺ wondered aloud if trouble was coming for him. Khadijah ﷺ, who knew him to be a man of integrity, comforted him and explained that Allah ﷻ would never let anything evil befall him. He was honest, charitable and upright. If something was to come, it surely would not be bad.

IT'S ALL ABOUT ISLAM

After some time, Angel Jibreel ﷺ again came to Muhammad ﷺ. This time, he was more prepared for the otherworldly experience. When the Angel finished speaking, Muhammad ﷺ memorized the **Revelation** وَحِي from Allah ﷻ.

You, wrapped up in sheets! Stand (in prayer) at night, but not all night, maybe half, or a little less or more. Recite the Qur'an in slow, measured tones. Soon, We (Allah) will give you a heavy Message. Truly, getting up late at night is powerful for controlling (one's soul) and the best for forming words (of prayer and praise).
Surat Al Muzzammil (The Enshrouded One) 73: 1-6

﴿يَا أَيُّهَا الْمُزَّمِّلُ﴾ ﴿قُمِ اللَّيْلَ إِلَّا قَلِيلًا﴾ ﴿نِصْفَهُ أَوِ انْقُصْ مِنْهُ قَلِيلًا﴾ ﴿أَوْ زِدْ عَلَيْهِ وَرَتِّلِ الْقُرْآنَ تَرْتِيلًا﴾ ﴿إِنَّا سَنُلْقِي عَلَيْكَ قَوْلًا ثَقِيلًا﴾ ﴿إِنَّ نَاشِئَةَ اللَّيْلِ هِيَ أَشَدُّ وَطْئًا وَأَقْوَمُ قِيلًا﴾

سُورَةُ الْمُزَّمِّل 73: 1—6

Muhammad ﷺ had been a simple man in a remote and dusty trading town. Now, he was about to embark on a mission which would change the face of the world forever. Little did he know what hardships and adventures lay ahead.

1. How did Muhammad ﷺ react when Angel Jibreel ﷺ first appeared to him in the cave?
2. What did Angel Jibreel ﷺ tell him in the cave?
3. What did Muhammad ﷺ see while he was rushing home?
4. How did Khadijah ﷺ comfort him?

Define: Angel Jibreel ﷺ, Khadijah ﷺ, Revelation.
Reflect: What did the first revelation that Muhammad ﷺ received tell him about his future mission?
Act: The first commandment that Prophet Muhammad ﷺ received was to "Read." Make wudu', find a copy of the Qur'an and read a passage from it.

IQ Builders:
1. How does Allah ﷻ say He will reveal the Qur'an to Muhammad ﷺ in ayaat 76:23-24?
2. According to ayah 42:51, what are the three ways in which Allah ﷻ reveals His instructions to human beings?

6 How Was the Qur'an Recorded?

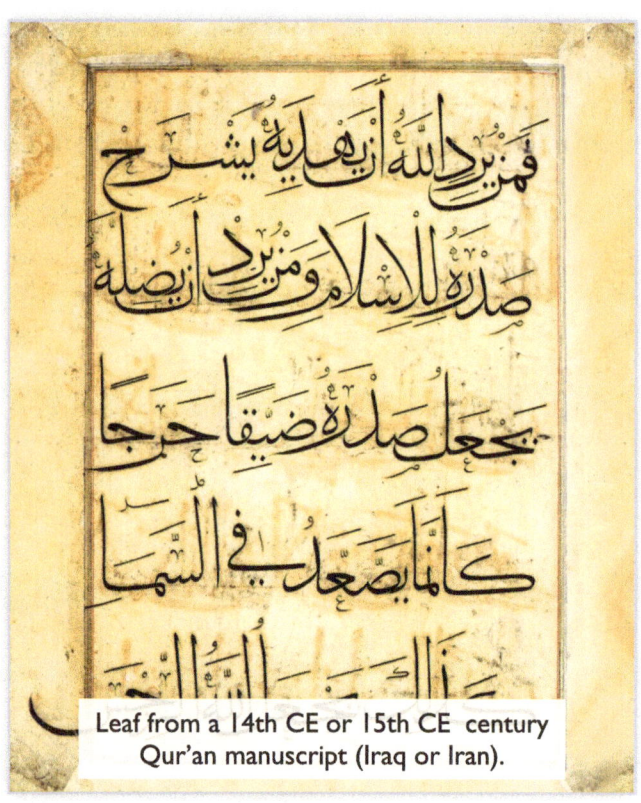

Leaf from a 14th CE or 15th CE century Qur'an manuscript (Iraq or Iran).

WHAT TO LEARN

Why has the Qur'an remained unchanged to this day, while other religious books have been tampered with?

VOCABULARY

Hijrah
'Umar bin Al Khattab رضي الله عنه

THINK ABOUT IT

How was the Qur'an preserved in the early days of Islam?

A. Who Recorded the Words of the Qur'an?

As the Blessed Prophet Muhammad ﷺ received the revelations from Allah عزَّ وجلَّ, he memorized the ayaat and then taught them to other people. In this way, the Qur'an was safeguarded because so many people immediately learned and discussed its message.

Additionally, the Prophet ﷺ received help from scribes, who were trained to write. Just as the Blessed Prophet ﷺ himself was receiving and speaking the revelation, these scribes would record the words on paper, leather or whatever else was available to write on.

An early source of Islamic history states that at one time, there was a total of 24 different scribes. The most important of these was Zayd bin Thabit رضي الله عنه, who also memorized the entire Qur'an.

We know the Qur'an was written down in the lifetime of the Blessed Prophet ﷺ and personally arranged by him under the instruction of Angel Jibreel عليه السلام. Many copies of the text were used for studying and teaching before and after the **Hijrah** هِجْرَة, the migration from Makkah to Al Madinah.

B. The Conversion of 'Umar bin Al Khattab رضي الله عنه

Perhaps you are familiar with the story of how **'Umar bin Al Khattab** رضي الله عنه عُمَرُ بْنُ الخَطّاب became a believer. When he learned that many people throughout Makkah were converting, 'Umar رضي الله عنه became angry. At that time, the idol-worshippers of Makkah were determined to crush Islam. During one of their meetings, 'Umar رضي الله عنه volunteered to kill Muhammad ﷺ. He then stormed through the streets, sword drawn, and vowed to murder the Blessed Prophet ﷺ.

A man who knew 'Umar رضي الله عنه saw the angry look on his face and asked him where he was going. When 'Umar رضي الله عنه replied that he was going to kill Muhammad ﷺ, the man told him, "Perhaps you should take care of your own house first. Your sister and brother-in-law have already accepted Islam."

When 'Umar heard this, he became more upset and ran off in the direction of his sister's house. When he got there, he heard someone reading, so he violently pushed in the door. He saw his sister, her husband and another Muslim sitting and reading aloud from a piece of paper. "Did you become a Muslim?" he yelled.

When his sister, Fatimah bint Al Khattab, replied that they had, he became enraged and began hitting Fatimah's husband. She grabbed 'Umar and tried to stop him from beating her husband.

'Umar swung around and hit his sister in the face. She fell to the ground in tears. She looked up at him and cried, "Do whatever you want to us! We are determined to die as Muslims!"

'Umar paused when he saw the blood on his sister's cheek. He felt terrible. He calmed down and stood silently, ashamed at what he had just done. After a minute, he asked to see the pages she had been reading. She told him to wash with water first. When he finished washing, he returned and was given the papers. On them were written verses from surat Ta Ha.

When he reached verse 14, he cried out, "Surely this is the Word of Allah! Take me to Muhammad right now!"

Khabbab, the other Muslim who was with them, stood up and declared, " 'Umar! Good news for you. It seems the prayer of the Holy Prophet, made last night, has been answered in your favor. He had prayed to Allah, 'Oh Allah, strengthen Islam with either 'Umar bin Al Khattab or 'Amr bin Hisham, whomever You please.'"

When 'Umar was brought to the Blessed Prophet, he was asked, " 'Umar, why have you come?" 'Umar replied, "I am here to accept Islam!" When the other Muslims heard these words, they shouted for joy. Calls of *Allahu Akbar* (Allah is the Greatest!) rang through the streets. The idol-worshippers were stunned. All it took was a few verses from the Holy Qur'an to change his heart—those pages and the will and guidance of Almighty Allah.

Ta Ha. We did not send down the Qur'an to you (Muhammad) to be (a source) for your distress but only as a reminder to those who fear (Allah). A revelation from the One Who created the Earth and space on high. (He is Allah) the Caring, and He is firmly established on the throne (of authority). To Him belongs whatever is in space and on Earth and everything in between them and all beneath the soil. Whether you declare (this message) aloud (or keep it a secret, it doesn't take away from His power) for surely He knows what is secret and what is hidden. Allah! There is no god but He! To Him belong the Most Beautiful Names! Has the story of Musa reached you? Behold, he saw a fire (on a mountain side) so he said to his family, "Wait here. I see a fire. Maybe I can bring you a lit branch (to make our campfire) or maybe I'll find some direction at the fire." But when he came to the fire, a voice was heard which said, "Musa! Certainly I am your Lord! Therefore, (in My presence) take off your shoes. You are in the sacred valley of Tuwa. I have chosen you, listen then to the inspiration (I send to you). Certainly, I am Allah: there is no god but I. So you should serve (only) Me and do your prayers for celebrating My praise. Certainly the Hour is coming. My design is to keep it hidden so every soul can receive its reward by the measure of its own action. Therefore, don't let people who disbelieve in this (message), who only follow their own lusts, divert you from (the truth); otherwise you will perish!" Surat Ta-Ha 20: 1-16

بِسْمِ اللَّهِ الرَّحْمَنِ الرَّحِيمِ ﴿طه﴾ ﴿مَا أَنزَلْنَا عَلَيْكَ الْقُرْآنَ لِتَشْقَىٰ﴾ ﴿إِلَّا تَذْكِرَةً لِّمَن يَخْشَىٰ﴾ ﴿تَنزِيلًا مِّمَّنْ خَلَقَ الْأَرْضَ وَالسَّمَاوَاتِ الْعُلَى﴾ ﴿الرَّحْمَنُ عَلَى الْعَرْشِ اسْتَوَىٰ﴾ ﴿لَهُ مَا فِي السَّمَاوَاتِ وَمَا فِي الْأَرْضِ وَمَا بَيْنَهُمَا وَمَا تَحْتَ الثَّرَىٰ﴾ ﴿وَإِن تَجْهَرْ بِالْقَوْلِ فَإِنَّهُ يَعْلَمُ السِّرَّ وَأَخْفَى﴾ ﴿اللَّهُ لَا إِلَٰهَ إِلَّا هُوَ لَهُ الْأَسْمَاءُ الْحُسْنَىٰ﴾ ﴿وَهَلْ أَتَاكَ حَدِيثُ مُوسَىٰ﴾ ﴿إِذْ رَأَىٰ نَارًا فَقَالَ لِأَهْلِهِ امْكُثُوا إِنِّي آنَسْتُ نَارًا لَّعَلِّي آتِيكُم مِّنْهَا بِقَبَسٍ أَوْ أَجِدُ عَلَى النَّارِ هُدًى﴾ ﴿فَلَمَّا أَتَاهَا نُودِيَ يَا مُوسَىٰ﴾ ﴿إِنِّي أَنَا رَبُّكَ فَاخْلَعْ نَعْلَيْكَ إِنَّكَ بِالْوَادِ الْمُقَدَّسِ طُوًى﴾ ﴿وَأَنَا اخْتَرْتُكَ فَاسْتَمِعْ لِمَا يُوحَىٰ﴾ ﴿إِنَّنِي أَنَا اللَّهُ لَا إِلَٰهَ إِلَّا أَنَا فَاعْبُدْنِي وَأَقِمِ الصَّلَاةَ لِذِكْرِي﴾ ﴿إِنَّ السَّاعَةَ آتِيَةٌ أَكَادُ أُخْفِيهَا لِتُجْزَىٰ كُلُّ نَفْسٍ بِمَا تَسْعَىٰ﴾ ﴿فَلَا يَصُدَّنَّكَ عَنْهَا مَن لَّا يُؤْمِنُ بِهَا وَاتَّبَعَ هَوَاهُ فَتَرْدَىٰ﴾ سُورَةُ طَه 20: 1–16

Questions to Answer

1. Why was 'Umar on his way to kill the Prophet?
2. What did 'Umar find in his sister's home?
3. What made 'Umar stop hitting the people in his sister's home?
4. What did his sister make him do before letting him see the Qur'an page?
5. From the story, what proof is there that the Qur'an was being written down from the beginning?
6. What was the great irony when 'Umar finally went to see the Prophet?

Define: Hijrah, 'Umar bin Al Khattab.

Reflect: What parallels are there between the story of Musa mentioned in surat Ta Ha and the mission of Prophet Muhammad?

Act: Search through the Qur'an for an ayah that resonates strongly with you. Find a friend or classmate and share the ayah with them, explaining why you connect so strongly with that verse.

IQ Builder: Summarize the meaning of 20:1-16 in your own words and explain how the message might have influenced 'Umar to accept Islam.

7. The Qur'an Never Changes

WHAT TO LEARN

The Qur'an is the only book in history that has survived unchanged for over 1,400 years. Why do you think that may be important?

VOCABULARY

Scribe Khalifa Sahaba
Tafseer Hafith Fus-ha

THINK ABOUT IT

How did Allah ﷻ protect the Qur'an?

The Protestant Bible	The Catholic Bible
Contains a total of 66 books.	Contains a total of 73 books.

Which one is the Word of God?

A. The Qur'an Is Protected

Allah ﷻ has said in the Qur'an that He is the One Who will protect His Book. No humans will ever be allowed to lose or change this last message as they lost and changed previous messages.

Indeed, Allah ﷻ has kept His promise. The Qur'an that we read today contains the same words and the same letters that were revealed directly to Prophet Muhammad ﷺ over 1,400 years ago. This is quite a miracle, especially when you consider that no other book has been preserved in this manner—not even the holy books of other religions.

Evidence that other religious books have been changed can be seen in the numerous variations of their texts. For example, the Protestant Bible contains a total of 66 books, while the Catholic Bible has 73 books. Some versions of the Bible contain chapters and verses that are not included in other versions. Other religions, including Buddhism and Hinduism, have sacred books whose authors are unknown.

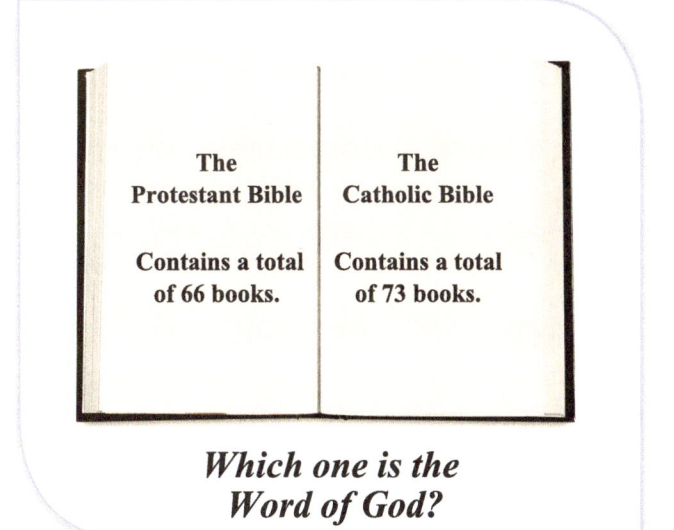

Only the Qur'an has survived through the centuries unchanged because, even today, people have not lost the ability to read it in its original language.

B. Arabic Is a Living Language

Sanskrit, ancient Greek, Aramaic or Hebrew are no longer used in the same way today as when they were written long ago. Yet, the Arabic of the Qur'an continues to live on through continued study and use by millions of people in their daily lives. The form of Arabic still spoken today includes the pure Arabic of the Qur'an, **Fus-ha** فُصْحَى, as well as informal dialects that have developed over time. Thus, Islam is quite distinguished from other religions in that both the original book, the Qur'an, exists, and the original language, Arabic, are still widely used today.

The entire Qur'an was written down in the lifetime of Prophet Muhammad ﷺ. It was personally arranged by him under the instruction of Angel Jibreel ﷺ, and Muslims have always memorized it in the same order. 'Uthman ﷺ reported that whenever a new verse was revealed, the Prophet ﷺ would call a **Scribe** كاتب, **One who was Appointed to Write** down the revealed words of the Qur'an. The scribes would write it down on leather, paper or any other material that could be used to record the holy words of the Qur'an. Then the Blessed Prophet ﷺ would instruct the person to put this ayah in the correct surat.

In addition, every year during the month of Ramadan, the Prophet ﷺ would recite the entire Qur'an from beginning to end with Angel Jibreel ﷺ. Its proper order was therefore no mystery.

Many of the **Sahaba** صحابة **Companions of Prophet Muhammad** ﷺ, not only memorized it completely, they also wrote it down and even added **Tafseer** تفسير **Commentary**. Thus, scholarship in Islam existed from the very beginning. When the Prophet ﷺ passed away, the whole Qur'an had already been written down on pieces of paper and leather. However, it was not yet gathered in book form.

C. The Danger of Losing the Qur'an

Abu Bakr ﷺ was the first **Khalifa** خليفة **Leader of the Muslim nation.** During his rule, a rebellion arose among some distant Arab tribes who wanted to leave the Islamic community and alter Islam to suit their needs. The Muslim leadership knew that this amounted to treason, so they organized armies to stop the sedition. During one battle with the rebels, at a place called Yamamah, nearly 70 of those who had memorized the Qur'an were killed.

'Umar ﷺ worried that if more people who memorized were killed or died, then the Qur'an might be lost, so he convinced Abu Bakr ﷺ that the Qur'an should be gathered in book form as a way of preserving it permanently.

Zayd bin Thabit ﷺ was responsible for overseeing this task. He was the Prophet's chief scribe and was himself a **Hafith (Hafiz)** حافظ, **One who has Memorized the Entire Qur'an**. He arranged the text of the Qur'an into its agreed-upon order and assembled it into one complete book.

Zayd ﷺ followed strict methods in his compilation, enlisting dozens of other *huffath* (plural of hafith) to verify his work to make sure everything was perfectly accurate. Abu Bakr ﷺ, who was also a hafith, confirmed that everything was correct. After Abu Bakr ﷺ passed away, 'Umar ﷺ took charge of the book, and when he passed away, the copy was kept with his daughter, Hafsah ﷺ, a widow of Prophet Muhammad ﷺ.

Keep in mind that, in addition to transcribing the Qur'an, thousands of Muslims were committing it to memory. As a result, the number of huffath was growing every year. In addition, every Muslim memorized some part of the Qur'an, and most people learned very large portions of it.

The written copy of the Qur'an did not have vowel markings or dots, nor were the ayaat separated and numbered. It was written in the Arabic letters of old, and any literate Arab back then could read it easily without such aids.

But as the Muslim world expanded into lands where the people learned Arabic as a second language, these new Muslims had difficulty learning the correct pronunciation of the text. According to a hadith of Prophet Muhammad ﷺ, the Qur'an was revealed in seven different dialects. Thus, different pronunciations and recitations of the Qur'an could be traced to the seven valid pronunciations of the Qur'an.

During the rule of 'Uthman ﷺ, the third khalifa, serious differences arose between the Syrians and Iraqis about how to pronounce the letters and words correctly. One Sahaba by the name of Hudhayfah ﷺ complained about this to 'Uthman ﷺ. Khalifa 'Uthman ﷺ consulted with the other Sahaba, and they agreed that something should be done to prevent such confusion.

D. The Official Qur'an Is Authenticated and Circulated

'Uthman, responding to this concern, charged that all copies of the Qur'an that represented different dialects be collected and destroyed. He again called upon Zayd bin Thabit and three other trusted Companions to reproduce and rewrite one copy of the Qur'an in the dialect that was best known at the time: the Qurayshi dialect.

Together, the four guardians borrowed the original complete copy of the Qur'an from Hafsah and transcribed many more copies of the Qur'an from it. Thus, the Qur'an was compiled in one pure and complete form, exactly as it was recited at the time of Prophet Muhammad.

Each major Muslim city was then sent a copy from which they could make more copies and spread the written Qur'an to other areas. At least two of these original copies of the Qur'an exist today. One is housed in the Topkapi Museum in Istanbul, Turkey; the other is in the city of Tashkent in Central Asia.

Miraculously, Allah protected His book through the actions of motivated and dedicated people. The Qur'an we use today is the same as the one circulated over 1,400 years ago.

During the rule of Khalifa Malik bin Marwan, the dots and vowel markings were added by Hajjaj bin Yusuf. He did this to make it easier for non-Arabs to learn and pronounce the words correctly.

We have been blessed by the fact that the revelation of Allah has been preserved and remains intact for everyone all over the world. Even to this day, Muslims memorize the Qur'an and study its meaning.

Every Muslim child learns at least a small part of the Qur'an. Many educated speakers of Arabic from all over the world use the style of Arabic in the Qur'an as a model to learn the language.

The Best Faith

The Blessed Messenger of Allah once asked a group of Sahaba, "Which person's faith (do you think) is the most pleasing (to God)?"

One person suggested that the angels had the most perfect faith. The Blessed Prophet replied, "But why shouldn't they believe when they are with their Lord?" Another person said that maybe the prophets had the best faith. The Blessed Messenger answered by saying, "Why shouldn't they believe when they have revelation descending upon them?"

Then another Sahabi suggested that maybe they themselves had the best faith. But the Blessed Prophet replied, "But why shouldn't you believe when I am among you?" Then he told the people with him, "The people whose faith pleases me the most are those who will come after my time who will find pages contained in a book (the Qur'an), and they will believe in what is contained within it."
(Al-Hakem)

قَالَ رَسُولُ اللهِ ﷺ: «أَتَدْرُونَ أَيَّ أَهْلِ الإِيمَانِ أَفْضَلُ إِيمَانًا؟ قَالُوا: يَا رَسُولَ اللهِ، المَلَائِكَةُ. قَالَ: هُمْ كَذَلِكَ، وَيَحِقُّ ذَلِكَ لَهُمْ، وَمَا يَمْنَعُهُمْ وَقَدْ أَنْزَلَهُمُ اللهُ المَنْزِلَةَ الَّتِي أَنْزَلَهُمْ بِهَا، بَلْ غَيْرُهُمْ، قَالُوا: يَا رَسُولَ اللهِ، فَالأَنْبِيَاءُ الَّذِينَ أَكْرَمَهُمُ اللهُ تَعَالَى بِالنُّبُوَّةِ وَالرِّسَالَةِ. قَالَ: هُمْ كَذَلِكَ، وَيَحِقُّ ذَلِكَ لَهُمْ، وَمَا يَمْنَعُهُمْ وَقَدْ أَنْزَلَهُمُ اللهُ المَنْزِلَةَ الَّتِي أَنْزَلَهُمْ بِهَا، بَلْ غَيْرُهُمْ، قُلْنَا: فَمَنْ هُمْ يَا رَسُولَ اللهِ؟ قَالَ: أَقْوَامٌ يَأْتُونَ مِنْ بَعْدِي فِي أَصْلَابِ الرِّجَالِ فَيُؤْمِنُونَ بِي وَلَمْ يَرَوْنِي، وَيَجِدُونَ الوَرَقَ المُعَلَّقَ فَيَعْمَلُونَ بِمَا فِيهِ، فَهَؤُلَاءِ أَفْضَلُ أَهْلِ الإِيمَانِ إِيمَانًا». رَوَاهُ الحَاكِمُ

IT'S ALL ABOUT ISLAM

Images of the earliest written version of the Qur'an.

Questions to Answer

1. When the Prophet ﷺ used to receive a revelation, what would he ask to be done?
2. Why did 'Umar ؓ want the Qur'an to be put into book form?
3. Who was placed in charge of compiling the Qur'an in book form, and why was he chosen?
4. Why were the vowel markings and dots added later on?
5. Do copies of the Qur'an that were made in the first generation of Islam still exist today? If so, where are they located?
6. Describe how each of the first three khulafa' participated in the preservation of the Qur'an.
7. What proof is there that the Prophet ﷺ himself arranged the proper order of the ayaat and suwar?

Define: Hafith, Sahaba, Fus-ha.

Reflect: Why do you think Prophet Muhammad ﷺ stated that the faith of those who were to come after his time would be most pleasing to him?

Act: Take two copies of the Qur'an prepared by different translators and compare them to one another. Create a chart that documents the similarities and differences.

IQ Builder: What does 2:23 state? How can this strengthen the proof that the Qur'an has been preserved in its purest form?

8 The Book of Miracles

WHAT TO LEARN

The Qur'an mentions scientific facts that were not known to man at the time of its revelation, such as the existence of other planets and galaxies. How do you think people in Arabia reacted when such verses were revealed?

VOCABULARY

Muhkamat   Mutashabihat

THINK ABOUT IT

What makes the Qur'an unlike any other book?

A. The Qur'an Is Unique

Allah ﷻ declares, *If this Qur'an were bestowed upon a mountain, it would crumble.* Surat Al Hashr (The Exile) 59:21

﴿لَوْ أَنزَلْنَا هَٰذَا ٱلْقُرْءَانَ عَلَىٰ جَبَلٍ لَّرَأَيْتَهُۥ خَٰشِعًا مُّتَصَدِّعًا مِّنْ خَشْيَةِ ٱللَّهِ ۚ وَتِلْكَ ٱلْأَمْثَٰلُ نَضْرِبُهَا لِلنَّاسِ لَعَلَّهُمْ يَتَفَكَّرُونَ﴾ سُورَةُ الحَشْرِ 59: 21

Indeed, the Holy Qur'an is a book of great power and miracles. No other book has been read or memorized more than the Qur'an. It moves people to action and brings joy and happiness to the hearts of the young and old, rich and poor. Many books have been written about the amazing qualities of the Holy Qur'an, from its perfect use of analogies and expressions to its melodic rhythm when recited aloud.

If it were a Book from anyone else besides Allah, you would have found many mistakes in it. Surat An-Nisa' (The Women) 4:82

﴿وَلَوْ كَانَ مِنْ عِندِ غَيْرِ ٱللَّهِ لَوَجَدُوا۟ فِيهِ ٱخْتِلَٰفًا كَثِيرًا﴾ سُورَةُ النِّسَاءِ 4: 82

There are no mistakes or errors in the Qur'an. It is a perfect book, and people have spent their entire lives studying even just one aspect of it.

Some people examine the many scientific statements, while others marvel at the perfect grammar. Some look for the hidden meanings of its verses, while others ponder the solutions given for mankind's problems in this life.

Allah ﷻ uses many words to describe the Qur'an, such as 'the Guidance الهُدى', 'the Good News البُشرى,' 'the Noble Message الرِّسَالَةُ النَّبِيلَة', 'the Standard المِنهاج', 'the Clear Book الكِتابُ الواضِح' and 'the Glorious Book الكِتابُ المَجيد'. It was revealed gradually to the Blessed Prophet Muhammad ﷺ, who could neither read nor write, over a period of 23 years.

43

IT'S ALL ABOUT ISLAM

B. A Guide for the Heart

The Qur'an is the most widely read and memorized book in the world, surpassing even the Bible, which has been in circulation far longer. It contains scientific details of which no human being knew at the time of Prophet Muhammad ﷺ. These facts did not come to light until more than a thousand years later.

As Allah indicates, *We have already sent down to you verses making things clear, an illustration from (the story of) people who passed away before you, and an admonition for those who fear (Allah).* Surat An-Noor (The Light) 24:34

﴿ وَلَقَدْ أَنزَلْنَا إِلَيْكُمْ ءَايَٰتٍ مُّبَيِّنَٰتٍ وَمَثَلًا مِّنَ ٱلَّذِينَ خَلَوْا۟ مِن قَبْلِكُمْ وَمَوْعِظَةً لِّلْمُتَّقِينَ ﴾ سُورَةُ النُّور 24: 34

The Prophet ﷺ memorized the entire message and thousands of his Companions did so as well. The Qur'an was committed to writing within his lifetime, and was checked and rechecked for accuracy in the earliest days of Islam. After the Prophet's ﷺ death, the message was gradually distributed in book form all over the world.

It has 114 chapters, or suwar, comprising approximately 6,208 ayaat, or verses. The verses cover a wide range of topics and themes that relate to the life of the present world and in the next life. Some verses are clear in meaning, **Muhkamat** مُحْكَمَات, while others are mystical or allegorical, **Mutashabihat** مُتَشَابِهَات, or those of deeper meaning. (3:7)

The ayaat are often referred to as **Makkan** مَكِّيّ or **Madinan** مَدَنِيّ revelations. That is, any revelations that came to the Prophet ﷺ while he was in the first phase of his mission, in Makkah, are called *Makkan suwar,* and any revelations that came to the Prophet ﷺ after his migration to Al Madinah are called *Madinan suwar.* The Makkan suwar deal primarily with Islamic beliefs and teachings, while Madinan suwar emphasize how to form and live within an Islamic society ruled through Islamic law.

Through the study of this book, millions have found a renewed sense of purpose in their lives. It is the book of guidance, of direction and of healing. No man or woman could have ever produced it, and no one can ever claim to understand all of its teachings.

It is the book that provides a clear and noble path for people to follow, in both their personal and spiritual affairs. It is unlike any other book in existence and the final message given to us by the Creator of the Universe.

Those who pay attention to what it says and implement its teachings are promised success in this life and the next, while those who reject it will ultimately fail.

Allah ﷻ Says of the Qur'an

When the Qur'an is read, listen to it with attention and hold your peace so you can receive Mercy. And bring your Lord to remembrance in your (very) soul, with humility and in reverence, without loudness in words in the mornings and evenings, and don't be negligent. Those who are near to your Lord don't hesitate to do Him service. They celebrate His praises and bow down before Him. Surat Al A'raf (The Heights) 7:204-206

﴿ وَإِذَا قُرِئَ ٱلْقُرْءَانُ فَٱسْتَمِعُوا۟ لَهُۥ وَأَنصِتُوا۟ لَعَلَّكُمْ تُرْحَمُونَ ﴾ ﴿ وَٱذْكُر رَّبَّكَ فِى نَفْسِكَ تَضَرُّعًا وَخِيفَةً وَدُونَ ٱلْجَهْرِ مِنَ ٱلْقَوْلِ بِٱلْغُدُوِّ وَٱلْءَاصَالِ وَلَا تَكُن مِّنَ ٱلْغَٰفِلِينَ ﴾ ﴿ إِنَّ ٱلَّذِينَ عِندَ رَبِّكَ لَا يَسْتَكْبِرُونَ عَنْ عِبَادَتِهِۦ وَيُسَبِّحُونَهُۥ وَلَهُۥ يَسْجُدُونَ ﴾ سُورَةُ الأعراف 7: 204-206

And We have sent down the Book to you, only because you may explain to them what they differed about, and (so that it may be) guidance and mercy for a people who believe. Allah sent down water from the heavens and revived the land with it after it was dead. Surely, in that there is a sign for a people who listen. Surat An-Nahl (The Bees) 16:64-65

﴿ وَمَآ أَنزَلْنَا عَلَيْكَ ٱلْكِتَٰبَ إِلَّا لِتُبَيِّنَ لَهُمُ ٱلَّذِى ٱخْتَلَفُوا۟ فِيهِ وَهُدًى وَرَحْمَةً لِّقَوْمٍ يُؤْمِنُونَ ﴾ ﴿ وَٱللَّهُ أَنزَلَ مِنَ ٱلسَّمَآءِ مَآءً فَأَحْيَا بِهِ ٱلْأَرْضَ بَعْدَ مَوْتِهَآ إِنَّ فِى ذَٰلِكَ لَءَايَةً لِّقَوْمٍ يَسْمَعُونَ ﴾ سُورَةُ النحل 16: 64-65

Read what is revealed to you of the (Qur'an) and establish prayer because prayer restrains (a person from doing) shameful deeds. Remembering Allah is the greatest (thing in life). And Allah knows what you do.

Don't argue with the People of the Book (the Jews and Christians) except in a better way, unless it be with the ones who are doing wrong, but even then, only say: "We believe in the revelation that came down to us and in the one that came down to you. Our God and your God is one, and it's to Him we bow."

And so We have sent down the book to you and some of the People of the book believe in it, even as some of these (Arabs do). Only the faithless reject Our signs. And you (Muhammad) were not (able) to recite a book before this (book came) nor are you (able) to write it with your own right hand (because you don't know how to write). If you (were a known writer before the Qur'an was revealed), then the vain people could have doubted.

Indeed, here are proven signs in the hearts of those who understand. Only the unjust reject Our signs. Yet they say: "Why are there no (miracles) sent down to him from his Lord?"

Tell them, "The signs are indeed with Allah, and I am indeed a clear Warner." Isn't it enough for them that We sent down to you the Book that is read to them? Indeed, in it is a mercy and reminder to those who believe. Surat Al 'Ankabut (The Spider) 29:45-51

> ﴿ ٱتْلُ مَآ أُوحِىَ إِلَيْكَ مِنَ ٱلْكِتَٰبِ وَأَقِمِ ٱلصَّلَوٰةَ ۖ إِنَّ ٱلصَّلَوٰةَ تَنْهَىٰ عَنِ ٱلْفَحْشَآءِ وَٱلْمُنكَرِ ۗ وَلَذِكْرُ ٱللَّهِ أَكْبَرُ ۗ وَٱللَّهُ يَعْلَمُ مَا تَصْنَعُونَ ۞ وَلَا تُجَٰدِلُوٓا۟ أَهْلَ ٱلْكِتَٰبِ إِلَّا بِٱلَّتِى هِىَ أَحْسَنُ إِلَّا ٱلَّذِينَ ظَلَمُوا۟ مِنْهُمْ ۖ وَقُولُوٓا۟ ءَامَنَّا بِٱلَّذِىٓ أُنزِلَ إِلَيْنَا وَأُنزِلَ إِلَيْكُمْ وَإِلَٰهُنَا وَإِلَٰهُكُمْ وَٰحِدٌ وَنَحْنُ لَهُۥ مُسْلِمُونَ ۞ وَكَذَٰلِكَ أَنزَلْنَآ إِلَيْكَ ٱلْكِتَٰبَ ۚ فَٱلَّذِينَ ءَاتَيْنَٰهُمُ ٱلْكِتَٰبَ يُؤْمِنُونَ بِهِۦ ۖ وَمِنْ هَٰٓؤُلَآءِ مَن يُؤْمِنُ بِهِۦ ۚ وَمَا يَجْحَدُ بِـَٔايَٰتِنَآ إِلَّا ٱلْكَٰفِرُونَ ۞ وَمَا كُنتَ تَتْلُوا۟ مِن قَبْلِهِۦ مِن كِتَٰبٍ وَلَا تَخُطُّهُۥ بِيَمِينِكَ ۖ إِذًا لَّٱرْتَابَ ٱلْمُبْطِلُونَ ۞ بَلْ هُوَ ءَايَٰتٌۢ بَيِّنَٰتٌ فِى صُدُورِ ٱلَّذِينَ أُوتُوا۟ ٱلْعِلْمَ ۚ وَمَا يَجْحَدُ بِـَٔايَٰتِنَآ إِلَّا ٱلظَّٰلِمُونَ ۞ وَقَالُوا۟ لَوْلَآ أُنزِلَ عَلَيْهِ ءَايَٰتٌ مِّن رَّبِّهِۦ ۖ قُلْ إِنَّمَا ٱلْـَٔايَٰتُ عِندَ ٱللَّهِ وَإِنَّمَآ أَنَا۠ نَذِيرٌ مُّبِينٌ ۞ أَوَلَمْ يَكْفِهِمْ أَنَّآ أَنزَلْنَا عَلَيْكَ ٱلْكِتَٰبَ يُتْلَىٰ عَلَيْهِمْ ۚ إِنَّ فِى ذَٰلِكَ لَرَحْمَةً وَذِكْرَىٰ لِقَوْمٍ يُؤْمِنُونَ ﴾ سُورَةُ ٱلْعَنكَبُوتِ 29: 45–51

Questions to Answer

1. How many suwar can be found in the Qur'an? How many ayaat?
2. What are three ways in which the Qur'an is unique?
3. How do we know that the Qur'an is from Allah?
4. What are the two types of ayaat, and how are they described in Surat 3, ayah 7?

Define: Muhkamat, Mutashabihat.
Reflect: Would 2:282 be considered a muhkamat or mutashabihat ayah? Explain your answer.
Act: Choose an ayah from the Qur'an that conveys something meaningful to you. Write it down and share why that ayah is special to you.

IQ Builders:
1. What does Allah say about the Qur'an in 17:88?
2. According to the ayaat contained in 18:1-2, what is the purpose of the Qur'an?
3. Allah gives us a beautiful example of His power to give as much revelation to humans as He wills. Explain this power according to 18:109.
4. What does Allah say about the Qur'an in 16:64? How is this illustrated in the very next ayah?

9 The Qur'an and Science

WHAT TO LEARN

What if you discovered an old computer inside a tomb that was thousands of years old? You would be astounded, because there's no way it could have been created at that time. The same is true of the Qur'an. It says things no one could have known long ago. Why do you think that is?

VOCABULARY

Signs   Munir   Siraj

THINK ABOUT IT

Why does Allah include scientific statements in the Qur'an?

A. A Scientist Speaks

"The relationship between the Qur'an and science is... a surprise, especially when it turns out to be one of harmony and not of discord."
–Dr. Maurice Bucaille, *The Bible, the Qur'an and Science.* (p.110).

After studying verses from the Qur'an that make reference to scientific subjects, the French scientist, Dr. Maurice Bucaille, was astounded. He noticed no discrepancies between the Qur'anic ayaat and modern scientific knowledge.

Indeed, the Qur'an is a book that not only provides guidance but also speaks of the natural world around us. Many studies prove that everything said in the Qur'an about science is accurate and consistent with what we know in science today. While this may not initially seem like anything special, when we remember that the Qur'an was revealed to Prophet Muhammad more than 1,448 years ago, it becomes a rather spectacular miracle.

Many of the things mentioned in the Qur'an about plants, animals, the Earth, space and humans were unknown at that time—it was completely new information.

What is even more spectacular is that the Blessed Prophet lived in the middle of Arabia, which was an area that had very limited exposure to the outside world. There were no schools, no scientists nor any universities.

But Allah doesn't make scientific statements in the Qur'an just to impress us. Instead, He uses them as **Signs** آيات for us to believe in Him and to follow the way of life that He wants for us, which is Islam.

In this chapter, we will explore a few of the many scientific statements in the Qur'an. If you are wondering what Muslims must have thought about these verses, which we are only beginning to understand today, remember that we are taught to believe in the Qur'an completely. If there is a part we don't fully understand yet, then we have to be patient and ask Allah to help us to discover the meaning.

He it is Who has sent down to thee the Book. In it are verses basic or fundamental (of established meaning); they are the foundation of the Book:

others are allegorical. But those in whose hearts is perversity follow the part thereof that is allegorical, seeking discord, and searching for its hidden meanings, but no one knows its hidden meanings except Allah. And those who are firmly grounded in knowledge say: "We believe in the Book; the whole of it is from our Lord" and none will grasp the Message except men of understanding. "Our Lord!" (They say), "Let not our hearts deviate now after Thou hast guided us, but grant us mercy from Thine own Presence; for Thou art the Grantor of bounties without measure. Our Lord! Thou art He that will gather mankind Together against a day about which there is no doubt; for Allah never fails in His promise." Surat Al 'Imran (The Family of 'Imran) 3: 7-9

﷽ هُوَ ٱلَّذِيٓ أَنزَلَ عَلَيْكَ ٱلْكِتَٰبَ مِنْهُ ءَايَٰتٌ مُّحْكَمَٰتٌ هُنَّ أُمُّ ٱلْكِتَٰبِ وَأُخَرُ مُتَشَٰبِهَٰتٌ ۖ فَأَمَّا ٱلَّذِينَ فِى قُلُوبِهِمْ زَيْغٌ فَيَتَّبِعُونَ مَا تَشَٰبَهَ مِنْهُ ٱبْتِغَآءَ ٱلْفِتْنَةِ وَٱبْتِغَآءَ تَأْوِيلِهِۦ ۗ وَمَا يَعْلَمُ تَأْوِيلَهُۥٓ إِلَّا ٱللَّهُ ۗ وَٱلرَّٰسِخُونَ فِى ٱلْعِلْمِ يَقُولُونَ ءَامَنَّا بِهِۦ كُلٌّ مِّنْ عِندِ رَبِّنَا ۗ وَمَا يَذَّكَّرُ إِلَّآ أُو۟لُوا۟ ٱلْأَلْبَٰبِ ﴾ ﴿ رَبَّنَا لَا تُزِغْ قُلُوبَنَا بَعْدَ إِذْ هَدَيْتَنَا وَهَبْ لَنَا مِن لَّدُنكَ رَحْمَةً ۚ إِنَّكَ أَنتَ ٱلْوَهَّابُ ﴾ ﴿ رَبَّنَآ إِنَّكَ جَامِعُ ٱلنَّاسِ لِيَوْمٍ لَّا رَيْبَ فِيهِ ۚ إِنَّ ٱللَّهَ لَا يُخْلِفُ ٱلْمِيعَادَ ﴾ سورة آل عمران 3: 7-9

Muslims have always embraced science and sought knowledge about the natural world. Allah ﷻ commands us to study the Universe so that we can recognize His power and strengthen our faith through this understanding. (2:164)

The next time you learn something fascinating about the world you live in, remember that it's a sign of Allah's ﷻ power, and that, insha'Allah, your dedication and faith in your Creator will increase because of it.

سبحان الله

Some Scientific Marvels of the Qur'an

Nearly all ants are females. Male ants are produced extremely infrequently and quickly die after mating. All the worker ants, as well as the queen ants, are females. Ants also communicate in their own "language." The Arabic word for 'ant' is النَّمْل, which is a masculine noun. No one in the world at that time even knew that ants had different genders, but in the Qur'an, Allah ﷻ says that Prophet Sulayman ﷺ heard an ant speaking to 'her' fellow ants قَالَتْ نَمْلَةٌ, telling them to run and hide to avoid being stepped on. The feminine form of the verb قَالَ is قَالَتْ, and is used in ayah 27:18. Thus, the ant is clearly described as female. Prophet Sulayman ﷺ is said to have been amused at "her speech." (27:19)

IT'S ALL ABOUT ISLAM

Salt water and fresh water do not mix easily. There is a barrier between them. (27:61; 55:19-22)

The moon is referred to as **Munir** مُنِير **Light Reflector**, while the sun is referred to as **Siraj** سِرَاج **Light Producer**. (25:61; 71:15-16; 78:12-13.)

Many species of spiders are solitary. The female may even eat the male after mating. Allah ﷻ mentions that spiders have the weakest homes of all. That doesn't mean just the webs, their family structure definitely needs improvement! (29:41)

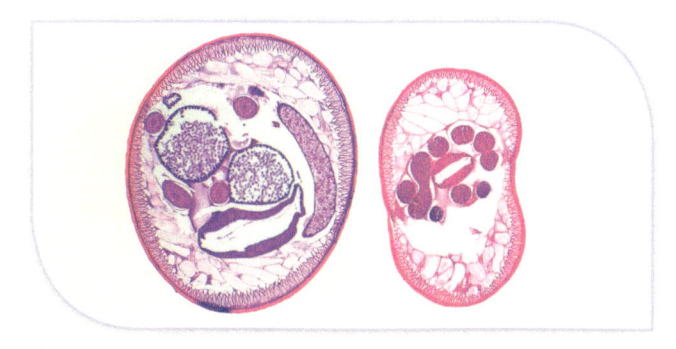

A pregnancy occurs only when the ova and sperm unite. Then the fertilized egg 'clings,' or 'alaq, in the womb. The fetus grows in stages until it is ready to be born. (23:14; 40:67; 75:37-38)

Water is the basis of all life. Allah ﷻ created all life from water. (24:45)

Everything was compacted together and then split apart. Gases spread throughout the Universe, and stars, planets and other entities were formed. (21:30; 41:11)

Plants have both male and female reproductive organs. All plants were created with paired organs. (13:3; 20:53; 22:5; 31:10; 36:36)

IT'S ALL ABOUT ISLAM

The action of the wind over the seas pulls moisture along and collects it in the clouds. The clouds are spread again by wind currents and then break up as rain falls down from them. (24:43; 30:48)

There is life on some other planets. Allah﷾ says that every creature in space and on Earth has to follow Him and that He spread life throughout space and Earth. (3:83; 19:93-95; 24:41; 23:17; 42:29; 30:26; 55:29; 65:12)

Humans can only break free of Earth's gravity and enter space with modern technology and powerful engines. Allah﷾ says humans can only venture into space with powerful tools to use. (55:33)

People have trouble breathing when they ascend to very high elevations. Their lungs become constricted. Even planes need pressurized cabins so people can breathe easily. (6:125)

Allahﷻ compares the state of an unbeliever to that of a person in the dark depths of the ocean. He cannot see his hand in front of his face and is under layers of darkness. Remember that the Prophet ﷺ had never even seen the ocean before, nor had anyone ever dived to the deep recesses of the ocean at that time. People didn't know at the time that the bottom of the ocean is dark. (24:40)

Questions to Answer

1. Why is it amazing that everything said about science in the Qur'an is true?
2. What does Allahﷻ say about the spider's home?
3. What does Allahﷻ tell us is the basis of all life?
4. To what does Allahﷻ compare the state of an unbeliever?

Define: Signs, Munir.

Reflect: Which scientific miracle from the Qur'an intrigues you the most and why?

Act: Memorize the dua' mentioned in surat Al 'Imran (The Family of 'Imran), verses 8-9. "Our Lord! Let not our hearts deviate (from the truth) after You have guided us and grant us mercy from You. Truly, You are the Bestower. Our Lord! Verily, it is You Who will gather mankind together on the Day about which there is no doubt. Verily Allah never breaks His Promise."

﴿رَبَّنَا لَا تُزِغْ قُلُوبَنَا بَعْدَ إِذْ هَدَيْتَنَا وَهَبْ لَنَا مِن لَّدُنكَ رَحْمَةً إِنَّكَ أَنتَ ٱلْوَهَّابُ﴾ ﴿رَبَّنَا إِنَّكَ جَامِعُ ٱلنَّاسِ لِيَوْمٍ لَّا رَيْبَ فِيهِ إِنَّ ٱللَّهَ لَا يُخْلِفُ ٱلْمِيعَادَ﴾

IQ Builders:

1. What does Allahﷻ say in 51:20-23 about why He mentions facts from science and nature?
2. What does Allahﷻ say in 6:38?
3. When a person rejects the scientific proof given by Allahﷻ, what does 6:37 say about it?

Literature Selection

Surat Ash-Shura (The Consultations): 42

Adapted from *The Holy Qur'an*
Arranged by Yahiya Emerick
(Explanatory words added in parentheses)

In the Name of Allah,
The Most Gracious, The Most Merciful

Ha Mim (1) 'Ayn Seen Qaf.* (2) And so, He's inspiring you (Muhammad), as He inspired the (ancient Prophets) who came before you, and Allah is All-Mighty and the Wise. (3) Whatever is in the Heavens and on Earth belongs to Him, He's the Exalted and the Most Great One. (4) The skies are nearly ripped to shreds above them, and the angels praise their Lord and pray for the forgiveness for all creatures on Earth. He is indeed the Forgiving and the Merciful, (5) but whoever looks for protector allies other than Him—Allah is Guardian over them—and you're not responsible for them at all. (6) And so, We've revealed to you a Qur'an in Arabic so you can warn "Um Al Qurah," the most important city (of Makkah), and all of the other (cities) beyond it, about the Day of Assembly that will arrive without any doubt. Some of them will be in Paradise, while the rest of them will be in the Raging Blaze. (7) If Allah had wanted to, He could have made all (the people of the Earth) into a single nation, but He (lets them differ and divide in order to test them), and also so that He can be merciful to whomever He wants, though the wrongdoers certainly aren't going to find any protector or rescuer to save them. (8)

Are they taking allies other than Him? Allah is the (only) One who can protect you, and He's the One who will bring the dead to life, for He has power over everything. (9) Whatever you're all arguing about, Allah will be the One to solve it. That is my Lord, Allah. I trust in Him and I turn myself towards Him (for guidance). (10) (He's) the Creator of the Heavens and the Earth, and He made you all into pairs (of male and female) among your own kind, even as He made cattle in pairs. That's how He made it possible for you to multiply. There's really nothing like Him at all, for He's the Listening and the Watchful. (11) The keys of the Heavens and the Earth belong to Him, and He extends or restricts the provision of whoever He wants to, for He knows about everything. (12) He has established the same way of life for you that He introduced to Noah—it's the same one that We're revealing to you, and the same one that We introduced to Abraham, Moses, and

---

* Al Huruf Al Muqatta'h الحُروف المُقَطَّعَة are unique letters that appear in the beginning of 29 suwar of the Qur'an. Muqatta'h means disjointed or unconnected letters. Their real meanings remain unknown and are considered by most Muslims to be known to Allah alone.

Jesus, namely to establish the (moral) way of life and not to be divided about it. The idol-worshippers find that what you're asking of them is hard, though Allah directs to Himself whoever He wants to, and He guides to Himself (all) who turn (their hopes towards Him). (13) (The people of the past) divided up (into many competing sects)—and that was after they already had knowledge (from Allah)! (They did it solely) out of selfish envy among themselves. If it wasn't for an order that your Lord had already decreed that gave (humanity) a fixed time limit, then the situation would have been resolved between them. (Later generations), who have inherited the Scriptures since then, are filled with uncertainty about (them). (14) So, on account of that, do continue to call them (to believe in the Qur'an), and remain committed (to the Cause) as you're commanded to and don't follow their whims. Tell them, "I believe in the Book that Allah has sent down. I am commanded to judge fairly between you. Allah is our Lord and your Lord. To us, are our deeds, and to you, are your deeds. There is no argument between us and you. Allah will bring us all together and the final return is back with Him." (15) Whoever argues about Allah after His (existence) has already been accepted (by all parties concerned) as arguing over nothing in Allah's sight. His anger is drawn over them and a strong punishment lies in reserve. (16) Allah's the One Who sent down the Book in all honesty and well-balanced (principles). And what will make you perceive? Perhaps the Hour is near. (17) The only ones who want it to come sooner are the ones who don't believe in it, but the faithful are in awe of it and know that it's a reality. Isn't it (true) that those who disregard the Hour are grossly mistaken? (18) Allah is More than Fair to His Servants. Allah is gracious to His servants; He gives the necessities of life to whoever He wants to, and He has the strength to do whatever He wants. (19) Whoever desires the harvest of the next life, We add to his harvest. Whoever desires the harvest of this world, We'll give him some of it, but he'll have no share of the next life. (20) Do they have "partners" (as powerful as Allah) who can make a religion for them without Allah's permission? If it wasn't for the order of Judgement, the issue would've already been decided between them, but the wrongdoers have a terrible punishment waiting for them. (21) You're going to see the wrongdoers trembling in fear for all the (sins) they've earned, and that is something they'll have to bear. The believers, however, who did what was morally right, will rest in the luxuries of Paradise. In their Lord's presence, they're going to have everything they wish for, and that's the greatest bounty! (22) That's the same one that Allah is giving the good news of to His servants who believe and do what's morally right. Say to them, "I'm not asking you for any reward for this, but at least extend to me the love that is due to a member of your own family!" Whoever accumulates any good (deeds), We will multiply the goodness within it, for Allah is Forgiving and Appreciative. (23) Are they saying, "He's making up lies about Allah?" If Allah had wanted to, He could have sealed up even your heart, but Allah blots out falsehood and proves, by His Own words, that the Truth is true, for He knows the secrets that lurk within (people's) hearts. (24) He's the One Who accepts repentance from His servants, and He also forgives sins, and He certainly knows whatever you're doing. (25)

He listens to the believers who do what's morally right and gives them an increase (in their fortune) from His largess—but, for the faithless, there is nothing but a terrible punishment. (26) If He ever increased the (financial) resources of His servants, they would surely go out of control all over the world, but He sends it down in increments as He wills, for He is ever aware and observant of His servants. (27) He's the One who sends down rain even after (people) have given up all hope for it, and He scatters His mercy (in every direction), for He is the Protector and the Praiseworthy. (28) Among His signs is the creation of the Heavens and the Earth, and all the living creatures that He scattered about, and He has the ability to collect them all together again when He wants to. (29)

Never Overlook Personal Responsibility

No misfortune comes upon you without it being the result of your own actions, but for many (of your mishaps) there is forgiveness. (30) And you can't escape (the results of your bad decisions) by running all over the world, for you have no one else who can help or protect you besides Allah. (31) Among His signs are the smooth sailing ships that ply through the oceans, looking like mountain peaks. (32) If He wanted to, He could stop the wind (that propels them), and they would be rendered immobile on the (ocean's) surface. Truly, there are signs in this (example) for all who persevere patiently and give thanks. (33) Or (if He wanted to), He could (sink those ships) as a (punishment) for (the sins) that (people) have earned, but He forgives many things. (34) and those who argue about Our signs, they will have no escape! (35) Whatever you're given in this world is only a trifle to use in this life, but whatever is with Allah is better and more lasting—(a reward) for the believers who put their trust in their Lord. (36) They avoid the most serious sins and shameful acts and forgive others, even when they're angry. (37) They respond to their Lord and establish prayers. They decide their communal affairs by consulting each other and spend (in Allah's Cause) out of what We have given them, (38) and they also defend themselves when they are wronged. (39) The payback for an evil (done to you) is (to get back) an equal (amount of compensation) from the (one who wronged you), unless a person forgives (the one who wronged them) and reconciles with him. His compensation is with Allah, for He does not love the wrongdoers. (40) If anyone defends themselves after they were wronged, they will not be blamed for it. (41) Blame will only be assigned against those who oppress people and defy all norms of justice in the Earth against all that is right, and a terrible punishment awaits them! (42) Whoever is patient and forgives (the wrongs that were done against them) is truly courageous, and that is worth considering deeply. (43)

Let Them Decide for Themselves

Whoever Allah leaves astray, there is no protector for them after that. You are going to see the wrongdoers say, just as they eye the punishment (ahead of them), "Isn't there any way to go back?" (44)

And You are going to see them brought to the front in utter humility for their shame, with eyes darting about. The believers will exclaim, "The losers are the ones who lost their own selves and their families on this Day of Judgement. Oh, how lasting a punishment the wrongdoers must endure!" (45) They will not have any protectors to help them in the sight of Allah, and anyone whom Allah leaves to stray will have no way (to escape). (46) Respond to your Lord before the Day comes when there will be no way to delay it, by Allah's (will). On that Day there will be no place for you to hide, nor will there be any chance for you to deny (your guilt). (47) If (people) turn away, then (it's not your fault), for We have not made you to be their keeper. Your duty is only to deliver (the message). And isn't it the case that whenever We give someone a taste of Our mercy, he celebrates, but when some misfortune befalls him, as a result of his own handiwork, he is truly thankless! (48) The control of the Heavens and the Earth belongs to Allah. He creates whatever He wants to, and bestows female children upon whom He pleases and male children upon whom He pleases, (49) or He bestows both males and females, while he leaves barren whom He wills, for He is full of knowledge and powerful. (50) It's beyond the majesty of Allah to speak to a human being, unless it's through inspired revelation, or from behind a veil, or through the agency of a message-bearer (like an Angel), who will reveal, with Allah's permission, whatever Allah wills him to, for He is highly exalted and wise. (51) And thus We've directed revelation to you by Our command. You didn't know what revelation and faith were (before being made a prophet), but We have sent down to you a light which you can use to guide whichever of Our servants that We will, and you are giving guidance towards a straight path (52)—the path of Allah—the One to Whom belongs whatever is in the Heavens and whatever is on Earth, and all affairs certainly will come back to Allah. (53)

Questions to Answer

1. Based on what you read above, how has Allah tried to reach us with His message?
2. Describe this chapter's three main points.

Unit 02 Review Exercise

VOCABULARY REVIEW

On a separate sheet of paper, write the definition of each word below.

1. Khalifa
2. Jibreel
3. Khadijah
4. Wahi
5. Signs
6. Scribe
7. Sahaba
8. Tafseer
9. Fus-ha
10. Hafith (Hafiz)
11. Surat
12. Zayd bin Thabit
13. Mutashabihah
14. Muhkamat

REMEMBERING WHAT YOU READ

On a separate sheet of paper, answer the following questions. Use complete sentences in your answers.

1. What happened to Muhammad while he was meditating in a cave outside Makkah?
2. Why do you think Muhammad was so frightened at first?
3. How did Khadijah comfort her husband after receiving his first revelation?
4. How did 'Umar become a Muslim and why was it ironic?
5. What do scribes do and for what purpose did the Blessed Prophet use them?
6. What choices did Allah give to humans that He gave to no other living creatures?
7. Why was it important to include verses that mention science in the Qur'an?

THINKING TO LEARN

On a separate sheet of paper, answer the questions below. Use complete sentences.

1. How has Allah tried to help humans choose their path wisely?
2. Why was it necessary for the Qur'an to be safe-guarded in the time of the first three khulafa'?
3. Describe how Zayd bin Thabit helped in the preservation of the Qur'an.
4. Describe three scientific miracles mentioned in the Qur'an and how they affect your belief in Islam.

UNIT 3
What Is Islam?

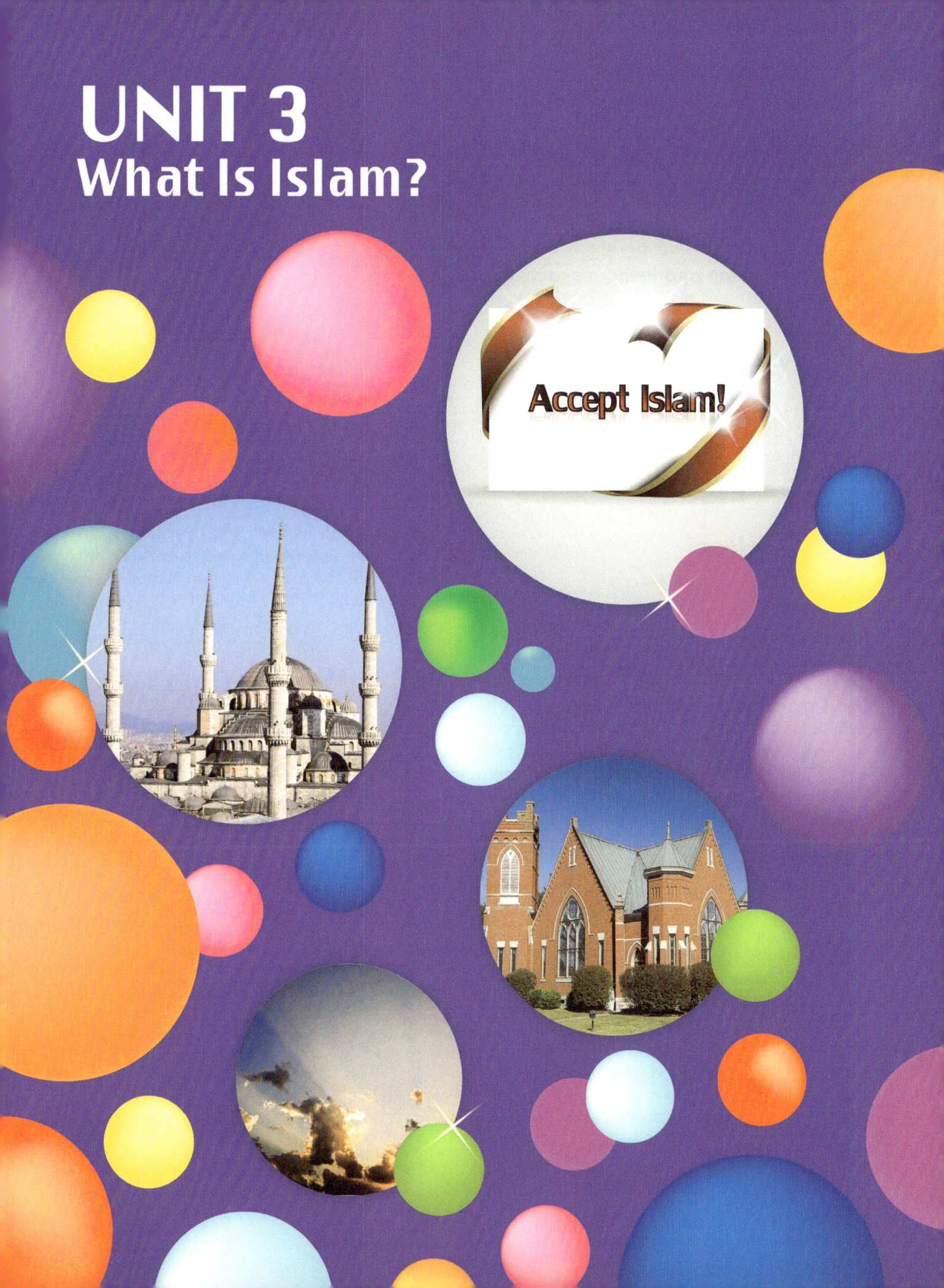

10 What Is Islam All About?

WHAT TO LEARN

What's the difference between being a Muslim by name and being a practicing Muslim?

VOCABULARY

Sect
Fitrah
Arkan al Islam
Arkan al Emaan

THINK ABOUT IT

What is real Islam?

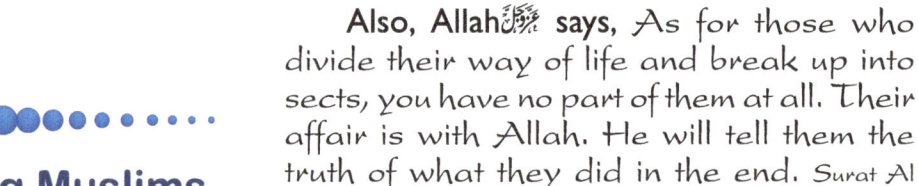

Sufi whirling.

A. Divisions among Muslims

Islam is one of the most misunderstood belief systems in the world. Is it a religion? Is it a culture? Is it a philosophy? There are people who treat Islam as if it were only one of those things and nothing else. Indeed, there seems to be as many versions of Islam as there are Muslim countries in the world. Everyone has their own way, and everyone feels they are following Islam correctly.

There are Sunni Muslims (including Traditionalists, Modernists, Sufis, Salafis, Wahhabis), Shi'a Muslims (including Zaidis, The Twelve Imams, Isma'ilis), 'Alawis, Ibadis, Druze, Nation of Islam and several others. Which **Sect** طائفة truly follows the authentic teachings of Islam?

Allah ﷻ is very harsh against those who make divisions. He said, Among those who split up their religion and became sects. Each group is happy with what it has before it. Surat Ar-Rum (The Romans) 30:32

﴿مِنَ الَّذِينَ فَرَّقُوا دِينَهُمْ وَكَانُوا شِيَعًا كُلُّ حِزْبٍ بِمَا لَدَيْهِمْ فَرِحُونَ﴾ سُورَةُ الرُّومِ 30: 32

Also, Allah ﷻ says, As for those who divide their way of life and break up into sects, you have no part of them at all. Their affair is with Allah. He will tell them the truth of what they did in the end. Surat Al An'aam (The Cattle) 6:159

﴿إِنَّ الَّذِينَ فَرَّقُوا دِينَهُمْ وَكَانُوا شِيَعًا لَسْتَ مِنْهُمْ فِي شَيْءٍ إِنَّمَا أَمْرُهُمْ إِلَى اللَّهِ ثُمَّ يُنَبِّئُهُم بِمَا كَانُوا يَفْعَلُونَ﴾ سُورَةُ الأنعام 6: 159

So this leaves the question: What is true Islam? Once Prophet Muhammad ﷺ said, "The Jews will be divided into 71 sects, the Christians into 72, and this community would eventually divide up into 73; they would all be in the fire except for one." When the people around him asked, "Which one was going to Paradise?" he replied, "that it was the one which would follow his example and that of his Companions." (At-Tirmidhi & Ibn Majah)

قَالَ النَّبِيُّ ﷺ: «افْتَرَقَتِ الْيَهُودُ عَلَى إِحْدَى وَسَبْعِينَ فِرْقَةً، وَافْتَرَقَتِ النَّصَارَى عَلَى اثْنَتَيْنِ وَسَبْعِينَ فِرْقَةً، وَسَتَفْتَرِقُ هَذِهِ الأُمَّةُ عَلَى ثَلَاثٍ وَسَبْعِينَ فِرْقَةً كُلُّهَا فِي النَّارِ إِلَّا وَاحِدَةً، قِيلَ: مَنْ هِيَ يَا رَسُولَ اللَّهِ؟ قَالَ: مَنْ كَانَ عَلَى مِثْلِ مَا أَنَا عَلَيْهِ وَأَصْحَابِي وَفِي بَعْضِ الرِّوَايَاتِ: هِيَ الْجَمَاعَةُ». رَوَاهُ التِّرْمِذِيُّ وَابْنُ مَاجَه

We are blessed as a community in that we have our original book and the complete record of the life and way of our Prophet ﷺ. If anyone comes and says "this" or "that" is Islam we can easily verify whether or not it's true. If it doesn't come from the Qur'an or Sunnah, then it can't be Islam. Thus, we use those two sources to explain what Islam really is. Sincere people seek to learn and practice the truth, and Allah ﷻ guides those who seek Him.

B. What Is the Definition of Islam?

Islam comes from the Arabic root word سَلَمَ, which means both 'surrender' and 'peace.' This name was given by Allah ﷻ in the Qur'an; therefore, this sets us apart from all other religious communities. Judaism, Christianity, Sikhism, Buddhism, Hinduism and all the other beliefs of the world were named by men for either a person or a place. Islam was given its name by Allah ﷻ himself. (6:162-163, 3:19)

The name Islam implies the following concept: by surrendering to Allah ﷻ, one can let go of all one's fears and earthly temptations to finally have peace in one's soul. Thus, Islam is surrendering your will to Allah ﷻ and finding peace. The synonym 'submission' is also used sometimes in place of 'surrender.'

Our **Fitrah** فِطْرَة **Basic Natural Way**, prompts us towards Allah ﷻ, so when we answer the call, we find contentment in our hearts. In contrast, wealth and riches don't bring us a sense of harmony and balance. Only by submitting ourselves to our Creator can we experience those feelings of contentment.

The Blessed Prophet ﷺ once remarked, "True wealth does not come from an abundance of things. True wealth comes from a contented heart." (Al Bukhari & Muslim)

قال النبي ﷺ: «لَيْسَ الْغِنَى عَنْ كَثْرَةِ الْعَرَضِ وَلَكِنَّ الْغِنَى غِنَى النَّفْسِ». رَوَاهُ الْبُخَارِيُّ وَمُسْلِمٌ.

According to the Qur'an, Islam is the way of life that Allah ﷻ designated for humanity, even as the rest of the Universe submits to His will. (41:11) Our task is to choose whether to accept it or not. Allah ﷻ declared, *Certainly the way of life acceptable to Allah is Islam (surrender to His Will) and those to whom the Book had been given did not show opposition until after knowledge had come to them, out of envy among themselves, and whoever disbelieves in the communications of Allah then surely Allah is quick in reckoning.* Surat Al 'Imran (The Family of 'Imran) 3: 19

﴿إِنَّ ٱلدِّينَ عِندَ ٱللَّهِ ٱلْإِسْلَٰمُ وَمَا ٱخْتَلَفَ ٱلَّذِينَ أُوتُوا۟ ٱلْكِتَٰبَ إِلَّا مِنۢ بَعْدِ مَا جَآءَهُمُ ٱلْعِلْمُ بَغْيًۢا بَيْنَهُمْ وَمَن يَكْفُرْ بِـَٔايَٰتِ ٱللَّهِ فَإِنَّ ٱللَّهَ سَرِيعُ ٱلْحِسَابِ﴾

سُورَةُ آلِ عِمْرَانَ 3:19

Anyone who follows his or her heart and seeks to submit to Allah ﷻ as his or her Creator is called a Muslim. Therefore, a Muslim is a person submitting to Allah ﷻ and seeking peace. It is Allah ﷻ Who revealed His messages to chosen guides throughout human history. Most of the names of these prophets, messengers, sages and seers are unknown to us today. (7:35) The culture in which they lived and the rituals they taught varied from place-to-place and time-to-time. Yet, no matter what rituals the people were given to follow and practice, the core message was always the same. It was always Islam. (6:42-45, 14:4)

IT'S ALL ABOUT ISLAM

He has ordained for you people the same religion as He had enjoined upon Nuh, and that which We have revealed to you (O prophet), and that which We had enjoined upon Ibrahim and Musa and 'Isa by saying, "Establish the religion, and be not divided therein." Arduous for the mushriks (polytheists) is that to which you are inviting them. Allah chooses (and pulls) toward Himself anyone He wills, and guides to Himself anyone who turns to Him (to seek guidance). *Surat Ash-Shura (The Consultations) 42:13*

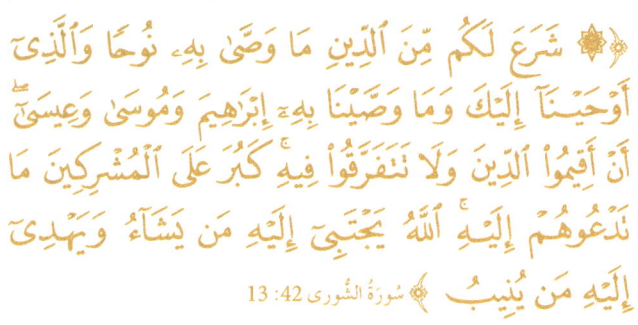

﴿ شَرَعَ لَكُم مِّنَ ٱلدِّينِ مَا وَصَّىٰ بِهِۦ نُوحًا وَٱلَّذِىٓ أَوْحَيْنَآ إِلَيْكَ وَمَا وَصَّيْنَا بِهِۦٓ إِبْرَٰهِيمَ وَمُوسَىٰ وَعِيسَىٰٓ أَنْ أَقِيمُوا۟ ٱلدِّينَ وَلَا تَتَفَرَّقُوا۟ فِيهِ ۚ كَبُرَ عَلَى ٱلْمُشْرِكِينَ مَا تَدْعُوهُمْ إِلَيْهِ ۚ ٱللَّهُ يَجْتَبِىٓ إِلَيْهِ مَن يَشَآءُ وَيَهْدِىٓ إِلَيْهِ مَن يُنِيبُ ﴾ سُورَةُ الشُّورَىٰ 42:13

For every Ummah (religious community) We have appointed a way of worship they are to observe. Therefore, they should never quarrel with you in the matter. And do call (them) to your Lord. Surely, you are on straight Guidance. *Surat Al Hajj (The Pilgrimage) 22:67*

﴿ لِكُلِّ أُمَّةٍ جَعَلْنَا مَنسَكًا هُمْ نَاسِكُوهُ ۖ فَلَا يُنَٰزِعُنَّكَ فِى ٱلْأَمْرِ ۚ وَٱدْعُ إِلَىٰ رَبِّكَ ۖ إِنَّكَ لَعَلَىٰ هُدًى مُّسْتَقِيمٍ ﴾ سُورَةُ الْحَجِّ 22:67

Every prophet taught Islam, or peaceful self-surrender to Allah. They all taught the good deeds and forbid the evil ones. (40:78)

Even though their religions didn't go by the name 'Islam,' they were all teaching the same basic principles, which Allah labeled 'Islam' in the Qur'an. Also, their messages were either lost or changed throughout the centuries, resulting in the current mosaic of religions that we have all over the world. (42:14)

C. The Final Message

The final message of Allah to humanity came in the year 610 CE, when Allah began revealing His final installment of guidance for us. This guidance, which is called the Qur'an, contains a complete description of the way of life ordained by Allah. Muhammad bin 'Abdallah, the prophet who bore this message, showed us how to implement it and gave us advice on how to be better followers of Allah.

When asked how he lived his life, 'Aishah, who was the wife of Prophet Muhammad, replied, "His character was the Qur'an." (Ahmad)

عَنْ أُمِّ الْمُؤْمِنِينَ عَائِشَةَ ﷺ لَمَّا سُئِلَتْ عَنْ خُلُقِ رَسُولِ اللهِ ﷺ، قَالَتْ: «كَانَ خُلُقُهُ الْقُرْآنَ». رَوَاهُ أَحْمَد

So when we talk about Islam, we must consult the Qur'an and the Sunnah every step of the way. Islam can be understood best by dividing it into three areas: Islamic beliefs, Islamic practices and Islamic duties.

D. The Six-Five-Three Program

There are six main beliefs, five main practices and three main duties. The six beliefs of Islam are listed in what is known as the **Arkan Al Emaan** أَرْكَانُ الإِيمَان **Pillars of Belief**. In Arabic it is said as follows:

60

There are several duties that a Muslim has to do, based on the commandments of Allah ﷻ in the Qur'an. Three main ones are described in this textbook:
1. *Da'wah* الدَّعْوَة (calling others to Islam)
2. *Jihad* الجهاد (striving in Allah's ﷻ Cause)
3. Encouraging good while forbidding evil الأمْرُ بِالمَعْرُوفِ وَالنَّهْيُ عَنِ المُنْكَرِ

These are all the features that make up the basic Islamic way of life. A person who seeks to be a good Muslim will make it a point to know and practice these things in order to gain the favor of their Lord. Any person who is following one part of Islam and skipping another is not being a true Muslim.

١. الإيمانُ باللهِ عَزَّ وجَلَّ
٢. الإيمانُ بالمَلائكةِ
٣. الإيمانُ بالكُتُبِ السَّماويَّةِ
٤. الإيمانُ بالرُّسُلِ
٥. الإيمانُ باليَوْمِ الآخِرِ
٦. الإيمانُ بالقَدَرِ خَيْرِهِ وشَرِّهِ

O you who have believed, believe in Allah and His Messenger and the Book that He sent down upon His Messenger and the Scripture which He sent down before. And whoever disbelieves in Allah, His angels, His books, His messengers, and the Last Day has certainly gone far astray. Surat An-Nisa' (The Women) 4: 136

﴿يَٰٓأَيُّهَا ٱلَّذِينَ ءَامَنُوٓا۟ ءَامِنُوا۟ بِٱللَّهِ وَرَسُولِهِۦ وَٱلْكِتَٰبِ ٱلَّذِى نَزَّلَ عَلَىٰ رَسُولِهِۦ وَٱلْكِتَٰبِ ٱلَّذِىٓ أَنزَلَ مِن قَبْلُ ۚ وَمَن يَكْفُرْ بِٱللَّهِ وَمَلَٰٓئِكَتِهِۦ وَكُتُبِهِۦ وَرُسُلِهِۦ وَٱلْيَوْمِ ٱلْءَاخِرِ فَقَدْ ضَلَّ ضَلَٰلًۢا بَعِيدًا﴾ سُورَةُ النِّسَاءِ 4: 136

Allah ﷻ declared, *Oh you who believe! Enter Islam wholeheartedly, and don't follow the path of the Shaytan. He is your declared enemy.* Surat Al Baqarah (The Cow) 2: 208

﴿يَٰٓأَيُّهَا ٱلَّذِينَ ءَامَنُوا۟ ٱدْخُلُوا۟ فِى ٱلسِّلْمِ كَآفَّةً وَلَا تَتَّبِعُوا۟ خُطُوَٰتِ ٱلشَّيْطَٰنِ ۚ إِنَّهُۥ لَكُمْ عَدُوٌّ مُّبِينٌ﴾ سُورَةُ البَقَرَةِ 2: 208

The five practices, also known as the **Arkan Al Islam** أرْكانُ الإسْلامِ **Pillars of Islam**, are given in detail. In Arabic it is said as follows:

١. الشَّهادَتانِ (شَهادَةُ أنْ لا إلَهَ إلَّا اللهُ، وأنَّ مُحَمَّدًا رَسُولُ اللهِ)
٢. الصَّلاةُ (إقامَةُ الصَّلاةِ)
٣. الزَّكاةُ (إيتاءُ الزَّكاةِ)
٤. الصَّوْمُ (صَوْمُ رَمَضانَ)
٥. الحَجُّ (حَجُّ البَيْتِ لِمَنِ اسْتَطاعَ إلَيْهِ سَبيلًا)

Our time here is short; we should make the most out of it for the sake of our own souls. Islam teaches that we all must approach our Lord by ourselves. In Islam, there are no intermediaries between us and Allah ﷻ. We don't need idols or saints to communicate with God, so what are we waiting for? (2:186)

They are listed in the following hadith of the Prophet ﷺ, the Prophet ﷺ once said, "Islam is founded on five things: Declaring that there is no god but Allah and that Muhammad is the Messenger of Allah, establishing Salah (prayer), giving Zakah (Charity), making Hajj (pilgrimage) to the House (the Ka'bah in Makkah) and fasting in Ramadan." (Al Bukhari & Muslim)

قالَ رَسُولُ اللهِ ﷺ: «بُنِيَ الإسْلامُ عَلَى خَمْسٍ شَهادَةِ أنْ لا إلَهَ إلَّا اللهُ وأنَّ مُحَمَّدًا عَبْدُهُ ورَسُولُهُ وإقامِ الصَّلاةِ وإيتاءِ الزَّكاةِ وحَجِّ البَيْتِ وصَوْمِ رَمَضانَ». رَواهُ البُخارِيُّ ومُسْلِمٌ

Will they wait until Allah comes to them in canopies of clouds with angels, and the issue is decided? Indeed, to Allah do all issues return. Surat Al Baqarah (The Cow) 2: 210

﴿هَلْ يَنظُرُونَ إِلَّا أَن يَأْتِيَهُمُ اللَّهُ فِى ظُلَلٍ مِّنَ الْغَمَامِ وَالْمَلَٰٓئِكَةُ وَقُضِىَ الْأَمْرُ وَإِلَى اللَّهِ تُرْجَعُ الْأُمُورُ﴾

سُورَةُ البَقَرَة 2:210

Islam is a complete way of life for any person, male or female, to follow. It touches upon our thoughts, emotions, senses and feelings. It guides us in this troubled world and gives us the hope we need to make it through each day.

Allah said, Declare to them (Muhammad), "If you love Allah, then follow me. Allah will love you and forgive you your sins." For Allah is the Forgiving and Merciful. Surat Al 'Imran (The Family of 'Imran) 3:31

﴿قُلْ إِن كُنتُمْ تُحِبُّونَ اللَّهَ فَاتَّبِعُونِى يُحْبِبْكُمُ اللَّهُ وَيَغْفِرْ لَكُمْ ذُنُوبَكُمْ وَاللَّهُ غَفُورٌ رَّحِيمٌ﴾

سُورَةُ آلِ عِمْرَان 3: 31

E. The Importance of Following Islamic Teachings

The effects of following this way of life are summed up best by our Creator. After mentioning that this life is short, Allah tells us that a better reward will come to those who do the following: Those (are the ones) who say, "Our Lord, surely we have believed, so forgive us our sins and save us from the punishment of the Fire," And those who are the patient, the truthful and the devout, who spend (in Allah's way) and who seek forgiveness in pre-dawn hours. Surat Al 'Imran (The Family of 'Imran) 3:16-17

﴿الَّذِينَ يَقُولُونَ رَبَّنَا إِنَّنَا ءَامَنَّا فَاغْفِرْ لَنَا ذُنُوبَنَا وَقِنَا عَذَابَ النَّارِ ۝ الصَّٰبِرِينَ وَالصَّٰدِقِينَ وَالْقَٰنِتِينَ وَالْمُنفِقِينَ وَالْمُسْتَغْفِرِينَ بِالْأَسْحَارِ﴾

سُورَةُ آلِ عِمْرَان 3: 16 – 17

Prophet Muhammad was the last messenger that Allah sent to Earth. In his last sermon, the Blessed Prophet confirmed what Allah told us in the Qur'an—that there will be no more revelations from Allah after this.

Muhammad is not a father of any of your men, but he is a messenger of Allah and the last of the prophets. And Allah has the Knowledge of every thing. Surat Al Ahzab (The Combined Forces) 33:40

﴿مَّا كَانَ مُحَمَّدٌ أَبَا أَحَدٍ مِّن رِّجَالِكُمْ وَلَٰكِن رَّسُولَ اللَّهِ وَخَاتَمَ النَّبِيِّۦنَ وَكَانَ اللَّهُ بِكُلِّ شَىْءٍ عَلِيمًا﴾

سُورَةُ الأَحْزَاب 33: 40

He told people that if they held onto the Qur'an and his Sunnah, then they would never go astray. Islam must be followed based on what these two sources contain.

Islam is the way of life that Allah will make prevail over all other ways of life. (61:8-9) Muslims are still human, however, and cannot be perfect. But in the end, God will look at our efforts and see how we balanced our lives with Islam.

Anyone who learns of this message is given the chance to discover it for themselves. No one can be forced to follow Islam. (2:256) It is an option for men and women to freely choose. But those who decide to reject it in this life will be losers on the Day of Judgement when we are shown the record of our lives. (53:31)

Who is more wrong than the person who is reminded of the signs of his Lord but turns away from them, forgetting the deeds which his hands have done? Surat Al Kahf (The Cave) 18:57

﴿وَمَنْ أَظْلَمُ مِمَّن ذُكِّرَ بِـَٔايَٰتِ رَبِّهِۦ فَأَعْرَضَ عَنْهَا وَنَسِىَ مَا قَدَّمَتْ يَدَاهُ﴾

سُورَةُ الكَهْف 18: 57

Allah's way of life for humanity is perfect and complete. To follow it is to be successful.

To deny it is to fail in the most important decision of your life.

Whoever seeks a faith other than Islam, it will never be accepted from him, and he, in the Hereafter, will be among the losers. Surat Al 'Imran (The Family of 'Imran) 3:85

﴿ وَمَن يَبْتَغِ غَيْرَ ٱلْإِسْلَٰمِ دِينًا فَلَن يُقْبَلَ مِنْهُ وَهُوَ فِى ٱلْءَاخِرَةِ مِنَ ٱلْخَٰسِرِينَ ﴾ سُورَةُ آلِ عِمْرَانَ 3 : 85

Questions to Answer

1. What makes someone a practicing Muslim?
2. Why are we a blessed community?
3. Why are there so many religions in the world?
4. What was the basic message taught by all the prophets in the past?
5. What are the Five Practices of Islam?
6. What are the Three Duties?

Define: Islam, Sect.

Reflect: Islam is derived from the root word سَلِمَ which means 'peace.' How can Islam bring peace to your heart? How have you already experienced this peace? What will you do to continue feeling peace throughout your life from Islamic beliefs and practices?

Act: Memorize the Arkan Al Emaan and Arkan Al Islam in Arabic and English.

IQ Builder:

1. What does Allah ﷻ tell us in 10:47 about previous prophets and how people changed their teachings?
2. Summarize the basic message described in 10:24-25.

Literature Selection

My Road to Islam

By Yahiya Emerick & Reshma Baig
From *The Seafaring Beggar and Other Tales*

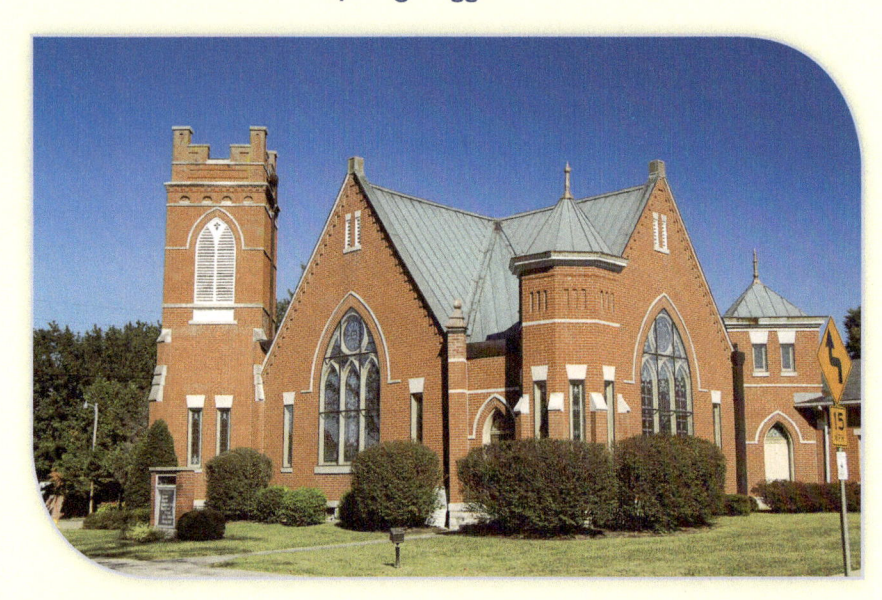

I was born into a typical, non-religious American family. I attended an average public school and had a relatively uneventful childhood. Religion was provided for me by my dear grandmother who saw to it that I went to a Baptist church with her every Sunday morning. This I did from the age of seven to about 16. Then my parents no longer made me go.

I liked the stories of the prophets that I was taught in her church, and I agreed with all the moral principles. But the religious ideology was a bit too vague for me to grasp. Compounding the problem, it seemed to me that there was no real direction in Christianity. What I mean is, beyond good ethics instruction, what exactly does Christianity have to offer in the way of solutions? Solutions to any problem require really defined teachings that can be implemented at any level, whether for the self, between neighbors, within societies or across whole countries.

But the religion that evolved from early Jewish activists, and later from the Greeks and Romans, seemed to me to have a vague foundation of right and wrong. I did not find, however, that it had a personal program to live by everyday, which is what I believe is needed for any true change to take place in a person. One emotional experience won't change your life forever. I also thought the preacher focused too much on negative things like punishment and Hell. But these things together were not sufficient reason for me to feel I needed something else. I was still fairly comfortable with the Baptist arm of Christianity. It was all I knew.

Then, one Sunday morning, the preacher said something that put my mind into a tailspin. He stated, in clear language, that Jesus is God! In 10 years of listening to sermons, that is the first time I heard that! I was always told he was a Servant of God, a Son of God... But never God, too.

I tried to rationalize this idea in my mind for months afterward: how could Jesus be the Son of God and then God at the same time? How can someone who was a man on Earth *ever* be the master of a Universe that is billions of light years wide? Why does God have to die before He can forgive our sins? If he were God, could he not just outright forgive us? Also, if there are three equal parts of God, each one a distinct person, then which part of God is in charge?

I was about 15 when this crisis of faith occurred, but I still remember it vividly as if I were right there. This was one of the two most significant events of my life. Disillusioned, I studied a little Zen and some Taoism after that, but I found them to be feel-good philosophies, not practical ways of life and guidance.

Zen Buddhism meditation.

The other essential event happened when I went away to college. Nabil gave me a Qur'an to take with me. Nabil had been my friend since childhood, and although he was Muslim, he had never really practiced up until that time. When we were growing up, we would sometimes argue about who had the better religion even though neither one of us knew much about our own faiths. But you know little kids. From those experiences, I made a mental note to read the Qur'an someday. Nabil started to practice Islam at that time, and I was open enough to agree to take a copy of this mysterious book with me.

Safely tucked away at school, I began to delve into the Qur'an. What I read had as tremendous an impact on my thinking as the preacher had so many years before. This time, however, I was shocked in a positive way. I finally found real answers to the questions that bothered me the most—answers to questions like, "Why are there so many religions? What is the real purpose of man? If God is the true Master, why can't His rules play a part in our politics?" and "What really happens when I die?"

The Qur'an explained itself to me with clear and intelligent reasoning. I was wonderstruck. In fact, one of the first new questions I began to ask was, "Why haven't I seen this book before? Who kept it from me?" I then raided the college library for books on Islam, took an Arabic language class and expanded my thinking in so many directions. An Irish-Muslim lady, Una, whom I met in my Arabic class, introduced me to a good brother from Jordan. He agreed to take me to the local masjid, and it was there that the full impact of Islam took hold of me.

Of course, it was Friday, the busiest day of the week, so I was very scared when we went in. But the brother, Musa, sensing my anxiety, took me into a side office and showed me how to perform salah. It felt really weird at first to bow on the floor, but soon it seemed like such a natural and pure way to revere the Creator.

Later, in Salat Al Jumu'ah, when the Muslims declared, "Ameen," after reading surat Al Fatihah, I was stirred to the very roots of my soul. "Such power," I thought. "And it only comes after relinquishing all your will to God."

I was moved to enter Islam some months before, but I didn't know how. There wasn't any da'wah going on around campus, nor were there any phone numbers to call. But when Musa took me to the Islamic Center in 1988, I knew I had found direction. My journey towards faith was over, and a new life was just beginning.

كل امرئ مباكسب رهين

Questions to Answer

1. What were some of the troubles that the author had with Christian beliefs?
2. How did he come into contact with the message of Islam?
3. Describe how you think it might have felt for the author to make salah for the first time.

11 Who Is a Muslim?

WHAT TO LEARN

What makes someone Muslim? Is it their name, their family heritage, their language, their beliefs or something else?

VOCABULARY

Kafir
Shahadah
Nifaaq
Munaafiqoon

THINK ABOUT IT

What is the real definition of a Muslim?

A. What Makes One a Muslim?

Islam has a definite concept of who and what a Muslim is.

Abu Huraira narrated that the Blessed Prophet said, "Every child is born following their Fitrah (i.e. they are a natural Muslim). It is the parents who make them a Jew, Christian or Zoroastrian (ancient Persian religion)." (Al Bukhari & Muslim)

عَنْ أَبِي هُرَيْرَةَ، أَنَّ رَسُولَ اللهِ ﷺ: «كُلُّ مَوْلُودٍ يُولَدُ عَلَى الْفِطْرَةِ، فَأَبَوَاهُ يُهَوِّدَانِهِ أَوْ يُنَصِّرَانِهِ أَوْ يُمَجِّسَانِهِ». رَوَاهُ الْبُخَارِيُّ وَمُسْلِمٌ

In other words, the culture we live in and the people around us have a strong influence on how our identity is formed.

We have already explored what Islam means and some of the features of this way of life. Anyone who accepts Allah as having no partners, believes in Allah as the Creator and then determines to live a life seeking the straight path towards their Lord, can be termed a Muslim. (16:9)

We live in a world full of cultures, languages, ideologies and social customs. Every day, children are born into one society or another, and the process of indoctrination into that culture begins.

What makes each of them a Muslim? Is it a Muslim-sounding name? Is it the clothes they wear? The food they eat? Is it the language they speak?

Sadly, the world is full of people who call themselves Muslims, but their identity is based more on cultural traditions than on Islamic teachings. Islam is not passed on from generation to generation by genetics. It is not a footnote attached to the end of a person's name. It doesn't reside in the type of clothes we wear, the food we eat or the culture in which we live.

> Not everyone is a Muslim just because they have a Muslim-sounding name or come from a traditionally Muslim country. A Muslim is a person who knows what Islam teaches and then follows those teachings. Anything else is just a name, and that really counts for nothing.

B. Who Is a Muslim?

To be a Muslim, a person must profess his or her belief and learn what this way of life requires. Each person must gain knowledge of the teachings of Islam and know how to behave in their daily life. A person who never sincerely declared that *There is no god but Allah, and that Muhammad is His Messenger* has never even entered Islam!

The **Shahadah** شَهَادَة **Statement of Faith** contains two parts that signify something unique. The first part, *I declare that there is no god but Allah*, affirms the truth that nothing in this life, be it money, idols or fame, should hold our allegiance more than Allah.

أَشْهَدُ أَنْ لَا إِلَهَ إِلَّا اللهُ وَأَشْهَدُ أَنَّ مُحَمَّدًا رَسُولُ اللهِ

The second part, *and I declare that Muhammad ﷺ is the Messenger of Allah*, indicates that we accept the Prophet ﷺ as our model, guide and spiritual leader. We want to emulate the way he spoke, behaved and lived. These are the basic understandings that every Muslim must have.

There is indeed a good model for you in the Messenger of Allah—for the one who has hope in Allah and the Last Day and remembers Allah profusely. Surat Al Ahzab (The Confederates) 33:21

﴿ لَقَدْ كَانَ لَكُمْ فِي رَسُولِ اللَّهِ أُسْوَةٌ حَسَنَةٌ لِّمَن كَانَ يَرْجُو اللَّهَ وَالْيَوْمَ الْآخِرَ وَذَكَرَ اللَّهَ كَثِيرًا ﴾ سُورَةُ الأَحْزَابِ 33: 21

C. Who Is a Kafir?

The word **Kafir** (plural Kuffar or Kafiroon) comes from the Arabic term **Kafara** كَفَرَ, which means to cover up or to hide something. A kafir is a person who covers up the truth and tries to hide it.

Allah ﷻ stated emphatically, *Therefore, avoid those who turn away from Our Message and who desire nothing but the life of this world. That is as far as knowledge will reach them. Certainly, your Lord knows best those who are astray from His path and, He knows those who are guided.* An-Najm (The Star) 53:29-30

﴿ فَأَعْرِضْ عَن مَّن تَوَلَّىٰ عَن ذِكْرِنَا وَلَمْ يُرِدْ إِلَّا الْحَيَاةَ الدُّنْيَا ﴾ ﴿ ذَٰلِكَ مَبْلَغُهُم مِّنَ الْعِلْمِ إِنَّ رَبَّكَ هُوَ أَعْلَمُ بِمَن ضَلَّ عَن سَبِيلِهِ وَهُوَ أَعْلَمُ بِمَنِ اهْتَدَىٰ ﴾ سُورَةُ النَّجْمِ 53: 29-30

While Allah ﷻ advises us to stay away from those who desire only this life, He reminds us that He Alone knows who is and is not guided. Therefore, it is not acceptable for Muslims to try to categorize other people. We never know who will become Muslim before their death or what might be in their hearts. These are secrets that only Allah ﷻ knows and He Alone is the Judge of all matters.

Allah ﷻ clearly points out that one can have different levels of faith. Allah ﷻ describes these different levels of faith with this example: *The (Bedouin) Arabs say, "We believe!" Declare to them, "You have no faith, but you only say, 'We are surrendered to Allah,' because emaan has not yet entered your hearts. But if you obey Allah and His Messenger, He will not lower any of your deeds, for Allah is the Forgiving, the Merciful." Only those are believers who have believed in Allah and His Messenger and have never since doubted. They have struggled with their wealth and their selves in the Cause of Allah. They are the sincere ones.* Surat Al Hujurat (The Dwellings) 49:14-15

﴿ قَالَتِ الْأَعْرَابُ آمَنَّا قُل لَّمْ تُؤْمِنُوا وَلَٰكِن قُولُوا أَسْلَمْنَا وَلَمَّا يَدْخُلِ الْإِيمَانُ فِي قُلُوبِكُمْ وَإِن تُطِيعُوا اللَّهَ وَرَسُولَهُ لَا يَلِتْكُم مِّنْ أَعْمَالِكُمْ شَيْئًا إِنَّ اللَّهَ غَفُورٌ رَّحِيمٌ ﴾ ﴿ إِنَّمَا الْمُؤْمِنُونَ الَّذِينَ آمَنُوا بِاللَّهِ وَرَسُولِهِ ثُمَّ لَمْ يَرْتَابُوا وَجَاهَدُوا بِأَمْوَالِهِمْ وَأَنفُسِهِمْ فِي سَبِيلِ اللَّهِ أُولَٰئِكَ هُمُ الصَّادِقُونَ ﴾ سُورَةُ الحُجُرَاتِ 49: 14-15

These ayaat demonstrate that there is a big difference between saying that one surrenders to Allah ﷻ and behaving as such. For those who are sincere believers, they never waver in their faith and also put all their resources into the Cause of Allah ﷻ.

To become a 'sincere believer,' as Allah ﷻ describes in the Qur'an, one must have belief, knowledge and actions that reflect those beliefs and teachings. If a person who thinks he or she is a Muslim has no faith in Islamic teachings and doesn't make Islamic learning and practices a part of daily living, then it is difficult for him or her to reach the level of faith that Allah ﷻ exalts in the Qur'an.

Yet, even though there are distinguished levels of belief that a Muslim can reach, it does not mean that we can go around calling other people 'kafir.' The responsibility of everyone's heart and soul is between them and Allah ﷻ. The Blessed Prophet Muhammad ﷺ forbade us from directly calling another Muslim a kafir unless they have said themselves that they reject Allah ﷻ.

What we must do, then, if we know of someone who is near Islam but is not following it the way it should be followed, we should call them to come closer to their Lord. We must use compassion, understanding and respect in our interaction with them because this was the way of Prophet Muhammad ﷺ and the main way in which we can reach their heart.

Invite others to the way of your Lord with wisdom and inspiring speech. Reason with them in a superior manner. Certainly, your Lord knows who has strayed from His path and who is guided. Surat An-Nahl (The Bees) 16:125

﴿ ادْعُ إِلَىٰ سَبِيلِ رَبِّكَ بِالْحِكْمَةِ وَالْمَوْعِظَةِ الْحَسَنَةِ وَجَادِلْهُم بِالَّتِي هِيَ أَحْسَنُ ۚ إِنَّ رَبَّكَ هُوَ أَعْلَمُ بِمَن ضَلَّ عَن سَبِيلِهِ ۖ وَهُوَ أَعْلَمُ بِالْمُهْتَدِينَ ﴾ سُورَةُ النَّحْل 16: 125

D. What Is a Munaafiq?

Another class of people who fall short of being believers are the **Munaafiqoon** مُنَافِقُون **Hypocrites**. These are people who claim to be believers in front of other Muslims. However, they disobey the commandments of Allah ﷻ and spend their energy in trying to divide people. (5:41, 9:124-125)

The Blessed Prophet ﷺ once said, "There are four signs which, if present in a person, show him to be a hypocrite. If someone has one of them, then he has one part of hypocrisy until he gets rid of it. These are: when he is trusted with something, he cheats; when he talks, he lies; when he promises, he breaks his promise; and when he argues, he insults." (Al Bukhari, Muslim)

قَالَ رَسُولُ اللهِ ﷺ : «أَرْبَعٌ مَنْ كُنَّ فِيهِ كَانَ مُنَافِقًا خَالِصًا، وَمَنْ كَانَتْ فِيهِ خَصْلَةٌ مِنْهُنَّ كَانَتْ فِيهِ خَصْلَةٌ مِنَ النِّفَاقِ حَتَّى يَدَعَهَا: إِذَا اؤْتُمِنَ خَانَ وَإِذَا حَدَّثَ كَذَبَ وَإِذَا عَاهَدَ غَدَرَ، وَإِذَا خَاصَمَ فَجَرَ». رَوَاهُ الْبُخَارِيُّ وَمُسْلِمٌ

Allah ﷻ describes them this way, *Among people are some who say, "We believe in Allah and the last day." But they don't really believe. They try to fool Allah and the believers, but they only fool themselves without realizing it. Their hearts are diseased, and Allah increases their disease because they were false to themselves. When they're told not to make trouble in the world, they answer, "We only want to make peace." But they're making trouble without realizing it. When they're told to believe like the other people believe, they say, "Should we believe like the fools?" But they're the fools without knowing it. When they meet the believers, they also say, "We believe." But when they're alone with their evil friends they say, "We're with you; we were only fooling them."* Surat Al Baqarah (The Cow) 2:8-14

﴿ وَمِنَ النَّاسِ مَن يَقُولُ آمَنَّا بِاللَّهِ وَبِالْيَوْمِ الْآخِرِ وَمَا هُم بِمُؤْمِنِينَ ﴿٨﴾ يُخَادِعُونَ اللَّهَ وَالَّذِينَ آمَنُوا وَمَا يَخْدَعُونَ إِلَّا أَنفُسَهُمْ وَمَا يَشْعُرُونَ ﴿٩﴾ فِي قُلُوبِهِم مَّرَضٌ فَزَادَهُمُ اللَّهُ مَرَضًا ۖ وَلَهُمْ عَذَابٌ أَلِيمٌ بِمَا كَانُوا يَكْذِبُونَ ﴿١٠﴾ وَإِذَا قِيلَ لَهُمْ لَا تُفْسِدُوا فِي الْأَرْضِ قَالُوا إِنَّمَا نَحْنُ

IT'S ALL ABOUT ISLAM

﴿مُصْلِحُونَ ۞ أَلَا إِنَّهُمْ هُمُ الْمُفْسِدُونَ وَلَٰكِن لَّا يَشْعُرُونَ ۞ وَإِذَا قِيلَ لَهُمْ ءَامِنُوا۟ كَمَا ءَامَنَ النَّاسُ قَالُوٓا۟ أَنُؤْمِنُ كَمَآ ءَامَنَ السُّفَهَآءُ ۗ أَلَآ إِنَّهُمْ هُمُ السُّفَهَآءُ وَلَٰكِن لَّا يَعْلَمُونَ ۞ وَإِذَا لَقُوا۟ الَّذِينَ ءَامَنُوا۟ قَالُوٓا۟ ءَامَنَّا وَإِذَا خَلَوْا۟ إِلَىٰ شَيَٰطِينِهِمْ قَالُوٓا۟ إِنَّا مَعَكُمْ إِنَّمَا نَحْنُ مُسْتَهْزِءُونَ ۞﴾
سُورَةُ البَقَرَةِ 2: 8 – 14

Hypocrisy is a dangerous thing. It is being a two-faced and a liar. Allah warns Muslims against becoming hypocrites in these words: Oh you who believe! Why do you say what you don't do? It's a hateful thing in Allah's sight to say what you don't do. Surat As-Saff (The Rank) 61: 2-3

﴿يَٰٓأَيُّهَا الَّذِينَ ءَامَنُوا۟ لِمَ تَقُولُونَ مَا لَا تَفْعَلُونَ ۞ كَبُرَ مَقْتًا عِندَ اللَّهِ أَن تَقُولُوا۟ مَا لَا تَفْعَلُونَ ۞﴾
سُورَةُ الصَّفِّ 61: 2 – 3

Allah has promised to punish the hypocrites unless they repent of their **Nifaaq نفاق Hypocrisy.** (4:142-146) He declared to them, Make no excuses. You became disbelievers (by mocking at Allah and His Messenger) after you had professed Faith. If We forgive some of you (who repent and believe), We shall punish others (who carry on their hypocrisy) because they were guilty. Surat Al Tawbah (Repentance) 9:66

﴿لَا تَعْتَذِرُوا۟ قَدْ كَفَرْتُم بَعْدَ إِيمَٰنِكُمْ ۚ إِن نَّعْفُ عَن طَآئِفَةٍ مِّنكُمْ نُعَذِّبْ طَآئِفَةًۢ بِأَنَّهُمْ كَانُوا۟ مُجْرِمِينَ ۞﴾ سُورَةُ التَّوْبَةِ 9: 66

The Blessed Prophet said, "The worst people in the sight of Allah on the Day of Resurrection will be the two-faced people. They appear to some people with one face and to other people with another face." (Al Bukhari)

قَالَ النَّبِيُّ ﷺ: «تَجِدُ مِنْ شَرِّ النَّاسِ يَوْمَ الْقِيَامَةِ عِنْدَ اللهِ ذَا الْوَجْهَيْنِ، الَّذِي يَأْتِي هَٰؤُلَاءِ بِوَجْهٍ وَهَٰؤُلَاءِ بِوَجْهٍ». رَوَاهُ الْبُخَارِيُّ

With these statements from Allah and the Blessed Prophet, we can determine that Muslims know what Islamic teachings are, believe in those teachings and practice them sincerely. They make Islamic practices a part of their life, and they stick together as a unified group. They have faith in Allah and place their hope in Him. (3:103)

Whoever does this is promised entrance into Paradise, prepared for those who voluntarily surrender their wills to Him. (9:71-72) We don't have to be perfect to be forgiven and rewarded by Allah. We merely have to be sincere and then make an effort to bring ourselves into alignment with His way of life.

That is the message of Islam: believe and try. That's all. That is what a true Muslim follows. That is what following the example of the Blessed Prophet Muhammad is all about. (3:102)

When the hypocrites come to you, they say, "We bear witness that you are indeed the messenger of Allah." Allah knows that you are really His messenger, and Allah testifies that the hypocrites are actually liars. They have made their oaths a shield, and thus they have prevented (others) from the way of Allah. Surely evil is what they have been doing. That is because they declared faith (in Islam apparently), then disbelieved (secretly). Therefore a seal has been set on their hearts, and thus they do not understand. Surat Al-Munafiqun (The Hypocrites) 63:1-3

﴿إِذَا جَاءَكَ ٱلْمُنَٰفِقُونَ قَالُوا۟ نَشْهَدُ إِنَّكَ لَرَسُولُ ٱللَّهِ وَٱللَّهُ يَعْلَمُ إِنَّكَ لَرَسُولُهُۥ وَٱللَّهُ يَشْهَدُ إِنَّ ٱلْمُنَٰفِقِينَ لَكَٰذِبُونَ ﴾ ﴿ٱتَّخَذُوٓا۟ أَيْمَٰنَهُمْ جُنَّةً فَصَدُّوا۟ عَن سَبِيلِ ٱللَّهِ إِنَّهُمْ سَآءَ مَا كَانُوا۟ يَعْمَلُونَ﴾ ﴿ذَٰلِكَ بِأَنَّهُمْ ءَامَنُوا۟ ثُمَّ كَفَرُوا۟ فَطُبِعَ عَلَىٰ قُلُوبِهِمْ فَهُمْ لَا يَفْقَهُونَ﴾ سُورَةُ الْمُنَافِقُونَ 63: 1–3

Questions to Answer

1. What two things make a person a practicing Muslim?
2. Explain why Islam is not based on a race or ethnic group.
3. What is the difference between a Kafir and a Munaafiq?

Define: Mu'min, Kafir, Munaafiq, Shahadah.

Reflect: Why do you think the Blessed Prophet Muhammad ﷺ forbade us from directly calling another Muslim a kafir unless they have said themselves that they reject Allah ﷻ?

Act: Review the four signs of a hypocrite. Pretend that someone who is displaying these signs has come to you for help. They want to know five tips for how to stay away from each behavior. Write down the tips that you would give them.

IQ Builders:

1. Why is it important for Muslims to avoid associating with the kuffar according to 8:73?
2. What are the signs of a hypocrite? How does that relate to the message in the Qur'an contained in 14: 24-26?
3. According to 8:20-23, what should Muslims do and what do hypocrites do?

12 Why Some Don't Believe

WHAT TO LEARN

Have you ever seen someone make a mistake, and they knew what they were doing was wrong? What would make someone act that way?

VOCABULARY

Da'wah   Taqwa

THINK ABOUT IT

Why do some people not believe?

A. The Guiding Light

Reading the Qur'an for the first time can change a person's perspective on life. Read the following passages to understand how it impacted one such person:

When I opened the Qur'an and began reading it for the first time, I was totally amazed. I had never read a book like that before. I didn't start at the beginning; rather, I just flipped to any old page and started browsing at random. What I read immediately touched a chord in my heart so deep I began to get nervous.

You see, the only book I had known all my life, which was said to be from God, was the Bible. But like most Christians, I felt that it wasn't really revelation from the Almighty. It seemed, instead, to be a collection of Jewish tribal history, unconnected anecdotes, myths and biographies.

It wasn't a unified book with a single purpose but was, instead, a book to read if you wanted to pass the time and maybe learn something about ancient mythology or legend. Even our own preachers told us it wasn't perfect and had mistakes in it. They said only having the 'Holy Ghost' in your heart could enable a person to learn from it. (9:30-31)

I could not accept such an answer.

So when I read the Qur'an, my eyes were opened. It was a book that spoke to me as a human. It wasn't a collection of other people's writings, but rather, it was a message from my Creator to me. It speaks to everyone who reads it. "Oh, you humans..." it says, or "Oh you who believe..."

And the content of the message strikes right into your heart and soul as if the One Who made it was sitting there telling you face-to-face what's going on in your world. Within a few weeks of reading the Qur'an, I decided I had to accept its teachings.

Now I thought that everyone would react the same way I did when they knew what was in the Qur'an. I told everyone I could about Islam: my friends, my co-workers, my relatives. I became a preaching machine. Maybe you could have called me 'Da'wah-bot' or something.

B. Problems in Conveying the Message

In my enthusiasm, I failed to see that not everyone was listening or even cared about knowing the reality of their lives and their purpose here. Some people told me they didn't want me to talk about Islam anymore, and others just listened politely and then went off to their next worldly diversion.

What was wrong? Here was a message to change a person's heart for the better! Here was the healing of hearts everyone desperately needed! Why didn't everyone who heard it accept it? I began to feel a little discouraged. Not with Islam, because I knew it was right, but with my own inability to convey the message. I paused my Da'wah دَعْوَة Islamic Outreach efforts and began to think. (3:186)

Then I started becoming more knowledgeable on the finer points of Islam and concentrated my energies towards calling "lost" Muslims back to the path of Islam. Although I thought this was a little easier, there were still some who didn't listen.

If I think I had it tough, imagine how hard-hearted the society must have been during the time of the Blessed Prophet Muhammad ﷺ when people first heard the Qur'an. The Blessed Prophet ﷺ was such a great man—how could anyone not believe him right away? I know that if I were there, I'd want to be the first to support the Prophet ﷺ. But why did some still refuse to believe even though they stood in the presence of one touched by angels?

C. Handling Objections

People have basic objections to Allah's ﷻ call that can be summarized and answered intelligently, but to overcome them and offer explanations, one must have knowledge of the Qur'an and other religions. See the chart at the end of this chapter for some of those objections and answers. Look up the ayaat from the Qur'an to see how Allah ﷻ answers these objections with utmost eloquence.

As you can see from the chart, there are a large number of objections to faith put forward by those who don't believe. The objections that have been raised from the most ancient days of human history are the same as those that are raised today. These objectors have chosen to disobey their hearts and their prophets and to leave this life losing the most important challenge of all. (7:174-177)

Those who reject faith, and die rejecting it, on them is the curse of Allah, the angels and of all humanity! Surat Al Baqarah (The Cow) 2:161

﴿ إِنَّ ٱلَّذِينَ كَفَرُواْ وَمَاتُواْ وَهُمْ كُفَّارٌ أُوْلَٰٓئِكَ عَلَيْهِمْ لَعْنَةُ ٱللَّهِ وَٱلْمَلَٰٓئِكَةِ وَٱلنَّاسِ أَجْمَعِينَ ﴾ سُورَةُ البَقَرَةِ 2: 161

The same situation occurred in the lifetime of the Blessed Prophet Muhammad ﷺ. The non-believers opposed him at every turn and made life unbearable at times. The idol-worshippers even resorted to incredible violence to try and silence the new message. But they were ultimately unsuccessful, for within a few years, people all over the world were flocking to this way of life.

Even though the message of Islam triumphed in the Middle East and much of Asia and Africa, the struggle with the disbelievers continued, as it does today. Hardly a moment goes by where the faith of a Muslim is not challenged by those around him or her. At every turn and in every hour, someone or something seeks to turn us from our Lord.

There is a great challenge faced by Muslims who live in non-Muslim countries. We are under the twin-pressures of external conflict and internal disunity. We are constrained to do things that compromise our faith, our morals, our family values and our faith in Allah ﷻ.

Many of the people of the Scripture (Jews and Christians) wish that if they could turn you away as disbelievers after you have believed, out of envy from their own selves even after the truth has become manifest unto them. But forgive and overlook till Allah brings His Command. Verily, Allah is Able to do all things. Surat Al Baqarah (The Cow) 2:109

IT'S ALL ABOUT ISLAM

﴿وَدَّ كَثِيرٌ مِّنْ أَهْلِ ٱلْكِتَٰبِ لَوْ يَرُدُّونَكُم مِّنۢ بَعْدِ إِيمَٰنِكُمْ كُفَّارًا حَسَدًا مِّنْ عِندِ أَنفُسِهِم مِّنۢ بَعْدِ مَا تَبَيَّنَ لَهُمُ ٱلْحَقُّ ۖ فَٱعْفُوا۟ وَٱصْفَحُوا۟ حَتَّىٰ يَأْتِىَ ٱللَّهُ بِأَمْرِهِۦٓ ۗ إِنَّ ٱللَّهَ عَلَىٰ كُلِّ شَىْءٍ قَدِيرٌ﴾ سُورَةُ ٱلْبَقَرَةِ 2: 109

At the same time, many of us have relatives who want us to make ethnic or national pride the basis of our identity rather than Islam. (2:272) It is as if we are stuck between two moving walls that are trying to crush us. (3:176)

If we understand and live Islam sincerely, Allah will provide us with an iron bar to place between the moving walls. The key is **Taqwa** تقوى **Awareness of Allah**. The more taqwa we develop, the stronger and more unyielding we will become. Solid taqwa is the one thing that bullets, bombs, torture, music videos, fashion and sin will never be able to destroy.

So if you're wondering what to do when you're faced with people who refuse to listen to the message of Islam, remember that the Blessed Prophet ﷺ had to face the same things—and worse.

Allah instructed him, *If they argue with you, tell them, "I have surrendered my whole self to Allah and so have those who follow me." And declare to the People of the Book (Jews and Christians) and to those who don't know, "Will you also surrender yourself (to Allah)?" If they do, then they will be on the right guidance. But if they turn away, your duty is only to convey the message. Allah sees all of His servants.* Surat Al 'Imran (The Family of 'Imran) 3:20

﴿فَإِنْ حَآجُّوكَ فَقُلْ أَسْلَمْتُ وَجْهِىَ لِلَّهِ وَمَنِ ٱتَّبَعَنِ ۗ وَقُل لِّلَّذِينَ أُوتُوا۟ ٱلْكِتَٰبَ وَٱلْأُمِّيِّـۧنَ ءَأَسْلَمْتُمْ ۚ فَإِنْ أَسْلَمُوا۟ فَقَدِ ٱهْتَدَوا۟ ۖ وَّإِن تَوَلَّوْا۟ فَإِنَّمَا عَلَيْكَ ٱلْبَلَٰغُ ۗ وَٱللَّهُ بَصِيرٌۢ بِٱلْعِبَادِ﴾ سُورَةُ آلِ عِمْرَانَ 3: 20

To better understand how to deal with those who reject Allah at every turn, it is a good idea

Taqwa is a shield.

to learn about the prophets, messengers and wise men and women Allah mentions in the Qur'an.

By reading their stories, we can gain a greater appreciation of the struggle ahead of us. We can remove worry from our minds, knowing that even better people than us had a hard time. Pay careful attention to how Allah brought peace to the hearts of His servants and know that Allah's message can bring peace to yours.

Oh humanity! There has come to you a direction from your Lord and a healing for your hearts and for those who believe, it is a guidance and a mercy. Declare, "In the blessing and mercy of Allah they should rejoice." That is far better than the treasures they hoard. Surat Yunus (Jonah) 10:57-58

﴿يَٰٓأَيُّهَا ٱلنَّاسُ قَدْ جَآءَتْكُم مَّوْعِظَةٌ مِّن رَّبِّكُمْ وَشِفَآءٌ لِّمَا فِى ٱلصُّدُورِ وَهُدًى وَرَحْمَةٌ لِّلْمُؤْمِنِينَ ۞ قُلْ بِفَضْلِ ٱللَّهِ وَبِرَحْمَتِهِۦ فَبِذَٰلِكَ فَلْيَفْرَحُوا۟ هُوَ خَيْرٌ مِّمَّا يَجْمَعُونَ﴾ سُورَةُ يُونُسَ 10: 57 - 58

الحمد لله

"Some Answers"
To the Objections of Non-Muslims

Allah only spoke to the Jews and only sent revelation to Jewish prophets.
Allah did give His message to the Jews, but He also sent messages to all the other nations. (2:83-85, 5:18, 5:41, 5:44, 61:5-8)

No belief in Allah or in an omnipotent creator of the Universe.
Allah gave us life, and signs in nature point to His existence. Only the blind refuse to see. Whether we believe in Him or not, He's there. (2:28-29, 6:104, 2:99, 11:13, 69:38-43, 34:31-32, 14:15, 10:4-20, 30:52-53)

Muhammad must have learned his message from someone or somewhere or copied it from the Bible.
Muhammad was illiterate; he neither knew how to read or write. The Qur'an mentions things that no one in that place or at that time could have known. There are similarities between the Bible and Old Testament because each revelation is from the same source. The other revelations either no longer exist or have been changed. (11:13, 16:103, 39:28, 62:2, 10:37-41)

'Isa (Jesus) was the last prophet sent to Earth. 'Isa was the son of God and/or God and that he came to die for man's sins, so no new prophets would be needed.
'Isa was a man. Allah was neither born not bears children. Allah forgives directly without an intermediary. 'Isa taught people to believe in one God and to do right (i.e., Islam). Christians broke up into sects because they lost the true teachings of 'Isa. Prophet 'Isa foretold the coming of Muhammad. (6:101, 6:159, 5:18, 5:116-117, 5:172, 9:30-31, 61:6, 112:1-4, 4:116, 17:42, 21:21-22, 13:16)

Faith has no place in the modern world where technology performs miracles everyday.
They only remember Allah when they're in trouble and afterwards they forget Him. People can only find real peace with Allah. (3:180, 10:12, 3:14-15, 2:212, 3:188, 13:28, 3:190, 2:204-206, 70:42, 2:257)

Eat, drink and live life to the fullest. Tomorrow we will die and that is the end. There is no afterlife nor a Day of Judgment.
It is only Shaytan which bids them to follow their lusts. All evil conduct will be paid back in the next life. Immoral people and the willfully disobedient will be stressed in this life and losers in the next. (2:168-169, 4:118-119, 2:15-16, 18, 3:185, 16:111, 2:256, 74:38, 7:33, 50:16-19, 2:204-206, 70:42, 2:257, 18:57, 7:28, 21:38-40, 7:53, 7:187, 18:55, 18:58-59, 14:10, 2:170, 5:104, 28:78-82, 15:13, 67:15-18, 90:4-7, 17:66-70, 13:26, 19:77-80, 5:100, 10:7-8, 10:48-56)

Why did Allah send a mortal man and not an angel or other supernatural forces to convey His message?
They can't believe a man would be chosen to bring Allah's messages, but who better to communicate on the rational level with other humans? How would there be a fair testing ground in any other case? If the world was populated by angels, He would have sent an angel to them as a messenger. (14:11, 14:17, 14:94-95, 13:43, 15:6-9, 64:56, 2:118, 21:2, 10:2-6)

They don't believe in a next life or that a Day of Judgement will come.
Allah gave us life to begin with. He can make us again and judge us. (17:49-50, 19:66-67, 17:9, 2:28, 6:94, 75:36-40, 50:1-15, 17:71-73, 10:37, 10:24, 10:31-36, 30:54)

They want to see supernatural proof such as angels, magic or miracles before they're convinced.
The Qur'an and nature are the greatest signs of all. Even if angels came or books appeared magically, they would only say it's magic or illusion anyway. (17:92-93, 13:27, 15:6-15, 6:7-9, 6:103, 21:5)

IT'S ALL ABOUT ISLAM

Suggested Qur'anic Wisdom				
1:1-7	The best surat and prayer.	17:66-72	Who really is in control?
6:1-50	Answering the unbelievers.	18:32-44	The gardener who forgot Allah.
13:8-17	What nature can teach us about Allah.	18:60-82	Prophet Musa and the Wise Man.
14:9-27	The Messengers call us to good.	24:35-40	Allah is the light.
35:1-26	Realizing our true relationship with Allah.	27:83-93	Reward or punishment?
49:1-15	How to be a true Muslim.	29:56-69	Remembering to be grateful to Allah.
56:1-98	A summary of the next life and what will happen to all.	34:37-39	How to get closer to Allah.
7:44-52	Conversations between those in Heaven and those in Hell.	40:28-44	The man who stood up to a pharaoh.
81:1-29	A final call to our hearts.	6:155-165	There are no excuses.
10:11-40	Here is your proof!	3:133-139	A message of hope.
59:18-24	The attributes of Allah.		

Questions to Answer

1. Think about the stories at the beginning of this lesson. How did reading the Qur'an affect those writers? Why do you think it affected them in that way?
2. Explain the two pressures facing Muslims who live in non-Muslim lands.
3. What can stop these pressures from negatively affecting Muslims in this situation?

Define: Kafir, Taqwa, Guidance.

Reflect: Why do you think Prophet Muhammad ﷺ advised us not to call another Muslim 'kafir'?

Act: Choose one of the items from the chart The Objections of the Non-Muslims and look up the ayaat mentioned for answering that particular objection. How do those ayaat answer the objections?

IQ Builders:

1. Summarize the conditions of the agreement Allah mentions in 9:111-112 for the believers?
2. What does Allah tell us in 17:89-93?
3. What is the message contained in 4:1?
4. What does 5:2 command us to do?
5. Write down three main points from 17:81-84 that relate to your life.

Unit 03 Review Exercise

VOCABULARY REVIEW

On a separate sheet of paper, write the definition of each word below.

1. Islam
2. Sunnah
3. Arkan Al Emaan
4. Arkan Al Islam
5. Kafir
6. Shahadah
7. Fitrah
8. Nifaaq
9. Taqwa
10. Da'wah

REMEMBERING WHAT YOU READ

On a separate sheet of paper, answer the following questions. Use complete sentences.

1. Why do you think we are advised not to break up into competing groups or sects?
2. What is the complete definition of the word 'Islam'?
3. What are the three duties of a Muslim, in addition to the Five Pillars?
4. Write down the meaning of the Arkan Al Emaan in English.
5. What are the Five Pillars of Islam? List them.
6. Why is it important to follow correct Islamic teachings?
7. What are the two sources of knowledge from our beloved Last Prophet ﷺ?

THINKING TO LEARN

On a separate sheet of paper, answer the questions below. Use complete sentences.

1. What is the only way of life acceptable to Allah ﷻ, and how do we know this?
2. Describe two objections non-Muslims may have to accepting Islam and explain the Qur'anic answer to each one.
3. How can nifaaq bring ruin and hardship to a person's life?

UNIT 4
The Islamic View of Creation

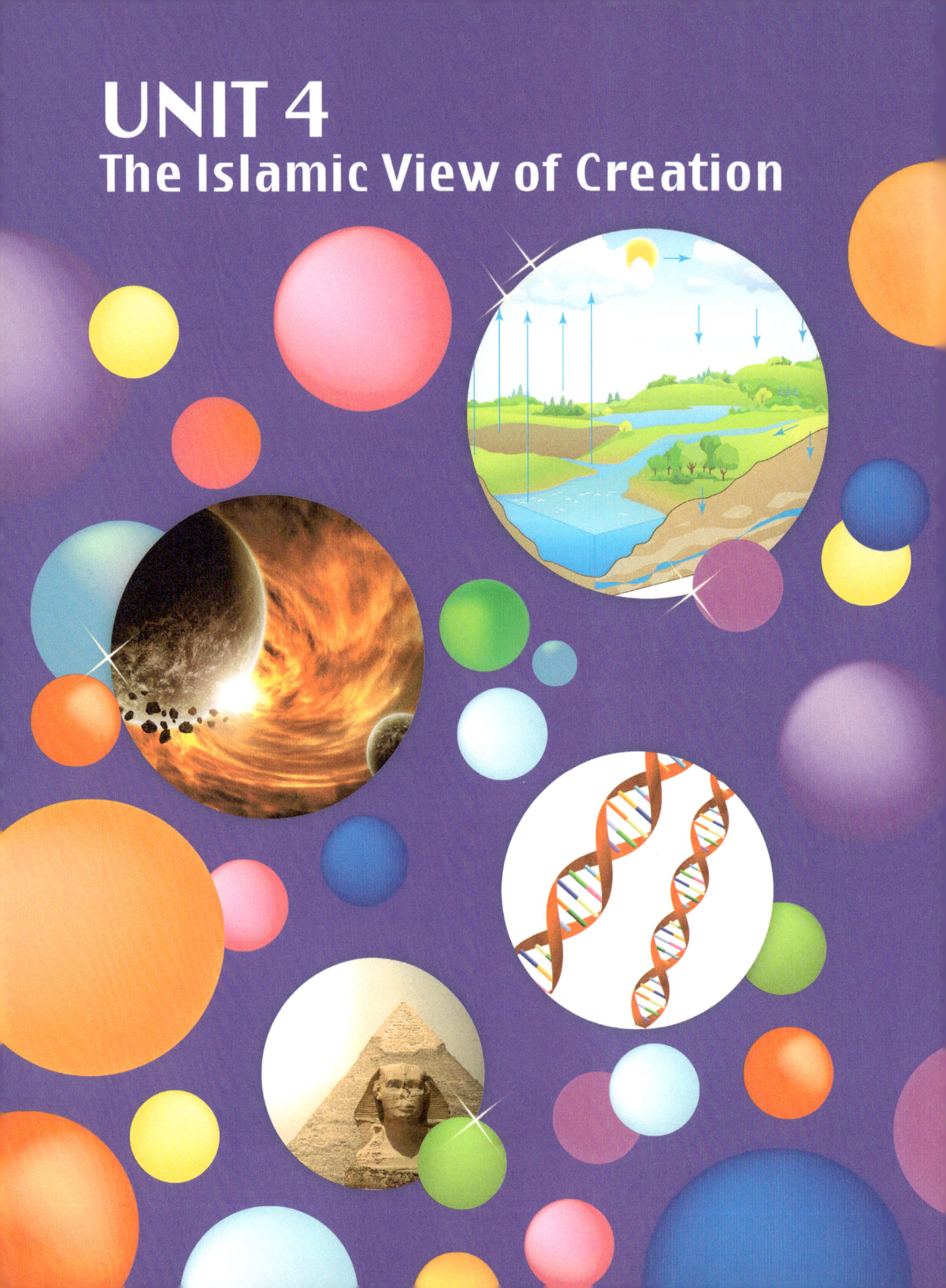

13 The Creation of the Universe

WHAT TO LEARN

The Qur'an gives an amazingly detailed description of how the Universe and Earth were formed. How do you explain that?

VOCABULARY

Big Bang Theory   Ozone Layer

THINK ABOUT IT

How did Allah create the Universe?

A. Why Does Allah Tell Us about Creating the Universe?

The Holy Qur'an is the book given to us by the Creator of the Universe. Allah knows us best and knows that humans can be very skeptical creatures.

Allah said, *If their aversion is too hard on you, then seek, if you can, a tunnel into the earth or a ladder unto the sky in order to bring them a sign. Had Allah so willed, He would have brought all of them to the right path. So never be one of the ignorant.* Surat Al An'aam (The Cattle) 6: 35

﴿وَإِن كَانَ كَبُرَ عَلَيْكَ إِعْرَاضُهُمْ فَإِنِ اسْتَطَعْتَ أَن تَبْتَغِيَ نَفَقًا فِي الْأَرْضِ أَوْ سُلَّمًا فِي السَّمَاءِ فَتَأْتِيَهُم بِآيَةٍ ۚ وَلَوْ شَاءَ اللَّهُ لَجَمَعَهُمْ عَلَى الْهُدَىٰ ۚ فَلَا تَكُونَنَّ مِنَ الْجَاهِلِينَ﴾

سورة الأنعام 6: 35

Allah, the Keeper of Wisdom, purposely provides many proofs in the Qur'an about His existence and creativity in guiding humanity. The diversity of all the proof strengthens the belief in Allah. We need proof, and Allah gives us that proof.

Assuredly the creation of the heavens and the earth is a greater (matter) than the creation of men: Yet most men understand not. Surat Ghafir (The Forgiver) 40:57

﴿لَخَلْقُ السَّمَاوَاتِ وَالْأَرْضِ أَكْبَرُ مِنْ خَلْقِ النَّاسِ وَلَٰكِنَّ أَكْثَرَ النَّاسِ لَا يَعْلَمُونَ﴾ سورة غافر 40: 57

Allah, of course, does not need us to follow Him or believe in Him. As He stated, *Allah can do without them and Allah is free of all needs.* Surat At-Taghabun (The Mutual Disillusion) 64:6

﴿وَاسْتَغْنَى اللَّهُ ۚ وَاللَّهُ غَنِيٌّ حَمِيدٌ﴾ سورة التغابن 64: 6

79

IT'S ALL ABOUT ISLAM

He merely provides proofs so that those who wish to can believe in Him; in turn, Allah ﷻ can reward them for their choice. Allah ﷻ is ready to forgive even those who act wrongly, if they but ask for His forgiveness.

Abu Huraira ﷺ narrated that Allah's Messenger ﷺ said, "When Allah completed the creation, He wrote in His Book which is with Him on His Throne, 'My Mercy overpowers My Anger.'" (Al Bukhari & Muslim)

عَنْ أَبِي هُرَيْرَةَ ﷺ قَالَ قَالَ رَسُولُ اللَّهِ ﷺ: «لَمَّا قَضَى اللَّهُ الْخَلْقَ كَتَبَ فِي كِتَابِهِ، فَهُوَ عِنْدَهُ فَوْقَ الْعَرْشِ إِنَّ رَحْمَتِي غَلَبَتْ غَضَبِي». رَوَاهُ الْبُخَارِيُّ وَمُسْلِمٌ

Among the proofs given in the Qur'an for us to learn from is a very detailed explanation of how the Universe was made and how the planets and stars were formed.

Of course, most people who lived at the Prophet's ﷺ time would never have understood what those ayaat really meant, but they accepted them and interpreted them as best they could.

Allah ﷻ instructs us to accept everything in the Qur'an, even if we don't understand it. As we gain more scientific knowledge about the Earth and its surrounding space and galaxies, our understanding of the Qur'an grows with each passing generation. As Allah ﷻ said, *But those firm in knowledge say, "We believe in it. All [of it] is from our Lord." And no one will be reminded except those of understanding.* Surat Al 'Imran (The Family of 'Imran) 3:7

﴿وَالرَّاسِخُونَ فِي الْعِلْمِ يَقُولُونَ آمَنَّا بِهِ كُلٌّ مِنْ عِنْدِ رَبِّنَا وَمَا يَذَّكَّرُ إِلَّا أُولُو الْأَلْبَابِ﴾ سُورَةُ آلِ عِمْرَانَ 3: 7

B. Modern Science and Islam

Modern day scientists are amazed by the complexity of the Universe. The sciences of astronomy, chemistry, astrophysics and molecular biology have pushed the limits of our knowledge ever further.

Who has created seven skies, one over the other. You will see nothing out of proportion in the creation of the Rahman (the All-Merciful Allah). So, cast your eye again. Do you see any rifts? Then cast your eye again and again, and the eye will come back to you abased, in a state of weariness. Surat Al Mulk (The Dominion) 67:3-4

﴿الَّذِي خَلَقَ سَبْعَ سَمَاوَاتٍ طِبَاقًا مَا تَرَى فِي خَلْقِ الرَّحْمَنِ مِنْ تَفَاوُتٍ فَارْجِعِ الْبَصَرَ هَلْ تَرَى مِنْ فُطُورٍ ۞ ثُمَّ ارْجِعِ الْبَصَرَ كَرَّتَيْنِ يَنْقَلِبْ إِلَيْكَ الْبَصَرُ خَاسِئًا وَهُوَ حَسِيرٌ﴾

سُورَةُ الْمُلْكِ 67: 3-4

These new discoveries have helped us better understand many Qur'anic ayaat. For example, in one part of the Qur'an, Allah ﷻ mentions that humans begin their life as an 'alaq in their mother's womb. The word literally means 'a clinging thing,' but no one in centuries past knew how that could be part of human development.

Created man from a clinging substance. Surat Al 'Alaq (The Clot) 96:2

﴿خَلَقَ الْإِنْسَانَ مِنْ عَلَقٍ﴾ سُورَةُ الْعَلَقِ 96: 2

Translators and scholars tried to explain this verse as meaning humans were clots of blood or some other such thing in the womb. But new discoveries in the last few years have shown that in the early stages of pregnancy, the fertilized egg actually attaches itself to the uterine wall and clings there as it is growing. Thus, modern knowledge unlocks another mystery that previous Muslims could only guess at.

To a startling degree, the same holds true in other Qur'anic revelations. When we study the ayaat of the Qur'an relating to the creation of the Universe, we come away astounded, especially since they agree with what has been discovered in only the last few decades.

The Qur'an does not give a single, unified essay on how the Universe began. Instead, in keeping with the Qur'anic method of teaching, different aspects of creation are mentioned in different places in order to give authority to the particular lesson being taught.

For example, in Surat At-Tariq (The Nightcommer) (86), Allah begins by mentioning the brightest star that appears in the sky at night, then uses it as a metaphor for how every human has an angel watching over them. In this manner, Allah uses physical aspects of nature to illustrate spiritual principles.

I swear by the sky and by the Night-Comer. And what may let you know what the Night-Comer is? The star of piercing brightness! There is no human being, but there is a watcher over him. So, let man consider of which stuff he is created. Surat At-tariq (The Nightcommer) 86:1-5

﴿وَٱلسَّمَآءِ وَٱلطَّارِقِ﴾ ﴿وَمَآ أَدْرَىٰكَ مَا ٱلطَّارِقُ﴾ ﴿ٱلنَّجْمُ ٱلثَّاقِبُ﴾ ﴿إِن كُلُّ نَفْسٍ لَّمَّا عَلَيْهَا حَافِظٌ﴾ ﴿فَلْيَنظُرِ ٱلْإِنسَٰنُ مِمَّ خُلِقَ﴾

سُورَةُ الطَّارِقِ 86: 1-5

C. The Qur'anic History of Creation

Each of the individual references to creation in the Qur'an can be pieced together to get a complete picture of how Allah's revelation explains the beginning of the Universe. As Muslims, however, we must not forget to look into the lesson taught in each passage. We must remember that the purpose for including these signs in the Qur'an is so that we can be enlightened spiritually as well as mentally.

Allah begins by stating that the Universe and planet Earth took six 'days' to create.

Indeed, your Lord is Allah, who created the heavens and earth in six days and then established Himself above the Throne. He covers the night with the day, [another night] chasing it rapidly; and [He created] the sun, the moon, and the stars, subjected by His command. Unquestionably, His is the creation and the command; blessed is Allah, Lord of the worlds. Surat Al A'raf (The Heights) 7:54

﴿إِنَّ رَبَّكُمُ ٱللَّهُ ٱلَّذِى خَلَقَ ٱلسَّمَٰوَٰتِ وَٱلْأَرْضَ فِى سِتَّةِ أَيَّامٍ ثُمَّ ٱسْتَوَىٰ عَلَى ٱلْعَرْشِ يُغْشِى ٱلَّيْلَ ٱلنَّهَارَ يَطْلُبُهُۥ حَثِيثًا وَٱلشَّمْسَ وَٱلْقَمَرَ وَٱلنُّجُومَ مُسَخَّرَٰتٍۭ بِأَمْرِهِۦٓ أَلَا لَهُ ٱلْخَلْقُ وَٱلْأَمْرُ تَبَارَكَ ٱللَّهُ رَبُّ ٱلْعَٰلَمِينَ﴾

سُورَةُ الأَعْرَافِ 7: 54

However, it must be remembered that in Arabic, the word يَوْم can mean **a day** as we know it, or it can mean any stage or period of time. As Allah points out, a day to Him can be a 1,000 years, 50,000 years or infinitely more.[1]

The creation of the planets, including Earth, took place in the last two periods of time. As Allah said, *Declare (O Muhammad): Do you disbelieve in the One Who created the Earth in two stages? Do you make others equal to Him? He is the Lord of all the worlds.* Surat Fussilat (Explained in Detail) 41:9

---

1 See 32:5 and 70:4. Many Muslim scholars have long known that the creation of the Earth was in six long stages and not in what we humans consider to be six days.

IT'S ALL ABOUT ISLAM

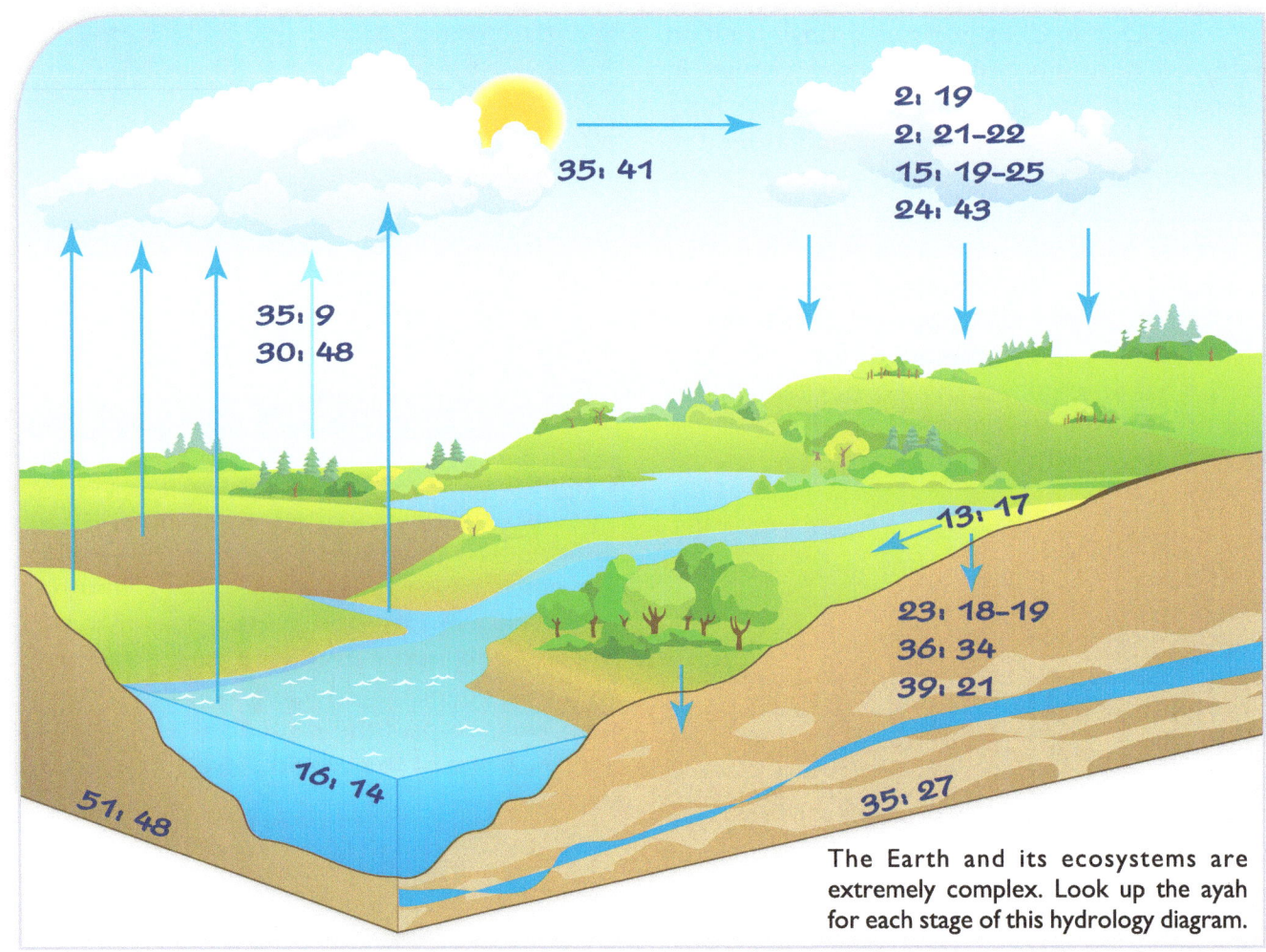

The Earth and its ecosystems are extremely complex. Look up the ayah for each stage of this hydrology diagram.

﴿ قُلْ أَئِنَّكُمْ لَتَكْفُرُونَ بِٱلَّذِي خَلَقَ ٱلْأَرْضَ فِى يَوْمَيْنِ وَتَجْعَلُونَ لَهُۥٓ أَندَادًا ۚ ذَٰلِكَ رَبُّ ٱلْعَٰلَمِينَ ﴾ سُورَةُ فُصِّلَتْ 41:9

The process of creation can be summarized as follows: all matter in the Universe was compacted together in one place. Then Allah ﷻ gave the command and it blew apart, scattering molecules and gases in all directions. This theory is what scientists refer to as **the Big Bang** الانفجارُ الكبيرُ. The force of this initial explosion keeps the Universe expanding.

Space was filled with matter, anti-matter and gases, which eventually combined into larger particles. These bits of matter eventually grew into asteroids, planets, stars and moons. Each object in interstellar space conformed to a set of physical laws that governed the trajectory of their orbits, so a regular pattern of rotation could be seen. (13:2, 21:33)

Stars ignited in a fury of radioactive fusion. They gave off light and heat, which brought warmth to those planets near them. (86:3) Small moons were captured in the orbit of larger planets. These moons developed a regular orbit around the planets, often reflecting light from the sun.

Finally, the planets themselves developed in a variety of ways, with fantastic geological formations and movements both above and below the surface.

Or the One who made the earth a place to settle and made rivers amidst it and made mountains for (making) it (firm), and made a barrier between two seas? Is there any god along with Allah? No, but most of them do not have knowledge. Surat An-Naml (The Ants) 27:61

IT'S ALL ABOUT ISLAM

﴿أَمَّن جَعَلَ ٱلْأَرْضَ قَرَارًا وَجَعَلَ خِلَٰلَهَآ أَنْهَٰرًا وَجَعَلَ لَهَا رَوَٰسِىَ وَجَعَلَ بَيْنَ ٱلْبَحْرَيْنِ حَاجِزًا أَءِلَٰهٌ مَّعَ ٱللَّهِ بَلْ أَكْثَرُهُمْ لَا يَعْلَمُونَ﴾ سُورَةُ النَّمْلِ 27: 61

The planet Earth, in particular, cooled near its outer layers, forming a thin crust made up of plates that moved and grated against each other. This allowed the Earth's surface to constantly erase the damage caused by occasional asteroid impacts. But the plate collisions also had the side effect of raising tall mountains and exposing the geological history of the planet.

Escaping gases from the ground and water warmed in the sunlight and eventually ascended to a high altitude where they formed a protective layer. This **Ozone Layer** طَبَقَةُ الأوزون shielded Earth from the harmful radiation and ultraviolet rays of the sun.

It is amazing that this scientific narrative is so similar to what Allah ﷻ revealed in the Holy Qur'an. Always remember that Allah ﷻ mentioned these things to convince us to be believers in Him. If He proves His words with things we have only recently discovered, how can we deny His message?

Qur'anic History of the Universe

Everything was compacted together and then Allah ﷻ made it split apart. Gases, matter and anti-matter spread throughout the Universe, and stars, planets, black holes, anti-matter geysers and other things were formed. This is called the Big Bang. (21:30; 41:11)

IT'S ALL ABOUT ISLAM

Allah ﷻ is expanding the size of the Universe; everything in it is constantly moving away from each other. (51:47)

Allah ﷻ created a protective canopy over the Earth that we call the ozone layer. It is constantly shielding us from harmful ultraviolet radiation. (21:32)

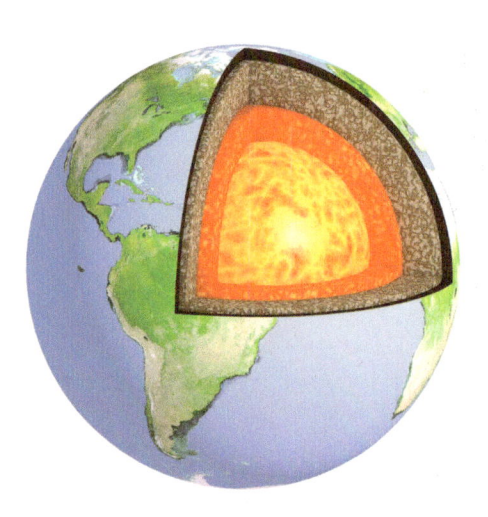

The Earth came into existence far before humans ever appeared. The different colored layers in the rock table provide us with a geological time line of our planet's history. (35:27-28, 40:64)

Allahﷻ spread the Earth out and caused the crust to form like a carpet over the surface of the planet. Then He created mountains in the Earth to keep it stable. The formation of mountains act as a kind of brake or buffer zone between the tectonic plates that make up Earth's crust. (71:19-20; 88:19-20; 78:6-7)

Questions to Answer

1. Why might Allahﷻ have put so many references to science in the Qur'an?
2. How have modern discoveries about the Universe helped in the understanding of the Qur'an?
3. Why doesn't the Qur'an give a single essay in just one surat about how the Universe was formed?
4. Why does Allahﷻ give us signs of His creativity?
5. What is the Big Bang Theory?
6. What is the function of the canopy over the Earth?

Define: Big Bang Theory, Ozone Layer.
Reflect: What can you do if you don't fully understand what an ayah means yet?
Act: Choose one modern discovery not mentioned in this chapter that has affected your belief in Islam and explain its impact on you.
IQ Builders:
1. What does Allahﷻ tell us in 22:54 about knowledge and faith?
2. When this life ends, what does Allahﷻ say will happen in 20:105-107 to the mountains?

14 Islam and Evolution

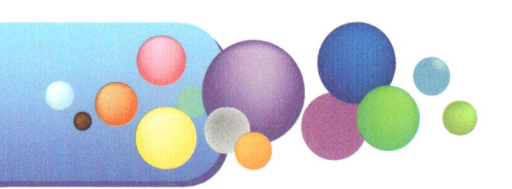

WHAT TO LEARN

Have you ever wondered what Islam says about evolution?

VOCABULARY

Sentient
Evolution
Creationism
Photosynthesis

THINK ABOUT IT

Where do dinosaurs and other ancient life forms fit into the Islamic worldview?

A. How Can We Know the World around Us?

As we have already learned, Islamic teachings imply that Earth and the Universe are very old. In addition, the Qur'an clearly states that one of the reasons Allah ﷻ made us intelligent and self-aware or **Sentient** واع, is so that we can discover the wonders of the natural world around us. In short, Allah ﷻ gave us a mission to investigate what He created.

There is so much we don't know or understand, even about how our own bodies work. With all these fantastic areas of knowledge to pursue, you would think that everyone would recognize their Lord. However, some still choose to keep their eyes closed. As Allah ﷻ said, *He created man from a drop, and soon he turned into a debating person, expressing himself openly.* Surat An-Nahl (The Bees) 16:4

﴿ خَلَقَ ٱلْإِنسَٰنَ مِن نُّطْفَةٍ فَإِذَا هُوَ خَصِيمٌ مُّبِينٌ ﴾

سُورَةُ النَّحْل 16:4

Thankfully, there are plenty of highly intelligent individuals that face life and learning with open minds. The world has many fine examples of great scientists and researchers who have put their faith in Allah ﷻ. Additionally, recent scientific discoveries are helping to complete our picture of the Universe, both past and present.

B. What Do We Know about the Origins of Life?

Today, scientists tell us that life began in the sea when simple molecules bonded together and became self-replicating, or self-producing. These single-celled organisms quickly took on the characteristics of what we know as algae.

They received their energy from the sun in a process termed **Photosynthesis** التَّرْكِيب الضَّوْئِيّ. As a result of this activity, new gases formed in the air, creating a viable environment for more complex forms of life.

As Muslims, we can either accept this theory, reject it or modify it according to what we know of Allah's ﷻ revelation. In this instance, it may be easier to accept the theory, since Allah ﷻ speaks of how He created all life from water and raised a protective canopy over the Earth. For theories that are not referenced in the Qur'an, we can study, research, test, reflect and then rest assured that Allah ﷻ knows best.

Scientists further tell us that over millions of years, the first organisms blossomed gradually into many different types and shapes, resulting in plant life, plankton, arthropods and simple fishes. Dinosaurs, higher creatures and mammals followed.

C. What Are Evolution and Creationism?

These discoveries do not necessarily undermine a healthy belief in Allah's ﷻ power as the Creator of all things. However some scientists have put forth a theory that says everything in the Universe, even life itself, happened all by chance and accident, without any divine intervention.

The name of this theory is **Evolution** تَطَوُّر, and its most famous advocate was a man named Charles Darwin (1809-1882). He was an Englishman who lived during the 19th century when Britain ruled most of the world. He spent a particularly long amount of time on the Galapagos Islands, located in the Pacific Ocean, examining birds, lizards and giant turtles.

Darwin came to believe that the variety of life in our world was due to what he called 'natural selection' and 'survival of the fittest.' He wrote his findings in a book entitled *On the Origin of Species*, which he published in 1859.

The book immediately caused a controversy in the Christian world because Christianity taught that God made life in an instant and that the Earth was the center of importance in the Universe. Some Christians also felt threatened by Darwin's teachings because they interpreted it to mean that everything happened without God's intervention. To this day, many Christians still oppose the teaching of evolution in schools.

Many Christians have advanced the idea of **Creationism** الخَلْق, or that God made everything all at once. This is opposed to most modern scientists who still promote evolution, or the independent, gradual and accidental creation of all things. Today, the two sides are as far apart as ever.

Islam and Science

The photosynthesis of primitive single-celled organisms aided in the development of a protective blanket of gases and electromagnetic layers around the Earth. Today there are seven layers to the sky. They are:

1. The Troposphere
2. The Stratosphere
3. The Mesosphere
4. The Thermosphere
5. The Ionosphere
6. The Magnetosphere
7. The Exosphere

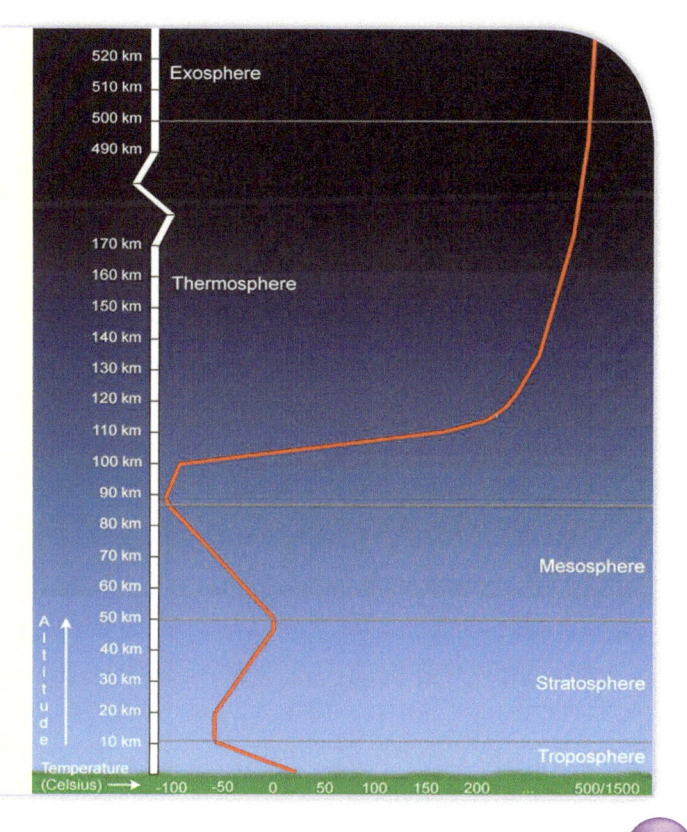

D. What Is the Islamic Perspective?

You may be surprised to learn that Muslims can agree with aspects of both sides of the debate on evolution. Islam teaches us that Allah's creation is vast and beyond our comprehension. We are also taught that the more we explore and learn, the more we will come to believe in Allah. That is the Islamic position.

So, we assert without any hesitation, that Allah caused the creation of the Universe and set up the laws for its functioning. As Allah said: Behold! In the creation of space and the Earth and in the changing of night into day are indeed signs for people of understanding. Those who remember Allah standing, sitting and lying down and contemplate the (wonders) of creation in space and Earth. (They declare) "Our Lord! You didn't create all of this for nothing. So save us from the punishment of the fire." Surat Al 'Imran (The Family of 'Imran) 3: 190-191

﴿إِنَّ فِي خَلْقِ ٱلسَّمَٰوَٰتِ وَٱلْأَرْضِ وَٱخْتِلَٰفِ ٱلَّيْلِ وَٱلنَّهَارِ لَءَايَٰتٍ لِّأُو۟لِى ٱلْأَلْبَٰبِ ﴿ ٱلَّذِينَ يَذْكُرُونَ ٱللَّهَ قِيَٰمًا وَقُعُودًا وَعَلَىٰ جُنُوبِهِمْ وَيَتَفَكَّرُونَ فِى خَلْقِ ٱلسَّمَٰوَٰتِ وَٱلْأَرْضِ رَبَّنَا مَا خَلَقْتَ هَٰذَا بَٰطِلًا سُبْحَٰنَكَ فَقِنَا عَذَابَ ٱلنَّارِ﴾ سُورَةُ آلِ عِمْرَانَ 3: 190 – 191

Science, then, increases our faith. It is wrong for anyone to close their eyes to what is right in front of them. For hundreds of years, people have been finding fossils, bones and ancient artifacts, which point to a hidden past we don't know much about. Allah even commands us to travel and learn from what we see.

We know that Earth existed long before the appearance of humans. Allah said, Wasn't there a long period of time before humans were even mentioned? Al 'Insaan (The Man) 76:1

﴿هَلْ أَتَىٰ عَلَى ٱلْإِنسَٰنِ حِينٌ مِّنَ ٱلدَّهْرِ لَمْ يَكُن شَيْـًٔا مَّذْكُورًا﴾ سُورَةُ الْإِنْسَانِ 76: 1

We also know from the geological timetable that Earth went through many ages before humans came here. Additionally, in the following ayaat that mentions this proof of Allah, we are given a very strong clue about the adaptability of life forms to their environment.

Allah said, Don't you see that Allah sends rain from the sky? With it We produce plants of various colors. And in the mountains are colored layers, white and red, of various tones and some black in hue. And so too, among humans, and crawling creatures, and cattle. They are of various colors. Those among Allah's servants who have knowledge truly fear Him, for Allah is Mighty and Forgiving. Surat Faatir (The Originator) 35:27-28

﴿أَلَمْ تَرَ أَنَّ ٱللَّهَ أَنزَلَ مِنَ ٱلسَّمَآءِ مَآءً فَأَخْرَجْنَا بِهِۦ ثَمَرَٰتٍ مُّخْتَلِفًا أَلْوَٰنُهَا وَمِنَ ٱلْجِبَالِ جُدَدٌۢ بِيضٌ وَحُمْرٌ مُّخْتَلِفٌ أَلْوَٰنُهَا وَغَرَابِيبُ سُودٌ ﴿ وَمِنَ ٱلنَّاسِ وَٱلدَّوَآبِّ وَٱلْأَنْعَٰمِ مُخْتَلِفٌ أَلْوَٰنُهُۥ كَذَٰلِكَ إِنَّمَا يَخْشَى ٱللَّهَ مِنْ عِبَادِهِ ٱلْعُلَمَٰٓؤُا۟ إِنَّ ٱللَّهَ عَزِيزٌ غَفُورٌ﴾ سُورَةُ فَاطِرٍ 35: 27 – 28

So while we agree with the Creationists who say Allah made the Universe, we disagree with them on how quickly it was constructed and with the position that Earth is the center of focus for the Creator. Allah declares Himself to be رَبُّ العالمين. Importantly, the word 'alameen in Arabic is plural, indicating more than one world or planet.

Because we do not reject the evidence presented to us by paleontologists or other scientists, we can accept some of what they say about the origins of life on Earth also. However, we disagree with those who say everything happened without Allah, by mere chance only.

IT'S ALL ABOUT ISLAM

The Earth may be as old as 4.5 billion years!

Allah ﷻ tells us in His Book that he is the source of all things, so this scientific evidence strengthens our faith in Him.

To Allah belongs the control of space and the Earth and Allah has power over all things. *Surat Al 'Imran (The Family of 'Imran) 3: 189*

﴿ وَلِلَّهِ مُلْكُ ٱلسَّمَوَٰتِ وَٱلْأَرْضِ وَٱللَّهُ عَلَىٰ كُلِّ شَىْءٍ قَدِيرٌ ﴾ سورة آل عمران 3: 189

Ours is the middle position; Allah ﷻ said we were created to be the middle community—never going to extremes.

And thus We have made you a medium (just) nation. *Surat Al Baqarah (The Cow) 2:143*

﴿ وَكَذَٰلِكَ جَعَلْنَٰكُمْ أُمَّةً وَسَطًا ﴾ سورة البقرة 2: 143

So we don't fully accept, based on the evidence, the final positions of both sides. Rather, we accept what appears to be true and reject what appears to be false from each. The Qur'an is our standard, our determiner. It has never let us down and it never will.

For a Muslim, then, the evidence of dinosaurs, trilobites and ancient algae is not a threat to our beliefs. Rather, it is a confirmation of the power of Allah ﷻ.

Allah created every creature from water. Of them are some that creep on their bellies, some that walk on two legs and some that walk on four. Allah creates what He wills, for He has power over all things. We have indeed sent signs that make things clear and Allah guides whom He wills to the straight way. *Surat An-Noor (The Light) 24: 45-46*

﴿ وَٱللَّهُ خَلَقَ كُلَّ دَآبَّةٍ مِّن مَّآءٍ فَمِنْهُم مَّن يَمْشِى عَلَىٰ بَطْنِهِۦ وَمِنْهُم مَّن يَمْشِى عَلَىٰ رِجْلَيْنِ وَمِنْهُم مَّن يَمْشِى عَلَىٰٓ أَرْبَعٍ يَخْلُقُ ٱللَّهُ مَا يَشَآءُ إِنَّ ٱللَّهَ عَلَىٰ كُلِّ شَىْءٍ قَدِيرٌ ۞ لَّقَدْ أَنزَلْنَآ ءَايَٰتٍ مُّبَيِّنَٰتٍ وَٱللَّهُ يَهْدِى مَن يَشَآءُ إِلَىٰ صِرَٰطٍ مُّسْتَقِيمٍ ﴾

سورة النور 24: 45 – 46

Who else but Allah could have made such a complex and mysterious Universe? Even the miraculous fertilization of an egg cannot convince some people to believe in the ingenuity of the Creator of the Universe. Allah ﷻ asked, Then what message will they believe in after this? *Surat Al Mursalat (Those Sent Forth) 77:50*

﴿ فَبِأَىِّ حَدِيثٍۭ بَعْدَهُۥ يُؤْمِنُونَ ﴾ سورة المرسلات 77: 50

The early surface of Earth suffered frequent volcanic eruptions and earthquakes.

89

IT'S ALL ABOUT ISLAM

Dinosaurs lived from 220 million years ago until 65 million years ago. We know of their existence through the discovery of fossils, bones and rock imprints. They are a sign of Allah's ﷻ creative will.

A Trilobite.

The fossil record is like a timeline. The deeper one digs into the Earth, the older and less complex the fossils get.

Questions to Answer

1. What has happened to the level of human knowledge in modern times?
2. Does Islam accept the existence of dinosaurs and other ancient life forms?

Define: Evolution, Creationism, Charles Darwin, Galapagos Islands.

Reflect: What position can a Muslim take in the debate between some Christians and scientists?

Act: Create a Venn diagram that compares and contrasts Creationism and Evolution. In the middle of the Venn diagram, describe the points that Islam agrees with.

IQ Builder:
What is Allah ﷻ telling us in 6:101?

15 The Origin of Humans

WHAT TO LEARN

Have you ever wondered why humans are the most advanced life form on Earth? Why do you think this is so?

VOCABULARY

Jinn   Ruh   Fitrah
Angels   Philosophers   Shaytan

THINK ABOUT IT

What is the meaning and purpose of our lives?

A. Who Are We?

Who are we? How did we get here? What is our purpose? Why are we here and where are we going?

Philosophers الفَلاسِفة have troubled themselves for thousands of years trying to answer these questions. When one **Philosopher** فَيْلَسوف believed that an answer was found, another would criticize the theory and replace it with something different. How can we know what it all means? How can we understand our origins?

Why not ask the One Who made us? Allah, the Creator of the Universe and Builder of Life, knows us best. So in order to understand why Allah chose humans over any other type of intelligent creature, we can consult the guidebook Allah left in our hands. In this book, we have the answers to all of our most important questions. The Qur'an is where we will return again and again as we explore the origin of humankind.

Oh Mankind! Have awareness of your Lord

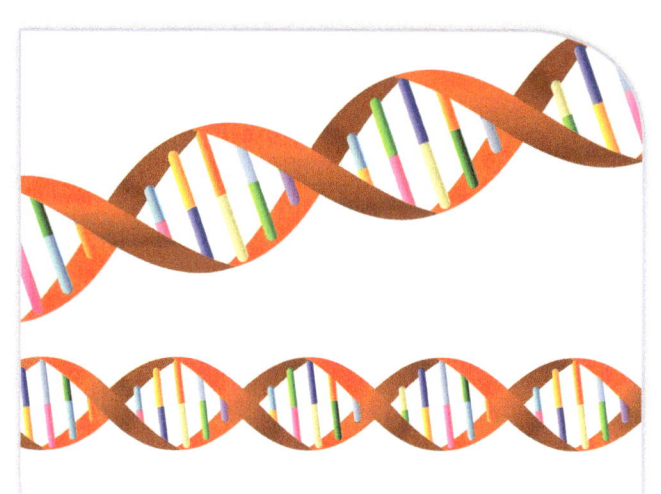

The wonder of DNA: it's like a blueprint for an organism and the building blocks of life.

Who created you from a single person and created for him a mate of similar nature. From the two He scattered countless men and women. Be aware of Allah, by Whom you demand your (human) rights. Respect the womb (of mothers) for Allah watches over you. *Surat An-Nisa' (The Women) 4:1*

﴿يَٰٓأَيُّهَا ٱلنَّاسُ ٱتَّقُوا۟ رَبَّكُمُ ٱلَّذِى خَلَقَكُم مِّن نَّفْسٍ وَٰحِدَةٍ وَخَلَقَ مِنْهَا زَوْجَهَا وَبَثَّ مِنْهُمَا رِجَالًا كَثِيرًا وَنِسَآءً ۚ وَٱتَّقُوا۟ ٱللَّهَ ٱلَّذِى تَسَآءَلُونَ بِهِۦ وَٱلْأَرْحَامَ ۚ إِنَّ ٱللَّهَ كَانَ عَلَيْكُمْ رَقِيبًا﴾ سُورَةُ النِّسَاء ٤:١

B. What Other Intelligent Life Exists?

Before humanity existed on Earth, Allah had already formed the physical Universe and populated it with angels and jinn. **Angels** مَلائكة are made from the elements of light and are created for carrying out Allah's will. The **Jinn** جن are made from the elements of fire and have a very limited interaction with mankind. They are intelligent like humans and generally exist only in their own dimension.

In time, Allah willed the creation of a third type of being. Before He initiated this new life form that would be called **Human** بَشَر, He first posed a question to everything

91

else in the Universe: Was anything willing to take responsibility for its actions? No. No other creation agreed. Only a certain type of spiritual matter, which would make up the human spirit, accepted the responsibility.

Allah said, We did offer the Trust to the heavens and the earth and the mountains, but they refused to bear its burden and were afraid of it, and man picked it up. Indeed he is unjust (to himself), unaware (of the end). Surat Al Ahzab (The Confederates) 33:72

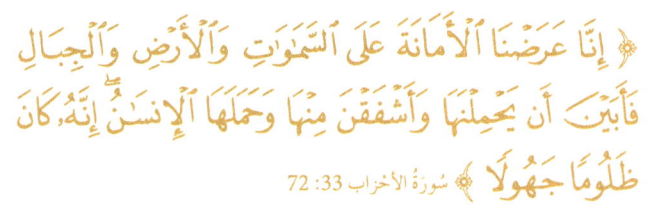

﴿ إِنَّا عَرَضْنَا الْأَمَانَةَ عَلَى السَّمَاوَاتِ وَالْأَرْضِ وَالْجِبَالِ فَأَبَيْنَ أَن يَحْمِلْنَهَا وَأَشْفَقْنَ مِنْهَا وَحَمَلَهَا الْإِنسَانُ إِنَّهُ كَانَ ظَلُومًا جَهُولًا ﴾ سُورَةُ الْأَحْزَابِ 33: 72

Thus, Allah announced that the unformed human spirit had accepted His challenge, and so He created this new species. The angels initially objected because, when they understood the full extent of the human's ability to choose to accept Allah or not, they thought that humans would create disorder and chaos. No one, they thought, should have the power to reject the order of the Universe.

But Allah knew what He was creating, and He fashioned humans in the form that He willed. Afterwards, He gave humans the faculties of sight, speech, hearing and reason. As Allah declared, He is the One Who created for you hearing, sight, feeling and understanding. Yet you are not very thankful. Surat Al Mu'minun (The Believers) 23: 78

﴿ وَهُوَ الَّذِي أَنشَأَ لَكُمُ السَّمْعَ وَالْأَبْصَارَ وَالْأَفْئِدَةَ قَلِيلًا مَّا تَشْكُرُونَ ﴾ سُورَةُ الْمُؤْمِنُونَ 23: 78

Allah then demonstrated to the angels that humans were created with superior qualities. He ordered the angels to bow to the first human, Adam, in respect. The angels all bowed because they always obeyed their Creator, but a jinn named Iblis remained still and did not bow.

When Allah questioned Iblis as to why he did not bow along with the angels, Iblis acted proud and arrogant. He exclaimed that he was made from the elements of fire, while the humans were made from the elements of Earth (clay).

Thereafter, Allah banished Iblis and those jinn who followed him. In retaliation, Iblis declared that he would mislead all humans into error and chaos if given the chance. But because Allah is the Master of all, Iblis had to ask Allah's permission. Allah accepted Iblis' request, saying that only those who rejected Him would be allowed to be misled by Iblis.

Recall when your Lord said to the angels, "I am going to create a human being from a ringing clay made of decayed mud. When I form him perfect, and blow in him of My spirit, then you must fall down before him in prostration." So the angels prostrated themselves, all together, Except Iblis (Satan). He refused to join those who prostrated. He (Allah) said, "O Iblis, what is the matter with you that you did not join those who prostrated?" He said, "I am not such that I should prostrate myself before a mortal whom You have created from a ringing clay made of decayed mud." He said, "Then, get out of here, for you are an outcast, And upon you is the curse up to the Day of Judgement." He said, "My Lord, then give me respite up to the day they (the dead) shall be raised." He (Allah) said, "Well, respite is given to you until the day of the Appointed Time." He said, "My Lord, since You made me go astray, I swear that I shall beautify for them (evils) on the earth, and shall lead all of them astray, Except those of Your servants from among them who are chosen (by You)." He (Allah) said, "This is the straight path leading to Me (that a person is chosen by Me through his good deeds). My servants are such that you have no power over them except those of the deviators who will follow you. And Jahannam (Hell) is the promised place for them all." Surat Al Hijr (The Rocky Tract) 15:28-43

﴿ وَإِذْ قَالَ رَبُّكَ لِلْمَلَٰٓئِكَةِ إِنِّى خَٰلِقٌۢ بَشَرًۭا مِّن صَلْصَٰلٍۢ مِّنْ حَمَإٍۢ مَّسْنُونٍۢ ﴾ ﴿ فَإِذَا سَوَّيْتُهُۥ وَنَفَخْتُ فِيهِ مِن رُّوحِى فَقَعُوا۟ لَهُۥ سَٰجِدِينَ ﴾ ﴿ فَسَجَدَ ٱلْمَلَٰٓئِكَةُ كُلُّهُمْ أَجْمَعُونَ ﴾ ﴿ إِلَّآ إِبْلِيسَ أَبَىٰٓ أَن يَكُونَ مَعَ ٱلسَّٰجِدِينَ ﴾ ﴿ قَالَ يَٰٓإِبْلِيسُ مَا لَكَ أَلَّا تَكُونَ مَعَ ٱلسَّٰجِدِينَ ﴾ ﴿ قَالَ لَمْ أَكُن لِّأَسْجُدَ لِبَشَرٍ خَلَقْتَهُۥ مِن صَلْصَٰلٍۢ مِّنْ حَمَإٍۢ مَّسْنُونٍۢ ﴾ ﴿ قَالَ فَٱخْرُجْ مِنْهَا فَإِنَّكَ رَجِيمٌۭ ﴾ ﴿ وَإِنَّ عَلَيْكَ ٱللَّعْنَةَ إِلَىٰ يَوْمِ ٱلدِّينِ ﴾ ﴿ قَالَ رَبِّ فَأَنظِرْنِىٓ إِلَىٰ يَوْمِ يُبْعَثُونَ ﴾ ﴿ قَالَ فَإِنَّكَ مِنَ ٱلْمُنظَرِينَ ﴾ ﴿ إِلَىٰ يَوْمِ ٱلْوَقْتِ ٱلْمَعْلُومِ ﴾ ﴿ قَالَ رَبِّ بِمَآ أَغْوَيْتَنِى لَأُزَيِّنَنَّ لَهُمْ فِى ٱلْأَرْضِ وَلَأُغْوِيَنَّهُمْ أَجْمَعِينَ ﴾ ﴿ إِلَّا عِبَادَكَ مِنْهُمُ ٱلْمُخْلَصِينَ ﴾ ﴿ قَالَ هَٰذَا صِرَٰطٌ عَلَىَّ مُسْتَقِيمٌ ﴾ ﴿ إِنَّ عِبَادِى لَيْسَ لَكَ عَلَيْهِمْ سُلْطَٰنٌ إِلَّا مَنِ ٱتَّبَعَكَ مِنَ ٱلْغَاوِينَ ﴾ ﴿ وَإِنَّ جَهَنَّمَ لَمَوْعِدُهُمْ أَجْمَعِينَ ﴾ سُورَةُ الْحِجْرِ 15: 28-43

C. Adam ﷺ and Hawwa

Meanwhile, Allah ﷻ placed Adam ﷺ and his mate, Hawwa, in a garden paradise with the one rule that they could not approach a particular tree. The tree itself was not special or magical, but merely a test for them. [2]

Iblis, who was renamed **Shaytan** شَيْطَان **Devil**, came into the garden and tempted the pair to eat from the tree. For their disobedience, Allah ﷻ drove them from their garden paradise and into the precarious world where they would have to fend for themselves.

The humans asked for Allah's ﷻ forgiveness. Allah ﷻ said, They (Adam and Eve) said: Our Lord! We have wronged our own souls. If you forgive us not and bestow not upon us your Mercy, we shall certainly be lost. Surat Al A'raf (The Heights) 7: 23.

﴿ قَالَا رَبَّنَا ظَلَمْنَآ أَنفُسَنَا وَإِن لَّمْ تَغْفِرْ لَنَا وَتَرْحَمْنَا لَنَكُونَنَّ مِنَ ٱلْخَٰسِرِينَ ﴾ سُورَةُ الأَعْرَافِ 7: 23

Allah ﷻ forgave them and informed them that whoever follows His guidance will be protected, but those who disbelieve His signs will be punished. (2:37-39)

All human beings today came from these first two people. How long ago were Adam ﷺ and

---

[2] It was Iblis who told Adam ﷺ and Hawwa that the tree was magical and contained powers. There are some other religious traditions that teach that the woman misled the man and that the pain of childbirth is punishment on the women for this sin. Still other traditions teach that this was the original sin, and the guilt of that sin is still carried by each human on Earth. Islam, on the other hand, says that both Adam ﷺ and Hawwa were equally responsible for disobeying Allah. Muslims believe that they asked for forgiveness, and Allah forgave them. No soul is ever responsible for the sins of another. (See 7:19-27)

Hawwa alive? Where was the garden paradise, and how did they live in the young, untouched wilderness? For these answers, we can turn to what archeologists and anthropologists have discovered. (16:43)

Scientists are in virtual agreement that every human being alive today can be traced back to the same ancestor couple. Genetic tests and DNA studies have confirmed that we are all one large extended family. The oldest known humanoid remains have been found in East Africa and date back about 3,000,000 years.

Those remains, however, are not entirely human in comparison to us today. Scientists have classified modern humans as Homo Sapiens, and the earliest bones of our particular species are around 150,000 to 200,000 years old. These first humans are said to have migrated out of Africa and into the Middle East and Europe about 60,000 years ago. They replaced earlier species and came to dominate the land completely.

Around 35,000 years ago, people began to form small communities. Then, approximately 7,000 years ago, people started to farm and cultivate the land they lived on, leading to the start of civilization as we know it today.

D. Why Did Humans Separate?

Allah explains that the earliest humans began as part of one small community but eventually split up because of disagreements. People soon became many nations that persistently rebelled against each other. Allah sent prophets to guide them, but most of them ignored the messages and continued their disobedience. Some of these ancient societies were destroyed for their wrongdoing.

All men used to be a single Ummah (of a single faith). Then (after they differed in matters of faith), Allah sent prophets carrying good news and warnings and sent down with them the Book of Truth to judge between people in matters of their dispute. But it was none other than those to whom it (the Book) was given who, led by envy against each other, disputed it after the clear signs had come to them. Then Allah, by His will, guided those who believed to the truth over which they disputed; and Allah guides whom He wills to the straight path. Surat Al Baqarah (The Cow) 2:213

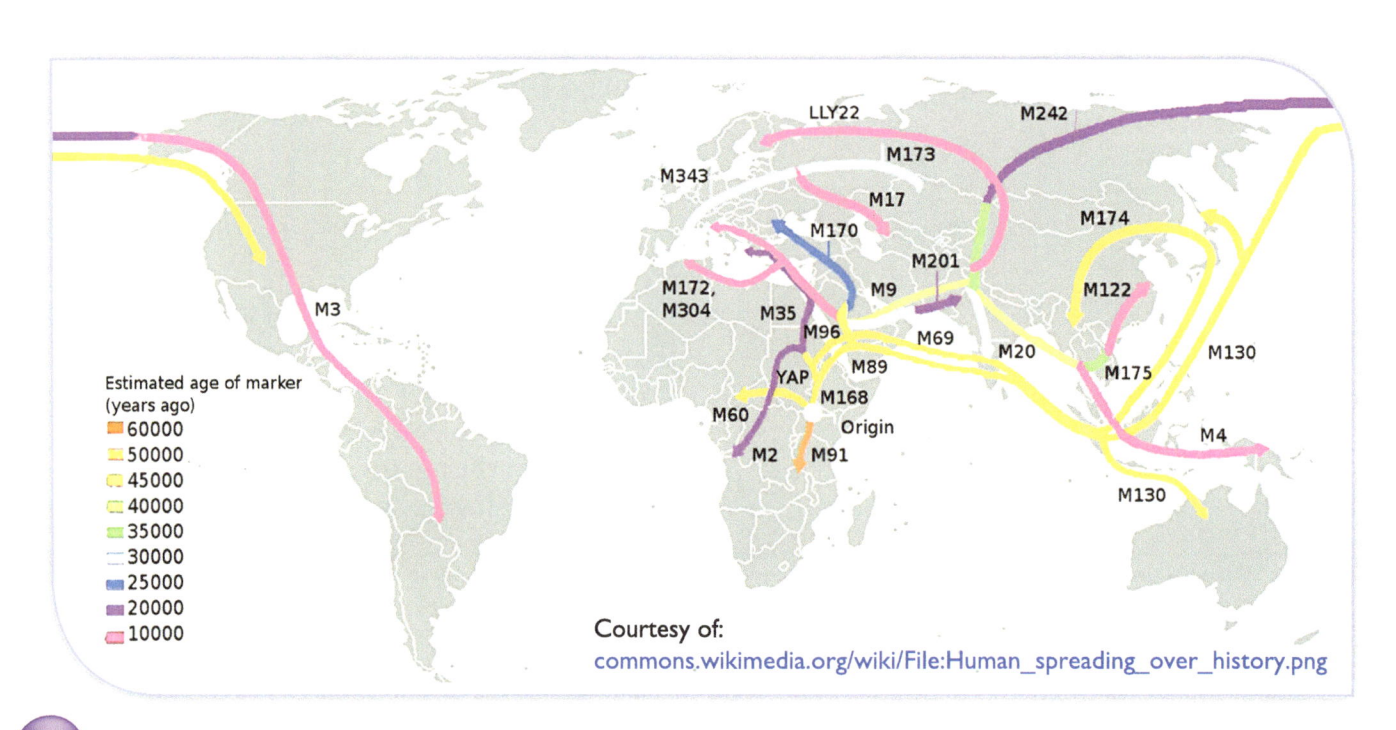

Courtesy of:
commons.wikimedia.org/wiki/File:Human_spreading_over_history.png

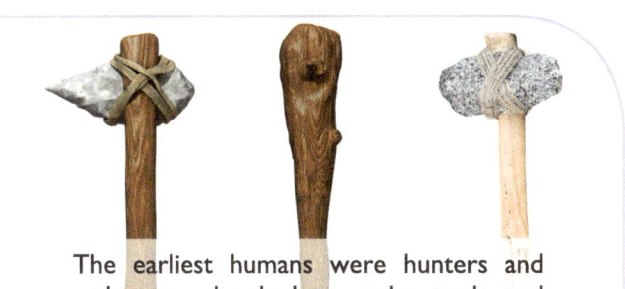

The earliest humans were hunters and gatherers who had to make tools and weapons in order to survive.

﴿كَانَ ٱلنَّاسُ أُمَّةً وَٰحِدَةً فَبَعَثَ ٱللَّهُ ٱلنَّبِيِّـۧنَ مُبَشِّرِينَ وَمُنذِرِينَ وَأَنزَلَ مَعَهُمُ ٱلْكِتَٰبَ بِٱلْحَقِّ لِيَحْكُمَ بَيْنَ ٱلنَّاسِ فِيمَا ٱخْتَلَفُوا۟ فِيهِۚ وَمَا ٱخْتَلَفَ فِيهِ إِلَّا ٱلَّذِينَ أُوتُوهُ مِنۢ بَعْدِ مَا جَآءَتْهُمُ ٱلْبَيِّنَٰتُ بَغْيًۢا بَيْنَهُمْۖ فَهَدَى ٱللَّهُ ٱلَّذِينَ ءَامَنُوا۟ لِمَا ٱخْتَلَفُوا۟ فِيهِ مِنَ ٱلْحَقِّ بِإِذْنِهِۦۗ وَٱللَّهُ يَهْدِى مَن يَشَآءُ إِلَىٰ صِرَٰطٍ مُّسْتَقِيمٍ﴾ سُورَةُ البَقَرَةِ 2: 213

How were Adam ﷺ and Hawwa, the first of this species, created? Was it a gradual process over time, or did Allah ﷻ place them on the Earth in some other way? It is clear from scientific discoveries that there were earlier, less-advanced and more ape-like humanoids on the Earth for at least 3,000,000 years. But scientists are at a loss to explain the appearance of Homo Sapiens.

The ability of modern humans to think, shape, plan, create art and change their environment is unprecedented in Earth's natural history. Anthropologists are constantly debating our origins. As Muslims, we know the answer: Allah ﷻ created us in what He terms the 'best of forms,' *We have created man in the best composition.* Surat At-Tin (The Fig) 95: 4

﴿لَقَدْ خَلَقْنَا ٱلْإِنسَٰنَ فِىٓ أَحْسَنِ تَقْوِيمٍ﴾ سُورَةُ التِّينِ 95: 4

We have abilities that make us aware of our surroundings, and the gift of reasoning, so we can understand and make sense of the world around us.

IT'S ALL ABOUT ISLAM

Allah has brought you forth from your mothers' wombs when you knew nothing, and He made for you ears, eyes and hearts, so that you may be grateful. Surat An-Nahl (The Bees) 16:78

﴿وَٱللَّهُ أَخْرَجَكُم مِّنۢ بُطُونِ أُمَّهَٰتِكُمْ لَا تَعْلَمُونَ شَيْـًٔا وَجَعَلَ لَكُمُ ٱلسَّمْعَ وَٱلْأَبْصَٰرَ وَٱلْأَفْـِٔدَةَ لَعَلَّكُمْ تَشْكُرُونَ﴾ سُورَةُ النَّحْلِ 16: 78

Additionally, we were made with a disposition to know Allah ﷻ. Specifically, our **Basic Natural Way** (feelings and inner sense), or **Fitrah** فِطْرَة, prompts us towards Allah ﷻ. After all, Allah ﷻ placed within us a spirit-material, or **Ruh** رُوح, which is created by Allah ﷻ. Allah ﷻ breathed the ruh into our bodies to create us, so why wouldn't we want to move closer to our original source? (15:29)

At the same time, humans have an earthly response system that compels us to satisfy our basic instincts. If you were to look at a model of the human brain, you could easily see the intertwining of these two aspects of our existence. Underneath our thinking, reasoning brain is what is known as the 'reptilian core' of our brain (known in brain anatomy as basal ganglia). That is where our basic instincts reside. Those who let their intelligence go to waste become a slave to their lower brain, which seeks only pleasure and the satisfaction of physical urges.

Humans are gifted with intelligence, but they can be seduced by their base desires. Shaytan whispers into people's minds, which can unfavorably tilt the balance in the wrong direction. Yet Allah ﷻ revealed His guidance to chosen people, called prophets, who called others back to the straight way.

By sending messengers, Allah ﷻ helps us learn how to fulfill our responsibilities, particularly in worshipping Allah ﷻ. If we choose to surrender to Allah ﷻ, then we become more worthy of a reward. If, however, we reject our

95

Creator and instead follow only our desires, we develop many vices, including greed, gluttony, hatred, envy and anger. In this instance, we will incur a punishment in the Hereafter. (4:147)

Our origins are ultimately known only to Allah, and when all mysteries are solved, we will look on in wonder and exclaim at the power of our Creator.

سُبْحَانَ اللهِ وَبِحَمْدِهِ سُبْحَانَ اللهِ الْعَظِيْمِ

Questions to Answer

1. Why did the angels object to the creation of humans?
2. What did Shaytan do that caused Adam and Hawwa to be removed from the garden?
3. What instruction did Allah give to Adam and Hawwa about future guidance?

Define: Jinn, Angels, Iblis, Shaytan.

Reflect: How did pride affect the response Iblis gave to Allah when Allah ordered all the creatures to bow to Adam?

Act: Memorize the dua' that Adam and Hawwa made to Allah to ask for forgiveness for their sin of eating from the forbidden tree. (7:23).

IQ Builders:

1. How did Allah show the angels that humans were superior according to 2:30-33?
2. What did Iblis promise to do to humans according to 7:16-17?

Literature Selection

Surat Az-Zukhruf (The Ornaments of Gold)

Adapted from *The Holy Qur'an*
Arranged by Yahiya Emerick
(Explanatory words added in parentheses)

In the Name of Allah,
The Most Gracious, The Most Merciful

Ha Mim.* (1) By the Book that makes things clear. (2) We made it an Arabic Qur'an so you could understand it. (3) It (originated) in the Mother of the Book "Umm Al Kitab," which is kept in Our presence, transcendent and full of wisdom. (4) Should we take Our message away from you (Arabs), simply because you're transgressing people? (5) Yet how many Prophets did we send to earlier civilizations? (6) No Prophet ever went anywhere without being mocked and ridiculed. (7) And so We destroyed (those nations), which were even mightier than this (one of yours). Thus, the example of earlier civilizations passes on. (8) Recognizing His Favors If you asked them, "Who created the Heavens and the Earth?" They would most likely reply, "They were created by the most Powerful and the most Knowledgeable One." (9) (And they would be right, for) He's the One Who spread the earth out for you and made many pathways throughout it so you can find the right direction. (10) (And He's the One Who) sends down sufficient rain from the sky to revive the dead land—and that's also how you'll be raised (up at the resurrection). (11) (He's also the One Who) created all living things in pairs, and He sent down (the knowledge of shipbuilding) so you could sail in ships, and (He's the One Who gave you) cattle, as well, so you could ride them, (12) sitting securely on their flat backs. Whenever you're sitting on (some mode of travel) you can say, "Glory be to the One Who subjected this to our (use), for we never could have mastered this by ourselves,(13) and we will certainly return to our Lord." (14)

They Claim Ignorance

Yet they have attributed to Him from His servants a portion.! Indeed, humanity is clearly (guilty of) suppressing (the truth)! (15) Has He given Himself daughters, (out of everything) He created, and then gave you the choice to have sons? (16) When one of them is told the good news of (the birth of a daughter)—the same thing that he so readily adds to the likeness of the Compassionate (God)—his face becomes downcast, and he's filled with terrible disappointment. (17) (Is it right that you would ascribe the qualities of a female), whom (you consider) to be raised merely as an ornament (for a man's life), and (whom you consider) to be incapable of speaking with directness, (with the qualities of God)? (18) And so they turn the angels into females, even though (the angels were made) only to serve God. Were they there when they were created? (If they were) then their evidence will be noted, and they will be questioned about it. (19) And then (the idol-worshippers) say, "If it had been the Compassionate (God's) will, then we would have never worshipped (any false gods)." However, they don't know what (they're saying), and they do nothing but guess. (20) Did We ever give them some scripture in the past that they're committed to? (21) No way! They're only (excuse is to) say, "This is the (religion) we found our forefathers following, so we're guiding ourselves according to their footsteps." (22) And this is how it's always been: whenever We sent a Warner before you to any nation, the well-to-do among them said, "This is the (religion) we found our forefathers following, so we're going to follow in their footsteps." (23) (And their Warner would always) say, "What! Even though I'm bringing you better guidance than what you inherited from your forefathers?" (To which the people would always) reply, "As far as we're concerned, we don't (believe) that you've been sent (on any mission at all)."(24) And so We took payback from them—and oh, how (stunning) was the closure of those who rejected (the truth)! (25) Abraham told his father and his people, "I'm free of what you're worshipping! (26) (I'm only going to serve) the One Who made me, for He's the One Who's going to guide me." (27) And (Abraham) left this doctrine to posterity so that (people) after his time could turn back (to God). (28)

The Myth of Silver and Gold

But no! I've given (the luxuries of this world) to these (ungrateful people), as well as to their forefathers, until even now when a clear Messenger (has come to them) bringing them the truth. (29) So now that the truth has come to them, they (deny it), saying, "It's just some kind of magic, and we reject it." (30) (These idol-worshippers of Makkah go one step further by) asking, "Why isn't this

Qur'an being sent down to someone important from either of the two (largest) cities (in the area)?" (31) Are they the ones who parcel out your Lord's mercy? In fact, We're the One who parcels out among them their resources in the life of this world. We promote some (people) above the rest in status so they can coerce labor from them, but the mercy of your Lord is far better than what they accumulate. (32) And if it wasn't for the fact that all (people) would (merge together) into one community (of greedy misers), then We would've given everyone who blasphemes against the Compassionate (God) silver roofs for their houses, and (silver) stairs upon which to climb, (33) and (silver) doors on their houses, and thrones (made of silver) to rest upon, (34) and golden ornament as well! But all of those are nothing but things to use in the life of this world. The next life, in God's view, is for those who were aware (of the difference). (35) Separation from God is the Root of All Evil. Whoever blinds himself to the remembrance of the Compassionate will have a devil assigned to him by Us to be his close companion. (36) They steer them away from the path even as they think they're being rightly guided. (37) (This goes on) until he comes back to Us and then says (to his devil), "If only we were as far apart as the east and then another east!" What a terrible companion (he had)! (38)
(Knowing then that) you were wrong won't help you at all on that Day, for you both will (have an equal) share in the punishment! (39) Can you make the deaf hear or show the way to the blind or to someone who is clearly wrong? (40) Even if We took you away from them, (as they wish to get rid of you), We would still get our due out of them, (41) and We might just show you what We've promised is coming to them, for We indeed have power over them. (42) So hold tight to the revelation that's coming down to you, for you're on a straight path. (43) Truly this (revelation) is the remembrance (intended) for you and your people, and soon you'll have to give an accounting (of how well you lived it). (44)

The Example of Moses

You should ask Our messengers who We sent before your time if We ever set up any gods for worship other than the Compassionate. (45) In the past, We sent Moses with Our signs to Pharaoh and his officials, and he said, "I'm a Messenger from the Lord of All the Worlds." (46) But (even though) He went to them with Our signs, they laughed at them. (47) We showed them sign after sign, with each one being more impressive than the last, until We finally seized them with (plagues) so they could (at least have a chance) to return (to God's path). (48) (In their fear) they cried out, "You wizard! Call upon your Lord for us by your covenant with Him (and remove these plagues from us), then we'll accept (your) guidance." (49) But (every time) We took away a punishment from them, they went back on their word. (50) And Pharaoh declared to his nation, "My people! Doesn't the kingdom of Egypt belong to me? Look at these rivers flowing underneath me. Don't you see them? (51) Aren't I better than (Moses), that vagabond who can't even speak properly? (52) Why isn't he wearing gold bracelets, and why isn't he flanked by angels in conjunction?" (53) This is how he made fools out of his people, for they obeyed him and were truly a rebellious nation. (54) When they provoked Us, We took Our due from them and drowned them all. (55) We caused them (to recede into history) and made them an example for those who would follow. (56)

The Example of Jesus

When the son of Mary is held up as an example, your people complain loudly (57) saying, "Are our gods better, (or that Jesus, whom the Christians worship)?" They're offering this (objection) against you for no other reason than (they like) to argue, or they're a very argumentative people. (58) (Jesus) was nothing more than a servant to whom We granted Our favor, and We made him an example for the Children of Israel. (59) If We had wanted to, We could've sent angels to live among you in the Earth who would've replaced you. (60) (Jesus) is a portent of the Hour (of Judgement), so don't doubt Its (coming), rather you should follow Me, for that is a straight path. (61) Don't let Satan steer you away, for he is your declared enemy. (62) When Jesus came with clear evidence (of the truth) he said (to his people), "I've come to you with wisdom so I can resolve those issues that cause you to differ, therefore be mindful of God and obey me. (63) Truly God is my Lord and your Lord, so serve Him alone, for that is a straight path." (64) However, sects arose over differences among them, (in spite of Jesus' best efforts), so ruin upon those who do wrong, (for they're going to suffer) from the punishment of a Dreadful Day. (65)

Paradise Described

Are they waiting for the Hour to come upon them all of a sudden, without their knowing? (66) Brothers will be enemies on that Day, except among those who were mindful (of God). (67) My servants! You won't have any fear on that Day, nor will you feel sorrow. (68) You're the ones who have believed in Our signs and surrendered (to Us) (69) so enter into Paradise—you and your spouses both—in jubilation. (70) Dishes (of food) and golden cups will be passed around among them! Everything that a soul could want will be there; everything that eyes could take pleasure in, and you will get to stay there forever! (71) This is the Paradise that you'll inherit (as a reward) for what you used to do (in the world), (72) and there will be an endless supply of delicious fruits for you to partake of. (73) Hellfire Described The wicked will remain in the punishment of Hellfire, (74) and its (torments) won't be lightened for them, even as they're engulfed by sorrow and despair. (75) But it's not that We're being unfair to them, rather, they're the ones who were unfair to themselves. (76) "Oh

Master!" They will cry out (to the Warden of Hell), "If only your Lord would put an end to us!" But they'll be told, "(No), for you must remain." (77) People Say Incredible Things About God And so We've brought the truth to you, (people of Earth), yet most of you have an aversion to reality. (78) Have they made some kind of plan (to thwart Us), when We're the One Who decides matters, (79) or do they think that We didn't hear their secrets and private meetings? Certainly not! Our messengers (angels) are very close, watching them (as they talk). (80) Tell them, "If the Compassionate had a son, then I would be the first to worship him." (81) Glory to the Lord of the Heavens and the Earth; the Lord of the Throne is (far removed) from what they're ascribing (to Him). (82) So leave them to quibble and play until they come upon their Day that they've been promised. (83) He's the One Who is God in the Heavens, and God on the Earth, and He is the Wise and the Knowing. (84) Blessed is the One Who controls the Heavens and the Earth and all in between them! He has the knowledge of the Hour, and you're all going to return back to Him. (85) The ones that they call upon besides God have no power to intercede, except for those who testified to the truth, and (God) knows who they were. (86) If you were to ask them who created them, they would be sure to say, "God did." So how come they're so far off the mark? (87) And (the Prophet) said, "My Lord Truly these are a people who won't believe!" (88) Then turn away from them and say, "Peace," but soon they'll know (the truth). (89)

Note: Look up Surat Az-Zukhruf (43) in the Qur'an. Also read it in Arabic if you can.

Questions to Answer

1. What is the excuse that idol-worshippers give to justify their practices, and how does the Qur'an prove that it is false?
2. Describe three main themes of this surat and give supporting details.
3. Why is it wrong to say that God has children?

16 Why Am I Here?

WHAT TO LEARN

Every human being has a unique personality, but we all share similar basic needs. Despite these similarities, why do some recognize their purpose in life while others do not?

VOCABULARY

Tawbah   Emaan

THINK ABOUT IT

What is the purpose of our life on Earth?

A. What Is Our Nature?

Humans were created with certain qualities such as self-awareness, intelligence, sight and feeling, which are our strengths. At the same time, humans have earthly desires and motivations that prompt them to seek satisfaction and fulfillment at any cost, are our weaknesses. These two competing forces operate in all of us, and when combined together in a balanced way, they can create what we may call the 'noble human drive.'

Our basic nature is one of good, and our hearts are constantly directing us to seek the higher power outside of ourselves. But Shaytan seeks to corrupt us and to turn us towards our base and low desires. Small thoughts, faint whispers, an urge, a flash of emotion—these are the means by which we can fall into the clutches of animalistic impulses.

Why should Shaytan be allowed to tempt us, and why should we have a feeling inside which calls us back towards Allah? Allah has declared that He created humans and jinn only to worship Him and obey His laws.

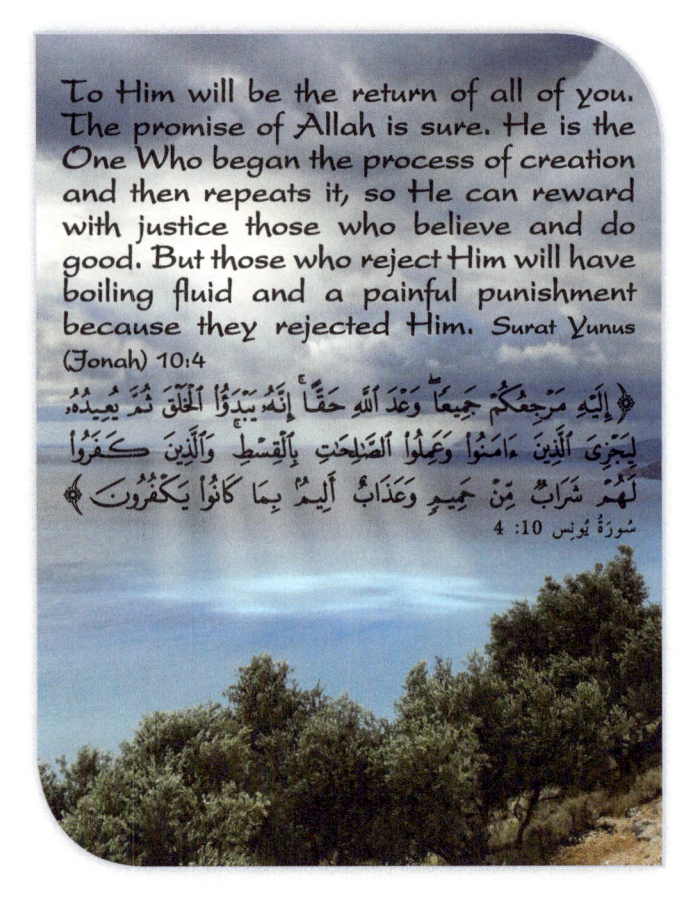

To Him will be the return of all of you. The promise of Allah is sure. He is the One Who began the process of creation and then repeats it, so He can reward with justice those who believe and do good. But those who reject Him will have boiling fluid and a painful punishment because they rejected Him. Surat Yunus (Jonah) 10:4

﴿إِلَيْهِ مَرْجِعُكُمْ جَمِيعًا وَعْدَ اللَّهِ حَقًّا إِنَّهُ يَبْدَأُ الْخَلْقَ ثُمَّ يُعِيدُهُ لِيَجْزِيَ الَّذِينَ آمَنُوا وَعَمِلُوا الصَّالِحَاتِ بِالْقِسْطِ وَالَّذِينَ كَفَرُوا لَهُمْ شَرَابٌ مِنْ حَمِيمٍ وَعَذَابٌ أَلِيمٌ بِمَا كَانُوا يَكْفُرُونَ﴾

سُورَةُ يُونُس 10: 4

I have only created jinn and humans so they can worship Me. Surat Ath-Thaariyaat (The Winds that Scatter) 51:56

﴿وَمَا خَلَقْتُ الْجِنَّ وَالْإِنْسَ إِلَّا لِيَعْبُدُونِ﴾ سُورَةُ الذَّارِيَات 51: 56

However, He gave to humans the expanded ability to choose whether or not to worship Him. The jinn have very limited interaction with mankind and are prone to arrogance, which has led them to disobedience.

If we can stop for a moment and consider the offer that Allah is holding out for us, we may be quite surprised. Allah has offered to us the ultimate bargain, available for all who will accept it.

You who believe, shall I lead you to a bargain that will save you from an awful punishment? It is that you believe in Allah and His Messenger and that you struggle in the Cause of Allah with your property and your selves. That is the best for you if you only knew. Then He will forgive you your sins and admit you to gardens beneath which rivers flow and to beautiful mansions in gardens of eternity. That is the supreme achievement! Surat As-Saff (The Rank) 61:10-12

﴿يَٰٓأَيُّهَا ٱلَّذِينَ ءَامَنُوا۟ هَلْ أَدُلُّكُمْ عَلَىٰ تِجَٰرَةٍ تُنجِيكُم مِّنْ عَذَابٍ أَلِيمٍ ۝ تُؤْمِنُونَ بِٱللَّهِ وَرَسُولِهِۦ وَتُجَٰهِدُونَ فِى سَبِيلِ ٱللَّهِ بِأَمْوَٰلِكُمْ وَأَنفُسِكُمْ ذَٰلِكُمْ خَيْرٌ لَّكُمْ إِن كُنتُمْ تَعْلَمُونَ ۝ يَغْفِرْ لَكُمْ ذُنُوبَكُمْ وَيُدْخِلْكُمْ جَنَّٰتٍ تَجْرِى مِن تَحْتِهَا ٱلْأَنْهَٰرُ وَمَسَٰكِنَ طَيِّبَةً فِى جَنَّٰتِ عَدْنٍ ذَٰلِكَ ٱلْفَوْزُ ٱلْعَظِيمُ﴾ سورة الصف 61: 10-12

B. Life Is a Great Test

Islam tells us that our purpose in life is to worship Allahﷻ, work in His cause and spread the message to those who still don't know or believe. By doing so, we will be rewarded with an existence in a place of eternal delight.

But what about the person who denies Allahﷻ and lives a life filled with selfish pleasure, only seeking to satisfy his or her desires? They live like they'll never die; they pass by the poor and don't care; they destroy their bodies with drugs, alcohol and tobacco; they spend their money on meaningless entertainment and treat their fellow human beings without consideration. Do they deserve to be rewarded also?

Those who don't place their hope in their meeting with Us (Allah), but are instead satisfied with the life of this world, and those who don't pay attention to Our signs, will be in the home of the fire because of what they earned. Those who believe and do good will be guided by their Lord because of their faith. Beneath them will flow rivers in gardens of happiness. They will call out, "Glory to You, Allah!" Their greeting will be "Peace." Their call will end with, "Praise be to Allah, the Lord of the Universe!" Surat Yunus (Jonah) 10:7-10

﴿إِنَّ ٱلَّذِينَ لَا يَرْجُونَ لِقَآءَنَا وَرَضُوا۟ بِٱلْحَيَوٰةِ ٱلدُّنْيَا وَٱطْمَأَنُّوا۟ بِهَا وَٱلَّذِينَ هُمْ عَنْ ءَايَٰتِنَا غَٰفِلُونَ ۝ أُو۟لَٰٓئِكَ مَأْوَىٰهُمُ ٱلنَّارُ بِمَا كَانُوا۟ يَكْسِبُونَ ۝ إِنَّ ٱلَّذِينَ ءَامَنُوا۟ وَعَمِلُوا۟ ٱلصَّٰلِحَٰتِ يَهْدِيهِمْ رَبُّهُم بِإِيمَٰنِهِمْ تَجْرِى مِن تَحْتِهِمُ ٱلْأَنْهَٰرُ فِى جَنَّٰتِ ٱلنَّعِيمِ ۝ دَعْوَىٰهُمْ فِيهَا سُبْحَٰنَكَ ٱللَّهُمَّ وَتَحِيَّتُهُمْ فِيهَا سَلَٰمٌ وَءَاخِرُ دَعْوَىٰهُمْ أَنِ ٱلْحَمْدُ لِلَّهِ رَبِّ ٱلْعَٰلَمِينَ﴾ سورة يونس 10: 7-10

We can see clearly that our life is a test. Allahﷻ knows our capacities, and He knows the future and the past. But for us, we will live and undergo a life that, in many ways, is like a final exam.

We are not here just to build large houses, make fortunes and have fun. Our lives are short, and we do not know if we'll live past tomorrow.

Our duty is to surrender to Allah'sﷻ perfect will and to do what is right in the world. Even Shaytan cannot force you to fall into error. You choose it for yourself. Allahﷻ said, But (Shaytan) had no authority over them, other than what We (allowed him to have), to test them to distinguish the one who believes in the next life from the one who doubts it. Your Lord watches over all things. Surat Saba' (Sheba) 34:21

﴿وَمَا كَانَ لَهُۥ عَلَيْهِم مِّن سُلْطَٰنٍ إِلَّا لِنَعْلَمَ مَن يُؤْمِنُ بِٱلْءَاخِرَةِ مِمَّنْ هُوَ مِنْهَا فِى شَكٍّ وَرَبُّكَ عَلَىٰ كُلِّ شَىْءٍ حَفِيظٌ﴾ سورة سبأ 34: 21

Allahﷻ asked us to enter Islam whole heartedly. Allahﷻ made us the khalifa on Earth, referring to human beings as successors in implementing Allah's message on this planet. We are here to create order and harmony—not to cause disorder and chaos. Allah warned us of this when He said, *Know, all of you, that the life of this world is only play and amusement, partying and bragging, and racing for more wealth and children. Here is an example: The rain and what it grows brings happiness to the gardeners. But soon (the plants) wither. You will see them become yellow and dry, eventually crumbling to dust. But in the next life, the destruction is even greater (for those who do wrong.) The forgiveness of Allah and the best reward (is better). What is the life of this world but materials of deception?* Surat Al Hadid (The Iron) 57:20

﴿ أَعْلَمُوا أَنَّمَا ٱلْحَيَوٰةُ ٱلدُّنْيَا لَعِبٌ وَلَهْوٌ وَزِينَةٌ وَتَفَاخُرٌ بَيْنَكُمْ وَتَكَاثُرٌ فِي ٱلْأَمْوَٰلِ وَٱلْأَوْلَٰدِ كَمَثَلِ غَيْثٍ أَعْجَبَ ٱلْكُفَّارَ نَبَاتُهُ ثُمَّ يَهِيجُ فَتَرَىٰهُ مُصْفَرًّا ثُمَّ يَكُونُ حُطَٰمًا وَفِي ٱلْأَخِرَةِ عَذَابٌ شَدِيدٌ وَمَغْفِرَةٌ مِّنَ ٱللَّهِ وَرِضْوَٰنٌ وَمَا ٱلْحَيَوٰةُ ٱلدُّنْيَا إِلَّا مَتَٰعُ ٱلْغُرُورِ ﴾ سُورَةُ الْحَدِيدِ 57: 20

C. How Should We Look at Our Lives?

The Blessed Prophet Muhammad once remarked, "Be in the world as though you were a stranger or a traveler." (Al Bukhari)

قَالَ رَسُولُ اللَّهِ ﷺ: «كُنْ فِي الدُّنْيَا كَأَنَّكَ غَرِيبٌ أَوْ عَابِرُ سَبِيلٍ».
رَوَاهُ الْبُخَارِيُّ

Take, for another example, the story the "Owner of the Garden" contained in Surat Al Kahf (The Cave) (18). In this story, there was a man who owned a huge tract of land and grew very wealthy. So much so that He even boasted one day, "I don't think this will ever end." But it did end, and a raging storm destroyed his land and ruined him. He was grief-stricken and cried out in sorrow. But did he think that the purpose of his life was to get rich?

The French writer Montaigne once remarked, "Fortune can destroy in a second what has taken long years to build." Sometimes it becomes difficult to remember that fortune and wealth can be destroyed in an instant, without warning. Allah remarked, *Wealth and children are the attractive things of this life, but good deeds are the things which last in the sight of your Lord, as the basis for reward and the best thing to rest your hopes on.* Surat Al Kahf (The Cave) 18:46

﴿ ٱلْمَالُ وَٱلْبَنُونَ زِينَةُ ٱلْحَيَوٰةِ ٱلدُّنْيَا وَٱلْبَٰقِيَٰتُ ٱلصَّٰلِحَٰتُ خَيْرٌ عِندَ رَبِّكَ ثَوَابًا وَخَيْرٌ أَمَلًا ﴾ سُورَةُ الْكَهْفِ 18: 46

Islam teaches that when you leave this life, you only take your **Emaan** إِيمَان **Faith** and your record of deeds with you. If you have faith in Allah and try your best to lead a moral life, then you will be rewarded by Allah. Even those who make mistakes and do wrong are able to receive Allah's rewards, if only they sincerely ask Allah for forgiveness and make **Tawbah** تَوْبَة **Repentance**. (48:13-14,)

Yet those who persistently disobey Allah should listen carefully to his warning. Allah said clearly, *Warn humanity of the day when the wrath will reach them. Then the sinners will say, "Our Lord, give us more time, even just a little. Then we'll listen to Your call and follow the prophets!" What?! Didn't you used to swear before that you would never perish?* Surat Ibrahim (Abraham) 14:44

﴿ وَأَنذِرِ ٱلنَّاسَ يَوْمَ يَأْتِيهِمُ ٱلْعَذَابُ فَيَقُولُ ٱلَّذِينَ ظَلَمُوا رَبَّنَآ أَخِّرْنَآ إِلَىٰٓ أَجَلٍ قَرِيبٍ نُّجِبْ دَعْوَتَكَ وَنَتَّبِعِ ٱلرُّسُلَ أَوَلَمْ تَكُونُوٓا أَقْسَمْتُم مِّن قَبْلُ مَا لَكُم مِّن زَوَالٍ ﴾ سُورَةُ إِبْرَاهِيمَ 14: 44

Once this short life is over, there will be no more time left to do things differently. Allah ﷻ reminds us that there are individuals who live their lives as if they will never die. But indeed, we will all die one day, even if we choose not to think about it. (56:57-62) Allah ﷻ can take us in our youth, during our adult lives or in our old age. It is all within His Power.

D. The Reality

Whatever we decide to do in life, the fact of the matter remains: life is short and temporary. Indeed, you and I are not permanent residents of the world.

To further bring this truth home to our hearts, what if it were possible to know the year in which you were going to die? How would such knowledge affect you? Would you think a little differently? Would your lifestyle change? Would your goals suddenly appear a little foolish or meaningless? Would you begin to question all those things you thought you were supposed to do, like wearing the coolest fashions, having the latest technology or doing things to impress others? Or would you now see them as unimportant? Would you suddenly have an overwhelming desire to follow Islamic teachings and believe in the Mercy of Allah ﷻ? I think most of us would probably listen intently to the words of Allah ﷻ when He says, *The example of those who deny their Lord is that their accomplishments are like ashes upon which the wind blows furiously on a stormy day. They have no power over what they earned. They were far from the real goal.* Surat Ibrahim (Abraham) 14:18

﴿مَثَلُ ٱلَّذِينَ كَفَرُوا بِرَبِّهِمْ أَعْمَـٰلُهُمْ كَرَمَادٍ ٱشْتَدَّتْ بِهِ ٱلرِّيحُ فِى يَوْمٍ عَاصِفٍ لَّا يَقْدِرُونَ مِمَّا كَسَبُوا۟ عَلَىٰ شَىْءٍ ذَٰلِكَ هُوَ ٱلضَّلَـٰلُ ٱلْبَعِيدُ﴾

سورة إبراهيم 14:18

We are created to surrender our will to Allah ﷻ. (39:11-12) To undergo a set of tests to determine if we are worthy of eternal rewards or eternal punishment. What we see before our eyes glitters but is temporal. Only those who seek to please Allah ﷻ in all that they do will ultimately succeed in the next life. (98:8)

'Ali bin Abu Talib ؓ once said: "People are asleep, and when they die, they will wake up." He was teaching us that some people are not aware of their purpose in life, and thus appear as though they are 'sleeping' through life.

Consider this example: Once the Blessed Prophet ﷺ was organizing an army to fight the idol-worshippers, but several people came forward asking to be excused from military duty.

Have you not seen those to whom it was said, "Hold your hands (from fighting) and be steadfast in Salah and pay Zakah." However, when fighting is enjoined upon them, then surprisingly, a group from them starts fearing people, as one would fear Allah, or fearing even more. They say, "Our Lord, why have you enjoined fighting upon us? Would you have not spared us for a little more time?" Say,

What is with you shall perish and what is with Allah shall last. And certainly, We shall bless those who observed patience, with their reward for the best of what they used to do. Surat An-Nahl (The Bees) 16:96

"The enjoyment of the world is but a little, and the Hereafter is far better for the one who fears Allah, and you shall not be wronged, even to the measure of a fiber." Surat An-Nisa' (The Women) 4: 77

﴿أَلَمْ تَرَ إِلَى ٱلَّذِينَ قِيلَ لَهُمْ كُفُّوٓاْ أَيْدِيَكُمْ وَأَقِيمُواْ ٱلصَّلَوٰةَ وَءَاتُواْ ٱلزَّكَوٰةَ فَلَمَّا كُتِبَ عَلَيْهِمُ ٱلْقِتَالُ إِذَا فَرِيقٌ مِّنْهُمْ يَخْشَوْنَ ٱلنَّاسَ كَخَشْيَةِ ٱللَّهِ أَوْ أَشَدَّ خَشْيَةً وَقَالُواْ رَبَّنَا لِمَ كَتَبْتَ عَلَيْنَا ٱلْقِتَالَ لَوْلَآ أَخَّرْتَنَآ إِلَىٰٓ أَجَلٍ قَرِيبٍ قُلْ مَتَٰعُ ٱلدُّنْيَا قَلِيلٌ وَٱلْءَاخِرَةُ خَيْرٌ لِّمَنِ ٱتَّقَىٰ وَلَا تُظْلَمُونَ فَتِيلًا﴾ سُورَةُ النِّسَاءِ 4: 77

Clearly, these people were afraid to die, and they selfishly thought only about living the life they thought they deserved. Then, we are all warned, *Wherever you are, death will find you; even if you are in mighty towers.* Surat An-Nisa' (The Women) 4: 78

﴿أَيْنَمَا تَكُونُواْ يُدْرِككُّمُ ٱلْمَوْتُ وَلَوْ كُنتُمْ فِى بُرُوجٍ مُّشَيَّدَةٍ﴾ سُورَةُ النِّسَاءِ 4: 78

You can't save yourself from death. This life is not a place you should think of as permanent—the next life is. Your purpose is to be tested, to try to build emaan that is as true as you can make it and to be the best you can be to those around you. (2:160 & 41:34)

...*and do not lose hope in the mercy of Allah. In fact, only the infidels lose hope in Allah's mercy.* Surat Yusuf (Joseph) 12:87

﴿...وَلَا تَا۟يْـَٔسُواْ مِن رَّوْحِ ٱللَّهِ إِنَّهُۥ لَا يَا۟يْـَٔسُ مِن رَّوْحِ ٱللَّهِ إِلَّا ٱلْقَوْمُ ٱلْكَٰفِرُونَ﴾ سُورَةُ يُوسُفَ 12: 87

Think about it, if you can keep yourself from being a slave to worldly things, then nothing that happens in this life can pull you into depression or hopelessness. You may feel sad if something tragic happens, but you never lose hope. Suicide, drug abuse, drunkenness, arguing, fighting and stress are all indicators of being far from Allah. A person can lose their fears and worries by implementing Islam fully in their lives.

Our lives do not end with death. Sure, our physical bodies perish and decay, but the spirit, that ruh, which Allah breathed into us, is quickly released into the other world. It crosses over and quickly learns the outcome of the decisions it made in this life.

Allah declared, *Indeed, Allah is the reality. It is He Who gives life to the dead,*

and it is He Who has power over all things. Surat Al Hajj (The Pilgrimage) 22:6

﴿ذَٰلِكَ بِأَنَّ ٱللَّهَ هُوَ ٱلْحَقُّ وَأَنَّهُۥ يُحْىِ ٱلْمَوْتَىٰ وَأَنَّهُۥ عَلَىٰ كُلِّ شَىْءٍ قَدِيرٌ﴾ سُورَةُ الحَجّ 22: 6

The purpose of our lives can best be summed up in the words of a man who thought much about it and realized the truth: I wouldn't be reasonable if I didn't worship the One Who created me and to Whom I will return. Surat Ya-sin 36:22

﴿وَمَا لِىَ لَا أَعْبُدُ ٱلَّذِى فَطَرَنِى وَإِلَيْهِ تُرْجَعُونَ﴾ سُورَةُ يس 36: 22

Which are you interested in: gardens of eternity or the punishment of a fire? A life of contentment or a life of depression? We are all given the tools to complete our test of life successfully. (3:90-91)

You only have one chance to get your life's record right. Make your decision wisely. That's why you're here. (6:30-32)

Our beloved Prophet ﷺ once said, "Allah forgives the person who commits a sin (then feels ashamed of it), purifies himself, offers a prayer and seeks His forgiveness." Then the Prophet recited these verses from the Qur'an: Those who, when they do an evil thing or wrong themselves, but then remember Allah and implore forgiveness for their sins—and who can forgive sins except Allah?—And who do not knowingly repeat (the bad deed) they did, the reward for that kind of person will be forgiveness from their Lord and gardens underneath which rivers flow. They will live there forever, a bountiful reward for those who work (in Allah's way) (3:135-136)." (Abu Dawud)

قَالَ حَبِيبُنَا ﷺ: «مَا مِنْ عَبْدٍ يُذْنِبُ ذَنْبًا فَيُحْسِنُ الطُّهُورَ ثُمَّ يَقُومُ فَيُصَلِّي رَكْعَتَيْنِ ثُمَّ يَسْتَغْفِرُ اللهَ إِلَّا غَفَرَ اللهُ لَهُ». ثُمَّ قَرَأَ هَذِهِ الْآيَةَ: ﴿وَٱلَّذِينَ إِذَا فَعَلُوا۟ فَٰحِشَةً أَوْ ظَلَمُوٓا۟ أَنفُسَهُمْ ذَكَرُوا۟ ٱللَّهَ فَٱسْتَغْفَرُوا۟ لِذُنُوبِهِمْ وَمَن يَغْفِرُ ٱلذُّنُوبَ إِلَّا ٱللَّهُ وَلَمْ يُصِرُّوا۟ عَلَىٰ مَا فَعَلُوا۟ وَهُمْ يَعْلَمُونَ ۞ أُو۟لَٰٓئِكَ جَزَآؤُهُم مَّغْفِرَةٌ مِّن رَّبِّهِمْ وَجَنَّٰتٌ تَجْرِى مِن تَحْتِهَا ٱلْأَنْهَٰرُ خَٰلِدِينَ فِيهَا وَنِعْمَ أَجْرُ ٱلْعَٰمِلِينَ﴾ 3: 135–136. رَوَاهُ أَبُودَاوُدَ.

If anyone does good deeds, be they male or female, and has emaan, they will enter Paradise and no injustice will be done to them at all. Surat An-Nisa' (The Women) 4: 124

﴿وَمَن يَعْمَلْ مِنَ ٱلصَّٰلِحَٰتِ مِن ذَكَرٍ أَوْ أُنثَىٰ وَهُوَ مُؤْمِنٌ فَأُو۟لَٰٓئِكَ يَدْخُلُونَ ٱلْجَنَّةَ وَلَا يُظْلَمُونَ نَقِيرًا﴾ سُورَةُ النِّسَاء 4: 124

The Blessed Prophet ﷺ once said, "Whoever intends to do something good is rewarded by Allah with one good deed for it. If he or she then does that good thing, Allah rewards him or her from ten to seven hundred times. Whoever intends to do something wrong, but doesn't do it, is also rewarded by Allah one good reward. If he or she does that bad thing, he or she is accounted with only one bad deed." (Al Bukhari & Muslim)

عَنْ رَسُولِ اللهِ ﷺ: «مَنْ هَمَّ بِحَسَنَةٍ فَلَمْ يَعْمَلْهَا كَتَبَهَا اللهُ عِنْدَهُ حَسَنَةً كَامِلَةً، وَإِنْ هَمَّ بِهَا فَعَمِلَهَا كَتَبَهَا اللهُ عِنْدَهُ عَشْرَ حَسَنَاتٍ إِلَى سَبْعِمِائَةِ ضِعْفٍ إِلَى أَضْعَافٍ كَثِيرَةٍ، وَإِنْ هَمَّ بِسَيِّئَةٍ فَلَمْ يَعْمَلْهَا كَتَبَهَا اللهُ عِنْدَهُ حَسَنَةً كَامِلَةً، وَإِنْ هَمَّ بِهَا فَعَمِلَهَا كَتَبَهَا اللهُ سَيِّئَةً وَاحِدَةً». رَوَاهُ البُخَارِيُّ وَمُسْلِمٌ.

IT'S ALL ABOUT ISLAM

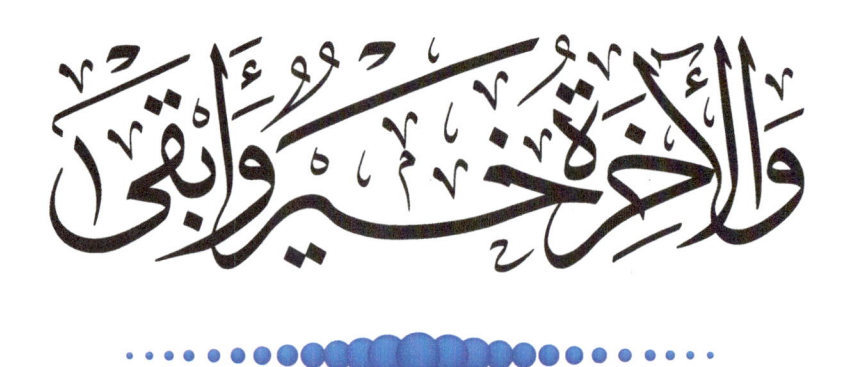

وَالْآخِرَةُ خَيْرٌ وَأَبْقَىٰ

Questions to Answer

1. What is the bargain Allah is offering us?
2. How is a good person different from an evil person?
3. What happened in the story of the Owner of the Garden?
4. Why should our focus in life not be the gaining of riches and wealth?
5. What will happen to us in the next life?
6. Why should we not fear death if we have faith in Allah and live a life that is good?

Define: Emaan, Tawbah.

Reflect: The Blessed Prophet once said, "Hearts can get rusty, just like metal. When the people asked how that can be prevented, the Prophet replied, By remembering that you will die someday and by reading the Qur'an." (Al Baihaqi)

قَالَ رَسُولُ اللهِ ﷺ: «إِنَّ هَذِهِ الْقُلُوبَ تَصْدَأُ، كَمَا يَصْدَأُ الْحَدِيدُ إِذَا أَصَابَهُ الْمَاءُ، قِيلَ: يَا رَسُولَ اللهِ، وَمَا جِلَاؤُهَا؟ قَالَ: كَثْرَةُ ذِكْرِ الْمَوْتِ، وَتِلَاوَةُ الْقُرْآنِ». رَوَاهُ الْبَيْهَقِيُّ

How do you think those two things keep your emaan fresh?

Act: Think of an action or activity in your life that takes you further away from Allah (i.e. lying, arguing or being addicted to TV, games, social media, email, etc). Commit to refraining from that activity from today onwards and take specific steps that help you stick to this goal. Write down both the goal and the steps you will take in a place visible to you. Revisit the goal often to make sure you are sticking to it.

IQ Builder: How does Allah describe the life of this world in 57:20?

Say (on My behalf), "O servants of Mine who have acted recklessly against their own selves, do not despair of Allah's mercy. Surely, Allah will forgive all sins. Surely, He is the One who is the Most-Forgiving, the Very-Merciful. Turn passionately towards your Lord, and submit to Him before the punishment comes to you, after which you will not be helped. And follow the best of what has been sent down to you from your Lord before the punishment comes to you suddenly when you do not even expect." Lest someone should say, "Pity on me, because I fell short in respect of (observing the rights of) Allah and, in fact, I was one of those who mocked," Or (lest) someone should say, "If Allah were to show me the way, I would have surely been among those who fear Allah," Or (lest) someone should say when he sees the punishment, "Would that I have a chance to return, so that I may become one of those who are good in their deeds." No! My verses had reached you, but you called them untrue, and waxed proud and became of those who disbelieved. And on the Day of Judgement, you will see those who had forged lies against Allah (in a state) that their faces are turned black. Is it not that in Jahannam there is an abode for the arrogant? And Allah will save the God-fearing (from Jahannam), with utmost success granted to them such so as no evil will touch them, nor will they grieve. Surat Az-Zumar (The Groups) 39:53-61

﴿ قُلْ يَا عِبَادِيَ الَّذِينَ أَسْرَفُوا عَلَىٰ أَنفُسِهِمْ لَا تَقْنَطُوا مِن رَّحْمَةِ اللَّهِ ۚ إِنَّ اللَّهَ يَغْفِرُ الذُّنُوبَ جَمِيعًا ۚ إِنَّهُ هُوَ الْغَفُورُ الرَّحِيمُ ﴾ ﴿ وَأَنِيبُوا إِلَىٰ رَبِّكُمْ وَأَسْلِمُوا لَهُ مِن قَبْلِ أَن يَأْتِيَكُمُ الْعَذَابُ ثُمَّ لَا تُنصَرُونَ ﴾ ﴿ وَاتَّبِعُوا أَحْسَنَ مَا أُنزِلَ إِلَيْكُم مِّن رَّبِّكُم مِّن قَبْلِ أَن يَأْتِيَكُمُ الْعَذَابُ بَغْتَةً وَأَنتُمْ لَا تَشْعُرُونَ ﴾ ﴿ أَن تَقُولَ نَفْسٌ يَا حَسْرَتَىٰ عَلَىٰ مَا فَرَّطتُ فِي جَنبِ اللَّهِ وَإِن كُنتُ لَمِنَ السَّاخِرِينَ ﴾ ﴿ أَوْ تَقُولَ لَوْ أَنَّ اللَّهَ هَدَانِي لَكُنتُ مِنَ الْمُتَّقِينَ ﴾ ﴿ أَوْ تَقُولَ حِينَ تَرَى الْعَذَابَ لَوْ أَنَّ لِي كَرَّةً فَأَكُونَ مِنَ الْمُحْسِنِينَ ﴾ ﴿ بَلَىٰ قَدْ جَاءَتْكَ آيَاتِي فَكَذَّبْتَ بِهَا وَاسْتَكْبَرْتَ وَكُنتَ مِنَ الْكَافِرِينَ ﴾ ﴿ وَيَوْمَ الْقِيَامَةِ تَرَى الَّذِينَ كَذَبُوا عَلَى اللَّهِ وُجُوهُهُم مُّسْوَدَّةٌ ۚ أَلَيْسَ فِي جَهَنَّمَ مَثْوًى لِّلْمُتَكَبِّرِينَ ﴾ ﴿ وَيُنَجِّي اللَّهُ الَّذِينَ اتَّقَوْا بِمَفَازَتِهِمْ لَا يَمَسُّهُمُ السُّوءُ وَلَا هُمْ يَحْزَنُونَ ﴾ سُورَةُ الزُّمَرِ 39: 53-61

Unit 04 Review Exercise

VOCABULARY REVIEW

On a separate sheet of paper, write the definition of each word below.

1. Shaytan
2. Evolution
3. Photosynthesis
4. Jinn
5. Ruh
6. Fitrah
7. Ozone Layer
8. Test
9. Sentient
10. Tawbah
11. Emaan

REMEMBERING WHAT YOU READ

On a separate sheet of paper, answer the following questions. Use complete sentences in your answers.

1. What does Islam say about the purpose of the creation of the Universe?
2. In what ways do Islam and modern science agree on our knowledge of the Universe?
3. What is the debate between some Christians and scientists?
4. What does Islam say about the appearance of humans on this planet?
5. How does reflecting on death help us become better Muslims?
6. Why did the first humans separate and scatter all over the world?
7. Who were Adam and Hawwa and what happened to them?
8. Describe the test that humans must pass to achieve Paradise in the next life.
9. How has Allah helped humans choose their path wisely?

THINKING TO LEARN

On a separate sheet of paper, answer the questions below. Use complete sentences.

1. What are some worldly desires that can make us forget about our true purpose in life? How might these desires deter us from living our lives as Allah says we should?
2. Which saying of the Blessed Prophet Muhammad from this lesson resonates most with you about your purpose in life? Explain your answer in 4–5 sentences.

UNIT 5
Tales of Ancient Days

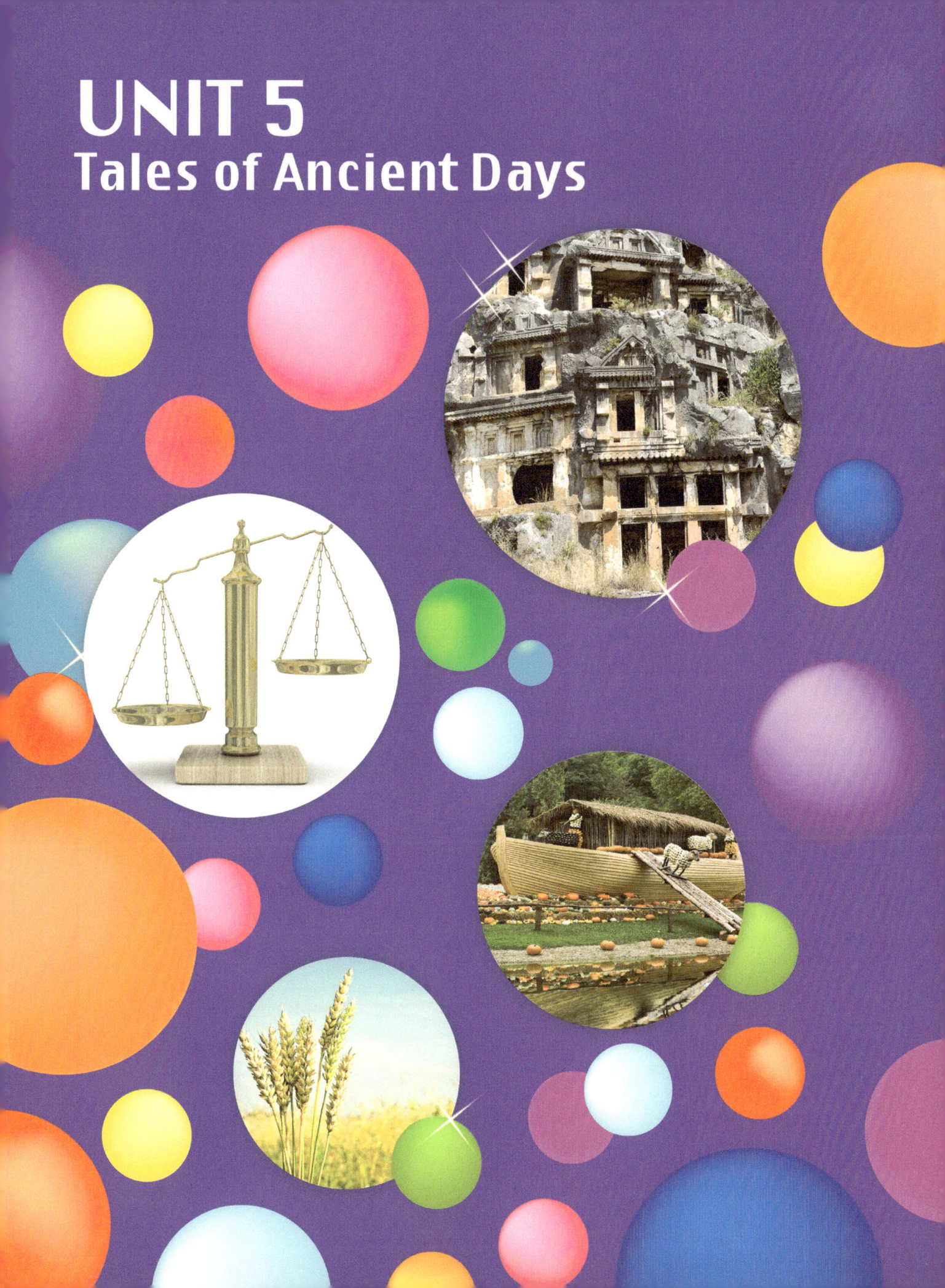

17 Who Were Adam ﷺ & Hawwa?

WHAT TO LEARN

Imagine being the first human being on the planet. How would you feel? Everything you saw would be the first time a human had ever looked upon it. There would be no pollution or annoying noise. You'd have complete freedom to do as you pleased. The only rule would be to not go near one, single tree...

VOCABULARY

Adam ﷺ   **Habeel**   **Qabeel**
Hawwa

THINK ABOUT IT

What was the experience of our earliest ancestors?

A. The First Humans

You have already learned that Allah ﷻ offered the responsibility of free will to the rest of the Universe and that all animate and inanimate things declined, knowing what a huge burden it would be.

Then Allah ﷻ offered this trust to the unformed human soul, and the soul accepted. Therefore, Allah ﷻ announced that He was going to create a khalifa. When the angels realized what choices and actions would be available to humans, they worriedly asked Allah ﷻ if it would be good for Earth. "Will you place there a creature who will create disorder and shed blood?" they asked. Surat Al Baqarah (The Cow) 2:30

Allah ﷻ, ever well aware, told them that He knew what they did not. He even added that they will soon be ordered to bow down to humans. (38:71-72) Then He caused humans to form.

When **Adam** آدَم ﷺ and **Hawwa** حَوَّاء awakened to a fully conscious mind, Allah ﷻ gave them the awareness and understanding of their environment and the world around them.

Then Allah ﷻ commanded the angels to explain the significance of the earthly environment, but they could not. So Allah ﷻ proved to the angels that Adam ﷺ was capable of understanding his environment in ways the angels could not. The angels were amazed and bowed in respect to Adam ﷺ when Allah ﷻ ordered them to. (2:31-34)

Another race of beings, which Allah ﷻ had created before humans, was the jinn. One of these jinn, by the name of Iblis, was watching the angels bow. He stood stiffly as they bowed. (18:50)

Allah ﷻ questioned him, "O Iblis, Why didn't you bow along with the angels?" Surat Al Hijr (The Rocky Tract) 15:32

Iblis was full of vanity and pride; he exclaimed, "You made me from fire and him from dirt." Surat Al A'raf (The Heights) 7:12

112

Iblis thought he was too good to bow to a creature made from dirt (water, carbon and other elements of the earth).

Allah ﷻ commanded Iblis to go away, but Iblis foolishly challenged Allah ﷻ by saying, "O my Lord! Because you misled me, I shall indeed adorn the path of error for them (mankind) on the earth, and I shall mislead them all." Surat Al Hijr (The Rocky Tract) 15:39

Allah ﷻ responded with His own challenge, saying Iblis could remain alive until the Day of Judgement and could try to carry out his sinister pledge. Then Allah ﷻ said, "Over My servants you will have no authority, except with the ones who put themselves in the wrong and follow you." Surat Al Hijr (The Rocky Tract) 15:42

Iblis arrogantly declared that he would create false desires in humans to lead them away from the truth. (4:119) So Allah ﷻ warned Iblis that if any humans chose to believe in him, then they would enter Hellfire along with all the evil jinn who dared to defy Allah ﷻ. (4:121)

Iblis left to carry out his plans, confident of his victory. But Allah ﷻ had equipped humans with defenses that Iblis, also known as Shaytan, never knew they had: intellect and the ability to reason.

Meanwhile, Adam ﷺ continued to live in the Garden with his wife, Hawwa, whom Allah ﷻ had also created. They lived a wonderful life of rest, enjoyment and satisfaction.

Allah ﷻ gave them only one rule to follow: stay away from one particular tree, while warning them of the dangers of Shaytan. Allah ﷻ said, "This is an enemy to you and your mate." Surat Ta-Ha 20:117

Some time later, Shaytan came into the Garden and began to whisper to the couple. He approached Adam ﷺ and Hawwa and started tempting them with his lies. (4:120)

He told them that if they ate from the forbidden tree, they would be powerful and live forever.

He said, "Oh Adam, shall I lead you to the tree of Eternity and to a kingdom that never decays?" Surat Ta-Ha 20:120

After some time, their desires got the better of them, and they ate from the forbidden tree. As soon as they ate, they realized their mistake and tried to hide. They began to feel embarrassed by one another's bodies and tried to cover themselves with leaves. (20:121)

B. Allah's ﷻ Forgiveness

Allah ﷻ knew what they had done, as He is All Seeing and All Knowing. He expelled Adam ﷺ and Hawwa from the Garden and ordered them to live out their lives on Earth. But Allah ﷻ is Merciful and soon taught them how to repent and ask for forgiveness for their deeds.

They said: "Our Lord, we have wronged ourselves, and if you don't forgive us and have mercy on us, we will surely be lost." Surat Al A'raf (The Heights) 7:23

Adam ﷺ and Hawwa earnestly asked for Allah's ﷻ forgiveness, and He granted them their request. (3:135) Then Allah ﷻ assured them, "If, and it will happen, there comes to you guidance from Me, whoever follows My guidance will not lose his way, nor fall into despair. But whoever turns away from My guidance, certainly he will have a life narrowed down and We will raise him up blind on the Day of Judgement." Surat Ta-Ha 20:123-124

Adam ﷺ and Hawwa took this simple instruction and lived out their lives according to Allah's ﷻ command. In time, they had two sons, **Habeel** هابيل **Abel** and **Qabeel** قابيل **Cain**.

Allah made Adam His first prophet, or guide for humanity. It was Adam's duty to teach his children to fear Allah and to obey His commands out of love for Him. His wife and children were his first followers.

Adam's two oldest sons decided that they wanted to present an offering to Allah to show their devotion. One day, they went out and each set up a small stone altar, or platform, upon which to offer their gift to Allah.

Both Qabeel and Habeel presented their offerings, but Qabeel looked over at his brother's altar in jealousy and envy. Finally, he felt convinced that Allah accepted only his brother Habeel's offering.

In a jealous rage, Qabeel threatened to kill his younger brother. Habeel merely protested that Allah only accepts the offerings of those who are good. (5:27)

Habeel then tried to admonish his brother by saying, "If you raise your hand against me, it is not for me to stretch my hand against you to kill you, for I fear Allah, the Lord of the Worlds. As for me, I want you to take my sin on yourself as well as your sins, for you will be a dweller of the fire. The only reward for people who do evil." Surat Al Ma'idah (The Table) 5:28-29

Qabeel's rage exploded in a blind fury! He attacked his younger brother and murdered him mercilessly. He was the world's first murderer.

After realizing what he had done, Qabeel was filled with regret. He had let his passion and envy rule his mind and had forgotten his reason, instead listening to the whisperings of Shaytan. He even tried to hide the body as he didn't know what to do with it.

While thinking about what to do, he saw a black raven scratching at the ground as if digging for something. As Qabeel watched the raven dig, he cried out, "Woe is me! If only I could be like this raven and hide the shame of my (murdered) brother." Surat Al Ma'idah (The Table) 5:31

He realized he could bury his brother's body. He dug a hole in the earth and covered his dead brother with dirt. Thus, the prophecy of Allah found its fulfillment. Allah said that humans could be enemies to each other on Earth. In time, after Prophet Adam passed away, his descendants split up into groups and went in different directions.

All the people were no more than a single community; later, they differed. But for a word from your Lord that had already come to pass, a decisive judgement would have been made about their mutual differences. Surat Yunus (Jonah) 10:19

﴿ وَمَا كَانَ النَّاسُ إِلَّا أُمَّةً وَاحِدَةً فَاخْتَلَفُوا وَلَوْلَا كَلِمَةٌ سَبَقَتْ مِن رَّبِّكَ لَقُضِيَ بَيْنَهُمْ فِيمَا فِيهِ يَخْتَلِفُونَ ﴾ سُورَةُ يُونُسَ 10:19

The story of Prophet Adam is ancient, but the lessons continue to play out to this very day. Allah sent many guides to the children of Adam in the generations to come. Some prophets and messengers were followed by their people, and some were not. All of those who lived before us are awaiting judgement. We must follow the guidance of Allah as left to us by His last Messenger or lose in this life and the next.

Questions to Answer

1. Why did the angels react with concern when they heard that Allah was going to create human beings with free will?
2. How did Allah show the angels that Adam was superior to them? Describe the scene.
3. Who was Iblis, and what did he say to Allah about humans?
4. How did Adam and Hawwa come to Earth?
5. What was the conflict between Qabeel and Habeel, and what happened in the end?
6. Who or what did Allah promise to send the people of the future to help them in their struggle against Shaytan?

Define: Hawwa, Qabeel.
Reflect: The name 'Iblis' means 'he despaired,' and the name 'Shaytan' means 'to separate from.' How does each name relate to this jinn's actions?
Act: Knowing that Shaytan will try to tempt you, what are some things you can do to protect yourself from his snares? Make a list and share it with at least one classmate.
IQ Builder: Read the exact translation from the Qur'an about the story of Adam and Hawwa. Find relevant passages by using the index of your Qur'an.

18 Nuh ﷺ and the Great Flood

WHAT TO LEARN

Jews and Christians say that the flood during the time of Prophet Nuh ﷺ (Noah) covered the entire world. Geologists and archeologists have proven that the world was never completely covered by water in the last billion years. The Qur'an, on the other hand, merely states that it was the people of Nuh ﷺ and their region that were destroyed in the flood. This is an example of how the stories in the various Holy Books are similar. However this demonstrates that the Qur'anic version is more scientifically correct.

VOCABULARY

Nuh ﷺ   Prehistoric
Mount Judi

THINK ABOUT IT

How did Prophet Nuh ﷺ try to convince his people?

A. The Human Saga

We have learned in previous lessons that the descendants of Adam ﷺ spread out in all directions across the globe. Some groups, or tribes, migrated to Europe, while others migrated to Asia, South America and even as far as Australia.

By exploring caves, archeologists have discovered evidence of human habitation on every continent. They have found rock paintings, tools and burial sites. Ancient campfires, dating back tens of thousands of years, have also been unearthed.

As Allah ﷻ tells us, *Many were the ways of life that have passed away before you. Travel over the Earth and see what was the end of those who rejected.* Surat Al 'Imran (The Family of 'Imran) 3:137

﴿قَدْ خَلَتْ مِن قَبْلِكُمْ سُنَنٌ فَسِيرُوا فِى ٱلْأَرْضِ فَٱنظُرُوا۟ كَيْفَ كَانَ عَـٰقِبَةُ ٱلْمُكَذِّبِينَ﴾ سُورَةُ آلِ عِمْرَان 3: 137

There is so much we will never know about ancient humans and their ways—so many names, and deeds of valor and of cowardice. How many great men and women arose and put their lives on the line, bettering humanity? And how many evil people, who rebelled against all goodness, worked their plots and schemes?

At the beginning of human existence people did not know how to write. We call this time period the **Prehistoric** قَبْلَ التَّارِيخ period as we have nothing of historical documentation written down. Writing was only invented about 6,000 to 7,000 years ago.

We will never know the names of the countless prophets that Allah ﷻ sent to the various peoples. Nevertheless, Allah ﷻ has revealed some of their stories to us in the Qur'an to illustrate the eternal struggle between good and evil that began between Prophet Adam ﷺ and Iblis the Shaytan.

One of these stories from prehistoric times is that of Prophet **Nuh**ﷺ نُوح **Noah** and his efforts to bring his people out of darkness and ignorance. We are uncertain of how many years passed between the time of Prophet Adam ﷺ and the time of Prophet Nuh ﷺ. Perhaps as many as 100,000 years may have elapsed, for we know that Nuh's ﷺ people were sophisticated enough to live in villages and were skilled in farming.

We can, perhaps, assign a rounded figure of his era to between 5,000 and 10,000 years ago. The geographic location seems to be somewhere in ancient Mesopotamia, where, indeed, some of the world's oldest farming villages have been discovered.

B. How Did Idol-worship Develop Among Nuh's ﷺ People?

Idol-worship was a well-established tradition when Nuh ﷺ was born into his small farming village. The crude statues may have been prominently displayed in the center of the village, framed by the rising mountains all around the large, fertile valley.

The Blessed Prophet Muhammad ﷺ explained how the worship of idols was adopted by Nuh's ﷺ ancestors. In a hadith, he explained that there were five famous people who lived in the remote past. They each had many followers and exerted a great influence in their villages.

Their names were **Wud** وَد, **Suwa'** سَوَاع, **Yaghuth** يَغوث, **Ya'uq** يَعوق and **Nasra** نَسرا. They each lived at different times and were known for different qualities. After they passed away, legends and stories developed around them. These stories were passed on by village storytellers from generation to generation.

Some people went so far as to build statues to honor and remember famous individuals. As generations passed, Shaytan introduced the idea to them that their forefathers actually worshipped these images.

Slowly, people began to believe that these idols were real gods who made the rains fall that nourished their crops. In time, rituals and prayers were introduced, and people virtually forgot about the Supreme Being, Allah ﷻ.

It was during this time that Allah ﷻ chose a righteous man named Nuh ﷺ to spread His guidance and message. A simple villager was chosen to proclaim Allah's ﷻ message to a network of farming villages steeped in ignorance. We record his story directly from the Qur'an.

C. The Mission Begins

Allah sent Nuh to his people with this mission: Warn your people before there comes to them a terrible Penalty. So Nuh announced, "My People! I am a clear Warner sent to you with the message that you should serve Allah, fear Him, and obey me. And Allah will forgive you your sins, and will respite you to an appointed term. Indeed when Allah's term comes, it is not deferred, if you only know!" Surat Nuh (Noah) 71:1-4

Then Nuh ﷺ went from village to village with his message, Surely We sent Nuh to his people. So he said, "My people! Serve Allah! You have no other god but

Him. I fear for you the punishment of an awful day!" The chiefs of his people said, "Indeed we see you in an obvious error." He said, "O my people, there is no error in me, but I am a messenger from the Lord of all the worlds. I am only carrying out the duties of My Lord's mission. My advice is sincere to you, and I know things from Allah that you don't. Don't you ever consider that there is coming to you a message from your Lord through a man of your own people? You are warned so you may fear Allah and receive His mercy." Surat Al A'raf (The Heights) (7:59-63)

But the leaders were firm in their position and argued against Nuh in front of the people. They said, "We don't see you as anything more than a man like us. The only people who seem to be listening to your message are the poor and foolish. We don't see anything in you that is any better than us. We think you are a liar!"
Nuh replied, "My people! Consider if I have a sign from my Lord and that He sent mercy to me from Himself. But the mercy is hidden from your eyes. Should we force you to accept it if you hate it? My people! I'm not asking for any money in return. My reward is from none but Allah. And I won't drive away anyone who believes for they will surely meet their Lord, and I think you are the ignorant ones!" Surat Hud 11:27-29

"My people! Who would help me against Allah if I drove the (poor) away? Won't you listen? I'm not telling you that I have the treasures of Allah, nor do I know what is hidden, and I'm not an angel. And I don't say that the people you consider poor will be denied good from Allah. Allah knows best what is in their souls. If I (turned the poor believers away) then I would be a wrong-doer." Surat Hud 11:30-31

The leaders stood forth among the people and declared, "Nuh! You have argued with us and lengthened our dispute too long. We dare you to bring on us what you threaten us with, if you are truthful." Nuh replied, "Truly Allah will bring it on you if He wills, and then you won't be able to stop it. My words to you will not help you, as much as I like to give you good advice. If Allah wills to let you stray, He is your Lord, and you will return to Him." Surat Hud 11:32-34

D. Nuh's Despair

Nuh, in his despair, prayed to Allah. He said, "My Lord! I've called to my people night and day, but my calling only increases (their) flight (from the truth). And every time I call to them so You might forgive them, they thrust their fingers in their ears, cover themselves up with their cloaks and they grow stubborn and give themselves up to arrogance." Surat Nuh (Noah) 71:6-7

Nuh continued his plea to Allah, "So I have called to them aloud. Further, I have spoken to them in public and secretly in private saying, Ask forgiveness from your Lord, for He is Forgiving. He will send rain to you in abundance; give you increase in wealth and sons, and bestow on you gardens and rivers (of flowing water). What's the matter with you that you don't place your hope for kindness and perseverance in Allah, seeing that He is the One Who created you in (the womb) in stages? Don't you see how Allah created the seven skies, one above the other, and made the moon a light in their midst and made the sun as a lamp? Allah has produced you from the Earth, growing (gradually), and, in the end, He will return you into the (Earth) and raise

you forth (again at the Resurrection). Allah has made the Earth for you as a carpet (spread out) that you may go about on spacious plains."
Nuh said, "My Lord! They have disobeyed me and they follow (men) whose wealth and children give them nothing but loss. And they have planned a tremendous plot, and they have said (to each other), 'Don't abandon your gods; don't abandon Wud or Suwa nor Yaghuth, Ya'uq or Nasr.' They have already misled many, and You grant no increase to the wrongdoers except in straying (from their goal)." Surat Nuh (Noah) 71:8-24

Allah revealed the following message to Prophet Nuh, "None of your people will believe except those who have already believed. So don't worry over their actions any longer. Build a ship under Our sight and Our direction and don't call on Me anymore about those who are in sin, for they are going to be overwhelmed." Surat Hud 11:36-37

Nuh began building a ship right away (in the mountain valley). Every time the leaders of his people passed by, they ridiculed him harshly. Even his wife disbelieved in him! Nuh would reply, "If you ridicule us now, we will look down on and ridicule you also. Soon you will know who will have a punishment that will cover them in shame, on whom will be an ever-lasting punishment!" Surat Hud 11:38-39

When the time was right, Allah's command came, and the springs of the Earth gushed forth. Allah commanded Nuh, "Board the ship and take two of each kind (of local farm animals), a male and female, and your family, except those who had the word decreed against them, and also take the believers." But there were only a few who believed with him. So Nuh announced, "Board the ship whether it moves or not. My Lord is the Forgiving and Merciful." Surat Hud 11:40

And Nuh said: "My Lord! Don't leave any unbelievers in the land! For, if You do leave (any of) them, they will mislead Your servants and will breed none but wicked, ungrateful people. My Lord, forgive me, my parents, and all who enter my house in faith, and (all) believing men and believing women. To the wrongdoers, grant no increase but in punishment!" Surat Nuh (Noah) 71:26-28

Then the ship rose on the water whose waves swelled like mountains. Prophet Nuh saw his son on a mountainside and called out to him, "My son, get on board with us and don't be with the unbelievers!" His son shouted back, "I will climb a mountain and be saved from the water!" Nuh replied, "Today nothing can save you from the command of Allah, except those who He has mercy on!" Then the waves came between them and his son was one of those overwhelmed by the flood. His wife, who disbelieved, was also lost. Surat Hud 11:42-43

After many days, the command went out, "Oh Earth, swallow your water. Oh sky, withhold."

The water subsided, and the matter was ended. The ship rested on a place called **Mount Judi** جَبَل الجُودِيّ, and the word went forth, "Away with those who do wrong!"

Prophet Nuhﷺ called upon his Lord saying, "My Lord! Surely my son was a member of my family, and Your promise is true. You are the best judge."

Allahﷻ revealed to him: "Nuh, He is not of your family because his conduct was evil. So don't ask Me about what you don't know. I give you good advice so you won't be ignorant."

Nuhﷺ said, "My Lord! I seek protection with You, so I won't ask You about things I don't understand. Unless You forgive me and have mercy on me, I'll be lost."

Allahﷻ said, "Nuh, come down (from the ship) with peace from Us, and a blessing is on you and on some of the nations who will come from those with you. There will also be nations to whom We shall grant treasures, but in the end a painful punishment from Us will reach them (if they fall into evil)." Surat Hud 11:44-48

E. The Conclusion

The story of Prophet Nuhﷺ is one of the most dramatic and intense stories in the Holy Qur'an. For hundreds of years, he tried in every way he could think of, to convince his people to give up sin and idol-worship. But time and time again, they arrogantly refused him and those who believed with him.

Prophet Nuhﷺ even lost of one of his sons and his wife because they refused to enter the safety of the ship when the valley was about to be flooded. In the end, Allahﷻ informed Prophet Nuhﷺ that if a family member is a sinner, you no longer have any ties to him or her. (9:23)

Researchers have been searching for the ship, or 'Ark,' of Nuhﷺ, for generations. The ship is most likely located on a mountain near northern Iraq or southeastern Turkey. The ancient name of this unknown mountain is Mount Judi. (54:15)

There are numerous lessons to learn from Nuh's story and many points to ponder. Ultimately, we understand that the penalty will come, and those who are steeped in sin and ignorance will suddenly find their time is up.

Questions to Answer

1. How did Nuh's people become idol-worshippers?
2. When Allah made Nuh a prophet, he began his mission by trying to reason with his people in a number of different ways. List three arguments Nuh used.
3. When Prophet Nuh saw he was not convincing them after trying for so long, what did he say to Allah?
4. When the flood came, what happened to Prophet Nuh's son, and what did Allah later say about it?

Define: Mount Judi, Prehistoric

Reflect: How did idol-worship begin amongst Nuh's people? How does this relate to the way in which rumors, or other false information, spread among people?

Act: In order to understand how messages can be changed from the original, play the "telephone game" in a same-gender group of 5-10 people. One person will begin the game by whispering a statement to the person to their right, and so forth. When the last person is reached, he/she should state out loud what he/she heard. The person who made the original statement can then share what was actually said.

IQ Builders:

1. The leaders of the villages rejected Prophet Nuh's call. What three reasons did they give for rejecting him in 11:27?
2. What were the three accusations the leaders made against Nuh, and how did he answer each one according to 11:28-31?
3. The leaders managed to keep most of the people from accepting Nuh's message, even Nuh's own wife ridiculed him! What challenge did they make to him in 11:32-33?

19 Hud ﷺ: The Ancient Prophet

WHAT TO LEARN

There are many names we remember in history and social studies books—the names of great leaders, religious figures and heroes. Did you know that some of them have been sent by Allah ﷻ as messengers or warners?

VOCABULARY

Hud
Iram
Ubar
The Empty Quarter
'Aad

THINK ABOUT IT

What are the signs of a Prophet of Allah, and how can we understand who might qualify?

A. The Ancient Prophets

Allah ﷻ sent a prophet or messenger to every community. He did this so that everyone would have a fair chance to hear His message and then decide freely whether to accept it or not.

Even though later generations often corrupted or changed the message of a particular prophet, the true spirit of the message remained in one form or another. If the message was completely lost, then Allah ﷻ would send another prophet to confront the falsehood and re-establish the truth.

Not all the stories of the prophets are recorded or clear in history after the time of Nuh ﷺ. Allah ﷻ only includes the stories of *some* of the prophets in the Qur'an to illustrate lessons and points He wishes to explain to us.

Because the invention of writing was still unknown at the time of Nuh ﷺ, and for thousands of years afterwards, we must rely on what Allah ﷻ and our historians tell us about that age of humanity.

In this lesson, we will next explore the story of Prophet **Hud** ﷺ هود as he tried to bring truth to his community.

Ancient Seals

B. The Lost City of Iram

The archeologist removed his hat and poured a cup full of sand out of it. The last sandstorm was terrible, and the men were still digging the trucks out from under the piles of yellow, granulated sand.

The band of archeologists came to the trackless Arabian desert to uncover something captured by a satellite photo, what appeared to be an ancient road leading to **The Empty Quarter** الرُبْعُ الخالي region of southeastern Arabia.

It was so hot and dry there that very little lived within a hundred miles of where they stood. Few trees, shrubs or even lizards could survive here for very long. A few moments later, the archeologist climbed over a sand dune to get his bearings.

When he cleared the top of the rise, he

nearly dropped his canteen in astonishment! There before him, like a dead giant, lay the blackened ruins of a long-dead city made of stone.

What used to stand as a fantastic city 6,000 years ago now was cracked and crumbled.

"My God," he must have muttered. "No one could have survived that!"

What the archeologist was referring to was the obvious devastation that had struck the city. The towers were beaten and broken, the walls were buried in sand. The surrounding terrain for hundreds of miles was barren and dry.

The lost city of **Iram**, also known as **Ubar**, was finally uncovered in 1992 after lying buried under the sand for over 5,000 years. What makes this find even more exciting is that the Qur'an gives the story of this city and its inhabitants, the **'Aad people** قَوْمُ عَاد. The Qur'an even described the mighty towers which ringed the city.

Of Iram, the men of tall pillars, likes of whom were never created in the lands. Surat Al Fajr (The Dawn) 89:7-8

﴿إِرَمَ ذَاتِ ٱلْعِمَادِ﴾ ﴿ٱلَّتِي لَمْ يُخْلَقْ مِثْلُهَا فِي ٱلْبِلَٰدِ﴾

سُورَةُ الفَجْرِ 89: 7-8

C. Who Were the 'Aad?

The 'Aad people ruled over a mighty trading city whose main products were frankincense and myrrh, two valuable fragrances. Their city was also an important stop along the trade route from the coast near the Indian Ocean to Palestine and beyond.

The ancient Greek geographer, Claudius Ptolemy, heard the legends of this lost city and correctly guessed that it lay somewhere in the southern Arabian peninsula. But already by his time, the city had laid in ruins for thousands of years.

Allah describes the 'Aad people thus, *(Remember) the 'Aad and the Thamud. Clearly, will their (fate) appear to you from the traces of their buildings. The Shaytan made their deeds pleasing to them and kept them back from the way, though they were gifted with intelligence and skill.* Surat Al 'Ankabut (The Spider) 29:38

﴿وَعَادًا وَثَمُودَا۟ وَقَد تَّبَيَّنَ لَكُم مِّن مَّسَٰكِنِهِمْ وَزَيَّنَ لَهُمُ ٱلشَّيْطَٰنُ أَعْمَٰلَهُمْ فَصَدَّهُمْ عَنِ ٱلسَّبِيلِ وَكَانُوا۟ مُسْتَبْصِرِينَ﴾

سُورَةُ العَنكَبُوتِ 29: 38

The 'Aad people took their mighty wealth and power to be a sign of their unmatched strength. All travelers had to pass through their city and pay homage to their idols. The countryside was full of fields, farms and springs of water. The weather was always pleasant and mild. They lived a very good life indeed.

Allah states, *The 'Aad behaved arrogantly in the land, against all right. They boasted, "Who is superior to us in power?" But didn't they see that Allah, who created them, was superior to them in strength? But they continued to reject our signs.* Surat Fussilat (Explained in Detail) 41:15

﴿فَأَمَّا عَادٌ فَٱسْتَكْبَرُوا۟ فِي ٱلْأَرْضِ بِغَيْرِ ٱلْحَقِّ وَقَالُوا۟

Ruins of the people of 'Aad in Oman.

مَنْ أَشَدُّ مِنَّا قُوَّةً أَوَلَمْ يَرَوْا أَنَّ اللَّهَ الَّذِي خَلَقَهُمْ هُوَ أَشَدُّ مِنْهُمْ قُوَّةً وَكَانُوا بِآيَاتِنَا يَجْحَدُونَ ۞ سورة فصلت 41:15

It was indeed a powerful city-state. With their wealth, they were able to construct tall buildings and guard towers of sizes that were unheard of at the time. But their wealth was not obtained by completely honest means.

They oppressed the surrounding villages and tribes and raised high taxes on those they controlled. They were tyrants and many who fell under their influence suffered from terrible injustice.

It was in this place that Allah chose a man by the name of Hud to be His prophet. Hud was born either within the city itself or in the countryside. We know nothing of his childhood or what events shaped and molded his character.

We do know that he was honest, upright, and strong. He had to be for all the opposition he received. When he began his mission, he tried to shock his people by exposing the truth of which they were unaware.

D. The Mission Begins

Prophet Hud declared, "Won't you have awareness of Allah? I am a Messenger to you that you can trust. So be aware of Allah and obey me. I'm not asking for any reward from you. My reward is only from the Lord of the Universe." Surat Ash-Shura (The Consultations) 26:124-127

Then he pointed out to the people their mighty city and asked the question, "Do you build a monument on every high place to amuse yourselves? Are you making your fine buildings in the hope of living there (forever)? And when you apply your strong hand, do you enforce it like you had absolute power? Now be aware of Allah and obey me." Surat Ash-Shura (The Consultations) 26:128-131

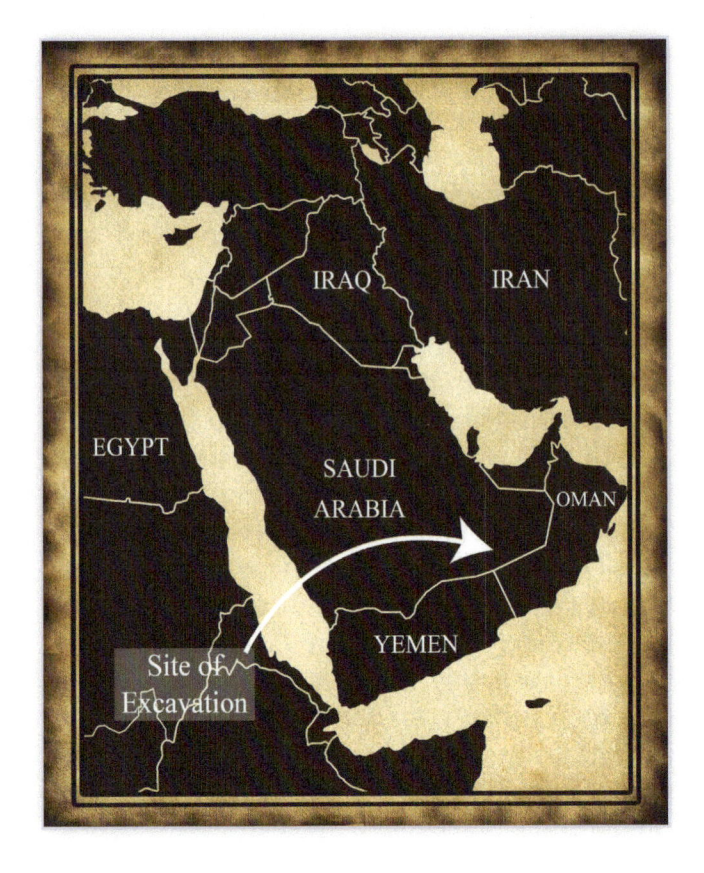

Then, after mentioning the rewards they would earn from Allah for following His will, Hud waited for their answer. The people began to shout and raise their fists. Finally, the leaders of the city announced, "It's all the same whether you advise us or not! You're only talking in the same way the ancient people did, and we're not about to be punished." Surat Ash-Shura (The Consultations) 26:136-138

Hud was not to be outdone so easily. On another occasion, he announced in public, "My people! Serve Allah! You have no other god but Him. (Your other gods) are nothing but made up things. My people! I'm asking for no reward from you. My reward is from the One Who made me. Won't you understand? My People! Ask forgiveness from your Lord and turn to Him. He will send you rain and add strength to your strength, so don't go back into sin!" Surat Hud 11:50-52

IT'S ALL ABOUT ISLAM

Incan idol.

The crowds shouted back at him and the leaders answered, "Hud! You haven't brought us any proof, and we won't desert our gods just on your word. We refuse to believe you!" Surat Hud 11:53

Then the leaders insulted Prophet Hud and made the people laugh at him. They said, "We think some of our gods must have made you crazy!" Hud replied,"I call Allah to witness, and you see also that I am free from the sin of making partners with Him. So plan your worst against me, and give me no chance. I put my trust in Allah, my Lord and your Lord! Nothing moves without Him having a hold on its forelock. Indeed, my Lord is on the straight track." Surat Hud 11:54-56

Then Hud issued this warning, "If you turn away, at least I gave you the message that I was sent with. My Lord will make another nation succeed you, and you won't harm Him in the least, for my Lord is a guardian over all things." Surat Hud 11:57

The enraged 'Aad insulted him and those who followed him. They said, "We think you're crazy and a liar!"

Hud could only answer, "My people! I'm not crazy, but I'm a Messenger from the Lord of the Universe." Surat Al A'raf (The Heights) 7:67

Then Prophet Hud tried one last time to reason with them. He announced, "Aren't you amazed that there has come to you a message from your Lord through a man of your own people, to warn you? Remember that He made you successors after the people of Nuh and gave you power among the nations. Remember the benefits from Allah so you can prosper." Surat Al A'raf (The Heights) 7:69

The leaders gave their final answer: "Do you come to us and tell us to serve only Allah and to give up the religion of our fathers? Bring on us what you threaten us with if you are telling the truth!" Surat Al A'raf (The Heights) 7:70

Hud raised his arms and said his last to his people, "The punishment and anger are already coming upon you from your Lord. Don't argue with me about the names (of idols) you invented. You and your ancestors had no authority from Allah (to make them up.) Then wait and see. I am also waiting with you." Surat Al A'raf (The Heights) 7:71

E. The End of the 'Aad

With their own tongues, the majority of the 'Aad chose to reject Allah and embrace destruction. They dared Allah to bring the punishment on them in this life.

They sat smug and secure in their mighty fortress and thought Hud was crazy and a nuisance. But while the 'Aad were sitting

IT'S ALL ABOUT ISLAM

comfortably in their homes, Allah ﷻ sent the message to Prophet Hud ﷺ to gather his followers and leave the city, never to return.

Soon, without warning, a terrible wind arose in the moonlit countryside, tearing trees from their roots and raising the dirt and sand high in the sky. As the huge storm swelled and loomed over the city, the people must have thought it was nothing more than a mid-season disturbance.

So, when they saw it as a cloud proceeding towards their valleys, they said, "This is a cloud that will bring us rain." No, it is the very thing you asked to hasten up—a wind in which there is a painful punishment that will destroy every thing with the command of its Lord! So they became such that nothing remained to be seen except their dwelling places. This is how We punish the guilty people. Surat Al Ahqaf 46:24-25

The sky turned darker, and the people in the streets looked up nervously as the black cloud raised itself over the horizon. The leaders in their luxurious rooms must have looked around at each other, thinking it would pass.

People shuttered their windows, and the horses and camels began to cry and stamp. The violent storm tore whole caravans out of its path, and finally descended upon the city, perhaps with more force than a tornado.

The sand covered the streets, and windows and doors were knocked off their hinges. The people were buffeted with flying rocks and debris, running about in the streets in panic.

Sounds of choking, pelting, screaming and cursing could be heard as the people trampled each other and scattered in all directions. The fierce storm raged for seven nights and eight days as the earth rumbled. In the end, nothing living was left, and all the wells, streams and farmlands were covered over with a thick layer of sand.

And as for 'Aad, they were destroyed by a violent windstorm, that He imposed on them for seven nights and eight consecutive days; so you could see them thrown on the ground, as if they were trunks of hollow palm-trees. Now, do you see any remnant of them? Surat Al Haaqqa (The Reality) 69:6-8

﴿وَأَمَّا عَادٌ فَأُهْلِكُوا بِرِيحٍ صَرْصَرٍ عَاتِيَةٍ ۝ سَخَّرَهَا عَلَيْهِمْ سَبْعَ لَيَالٍ وَثَمَانِيَةَ أَيَّامٍ حُسُومًا فَتَرَى الْقَوْمَ فِيهَا صَرْعَى كَأَنَّهُمْ أَعْجَازُ نَخْلٍ خَاوِيَةٍ ۝ فَهَلْ تَرَى لَهُم مِّن بَاقِيَةٍ﴾ سُورَةُ الحَاقَّةِ 69: 6-8

With the city destroyed, and mountains of sand covering hundreds of miles, the traders' traditional routes were abandoned. As the centuries passed, people remembered the city in legend only. Such was the end of the people of 'Aad.

أستغفر الله

Questions to Answer

1. Why would Allah send a new prophet to a people?
2. What were archeologists looking for in the Arabian desert in 1992?
3. What gave them the clue to its location?
4. What is so fascinating about this discovery as far as Muslims are concerned?
5. What were the two main products of the ancient city of Iram?
6. What crimes did the 'Aad people commit? List three.
7. Give three responses that Prophet Hud's people gave him.
8. Why did his people not want to give up their idols?
9. What did the people dare Allah to do?
10. How was the city destroyed?

Define: Iram, Ubar, The Empty Quarter.

Reflect: What are some of the methods that Prophet Hud used to encourage his people to have awareness of Allah?

Act: Research five interesting facts about the city of Iram. Prepare the information in a visually-appealing presentation that you will share with your peers.

IQ Builders:
1. Read 22:45-46 and then use these ayaat to explain the significance of the 'Aad story, along with the importance of the discovery of their ancient lost city.
2. How did Prophet Hud begin his preaching, according to 26:124-127?

Skill Builder

The Tools of Archaeology

Imagine finding the ruins of an ancient city, lost for thousands of years. The passage of many centuries has brought wind and rain through its streets, destroying many buildings. Eventually, all that is left of the city are crumbled walls and scattered artifacts. As more time passed, soil covered much of the site, and brush and grasses cover what remains. The archaeological record of the city is sealed within layers of Earth.

But then all of a sudden, you happened to find it while digging a plant out of the top of a mound. When your shovel hit stone, you knew something was strange. As you cleared away more dirt, you could see that the stones had been placed there in a clear pattern. It must have been made by human hands!

You call the local museum, which sends a team of archaeologists to the site. The first thing they do is assess or determine the important points of the situation. Then they plan their excavation. Excavation is the process of digging up the remains of the past.

You watch them as they work. Perhaps you remember the *ayah* from the Qur'an where Allahﷻ tells us to study the past so we can learn the lessons of history and become better Muslims. (22:46-48, 27:69-70)

The archaeologists carefully remove the earth, layer by layer. They divide the surface of the site into squares with grids made of strings tied to small stakes. As they dig, they carefully record the exact location of every object they find.

Any man-made object they find is called an 'artifact'. Artifacts are carefully tagged, noted and then shipped to a museum for study. There the archaeologists try to determine the age of the pieces they found. Dating can be accomplished in a number of different ways.

First of all, the artifacts can be culturally dated, or compared with other items from a similar time period. For example, if you found a Chinese coin with the name of a certain leader stamped on it, then you would know approximately when it was made.

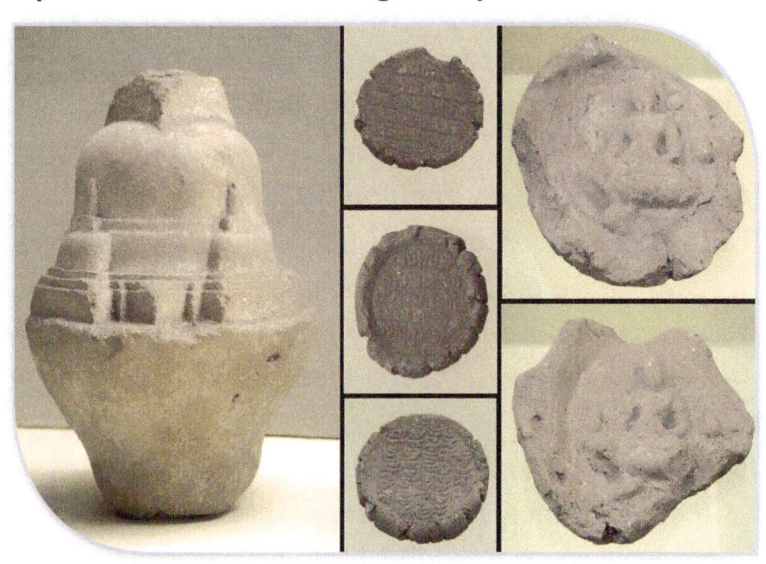

If you found a cedar log in the wall of an ancient home where no cedar trees have ever grown, then you can be sure that trade with Phoenicians took place. Since we already know when the Phoenicians existed, we can get an idea of how old the settlement must be. This technique works with most objects of art, pottery and currency.

The second method of dating is known as scientific dating. The main method used by most archaeologists today is called 'radiocarbon dating.' In this method, the measurement of the radioactive carbon within an object is used to determine the age of the object. This method can only be used to date objects that were once living, such as wood or human bones.

Here's how radiocarbon dating works. Every living thing absorbs carbon from the atmosphere. A small amount of the carbon is radioactive. When the plant or animal dies, it stops absorbing carbon. From the moment it dies, the carbon starts to decay at a known rate. This method is not perfect, however, because it only works on objects older than 1,000 years and younger than about 60,000. Radiocarbon dating needs a measurable rate of decay that is still detectable but not too fresh.

After objects have been classified, sorted and dated, then the next job begins: figuring out who the people were, how they lived and how they disappeared. It is this part of the story that should be the most important to us for as Allah said, *When the stated term of a nation is over, there is no one who can prolong it. Surat Al A'raf (The Heights) 7:34*

﴿ وَلِكُلِّ أُمَّةٍ أَجَلٌ فَإِذَا جَاءَ أَجَلُهُمْ لَا يَسْتَأْخِرُونَ سَاعَةً وَلَا يَسْتَقْدِمُونَ ﴾ سُورَةُ الأعراف 7: 34

The study of archaeology is the story of humanity's acceptance or rejection of their Lord.

The Blessed Prophet ﷺ once advised that we should never pass by the ruins of ancient peoples without crying, to remember so that their fate might not overtake us. Who were the ancient prophets, and did their people accept or reject the message? Only Allah knows. Perhaps we can discover something about these ancient people as we sift through the story of our past.

Exercises

Answer the questions below.

1. How does an archaeologist prepare a site for excavation?
2. What are the two methods of dating artifacts and bones?
3. How should a Muslim archaeologist view his or her work?
4. Do you have a favorite archaeological discovery? What is it?

20   The Quest of Ibrahim ﷺ

WHAT TO LEARN

What would make a person abandon the religion of his father? What if changing your religion meant that you would suffer punishment and exile? Sometimes there is no price too high to pay for the truth.

VOCABULARY

Azar   Namrud
Suhuf   Ishaq
Zamzam

THINK ABOUT IT

Why did Ibrahim ﷺ want to leave the land of his birth?

A Ziggurat.

A. Claimed by Three, Followed by One

There is one ancient prophet who is revered in the world today by the followers of three distinct spiritual traditions. The Jews hold him as their forefather; the Christians respect him as a prophet, and the Muslims love him as one of the greatest of Allah's ﷻ chosen guides to humanity.

The name of this prophet is **Ibrahim** ﷺ إبراهيم, also known as **Abraham** in the English-speaking world. He lived in ancient Mesopotamia around 1900 BCE. But who can claim his legacy? Who can say that they are following in the footsteps of Prophet Ibrahim ﷺ? As you follow his story in this lesson, you will begin to see that, although he is claimed by three groups, one follows his example and lives by his example more closely than the others.

B. An Idol for Sale

"Idols! Get your idols here!" the young man cried as he hoisted a small stone carving over his head.

"Only five silver pieces! Get your idols here!" He had been walking around the splendid city of Ur all morning, trying to sell the small idols his father, **Azar** آزر the idol-maker, sent with him. He had only one left to sell and knew that he couldn't return home until they were all sold.

He wasn't having much success getting rid of the last one, though. The streets were busy with traders, shoppers, incoming caravans and any number of other colorful sights. The young man, whose name was Ibrahim ﷺ, looked up at the hot sun in the sky and felt a sudden flash of heat.

He decided to go down to the banks of the Euphrates river to cool off. As he passed through the city gates, he must have been awe-struck to see the endless fields of barley and wheat. If he turned around and looked back at the city, he might have seen the mighty Ziggurats, or 'step-temples,' of the gods. But he continued forward since he was focused on a different goal.

130

When he reached the brisk water, he put the idol on the ground and waded into the refreshing river. After he cooled off, he returned to shore and got ready to leave.

He picked up the idol and was about to go when a strange thought entered his mind. If that idol his father made was really a god, what power did it have? What could it do? Everyone prays to them and worships them, but what power could they wield?

Almost without thinking, Ibrahim ﷺ swung the idol over his head and threw it in the river. "If you have power," he must have thought, "then save yourself."

But the idol merely hit the water with a splash and sank quickly in the shallow waters. Ibrahim ﷺ was scared for a moment. He thought for sure that a thunderbolt would strike him or something. He waited tensely and watched. Nothing happened.

Finally, he waded out in the river and fished the idol off the bottom. He held it up and looked at it. It still had the same expression on its face as before—only this time, it was all wet.

"Hmm," he thought. "You can't even save yourself." At that moment, Ibrahim ﷺ knew the idols were a lie.

C. Ibrahim's ﷺ Search for Truth

Ibrahim ﷺ spent the next few days in restless thought. He no longer felt good about selling the idols that his father made. When he began to avoid his shop, his father thought he was going through a stage that would soon pass.

Finally, Ibrahim ﷺ could stand it no longer. He confronted his father and said, "Do you take idols for gods? I see you and your people making a big mistake." Surat Al An'aam (The Cattle) 6:74

After that, Ibrahim ﷺ began to spend much of his time out in the fields, alone. He wanted to know what his life meant. What was it all for? He looked around for something more powerful than an idol.

He began to stare at the night sky. Then he saw a bright star. He declared, "This is my lord." But when it set, he lamented, "I don't love those who set." When he saw the moon rising in splendor, he said, "This is my lord." But when it set, too, he said, "Unless I'm guided by the True Lord, I will probably be lost." When he saw the sun rising up, he said, "This is my lord. This is greater." But when it set, he said: "O my people! I am indeed free from all that you join as partners." **He began to tell people, "For me, I have set my face firmly towards the One who created the skies and the Earth. I will never make partners with Allah."** Surat Al An'aam (The Cattle) 6:76-79

D. Azar, the Idol-maker

Ibrahim returned to his home and said to his father, "Father! Why do you serve what can't hear or see or do any good for you? My father! I have gained some knowledge that you don't have, so follow me. I will guide you to a way that is right. My father! Don't serve Shaytan, for he is a rebel against the Merciful God. My father! I'm afraid that a punishment might strike you from the Merciful God because you've become a friend to Shaytan."
His father replied, "Do you hate my gods, Ibrahim? If you don't stop this, I'll stone you to death. Now get away from me for a good long time!"
(Before leaving), Ibrahim told him, "Peace be to you. I will pray to my Lord for your forgiveness. He is good to me. And I will turn away from you and those you call upon besides Allah. I will call on my Lord, and maybe by my prayers I won't be left without blessings." Surat Maryam (Mary) 19:42-48

E. The Public Battle

Ibrahim asked his father and his people, "What are these images you worship so much?" They replied, "Our ancestors worshipped them also." Ibrahim replied, "Then you're making a big mistake, and your ancestors did also." The people answered, "Have you brought us the truth, or are you only joking?" He replied, "No! Your Lord is the Lord of the skies and the Earth. He created them, and I testify to it. By Allah! I have a plan for your idols when you're not looking." Surat Al Anbiya' (The Prophets) 21:52-57

But his people did not listen to him and teased him harshly.

Then he glanced up at the stars and cried, "I'm hurt (in my heart)." So they turned away from him and left him alone. He approached their idols and addressed them, "Why don't you eat the offerings placed before you? Why don't you speak?" Surat As-Saaffat (Those Set in Ranks) 37:88-92

Then, when the day of a great festival came, the people left the city and ventured out in the fields for their celebrations. With the temple unguarded, the time came for Ibrahim to act. He fell upon the idols and broke them to pieces, all except the biggest one. Surat Al Anbiya' (The Prophets) 21:58

When the people returned and saw what had happened, they were enraged and tried to find out who did it. The priests asked, "Who has done this to our gods? He must be an evil man." Some people said, "We heard of a boy who talked about them. His name is Ibrahim." (The priests) said, "Then bring him before the eyes of the people so they can see him." (When he was brought) they asked, "Are you the one who did this to our gods, Ibrahim?" He answered, "Their

IT'S ALL ABOUT ISLAM

biggest idol must have done it! Ask them (the broken idols), if they can speak." Then the people turned to themselves and said, "We're certainly foolish." Then they were filled with shame. They said, "You know full well the idols can't speak." Ibrahim then declared, "So why do you serve, besides Allah, things that can do you no good or bad? To heck with you and the things you worship besides Allah. Don't you have any sense?" Surat Al Anbiya' (The Prophets) 21:58-67

They were filled with anger and rage, and one of them shouted, "Build a fire and throw him in the burning flames!" Surat As-Saaffat (Those who set the Ranks) 37::97

When they threw him in, they shouted, "Burn him and protect your gods if you can!" We (Allah) ordered, "Oh fire! Be cool and a safe place for Ibrahim." When they saw the miracle, they were wonder-struck. Then they thought about another plan (to get rid of him), but We (Allah) made them the ones who lost the most. Surat Al Anbiya' (The Prophets) 21:68-70

F. The Showdown with Namrud

Meanwhile, Ibrahim ﷺ was receiving revelation from Allah ﷻ, which he began to write on scrolls of leather. This book is called the **Suhuf** صُحُف **Scrolls** of Ibrahim ﷺ.

Ibrahim's ﷺ curiosity and thirst for knowledge is best illustrated by the following incident.

Once Ibrahim said to Allah, "My Lord! Show me how You give life to the dead."
Allah answered him, "Don't you believe?"
"I do," Ibrahim answered. "I only want to satisfy my own curiosity."
Allah replied, "Take four birds and train them to obey you. Then put one of them on each hill and call them to you. They will come to you quickly. By this know that Allah is the Powerful and Wise." Surat Al Baqarah (The Cow) 2:260

﴿وَإِذْ قَالَ إِبْرَٰهِـۧمُ رَبِّ أَرِنِى كَيْفَ تُحْىِ ٱلْمَوْتَىٰ قَالَ أَوَلَمْ تُؤْمِن قَالَ بَلَىٰ وَلَـٰكِن لِّيَطْمَئِنَّ قَلْبِى قَالَ فَخُذْ أَرْبَعَةً مِّنَ ٱلطَّيْرِ فَصُرْهُنَّ إِلَيْكَ ثُمَّ ٱجْعَلْ عَلَىٰ كُلِّ جَبَلٍ مِّنْهُنَّ جُزْءًا ثُمَّ ٱدْعُهُنَّ يَأْتِينَكَ سَعْيًا وَٱعْلَمْ أَنَّ ٱللَّهَ عَزِيزٌ حَكِيمٌ﴾ سورة البقرة 2: 260

He continued his mission of teaching and calling people away from the idols. With the grace of Allah ﷻ, he managed to convince quite a few people, including some of his own family members. His nephew Lut ﷺ became a firm supporter.

But Ibrahim's ﷺ enemies launched a dangerous plot. They informed the city authorities that idol-worship was being subverted, and eventually news reached the King of Ur, **Namrud** نَمْرُود. He was briefed about this man who rejected the gods. Namrud ordered Ibrahim ﷺ to be brought before him.

When the young man was taken to the palace, he was thrown in a great room. There before him, surrounded on both sides with

133

Detail of winged human-headed lion from the kingdom of Namrud - British Museum.

his nobles and soldiers, was the great King Namrud. Ibrahim neither bowed nor uttered any words of worship to the self-proclaimed god-king. Namrud must have felt insulted.

Do you not know the one who argued with Ibrahim about his Lord, because Allah had given him kingship? When Ibrahim said, "My Lord is the One Who gives life and brings death," he said: "I give life and I bring death." Said Ibrahim, "Allah brings the sun out from the East; now, you bring it out from the West." Here, baffled was the one who disbelieved, and Allah does not bring the wrongdoers to the right path. Surat Al Baqarah (The Cow) 2:258

Namrud knew he could not answer the challenge, and he was silent. But instead of realizing the limitation of his power, he ordered Ibrahim removed from his court.

Ibrahim knew he was no longer welcome in Mesopotamia, the land between the two rivers. Not even his own father was on his side. So when Allah gave the command to leave, Ibrahim gathered his followers and left. He secretly headed West towards a land that Allah promised would be blessed for all nations. (21:71)

Just before setting out, however, he asked Allah to forgive his father, just like he promised his father he would, because Ibrahim was very tender-hearted. But Allah will not forgive those who choose to do wrong. (9:114)

G. Two Men Who Parted

Ibrahim traveled for weeks towards his new home, but along the way, he found that there were too many people in his group. Some people were close to Lut and quarreled with Ibrahim's close companions.

After discussing the situation, it was decided that the two groups would separate. Lut took his people and headed for the Cities of the Plain, while Ibrahim continued on into Palestine.

Ibrahim settled on a decent patch of land and organized his followers into a tight-knit community. He married a woman named Sarah and watched over his people. He received Allah's messages and established a viable spiritual life and tradition in the people.

H. Isma'il and Ishaq

For many years Ibrahim lived with Sarah, but she bore him no children. She seemed to be barren. Because it was important for Ibrahim to have heirs to teach his knowledge to, he married Hajar, Sarah's maid servant, as a second wife. Ibrahim and Hajar were blessed with a boy they named 'Isma'il. (37:101)

A short time later, Allah sent His angels, disguised as men, to visit Ibrahim's home. They greeted him with the words of peace, and he, thinking they were travelers, prepared a tray of meat for them. When they didn't eat, he felt uneasy about them. But they told him not to fear.

In time, Sarah bore a son named **Ishaq** إسْحَق. She loved him greatly. Later, Allah ﷻ instructed him to settle Hajar ؏ and her son 'Isma'il ؏ in another land that needed a prophet: a role that Isma'il ؏ would later fulfill.

I. The Valley of Bakka

Ibrahim ؏ journeyed south for about two weeks into the Arabian peninsula, until he found a barren valley. It was here that he was told to leave Hajar ؏ and Isma'il ؏. He gave them a few supplies and then returned north to Palestine.

As you read in the lesson on Hajj, Hajar ؏ and Isma'il ؏ soon ran out of water and were nearly overcome in the heat. Allah ﷻ gave them a well known as **Zamzam**, which enabled them to survive. The water source also gave them a valuable commodity they could trade with passing nomads. A few desert tribes began to move into the valley as it now had a water supply. When Ibrahim ؏ returned for a visit, he was amazed at how things had developed. He knew Allah's ﷻ plan was the right one.

In time, 'Isma'il ؏ grew into a fine young man and brought great pleasure to his parents. Ibrahim ؏ loved his son dearly, and that would be his next test. Ibrahim ؏ saw in a dream that he was sacrificing his son. When he told him of it, the boy said, "My father! Do what you have been commanded to do. I will be, if Allah wills, patient." So when they both

They declared, "We have been sent against the people of Lut." Surat Hud 11:70

If you remember, Lut ؏ had parted ways with Ibrahim ؏ and went to the Cities of the Plain. There, he became a prophet to the people. However, many refused to listen to him, including members of his own family. Now was the time Allah ﷻ would deal with those wrong-doers.

Then the angels told Ibrahim ؏ that he was going to have a son with his first wife, Sarah. Sarah was standing in the door and laughed when she heard what the angels said. She was old and never thought she would have a child.

She said, "Oh me? How can I have a child, given that I'm an old woman and my husband here is an old man? That would be a miracle!" The angels replied, "Are you amazed at Allah's command? The grace of Allah and His blessings are upon you, people of this house. For He is indeed praiseworthy and full of glory!."
Surat Hud 11:71-73

Before leaving, Ibrahim ؏ begged the angels to spare Lut ؏ and his people. The angels told him not to appeal against Allah's ﷻ command, and then they left. (11:77-83)

Bakkah was a barren valley.

135

surrendered their wills (to Allah), and he had lain him on his forehead, We called out to him, "Ibrahim! You have fulfilled the (requirements) of the vision already." This is how We reward those who do right. For this was clearly a great test for him. Surat As-Saaffat (Those who set the Ranks) 37:102-106

They found an animal nearby, a ram perhaps, and sacrificed it instead. Ibrahim showed that he was ready to give up everything he loved in this life for the sake of Allah.

Ibrahim and Isma'il built the foundations of the building we would later call the Ka'bah. Ibrahim, sensing that this town would eventually become a center for prayer to Allah, made the following dua':

My Lord! Make this city one of peace and security. Preserve me and my children from worshipping idols. My Lord! Idols have led many people astray. Whoever follows my example is of me, and whoever disobeys me—still, only You are Forgiving and Merciful. Ibrahim (looked around him and continued his prayer) My Lord! I have brought some of my descendants to live in a valley that has never been farmed, to live by Your Sacred House, in order,

our Lord, that they may establish prayer. So fill the hearts of some people with love towards them and feed them with fruit so they will give thanks. Surat Ibrahim 14:35-37

Then Ibrahim thanked Allah for his children and prayed that his plea would be accepted. In time, Allah made Isma'il a prophet, and he led the first community in the valley of Bakka, later renamed Makkah. (19:54-55)

J. Who Follows Ibrahim's Example?

Jews, Christians and Muslims all revere Prophet Ibrahim. But while everyone loves him, who has remained faithful to his example? The Holy Qur'an declares:

The same way of life has been established for you (Muslims) that was established for Nuh. It is the same inspiration to you that We (Allah) gave to Ibrahim, Musa and 'Isa, that you should stick strongly to your way of life and make no divisions in it. Surat Ash-Shura (The Consultations) 42:13

﴿ شَرَعَ لَكُم مِّنَ ٱلدِّينِ مَا وَصَّىٰ بِهِۦ نُوحًا وَٱلَّذِىٓ أَوْحَيْنَآ إِلَيْكَ وَمَا وَصَّيْنَا بِهِۦٓ إِبْرَٰهِيمَ وَمُوسَىٰ وَعِيسَىٰٓ أَنْ أَقِيمُوا۟ ٱلدِّينَ وَلَا تَتَفَرَّقُوا۟ فِيهِ ﴾ سُورَةُ الشُّورَىٰ 42: 13

Prophet Ibrahim was given the same inspiration as the later prophets. He rejected idol-worship, stood up for justice, called people to the truth and obeyed Allah's commands. Allah declares: Ibrahim was neither a Jew nor a Christian. But he was upright, a Muslim and was not one of those who associate partners with Allah. The closest of people to Ibrahim are those who followed him, this prophet and those who believe, and Allah is the Guardian of all believers. Surat Al 'Imran (The Family of 'Imran) 3:67-68

Who follows Prophet Ibrahim ﷺ?

﴿مَا كَانَ إِبْرَاهِيمُ يَهُودِيًّا وَلَا نَصْرَانِيًّا وَلَٰكِن كَانَ حَنِيفًا مُّسْلِمًا وَمَا كَانَ مِنَ ٱلْمُشْرِكِينَ ۝ إِنَّ أَوْلَى ٱلنَّاسِ بِإِبْرَاهِيمَ لَلَّذِينَ ٱتَّبَعُوهُ وَهَٰذَا ٱلنَّبِيُّ وَٱلَّذِينَ ءَامَنُوا۟ ۗ وَٱللَّهُ وَلِيُّ ٱلْمُؤْمِنِينَ﴾ سُورَةُ آلِ عِمْرَانَ 3: 67 – 68

Prophet Ibrahim ﷺ called all people to Allah's ﷻ way of life. This is unlike some followers of Judaism, who believe that they alone are God's chosen people, to the exclusion of all others. (4:49-50) Additionally, Ibrahim ﷺ always preached the Oneness of Allah ﷻ, in contrast to the concept of the Trinity that most Christians believe in today. Some Christians go even further and erect statues or make paintings of their god, which is a practice forbidden by their Ten Commandments.

If Prophet Ibrahim ﷺ were to come back in the world today, who do you think he would choose to be among? Who would seem faithful to his way?

Say, Allah has told the truth. So, follow the Faith of Ibrahim, the upright one. He was not one of those who ascribe partners to Allah. *Surat Al 'Imran (The Family of 'Imran) 3:95*

﴿قُلْ صَدَقَ ٱللَّهُ ۗ فَٱتَّبِعُوا۟ مِلَّةَ إِبْرَاهِيمَ حَنِيفًا وَمَا كَانَ مِنَ ٱلْمُشْرِكِينَ﴾ سُورَةُ آلِ عِمْرَانَ 3: 95

IT'S ALL ABOUT ISLAM

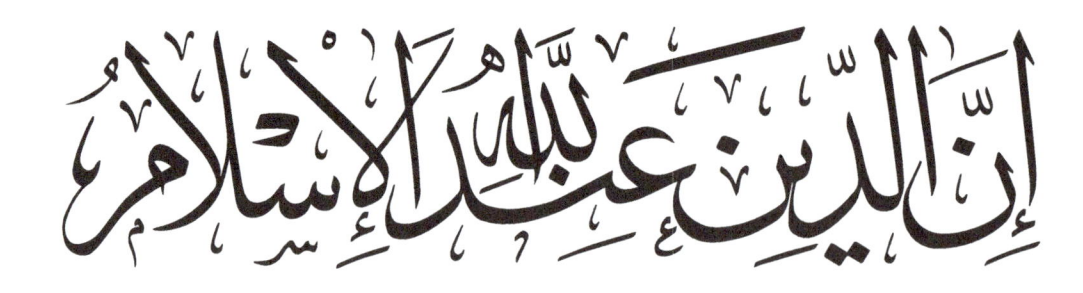

إِنَّ الدِّينَ عِندَ اللَّهِ الْإِسْلَامُ

Questions to Answer

1. Where was Ibrahim born?
2. How did he come to reject idol-worship?
3. How did he show his people that idol-worship was not a correct practice?
4. Who was Namrud, and what happened with him?
5. Why did Prophet Ibrahim take Hajar and his son Isma'il to the Arabian desert?
6. Why did Prophet Ibrahim and his son Isma'il build the Ka'bah?

Define: Bakkah, Zamzam, Ziggurat.

Reflect: The lesson of Ibrahim and his dream was about sacrifice. In light of this, what are you willing to give up for Allah's sake? How does this principle relate to the Hajj Muslims perform every year?

Act: Create a visual display that lists at least three similarities and three differences between Islam, Christianity and Judaism.

IQ Builders:

1. Read surat 11:77-83 and summarize what happened to Lut and his people.
2. Jews and Christians claim that Prophet Ibrahim was their prophet, to the exclusion of others. What does Allah tell them in 3:65-68?
3. Describe three main points in the public speech of Prophet Ibrahim in 26:70-82.

21 The Three Unknown Prophets

WHAT TO LEARN

Sometimes it takes more than one person to convince people of their need to understand. Have you ever had to have a friend help you in an argument with someone else? Here's the story of two prophets who had such a tough time that they needed another prophet to help!

VOCABULARY

Authentic   Anonymous

THINK ABOUT IT

What message was given to the people by each prophet? How did the people respond to those prophets sent to them?

Biblical city ruins in Jordan.

A. The Prophets to the World

Islam teaches that Allah﷾ sent prophets and messengers to every nation. The last of these was Prophet Muhammad ﷺ whose message was meant for the whole world and would be protected.

We study any world religion, which was founded before the mission of Prophet Muhammad ﷺ, we must investigate whether it was started by an **Authentic** حَقِيقيّ prophet or not.

Any religion started after the time of Allah's﷾ last Messenger ﷺ is completely a false invention, as the Blessed Prophet ﷺ said that after him there would be no more revelations from Allah﷾ to the world.

So we are interested in researching the history of ancient societies to identify the names and teachings of whatever spiritual guides were in existence long ago. But sometimes we will never be able to discover the names of those prophets. Most of the prophets, in fact, will always remain **Anonymous** مَجْهول with their true identity never to be known. (40:78)

B. The Three Unknown Prophets

In the Qur'an, Allah﷾ gives us the story of the Three Prophets He sent to the same city, at the same time. No names are given, and the city's location and identity also remain a mystery.

What makes this story all the more intriguing is that an ordinary person takes up the cause of the Three Prophets and tries to convince his people to follow them, with surprising results.

Was the city an ancient Mayan or African town? Was it in Asia or North America? Perhaps it was Cahokia, near the Mississippi river, or Meroe, along the Nile. We will possibly never know in this life. But the important thing is the lesson taught by the preaching of the man who obeyed the call of Allah﷾. Let's look at their story.

C. The Companions of the City

Cite to them the example of the People of the Town, when the messengers came to it. When We sent to them two (apostles), and they rejected both of them, so We confirmed them with a third one. So they said, "We are sent to you."
They (the people of the Town) said, "You are no more than human beings like us, and the Rahman (the All-Merciful Allah) has not sent down anything. You are but telling a lie."
They (the messengers) said, "Our Lord knows that we are undoubtedly sent to you. Our obligation is no more than to convey the message clearly."
They (the People of the Town) said, "We take you as a bad omen for us. If you do not desist, we will certainly stone you, and you will be afflicted by a painful punishment from us."
They said, "Your bad omen is with yourselves. (Do you take it as bad omen) if you are given good counsel? Rather, you are a people who cross all limits."
And there came a man rushing from the farthest part of the city. He said, "O my people, follow the messengers. Follow those who do not claim any reward from you and who are on the right path. What excuse do I have if I do not worship the One who has created me and to whom you will be returned? Shall I adopt those gods besides Him whose intercession, if Rahman (the All-Merciful Allah) intends to do harm to me, cannot help me in the least, nor can they come to my rescue? In that case, I will be in open error indeed. Undoubtedly I have believed in your Lord so listen to me." (Thereafter, when his people killed him) it was said to him, "Enter the Paradise." He said, "Would that my people knew how my Lord has forgiven me and placed me among the honored ones!" Surat Ya-sin 36:13-27

D. The End of the City

The wicked people of the city were no doubt rejoicing in driving away Allah's Messengers and all those who dared to believe. Now they felt that they could return to their old ways, oppressing their neighbors and cheating and stealing from them.

But Allah decreed the end of that civilization, and they lost their chance to save themselves from the punishment of the Next Life.

As Allah said, "We didn't send against his people any forces from the sky, nor did We need to do so. It took no more than a huge explosion, and they lay still." Surat Ya-sin 36:28-29

The ruins of Old Ma'rib.

In conclusion, Allah ﷻ gives us a telling statement about the state of most people on Earth. He announces, *"Alas for the servants! When a Messenger comes to them, they mock him. Don't they see how many generations before them We destroyed? None of them will return. Each one will be brought before Us (for judgement)."* Surat Ya-sin 36:30-32

We will never know the identity of the Three Messengers, the Advocate or their city. But we do know who the real winners were in the end—not the people who enjoyed their sinful way of life for a few moments more but the ones who surrendered their wills to Allah ﷻ and held true to their faith. Let us follow the lesson of those who always surrender to Allah ﷻ.

Questions to Answer

1. What do we know about the people and the city of the Three Unknown Prophets?
2. How did the people respond to the first two Messengers?
3. How did they respond when a third Messenger was sent to them by Allah ﷻ?
4. What accusations did the people of the city make against the Messengers?
5. Who was the Advocate?
6. What arguments did the Advocate make to the people?
7. What happened to him?
8. What was the fate of the city in the end?

Define: Anonymous, Authentic.

Reflect: What are three lessons that can be learned from this story?

Act: The Advocate stood out against falsehood, even though it cost him his life. List five causes that you believe in strongly and would like to stand up for. Then choose one of those causes and create a detailed plan for how you will become an 'Advocate' for them. Begin to implement your plan today.

IQ Builders:

1. What does Allah say about people and His signs in 36:46?
2. How is 39:17-18 descriptive of the Advocate?

22. The Story of Yusuf ﷺ

WHAT TO LEARN

No matter how bad your life may seem, there is always the possibility it may turn around in an instant. The key is to always be prepared to seize your opportunities, never give up your faith and never fail to take action.

VOCABULARY

Ya'qub   'Aziz Misr
Benjamin

THINK ABOUT IT

How did Yusuf ﷺ turn his situation around with Allah's ﷻ help?

A. Who was Yusuf ﷺ?

Allah ﷻ describes the saga of Prophet Yusuf ﷺ as the most beautiful of all stories. Indeed, anyone who has read it comes away with a feeling of excitement and wonder.

The most amazing adventures befell one young man who lived around 1600 BCE, and these adventures tested his faith to the limits. But who is Yusuf ﷺ, and where did he come from?

Ibrahim's ﷺ son Ishaq ﷺ, who remained in Palestine, had a child named **Ya'qub** ﷺ يَعْقُوب **Jacob**. In turn, Ya'qub ﷺ had 12 sons and many daughters. One of these sons was named Yusuf ﷺ. He and his baby brother **Benjamin** بنيامين were both from the same mother. The 10 other brothers were from a different mother.

To tell the story of Yusuf ﷺ in words other than Allah's ﷻ would be a great injustice. We will relate the story of Yusuf ﷺ directly from the verses in surat Yusuf (Joseph). Prepare yourselves for a most beautiful story!

B. The Strange Dream

We are now going to tell you the most beautiful of all stories in Our revealing this portion of the Qur'an. You did not know this story before. *Surat Yusuf (Joseph) 12:3*

Yusuf told his father, "Father! I saw (in a dream) 11 stars and the sun and the moon all bowing themselves to me!"
My son, his father replied, "Don't tell this dream to your brothers because they might plan against you (out of jealousy). Shaytan is the enemy of people! I believe your Lord will choose you and teach you how to understand dreams. He will complete His blessing upon you and upon the descendants of me, Ya'qub, even as He completed it to your fore-fathers, Ibrahim and Ishaq, before! Allah has all knowledge and wisdom."
Certainly, in the example of Yusuf and his brothers are lessons for people who look for truth. *Surat Yusuf (Joseph) 12:4-7*

One day Yusuf's older brothers complained amongst themselves, "Our father loves Yusuf and his younger brother (Benjamin) more than us, even though we are just as good! Our father is obviously out of his mind!" Surat Yusuf (Joseph) 12:8

Then one of the brothers suggested, "So let's kill Yusuf or send him away to some far off land. Then our father will give us all his attention. There will be plenty of time to be good later!" Surat Yusuf (Joseph) 12:9

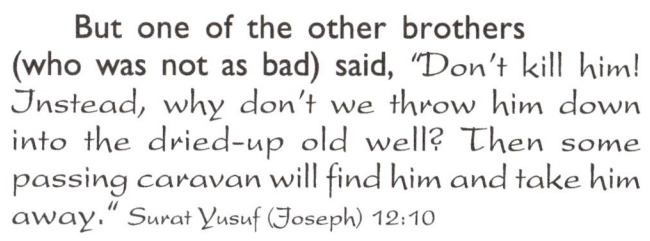

But one of the other brothers (who was not as bad) said, "Don't kill him! Instead, why don't we throw him down into the dried-up old well? Then some passing caravan will find him and take him away." Surat Yusuf (Joseph) 12:10

After they agreed to this plan, the brothers went to their father and asked permission to take Yusuf out for a day of fun. When their father hesitated, they complained, "Father! Why don't you trust Yusuf with us? We really love him. Send him with us tomorrow to enjoy himself and play. We'll take good care of him." Their father replied, "It worries me that you want to take him out. I'm afraid that a wolf might eat him while you're not looking." They answered, "If a wolf were to eat him while we are so large a group, then we would have to be eaten first!" Surat Yusuf (Joseph) 12:11-14

So, they took Yusuf out with them. But secretly they had all decided to throw him down the dried-up well. When they seized Yusuf and threw him into the dark hole, We (Allah), told him in his heart, "One day you will bring out the truth about this plan of their's when they won't even know you." Surat Yusuf (Joseph) 12:15

The brothers returned home in the early part of the night crying, "Oh father! We went racing with each other and left Yusuf alone to watch our things. Then a huge wolf came and ate him. But you'll probably never believe us even though we're telling the truth." Then they pulled out his shirt, which they had secretly stained with false blood. Ya'qub said, "No! You must have made up a story to use. I can only wait patiently against what you claim. It is Allah whose help is sought against what you describe." Surat Yusuf (Joseph) 12:16-18

C. The Journey to Egypt

Later that day, a caravan of travelers was passing by and decided to send their water-boy to the well for water. When he let down his bucket into the well. He shouted, "Hey! Look! Good news! Here is a fine young boy!" Then they hid him like merchandise! But Allah knows what they were doing! They sold him (in Egypt) for the miserable price of a few counted silver coins. They considered him of little value. Surat Yusuf (Joseph) 12:19-20

The man who bought him, 'Aziz Misr عَزِيزُ مِصْرَ, took the boy home and said to his wife, Wife of 'Aziz Misr, "Treat him well because he might bring us some good, or we could even adopt him as a son." In this way, We settled Yusuf in a new land so We could teach him how to interpret dreams. Allah has full power and control over His plans, but most people don't realize it. Surat Yusuf (Joseph) 12:21

When Yusuf (grew to be a young man,) We gave him strength and knowledge. This is how We reward those who do right. But (Wife of 'Aziz Misr) was attracted to him and wanted to seduce him and change his nature. One day she bolted the doors and said to him, "Now come to me!"
"Allah forbid!" cried Yusuf. "Your husband is my master! He's the one who made my life here bearable! Nothing good comes to people who do wrong!" But she desired him greatly, and he would have desired her, but he remembered the signs of his Lord. We turned him away from (all) shameful deeds. He was one of Our sincere servants. Surat Yusuf (Joseph) 12:22-24

So, they both raced each other to the door, and she tore his shirt from behind. (When Yusuf flung the door open) there, in front of them, stood her husband. She said, "What other punishment can there be for a man trying to seduce your wife but prison or a painful beating!" "But she's the one who tried to seduce me away from my own self!" cried Yusuf.

'Aziz Misr couldn't make up his mind because he was fond of both Yusuf and his wife, so a witness from her family observed that if his shirt was ripped from the front, then she is truthful and he is a liar! But if his shirt is torn from the back, then she is the liar and he is telling the truth! Surat Yusuf (Joseph) 12:25-27

When he saw that Yusuf's shirt was indeed torn from the back, he said, "This is certainly your trickery, O woman. Great is the trickery of you women indeed. O Yusuf ignore this matter, and you (O woman), seek forgiveness for your sin, for you were guilty in fact." Surat Yusuf (Joseph) 12:28-29

D. Wife of 'Aziz Takes Revenge

When the details of what happened reached other people, the women of the city began to gossip, The wife of the great minister was trying to seduce her own slave from himself. He must have inspired her with violent love. She's clearly going out of her mind! Soon (Wife of 'Aziz Misr) heard of their malicious talk. She decided to invite the (gossiping) women to visit her, and she prepared a banquet for them. She had a knife placed at each of their seats (and while they were cutting their food); she called out to Yusuf, "Come here before us." When the ladies saw him, they were amazed by his handsome features. In their amazement, they cut right through (their fruit) to their hands. They exclaimed,

"Allah save us! He is no mortal! This is none other than a noble angel!" Surat Yusuf (Joseph) 12:30-31

Wife of 'Aziz Misr announced triumphantly, "There, before you, is the man you teased me about! I tried to seduce him from his nature, but he got away from me and is still innocent! But now if he doesn't do what I say, he will be thrown into prison with the worst criminals!" Surat Yusuf (Joseph) 12:32

"My Lord!" He cried out. "Prison is better than what they are calling me towards. Unless you turn their trap away from me, I might become attracted to them and act like an ignorant fool."
So his Lord heard (his prayer) and turned their trap away from him. Certainly, He hears and knows (all things). Then it occurred to the husbands of the women, after they heard what their wives wanted Yusuf for, that it would be best to put him in prison for a while. Surat Yusuf (Joseph) 12:33-35

E. The Prisoners' Dreams

Along with Yusuf were two other men in prison. The first one said, "I see myself (in a dream) pressing wine." The second one said, "I see myself (in a dream) carrying bread on my head with a swarm of birds eating from it." So they asked Yusuf, "Tell us the meaning of these (strange dreams) because we can tell that you're a good person." Surat Yusuf (Joseph) 12:36

Yusuf answered, "Before your next meal comes, I will reveal to you the meaning of (your dreams) prior to the events actually happening. This is part of what my Lord has taught me. I've given up the ways of people who disbelieve in Allah and who even deny the next life. I follow the ways of my fathers: Ibrahim, Ishaq and Ya'qub. We never made any partners with Allah. This comes from the grace of Allah upon us and to other people though most people are not thankful." Surat Yusuf (Joseph) 12:37-38

Then he said, "My two fellow companions of the prison! I ask you, 'Are many gods arguing among themselves better or Allah the One, Supreme?' If you don't serve Him, then you serve nothing but names which you and your fathers made up. Allah gave no permission for anyone to do that. The right to command is for none but Allah. And He has commanded that you serve nothing but Him. That is the straight way of life, but most people don't understand." Surat Yusuf (Joseph) 12:39-40

"My two fellow companions of the prison!" he continued, "as for the first one of you, he will again pour out the wine for his master to drink. As for the other, he will be hung from a stake and the birds will eat off his head. The matter you two asked me about has been decided." Yusuf quietly whispered to the one he knew was going to be released, "Mention me to your master." But Shaytan made the man forget about it. So Yusuf lingered in prison a few more years. Surat Yusuf (Joseph) 12:41-42

F. The King of Egypt

One day, the king of Egypt [3] called to his ministers, "I saw (in a dream) seven fat cows being eaten by seven skinny ones, and seven green ears of corn and seven others withered. Ministers, tell me what my vision means if you can understand dreams." They replied, "It's a confused bunch of symbols. We are not skilled in figuring out the meaning of dreams." But the king's wine-pourer, who had been released (from prison), and who now remembered (Yusuf) after so long said, "I will tell you what it means. Send me (to the one who can solve this riddle)." Surat Yusuf (Joseph) 12:43-45

When the man arrived at the prison, he went to Yusuf's cell and said, "Yusuf! Man of truth! Tell us the meaning of seven fat cows being eaten by seven skinny ones, and of seven green ears of corn followed by seven withered ones. Tell me, so I can return to the people, and they will understand."

Yusuf answered, "For seven years you will diligently grow crops like you always do, but when you harvest them, leave all the grains on the stalk except the little that you must eat. Then, after this will come seven dreadful years (of bad harvests) in which you will live off of what you stored in advance, saving only small, guarded supplies. Then, after that period, a year will come in which the people will have abundant water, and they will press (juice and oil)." Surat Yusuf (Joseph) 12:46-49

When the wine-pourer returned with the meaning of the dream, the king said, "Bring that young man to me." The messengers went to the prison to release Yusuf, but he refused to leave his cell, saying, "Go back to your master and ask him, 'What are the ladies who cut their hands up to?' My Lord is aware of their trap." Surat Yusuf (Joseph) 12:50

The king then ordered the ladies who were involved to be gathered before him and asked, "What were your intentions when you tried to seduce Yusuf from his own self?" The ladies answered, "God save us! We don't know anything bad about him!" Then (Wife of 'Aziz Misr) said, "The truth is now clear to all. It was I who tried to seduce him from his nature. He is indeed true and virtuous." Surat Yusuf (Joseph) 12:51

---

[3] The ruler of Egypt during this story is always called a king مَلِك and not Pharaoh. But in the story of Prophet Musa, the ruler of Egypt is called Pharaoh فِرْعَون and not a king. This is because during Yusuf's stay in Egypt, the northern half of the country was being ruled by foreign invaders from the Middle East called 'Hyksos,' who ruled there between 1652 BCE and 1544 BCE. They were able to overpower Egyptian armies due to their superior weapons and tactics. Their chieftains were kings who at first rejected the worship of most of the Egyptian idols and required tribute from the real Egyptian Pharaohs, who were confined to the remote south of the country. When the native Egyptians, led by Prince Kamose of Thebes, finally threw the Hyksos out, they started their native, Pharaoh-based system again and at the same time made the Jews slaves. Thus, when Prophet Musa was there, many hundreds of years later, the ruler would be called Pharaoh. Allah's book is accurate even to the smallest details!

When Yusuf ﷺ was informed of the proceedings he said, "I wanted this (public hearing) so that (the minister, 'Aziz Misr,) would know that I did not betray him in his absence and that Allah will never guide the plan of betrayers. Nor do I absolve myself (of all blame); the human soul is certainly prone to evil unless my Lord gives His Mercy. Certainly, my Lord is Forgiving and Most Merciful." Surat Yusuf (Joseph) 12:52-53

Then the king commanded, "Bring him to me; I will take him to be my special servant." When Yusuf was brought, the king reassured him, "Be certain that today you are before me and that your position is firmly set with your honesty fully proved!" Yusuf said, "Put me in charge of all the storehouses in the land. I will guard them like one who knows their importance." Surat Yusuf (Joseph) 12:54-55

Thus, We put Yusuf in the position where he could take anything in the land he pleased. We give Our Mercy to whom We please, and We never let be lost the reward of those who do good. Certainly, the reward of the next life is the best for those who believe and are constant in doing good. Surat Yusuf (Joseph) 12:56-57

G. The Brothers Come Forth

The foretold famine struck, forcing people far and wide to go to Egypt to buy food. Among these came Yusuf's ﷺ brothers. When they came before his (court) to buy things, they didn't recognize him, although Yusuf instantly knew who they were. After he had given them the supplies, they needed, he told them, "Bring to me the youngest brother you have from the same father as yourselves. Don't you see that I give generously and that I provide the best hospitality? Now, if you don't bring him to me you will not get any more (grain) from me, nor shall you ever come near me again." Surat Yusuf (Joseph) 12:58-60

They answered, "We will certainly get our way from his father. Indeed we will do it." Then (Yusuf) said to his boys, "Put their goods in their camel-packs. Perhaps they will recognize it when they go back to their family; perhaps they will come again." Surat Yusuf (Joseph) 12:61-62

When the brothers returned to their father, they said, "Father! We won't get any more grain unless we take our youngest brother with us next time. So send (Benjamin) with us so we can get our supplies. We will take good care of him." "Shall I trust you with him when I had already trusted you with his brother (Yusuf) so long ago?" he replied. "But Allah is the best to take care of things, and He is the Most Merciful of all." Surat Yusuf (Joseph) 12:63-64

When they opened their baggage, they found their goods given back to them. They said, "Our father, what else should we want? Here are our goods given back to us, and we shall bring food to our family, protect our brother and add the measure of one camel more. That is an easy measure." Surat Yusuf (Joseph) 12:65

Ya'qub said, "I'll never send him with you unless you swear a special promise to me, in Allah's name, that you will be sure to bring him back unless you yourselves are trapped." After they had sworn their special promise he said, "Allah, be the Witness and Guardian over all that we say!"
Then he instructed his sons, "Don't enter the city all from the same road, but rather, each of you pick a different gate. Not that I can help you against Allah's plan with my advice. No one can command except Allah. In Him do I put my trust, and let everyone who trusts put their trust in Him." Surat Yusuf (Joseph) 12:66-67

And when they entered the city in the way their father had told them to, it did not help them in the least against (the plan of) Allah. It was just something Ya'qub felt he had to say. For he was, by Our teaching, very experienced. But most people don't know that. And when they came to Yusuf, he lodged his brother (Benjamin) with himself. He said, "Look, I am your brother! So do not grieve for what they have been doing." Surat Yusuf (Joseph) 12:68-69

H. Yusuf's Plan

When Yusuf had given them the supplies they needed, he (had his servant) put the drinking cup of the king into the youngest brother's saddlebag. Then, when the caravan was setting out for the return journey, he had a guard shout out after them, "Hey! You in the Caravan! Stop, you are thieves!" Surat Yusuf (Joseph) 12:70

The brothers halted their caravan and shouted back, "What are you missing?" The guards surrounded them and the leader replied, "We are missing the great cup of the king. Whoever finds it will get the reward of a load of valuables. I will do my duty and find it!" Surat Yusuf (Joseph) 12:71-72

The brothers said, "By God! You know we didn't come to make trouble in this country, and we're not thieves!" The guards answered, "What should be the punishment of this crime if we prove you're lying?" They replied, "The penalty should be that the owner of the saddle bag in which you find the item should be held as a slave to pay for the crime. This is how we punish criminals in our country." Surat Yusuf (Joseph) 12:73-75

(The guards called their master, Yusuf, over to the caravan) and he began to search the brothers' baggage. Then, when he opened the bag of (Benjamin), there was the missing cup of the king! This is how We (Allah) planned it for Yusuf. He couldn't hold his brother, according to the law of the king, except that Allah willed it (so). We increase (in wisdom) whoever We want to, but over all intelligent people is the All-Knowing. Surat Yusuf (Joseph) 12:76

The brothers cried out, "If he stole something, then you should know he had another brother who used to steal also."(Upon hearing their lies, Yusuf became angry) but he kept his feelings locked in his heart so as not to give away the secret to them. He simply said, "You are in the worst position, and Allah knows best the truth of what you claim!" They begged, "Great one! Listen to us! He has an old and respected father (who will grieve for him), so keep one of us in his place. We see that you are gracious in doing good." But Yusuf replied, "God forbid that we take anyone except the one who had our property. If we did so, we would be acting wrongly." Surat Yusuf (Joseph) 12:77-79

When they saw no hope of changing his mind, they held a meeting in private. The eldest among them said, "Don't you remember that we made a promise with our father, in Allah's name, and how before this we failed in our duty with Yusuf? As for me, I won't leave this land until my father allows me or Allah commands me, and He is the best to command. Go back to father and say, 'Father! Your son stole something. We say only what we know, and we could not guard against what we didn't expect! Ask at the town we passed through and in the caravan in which we returned, and (you will find) we are telling the truth'". Surat Yusuf (Joseph)12:80-82

When Ya'qub was informed, he cried out, "No! You just made up a story good enough to cover you! All I can do is be patient. Maybe Allah will bring them all back to me (in the end), for He is indeed full of knowledge and wisdom." Then he turned away from them and cried, "How great is my sadness for Yusuf." And his eyes became white and blinded with sorrow, and he fell into a silent daze. Surat Yusuf (Joseph) 12:83-84

The brothers said, "By Allah! Won't you ever stop remembering Yusuf, even until you reach the last moments of illness or until you die?" Ya'qub answered them, "I only complain about my problems and sorrow to Allah, and I know things from Allah that you don't. My sons! Go back to Egypt, ask about Yusuf and his brother and never give up hope of Allah's Mercy. Truly, no one despairs of Allah's Mercy except those who have no faith." Surat Yusuf (Joseph) 12:85-87

I. The Truth is Out!

When the brothers returned to Egypt and entered Yusuf's presence, they said, "Great one! Grief has come upon us and our family. We have only a little money, so give us full supplies, we beg you, and treat it as charity for us. Allah rewards the charitable." Yusuf answered, "Do you remember how you dealt with Yusuf and his youngest brother in your ignorance?" Surat Yusuf (Joseph) 12:88-89

(When they realized who Yusuf was) they asked, "Are you really Yusuf?"
"I am Yusuf, and this is my brother!" He replied (pointing to Benjamin). "Allah has been gracious to us. Whoever is righteous

and patient, Allah will never let their reward be lost, because they did right." Surat Yusuf (Joseph) 12:90

(The brothers began weeping) and cried out, "By Allah! Indeed Allah has preferred you above us! We are guilty of sin!" "There will be no shame put on you today," Yusuf replied. "Allah will forgive you, and He is the Most Merciful of all. Go and take my shirt, and put it over the face of my father. He will come to see clearly again. Then bring him and all your family back to me here." Surat Yusuf (Joseph) 12:91-93

After the caravan had left Egypt and was on its way home, Ya'qub exclaimed to the people around him, "I feel the presence of Yusuf. And don't think I'm senile." They said, "By Allah! You have an old wandering mind." But when the bringer of the good news came and put the shirt over Ya'qub's face, he immediately regained clear sight. Then he said, "Didn't I tell you that I know from Allah things you don't?" Surat Yusuf (Joseph) 12:94-96

Then the brothers begged, "Father! Ask forgiveness for our sins for we were truly at fault." "I will ask my Lord to forgive you" he replied. "For He is the Forgiving and Merciful." Then, (after they all traveled to Egypt) and came before Yusuf, he provided a home for his parents with himself and declared, "Enter Egypt in safety, if it please Allah."

He raised his parents high (in respect) and they all (his two parents and eleven brothers) fell down in prostration before him. He announced before them, "My Father! This is the fulfillment of the vision I had so long ago. Allah has made it come true! He was indeed good to me when He took me out of prison and brought you all here out of the desert even after Shaytan had caused jealousy between me and my brothers. Surely, my Lord understands better the mysteries of all He plans to do, for certainly He is full of knowledge and wisdom." Surat Yusuf (Joseph) 12:97-100

Yusuf continued saying, "My Lord! You have indeed given me some power and taught me how to understand visions. Creator of the skies and the Earth! You are my Protector in this world and in the next. Take my soul as one surrendering to Your Will. Join me with the righteous!" Surat Yusuf (Joseph) 12:101

This is one of the hidden stories, which We (Allah) reveal by inspiration to you. You were not there with them when they put the details together in weaving their plots. Yet most people will not believe, no matter how strongly you want them to. Surat Yusuf (Joseph) 12:102-103

Questions to Answer

1. Why were Yusuf's brothers jealous of him and Benjamin?
2. How did Yusuf's brothers get rid of him?
3. What did Wife of 'Aziz Misr do to make Yusuf run away from her?
4. Why was Yusuf thrown in prison?
5. How did he get out of prison?
6. What power was Yusuf given by the King of Egypt?
7. Why did Prophet Yusuf's brothers travel to Egypt?
8. How did Yusuf teach his brothers a lesson?
9. After Yusuf brought all of his family to Egypt, what did he say was the meaning of his dream that he had dreamt as a child?

Define: 'Aziz Misr, Benjamin.
Reflect: What is your favorite part of the story?
Act: Create a children's story book that recounts the beautiful story of Yusuf. Do not draw any characters, but illustrate it based on other aspects of the story.
IQ Builder: Choose a quote from surat Yusuf (Joseph) that resonates most with you. Explain your understanding of the quote, and explain how it impacts you personally.

Unit 05 Review Exercise

VOCABULARY REVIEW

On a separate sheet of paper, write the definition of each word below.

1. Habeel and Qabeel
2. Mount Judi
3. Prehistoric
4. 'Aad
5. Iram
6. Archaeology
7. Namrud
8. Ziggurat
9. Zamzam
10. Benjamin
11. Lut
12. Azar
13. 'Aziz Misr

REMEMBERING WHAT YOU READ

On a separate sheet of paper, answer the following questions. Use complete sentences in your answers.

1. What happened with Adam's two sons?
2. How did idol-worship develop among Nuh's people?
3. Describe three arguments Nuh made to convince his people of the truth.
4. How were the people of Prophet Nuh punished?
5. Why did Allah destroy the city of Iram?
6. Who were the 'Aad people?
7. How did Prophet Hud carry out his mission?
8. What are three lessons we can learn from the Story of Yusuf?
9. Why did Prophet Yusuf have to use a trick to have Benjamin detained?

THINKING TO LEARN

On a separate sheet of paper, answer the questions below. Use complete sentences.

1. How did Ibrahim realize idol-worship was false?
2. Why do you think Prophet Ibrahim won the showdown with Namrud?
3. Who was the Advocate and what happened to him?
4. How did Prophet Yusuf go from being a slave to a nobleman in Egypt?

UNIT 6
Bani Isra'il

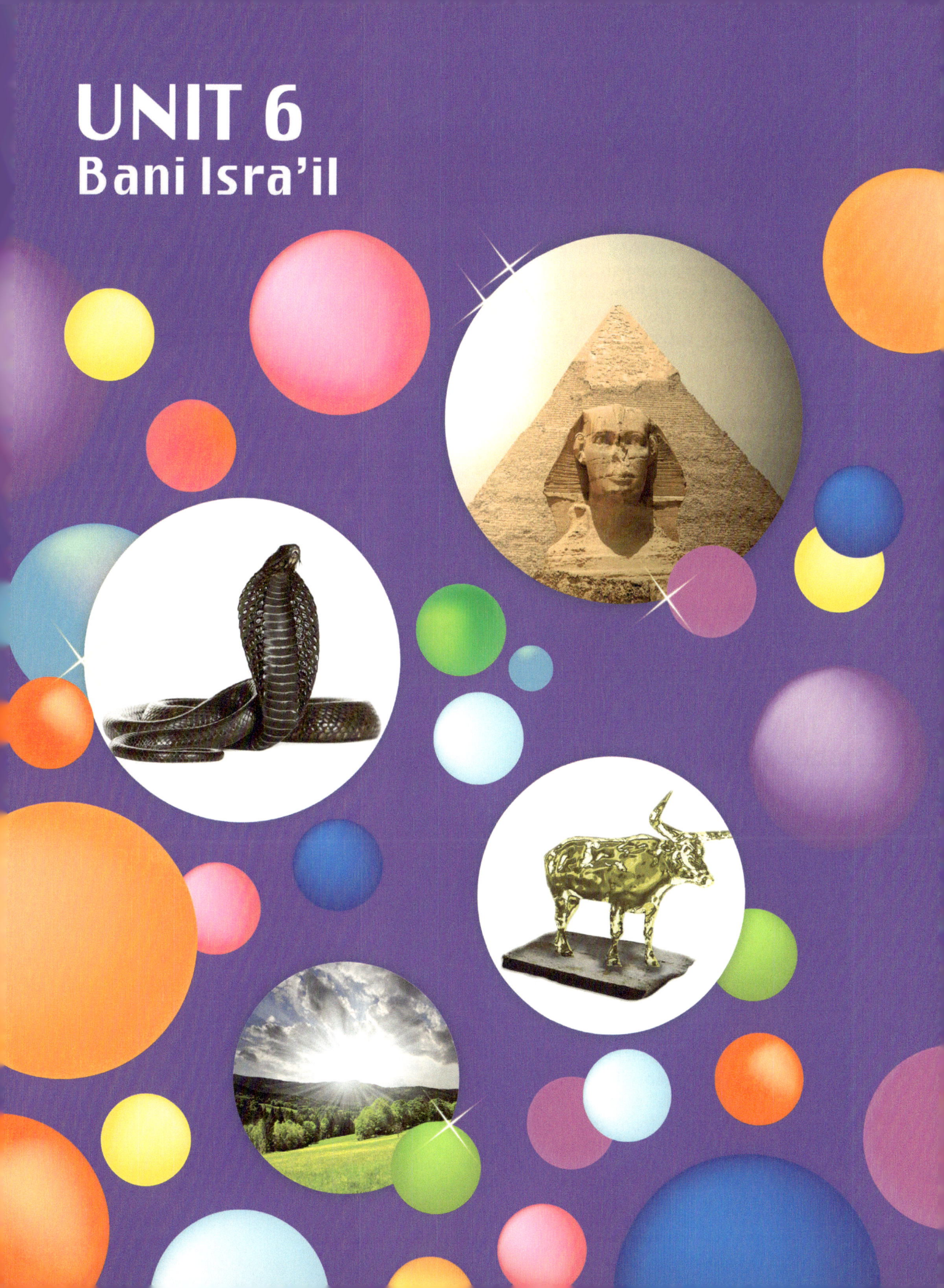

23 From the Nile River to the Desert

WHAT TO LEARN

How many times in history have people who were born into poor families risen to the top? In the case of Prophet Musa ﷺ, he not only rose to the top but also had many interesting adventures along the way.

VOCABULARY

Madyan   Pharaoh   Banu Isra'il
Asyah   Hebrews

THINK ABOUT IT

How did Prophet Musa ﷺ give da'wah to the Egyptians and his own people?

A. The Enslavement of the Hebrews

The family and tribe of Prophet Yusuf ﷺ, who were called **Banu Isra'il** بَنُو إِسْرَائِيل (the descendants of Prophet Jacob ﷺ), had all immigrated to Egypt in search of a better life. They were initially welcomed in the land by the rulers of Egypt, who were from the tribe called Hyksos. The Hyksos were invaders who only ruled Egypt for a short time.

When the Egyptians overthrew the invaders, they reinstituted their own people as kings of ancient Egypt: **Pharaohs** الفَرَاعِنَة, **Rulers** and mistreated the Hebrew immigrants. **Hebrews** العِبْرَانِيِّين, means literally **People from the Other Side**, as their forefather Ibrahim ﷺ had crossed from the other side of the Euphrates River and into Palestine long before this time.

Many Egyptians were resentful of the Hebrews. Over the course of many centuries, the descendants of Yusuf ﷺ and his people lost more and more rights.

Finally, by about 1500 BCE, they were reduced to the status of forced laborers, or slaves of the state. The Hebrews were in a miserable situation. What was far worse, however, was that they had forgotten most of what their forefathers had known about Allah ﷻ.

The Hebrews mostly followed Egyptian customs. Many even worshipped Egyptian idols, and they knew little of the good and moral way of life.

But no matter how much the Hebrews assimilated, the Egyptians still did not like these outsiders. In about the year 1200 BCE, the Egyptians saw that the Hebrew population was increasing at an alarming rate and sent forth a decree from the house of Pharaoh: all Hebrew baby boys must be killed.

And when Musa said to his people, "Remember Allah's blessing upon you when He delivered you from Pharaoh's people who had been inflicting a grievous torment on you, slaughtering your sons and leaving your women alive. In that there was a great trial from your Lord."
Surat Ibrahim (Abraham) 14:6

﴿وَإِذْ قَالَ مُوسَىٰ لِقَوْمِهِ ٱذْكُرُوا۟ نِعْمَةَ ٱللَّهِ عَلَيْكُمْ إِذْ أَنجَىٰكُم مِّنْ ءَالِ فِرْعَوْنَ يَسُومُونَكُمْ سُوٓءَ ٱلْعَذَابِ وَيُذَبِّحُونَ أَبْنَآءَكُمْ وَيَسْتَحْيُونَ نِسَآءَكُمْ ۚ وَفِى ذَٰلِكُم بَلَآءٌ مِّن رَّبِّكُمْ عَظِيمٌ﴾ سُورَةُ إبراهيم 14: 6

The Egyptians then proceeded to carry out this evil scheme, and although the Hebrews tried their best to resist, they were powerless in the face of the soldiers who went house to house obeying their master's wishes.

B. The Baby in a Basket

Allah had a plan to deal with the evil pharaoh. He sent a revelation to a certain Hebrew mother which included some very unusual instructions.

We inspired the mother of Musa saying, "Suckle him (Musa). Then once you fear about him, cast him in the river, and do not fear, and do not grieve. Surely We are going to bring him back to you and appoint him one of (Our) messengers." Surat Al Qasas (The Stories) 28:7

Later, when the soldiers were coming to her part of town, the woman took a basket of reeds and put her baby boy into it. She went down to the river and set the basket in the water. Perhaps with a bitter tear, she pushed the tiny craft out into the current and watched it float away. Allah then revealed to her that he would, indeed, be safe. (20:39)

As Allah would have it, the river brought the basket to one of Pharaoh's river-side palaces. **Asyah** آسيا, Pharaoh's wife, was amazed to see the basket and ordered it brought to her.

So the family of Pharaoh picked him up, so that he becomes for them an enemy and a (cause of) grief. Indeed Pharaoh, Haman and their armies were mistaken. And the wife of Pharaoh said, (to Pharaoh about Musa), "He may be a delight of eye for me and you. Do not kill him. It is hoped that he will be of benefit to us, or we will adopt him as a son." And they were not aware (of what was going to happen). Surat Al Qasas (The Stories) 28: 8-9

The mother of Musa (which is what Asyah named the infant) felt heartsick for her baby. She found out that a baby was brought into Pharaoh's household from the river, and that there were many stories told about it.

Her pain at losing her son almost made her go to Pharaoh and ask for him back. But Allah strengthened her heart so her belief could remain true. (28:10)

Musa's mother asked her daughter to go near the palace and try to keep an eye on what was happening with the baby as best she could.

Meanwhile, inside the palace, the baby refused to take milk from anyone. He was crying and hungry and in danger of dying unless someone could feed him. The servants of the palace looked frantically for anyone who could feed the baby.

Perhaps Musa's older sister heard someone talking as they were going out from the palace. She quickly thought to present herself saying, "I know of a family that can feed and raise him for you with great concern for his welfare." Surat Al Qasas (The Stories) 28: 12

Thus, Allah fulfilled his promise to Musa's mother and returned her child to her.

The waters of the Nile river carried the basket right past one of the palaces of Pharaoh. A servant fished it out of the water and brought the basket to Asyah.

However, she had to pretend that the baby was not hers, as the house of Pharaoh had a claim on him now. But at least she knew he was safe and that she would be able to be near him.

C. The Big Brawl

Musa ﷺ grew strong, and in time became a handsome and powerful young man. He was privileged to be a part of Pharaoh's household, and Asyah, his adopted mother, must have been very gracious to him.

It may have been hidden from Musa ﷺ for a time that he was a Hebrew and not an Egyptian, but it didn't matter, as he had the protection of Asyah behind him. He could go and do as he pleased.

But he was not arrogant or vain, nor did he go to the other Hebrews and act like he was better than them. His real mother had raised him with good values in her home, with his older sister and his brother Harun ﷺ. Perhaps she even revealed to him his true identity.

And when he reached his maturity and became perfect, We gave him wisdom and knowledge. This is how We reward those who are good in their deeds. Surat Al Qasas (The Stories) 28:14

One day, while Musa ﷺ was out walking in the city, he found two men fighting in a hidden area with no one else around. One was a Hebrew and the other, an Egyptian.

The Hebrew man called out to Musa ﷺ for help, and Musa ﷺ tried to intervene. During the scuffle Musa ﷺ hit the Egyptian, unintentionally killing him.

Musa ﷺ felt terrible and asked Allah ﷻ for forgiveness and mercy. Thanks to his mother's influence, Musa ﷺ believed in the oneness of God and rejected the Egyptian idols. Allah ﷻ forgave Musa ﷺ and settled his heart.

He (Musa) said, "O my Lord! As You have favored me, I will never be a supporter of the sinners." Surat Al Qasas (The Stories) 28:17

The next day, Musa ﷺ went out in the city again and saw the same Hebrew man he saved earlier. The man was fighting with another Egyptian. When the Hebrew asked for help again, Musa ﷺ shouted at him, "You're clearly a brawler!"

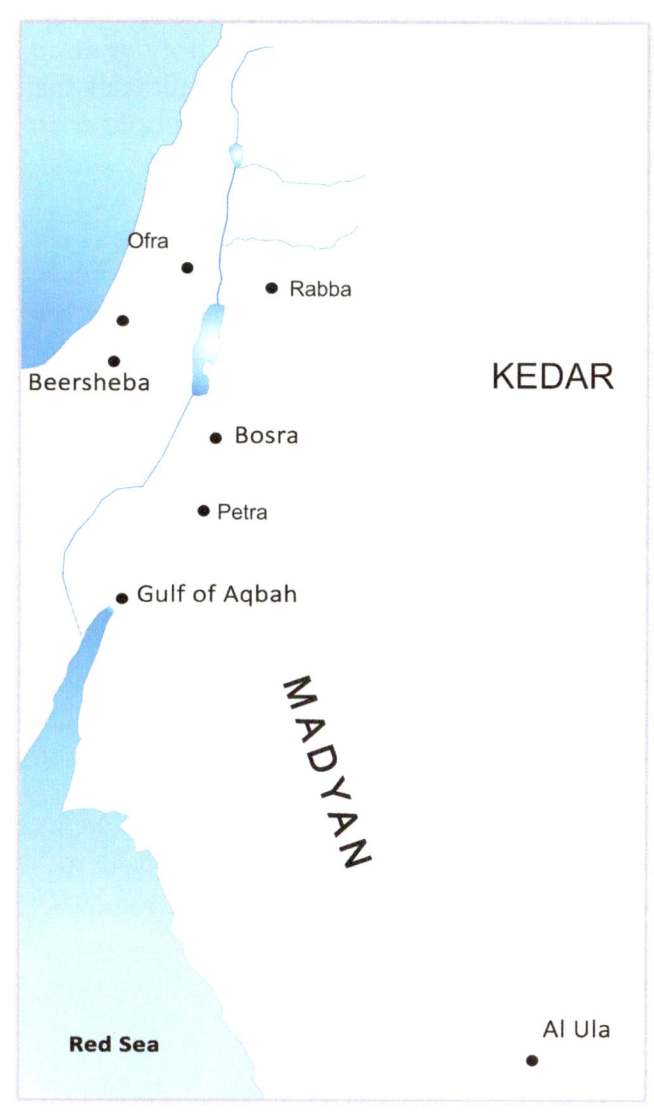

Then Musa ﷺ grabbed whatever supplies he could and escaped from Egypt. He headed east across the Sinai desert.

So, he went out of it (the city), looking around in a state of fear. He said, "O my Lord, save me from the cruel people." Surat Al Qasas (The Stories) 28:21

D. The Daughters of Madyan

Musa ﷺ traveled on until he reached **Madyan** مَدْيَن, a land located in the northern tip of the Arabian peninsula. Upon arriving out of the trackless wilderness, he said, *"I hope my Lord shows me an easy road." And when he arrived at the waters of Madyan, he found a large number of people watering (their animals) and found, aloof from them, two women keeping (their animals) back. He said, "What is the matter with you?" They said, "We cannot water (our animals) until these shepherds take (their animals) back after watering them, and our father is a very old man." Musa took the water buckets and watered the whole flock for the women. When he had finished, he returned to a shady spot and said, "My Lord! I am in need of any good You send me." Afterwards, one of the women came back to him, walking shyly, and said, "My father has invited you to a dinner so he can reward you for watering (our animals) for us." So when he (Musa) came to him (the father of the women) and narrated to him the whole story, the latter said, "Do not fear; you have escaped from the wrongdoing people."* Surat Al Qasas (The Stories) 28:22-25

So Musa ﷺ went to the camp of the old leader—who was actually Prophet Shu'aib ﷺ—and was invited inside. During the course of the dinner, Musa ﷺ told the old man all that had happened to him.

Musa ﷺ thought he would try to break up the fight, and when he came near the struggling men, the Egyptian said, *"Hey Musa! Are you going to kill me like you killed that man yesterday? You only want to be a tyrant in the land and not a peace-maker!"* Surat Al Qasas (The Stories) 28:19

Someone had found out about the dead man! Musa ﷺ knew he was in trouble. Then someone came running to Musa ﷺ and said, *"Hey Musa! The leaders are having a meeting about you, to order your execution. You have to get out of here. Take my advice! I mean it!"* Surat Al Qasas (The Stories) 28:20

One of his (daughters) suggested, "Dearest Father, hire him for wages. The best man to employ is one who is strong and honest." The father announced to Musa, "I want to marry you to one of my daughters. My condition is that you work for me for eight years, but if you stay for ten years, it will be a mercy from you (to me). But I don't want to put too big a burden on you. You will see that, as Allah wills, I am one of the righteous." Musa said, "Let that be the (deal) between me and you. Whichever length of time I work, don't have any ill feelings towards me. Let Allah be the witness to what we say." Surat Al Qasas (The Stories) 28:26-28

E. The Burning Bush

Musa married one of his daughters and worked for her father for the required number of years. When his obligation was over, he decided to strike out on his own. He packed up his belongings and headed for the Sinai Peninsula with his wife.

One evening, Musa was looking out from his camp, and he thought he saw a light on a nearby mountain. The mountain, known as Mount Tur, loomed over him like a monolith. He had to find out who was there.

He told his wife to remain in camp while he went to get some information from the one who started the fire. At the very least, he thought that he could bring a burning branch to start their own campfire.

Musa climbed the mountain until he reached a small valley within it. There he saw a small tree, or bush, that was on fire.

So when he came to it, he was called by a voice coming from a side of the right valley in the blessed ground, from the tree, saying, "O Musa, I am Allah, the Lord of the worlds." Surat Al Qasas (The Stories) 28:30

Musa was then commanded to remove his shoes because he was on holy ground. Allah gave Musa two secret miracles that would prevent Pharaoh or his people from harming him, "Throw down your stick." So when he saw it moving as if it were a snake, he turned back in retreat and did not look back. (Allah said to him), "O Musa come forward and do not fear; you are one of those in peace. Insert your hand into your bosom, and it will come out white without any evil (disease), and press your arm to your side for (removing) fear. Thus these are two proofs from your Lord (sent) to Pharaoh and his chiefs. Indeed they are transgressing people." Surat Al Qasas (The Stories) 28:31-32

Allah bestowed the gift of prophethood on him. Allah informs us, Remember when your Lord called Musa saying, "Go to the transgressing people, The people of Pharaoh. Do they not fear Allah?" He (Musa) said, "My Lord, I fear that they will reject me. My heart gets straitened, and my tongue is not fluent; so send for Harun. Moreover, they have (leveled) a

Mount Tur, where Allah spoke with Musa.

charge of offence against me, and I fear they will kill me."
Surat Ash-Shuaraa (The Poets) 26:10-14

Musaﷺ knew for certain what he had to do. He instructed his family to return to Madyan and remain there while he secretly traveled back to Egypt to meet up with his brother Harunﷺ. Then he would have to face the pharaoh of Egypt. But would he listen? Time would tell.

Questions to Answer

1. Why did the Egyptians dislike the Hebrews?
2. What plan did the Egyptians make to keep the Hebrew population down?
3. What was the revelation given to Musa'sﷺ mother telling her what to do?
4. Who found the baby, and what happened to him?
5. How did Musa'sﷺ mother get him back?
6. Why did Musaﷺ have to escape Egypt?
7. What act of kindness did Musaﷺ perform in Madyan? How was he rewarded?
8. What did Musaﷺ find while traveling with his family? What happened there?

Define: Madyan, Hebrews.

Reflect: The Prophet Musaﷺ asked Allahﷻ to let his brother Harunﷺ help him fulfill his mission. Has there been a time in your life where having someone with you strengthened your ability to complete a task?

Act: Memorize the two dua's that Prophet Musaﷺ made to Allahﷻ when he was in trouble. Say these dua's whenever you are in need of Allah'sﷻ help.

IQ Builders:
1. What did Allahﷻ tell Prophet Musaﷺ in 20:12-16?
2. How did Musaﷺ react when he saw his staff turning into a snake, according to 28:31?
3. What does Allahﷻ tell Prophet Musaﷺ to say in 28:37?

24 Prophet Musa the Leader

WHAT TO LEARN

What if you had to confront the most powerful man in the world? How would you feel?

VOCABULARY

Haman   Shaheed
Hieroglyphics

THINK ABOUT IT

How did Musa try to reason with the Pharaoh?

A. The Showdown with Pharaoh

Musa returned to Egypt in about the year 1225 BCE, almost ten years after he had barely escaped with his life. He met up with his brother, Harun, to whom Allah had also granted prophethood in order to help Musa. (19:53)

It didn't take long for Pharaoh to find out that Musa had returned. He ordered his men to bring Musa and his brother to him. His palace was a huge stone mansion filled with statues, **Hieroglyphics** الهيروغليفيّة **Ancient Egyptian Writing**, soldiers and priests.

When Musa was brought in front of Pharaoh, Asyah must have felt pained at the thought of what her husband might do to him.

The Pharaoh said, "Musa, didn't we love you and care for you as a child, and didn't you live many years with us? But then you did the crime you did! You're a thankless man!" Musa answered, "I did it back then, and I was wrong. So I ran away from you and feared you. But my Lord has since given me Judgement and made me one of His Messengers. And you say it was a favor, what you did for me, but you enslaved the Children of Isra'il!" Surat Ash-Shuaraa (The Poets) 26:18-22

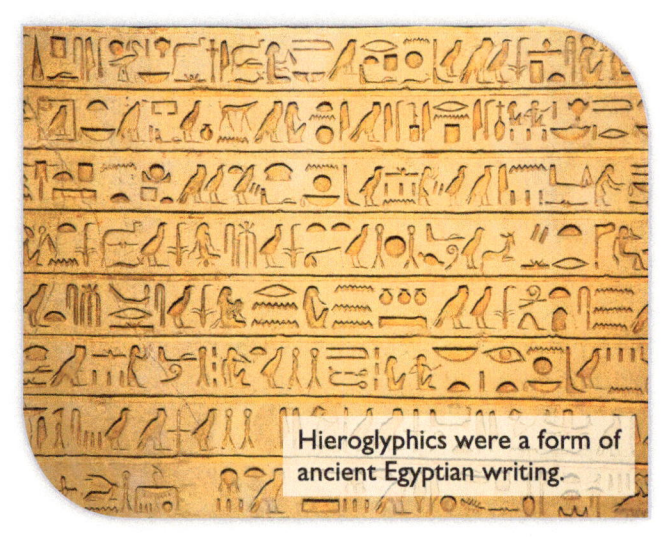

Hieroglyphics were a form of ancient Egyptian writing.

Musa then announced, "Pharaoh! I am a Messenger from the Lord of the Worlds! I say nothing but the truth about Allah. I have come to you from your Lord with a clear sign, so let the Children of Isra'il leave with me!" Surat Al A'raf (The Heights) 7:104-105

Pharaoh asked, "Who is this Lord of the Worlds?" Musa answered, "He is the Lord of the skies, the Earth, and all in between if you want to know." Pharaoh said to those around him, "Do you hear that!" Musa continued, "He is your Lord and the Lord of your ancestors, from the very beginning." Pharaoh said "This Messenger sent to you (Hebrews) is insane!" Musa said, "He is the Lord of the East and the West and all in between, if you only had sense!" Pharaoh declared, "If anyone makes any god other than me, I will imprison him!" Musa called out, "Even if I showed you clear proof?" Surat Ash-Shuaraa (The Poets) 26:23-30

The Pharaoh replied, "If you have really come with a sign, then show it if you're telling the truth." So Musa threw his staff down and then it became a real serpent. Then he pulled out his hand, and it glowed white (to everyone's eyes!) The Pharaoh's advisers whispered to their master, "He is a skilled sorcerer. His plan is to drive you from your kingdom." Then they asked each other, "What should we do?" One advisor said, "Delay him and his brother in suspense. Then send men to all the different cities to gather all our finest sorcerers." Surat Al A'raf (The Heights) 7:106-112

The day's meeting was adjourned, and Musa and Harun were probably allowed to go back among the Hebrews until the next meeting. Perhaps they spread the word that Allah's Messenger was among them and that they were about to be delivered from their difficulties.

B. The Sorcerers Speak

Whatever happened in the time after the first meeting, it was short, for when the Pharaoh of Egypt called the people to him, they had to move quickly.

Then Musa and Harun were summoned to the court of Pharaoh once more. On one side of the chamber stood Pharaoh's finest sorcerers and workers of magic.

The sorcerers came to Pharaoh. They said, "Of course we will be rewarded if we win?" The Pharaoh answered, "Yes, and of course, you will be among the closer ones (to me)." The sorcerers said, "Musa, will you go first or shall we?" He said, "You throw." So when they threw, they bewitched the eyes of the people, and made them frightened, and produced great sorcery. Surat Al A'raf (The Heights) 7:113-116

The sorcerers threw their sticks and ropes and chanted strange words, causing everyone to think that the sticks had become snakes.

So, when they had cast, Musa said, "All that you have brought is magic. Allah will certainly bring it to naught. Be assured that Allah does not set right the work of the mischief-makers." Surat Yunus (Jonah) 10:81

We revealed to Musa, "Throw your staff." Then all of a sudden, it began to swallow all that they had concocted. Thus the truth prevailed, and what they were doing became a nullity. So, they were overcome then and there and turned humiliated. Surat Al A'raf (The Heights) 7:117-119

When they realized that Musa's power was real while theirs was only illusion, the sorcerers fell to their knees and bowed. They cried, "We believe in the Lord of the Universe—the Lord of Musa and Harun!" Surat Al A'raf (The Heights) 7:120-122

Pharaoh was enraged! He shouted at them, "Do you believe in him without my permission? This must be a trick which you all planned in the city to make the people run away. Soon you will know (your fate). I will have your hands and feet cut off on opposite sides, and I'll have you killed on a stake." They replied, "For us, we will only be returned to our Lord. You only want to take revenge on us because we believe in the signs of our Lord that have come to us!" Then they prayed to Allah, "O our Lord, pour out patience upon us, and cause us to die as Muslims." Surat Al A'raf (The Heights) 7: 123-126

The meeting was again adjourned and Musa and Harun went back among their people. Meanwhile, the nobles of the court asked the Pharaoh, "Are you going to let Musa and his people cause chaos in the land and abandon your gods?" The Pharaoh ordered, "We will kill their male children (again) and keep their females alive. We have total power over them!" Surat Al A'raf (The Heights) 7: 127

When the threat was announced in the Hebrew areas of the city, Musa said to his people, "Seek help from Allah and be patient. Surely, the land belongs to Allah. He lets whomsoever He wills inherit it from among His servants; and the end-result is in favor of the God-fearing." But then his people started complaining against him, "We've had trouble both before and after you came to us!" Musa replied, "Maybe your Lord will destroy your enemy and make you survive in the Earth. Then He might test you by your actions." Surat Al A'raf (The Heights) 7: 127-129

C. The Arrogance of Pharaoh

And We seized the people of Pharaoh with years of famine and poor production of fruits so that they may learn a lesson. When good times came to them, they said, "This is our right." And if an evil touched them, they took it as an ill omen of Musa and those with him. Listen, their ill omen lies with Allah only, but most of them do not know. Surat Al A'raf (The Heights) 7: 130-131

The truth of Prophet Musa's teachings reached even to Egyptians, and some of Pharaoh's own people began to believe. One Egyptian man even challenged the Pharaoh and told him to listen to Musa's message. (40:28-35)

Pharaoh became more arrogant and ordered **Haman** هامان his second-in-command, to build a huge tower. The Pharaoh said, "Build me a huge palace so I can climb to the sky and touch the God of Musa, for I think Musa is a liar!" Surat Al Qasas (The Stories) 28:38

But the Egyptian man, who now believed in Allah, told the Pharaoh that even if he built up all the treasures in the world, it wouldn't matter, since everything in this life passes away. Although the Pharaoh tried to have the man killed for his insolence, Allah helped the man to escape. (40:38-45)

Meanwhile, Musa and Harun kept spreading the message of Allah's truth among Banu Isra'il; few truly believed, however. (10:83)

Then Allah instructed Prophet Musa and Harun to turn their homes into places of worship of Allah and to establish times of prayer. (10:87) This they did, and many more people began to learn about Allah and their duty to Him.

Before the next meeting with Pharaoh, Musa said, "Our Lord, You have given Pharaoh and his group glamour and riches in the worldly life, so that, our Lord, they mislead (people) from Your path. Our Lord, obliterate their riches and harden their hearts, so that they may not come to believe until they witness the painful punishment." Allah said, "The prayer of the two of you has been granted so stand firm, and never follow the way of the ignorant." Surat Yunus (Jonah) 10:88-89

Pharaoh boasted to Musa, "Whatever signs you bring against us from your magic, we will never believe you." Surat Al A'raf (The Heights) 7: 132

So Allah sent terrible plagues against the land, which caused many deaths. Locusts descended on the fields, devouring the crops; lice infected the city; frogs filtered into the city from the swamps; and, a mysterious blood-red color seeped out into the water. Pharaoh rejected the call, even after all this. (7:133)

After each plague, Pharaoh would beg Prophet Musa to stop and would promise that he would believe in him. But whenever the plague was removed, the Pharaoh would break his promise. (7:134-135)

D. The Woman Who Defied Pharaoh

After hearing all the exchanges between Musa and her husband, Asyah, the wife of Pharaoh, decided to take a stand of her own. She couldn't sit by silently any longer. She came to believe that Musa was a true prophet and that her husband was wrong. She said something that would make her husband very angry with her.

And Allah has cited for the believers the example of the wife of Fir'aun (Pharaoh), when she said, "My Lord! Build for me, in nearness to You, a palace in Paradise. Save me from the Pharaoh and his actions and save me from evil people." Surat At-Tahrim 66:11

Pharaoh was livid and ordered Asyah, his own wife, to be tortured until she broke. According to Salman Al Faresi, Allah sent invisible angels to spread their wings over her, shielding her from the pain and suffering of the torture. When she died, she became a **Shaheed** شهيد **Martyr**, someone who dies for the sake of Allah.

E. The Great Escape!

The arrogance of Pharaoh grew to the breaking point. He was surely going to order his soldiers to exterminate Musa and his people. So Allah sent the inspiration to Musa to organize his people for the great escape. (26:52)

Everyone was told to prepare to leave when the signal was given. As soon as the time came, all the Hebrews and the Egyptians who believed in Musa's message poured silently forth from their homes one night. They carried with them whatever they could and moved as quietly as possible.

By the time the dawn rose over the Egyptian countryside, Musa's entire people had evacuated and were heading towards Palestine. There were perhaps thousands of men, women and children. Few had any horses or mules, and many were weak or elderly and needed extra help in their journey.

When the Egyptians found out that they were gone, they informed Pharaoh. Allah mentioned, So Pharaoh sent into the cities (his) men to muster (people) saying,

IT'S ALL ABOUT ISLAM

Allah caused Musa and his followers to safely cross the Red Sea.

"These are a small band, and indeed they are enraging us. And we are a host, well-armed." Surat Ash-Shuaraa (The Poets) 26:53-56

Then Pharaoh arranged his army of spearmen, archers, charioteers, horsemen and foot soldiers and marched forth out of the city in pursuit of the fleeing Hebrews.

After several days of hard traveling, Musa led his people to an area of small, shallow lakes, just north of the Gulf of Suez. Perhaps they planned to thread their way through the narrow land corridors and enter Palestine secretly, but their plan was thwarted by Pharaoh's expert trackers.

In the distance, the Hebrews saw the huge dust cloud of an approaching army. Many panicked, and others cowered in fear, as their only escape route was blocked by water.

So they (the people of Pharaoh) pursued them (the people of Musa) at the time of sunrise. And when the two hosts saw each other, the companions of Musa said, "Surely we are overtaken." He said, "Never! Indeed with me is my Lord. He will guide me." My Lord is with me and He will give me guidance! Then Allah inspired Musa to hit the sea in front of them with his staff, and by a miracle of Allah, the waters parted, leaving a clear path across the bottom to the other side. Musa and Harun called to the people to run for their lives to the far shore, and they all did so. Surat Ash-Shuaraa (The Poets) 26:60-65

When Pharaoh and his army came upon the parted sea and saw the fleeing people, his arrogance pushed him to order his army in after them. He led the charge down into the corridor between the water, in full battle array.

After the last of Musa's people were safely on the other side, Allah sent the waves crashing down upon Pharaoh and his army, resulting in their death. Surat Ash-Shuaraa (The Poets) 26:65-67

With the help of Allah, Musa saved his people and brought the message of truth back to them. Along the way, he managed to convince quite a few Egyptians of Allah's truth as well. But now that the period of slavery was over, the real struggle was about to begin.

Questions to Answer

1. How did Pharaoh address Prophet Musa in their first meeting?
2. How did Prophet Musa answer him after Pharaoh listed all his favors given to him?
3. How did Prophet Musa describe Allah to Pharaoh?
4. What were two signs that Musa showed to Pharaoh?
5. What plan did Pharaoh's advisers come up with to defeat Prophet Musa?
6. Describe the match between the sorcerers and Prophet Musa.
7. What did the sorcerers do when the contest was finished, and what happened to them?
8. After Pharaoh threatened to kill the baby Hebrew boys again, how did the Hebrews respond to Musa in 7:127-129?
9. Who was Haman, and what did he do?
10. Who was Asyah, and what happened to her?
11. How did Prophet Musa escape with his people from Egypt?
12. How was Pharaoh's army defeated?

Define: Banu Isra'il, Hieroglyphics

Reflect: What are some lessons that you learned from this story? How do they relate to your life?

Act: Create a pictorial summary of the events described in this lesson. Avoid using or drawing human faces as Islamic traditions do not include making images of the prophets. The pictorial summary can be created using hand-made illustrations, print-outs from the internet, magazine cut-outs or a combination of all three.

IQ Builders:

1. Qarun, a wealthy Hebrew that worked for Pharaoh, came out and denounced Musa. What happens to him in 28:76-82?
2. Just before Pharaoh is drowned in the sea, he cries out. What does he say, and what does Allah say about it in 10:90-92?
3. What will happen to Pharaoh and his people on Judgement Day, according to 40:46-50?

25 The Wanderers

WHAT TO LEARN

Banu Isra'il wandered in the desert for years under the leadership of Prophet Musa. They disobeyed him at every turn, and only a few of them had true faith in Allah. It would take generations before they returned to the straight path.

VOCABULARY

Samiri   Tawrah
Al Khidr

THINK ABOUT IT

What problems did Musa encounter in leading Banu Isra'il?

From Egypt to the wilderness

A. Banu Isra'il and Musa

The Hebrews, or Banu Isra'il, were out of Egypt and safe from the hands of its rulers. Now what would they do? Prophet Musa was inspired by Allah to lead his people towards Mount Tur (also known in the West as Sinai) where he had received revelation the first time.

Along the way, problems were beginning to mount. As they passed near the lands of a small nation in the southern Sinai peninsula, Banu Isra'il noticed that idols were a part of the culture there. Allah said, We made the children of Isra'il cross the sea, then they came across a people sitting in devotion before their idols. They (the Israelites) said, "O Musa, make a god for us like they have gods." He said, "You are really an ignorant people. What these people are engaged in is sure to be destroyed and false is what they are doing." He said, "Shall I seek any one other than Allah as God for you, while He has given you excellence over the (people of all the) worlds." Surat Al A'raf (The Heights) 7:138-140

Within a few days, the huge group of people reached Mount Tur and began to settle themselves there. Prophet Musa put his brother Harun in charge and then went up the mountain with a few supplies to await the command of his Lord. (7:142) When Musa reached the sacred valley, called Tuwa, he made a small encampment and remained there for 40 days. After arriving, Musa asked of Allah a strange request.

When Musa came at Our appointed time and his Lord spoke to him, he said, "My Lord, show (Yourself) to me that I may look at You." He said, "You shall never see Me. But look at the mount. If it stays at its place, you will see Me." So when his Lord appeared to the mount, He made it smashed, and Musa fell down unconscious. When he recovered, he said, "Pure are You. I repent to You, and I am the first to believe (that no one can see You in this world)." He said, "Musa, I have chosen you above all men for my messages and for My speaking (to you). So, take what I have given to you, and be among the grateful." Surat Al A'raf (The Heights) 7:143-144

IT'S ALL ABOUT ISLAM

Prophet Musa ﷺ went up Mount Tur to await the command of his Lord.

Then Allah ﷻ explained to Musa ﷺ how he must lead the nation and instruct them. He also revealed laws to Musa ﷺ that he then carved onto thin stone slabs.

Finally Allah ﷻ revealed to him, Hold to these firmly, and order your people to follow as best they can these teachings. I will soon show you the final destination of the wicked. *Surat Al A'raf (The Heights) 7:145*

After receiving the laws of Allah ﷻ, Prophet Musa ﷺ gathered the small stone slabs and descended to where his people were camped. Allah's ﷻ last words to Musa ﷺ were that his people were being tested by **Samiri** سامِرِيّ, a man from the tribe of Banu Isra'il.

He (Allah) said, "We have then put your people to test after you (left them) and Samiri has misguided them." So, Musa went back to his people, angry and sad. He said, "O my people, did your Lord not promise you a good promise? Did then the time become too long for you, or did you wish that wrath from your Lord befalls you, and hence you broke your promise to me?" *Surat Ta-Ha 20:85-86*

B. The Golden Calf

When Prophet Musa ﷺ returned to his people, Allah's ﷻ warning was confirmed: Samiri had suggested to the people to make an idol of their own.

The people donated whatever jewelry, gold plates and serving vessels they had. They melted them in a fire and shaped it into the image of a small calf. Then they began to worship it. Only a few people realized it was a shameful thing to do. (7:148-149)

When Musa ﷺ came back into the camp and saw what was going on, he put the stone tablets down and then grabbed his brother Harun ﷺ by the hair.

When Musa returned to his people, angry and sad, he said, "How bad is the thing you have done in my absence! How did you act in haste against the command of your Lord?" He dropped down the tablets and grabbed the head of his brother, pulling him towards himself. He (Harun) said, "My mother's son, the people took me as weak and were about to kill me. So do not let the enemies laugh at me, and do not count me with the wrong-doers." *Surat Al A'raf (The Heights) 7:150*

Prophet Musa ﷺ addressed the people, saying, "My People! Didn't your Lord make a great promise to you? Did the promise seem far off, or did you wish for the wrath of your Lord to be upon you, and so you broke your promise to me?"

They replied, "We didn't break our promise to you as far as we could hold it. We were made to carry the ornaments of the people and throw them in the fire. This is what the Samiri told us to do. Then he made the image of a calf that seemed so crude."

167

Then (he and his followers) said, "This is your god and the god of Musa, but Musa has forgotten." Surat Ta-Ha 20:86-89

Musa asked Samiri why he did it, to which Samiri replied that his inner-self suggested that he do this. Musa ordered him banished from the camp. Then he melted the calf-idol down into small bits and sent people to throw the remnants of it into the sea. (20:95-97)

Musa immediately began to pray for Allah's forgiveness for himself and his brother. (7:151) Afterwards, he took up the tablets again and began to teach the people the laws that Allah made for them. (7:154)

Prophet Musa then chose 70 representatives from Banu Isra'il, and they gathered on Mount Tur to ask Allah's forgiveness for the rest of the people. The mountain quaked and Musa begged for forgiveness. Finally, Allah granted it after explaining that His mercy is stronger than His anger. (7:155-156 & 2:54)

C. The Rebellion against Prophet Musa

Prophet Musa then led the people away in the direction of Palestine. However, along the way, the people began to grumble and complain about the hardships of traveling. (2:61)

The mountain quaked when Banu Isra'il gathered on Mount Tur to ask Allah's forgiveness.

Prophet Musa had divided up the people into 12 tribes so that they could be better organized. When the leaders of the 12 tribes complained about the lack of water, Allah inspired Prophet Musa to hit a large rock with his staff, and 12 springs gushed out. (7:160)

When Allah commanded them to sacrifice a cow to show obedience to Him, they were so reluctant that it was clear they weren't genuine believers yet. (2:67-71)

Also along the way, Banu Isra'il entered several towns and disobeyed Prophet Musa's instructions about how to behave. (2:58-59) They broke the rules whenever Prophet Musa ordered them to obey Allah, and they made his task of leadership a difficult one. (7:161-166)

D. Musa and Al Khidr[4]

Prophet Musa, though an honored prophet, made mistakes. Once, after the leaders of Banu Isra'il had given him a particularly hard time, he stood up among them and said, "Who is the smartest man among the people? I am the smartest!"

Because Musa didn't say that Allah was the most knowledgeable of all, Allah led

---

[4] In this story, hadith from the Al Bukhari collection and the story from Surat Al Kahf (The Cave), number 18 in the Qur'an, are combined as the two complement each other.

him on a quest to learn wisdom. Allah told him to go to the coast of the Red Sea where it meets the Gulf of Aqaba and the Gulf (of modern day Suez) and look for a person there who was more learned than even he.

Prophet Musa asked Allah, How can I find him? Allah instructed, take a fish in a basket, and you will find him where you lose that fish. So Musa set out with his servant-boy Yusha' on the mysterious journey to find the wisest man in the world.

Musa said to his servant, "I won't give up (my search for the wise man) until I reach the meeting of the two seas, or until I've traveled for years!"
And when they reached the place where the two seas met, the servant forgot about the fish (they brought for lunch). It (miraculously) shot straight into the water (and got away).
After they traveled on further, Musa said to his servant, "Bring us our meal, for we have been traveling hard."
But the servant answered, "Didn't you see what happened when we rested on the rocks (by the sea)? I forgot to tell you about the fish. Only Shaytan could have made me forget to tell you. The fish jumped into the sea in a miraculous way!"
Musa cried, "That was the (sign) we were seeking." Then they retraced their path back (to where they were before).
There, they found one of Our servants on whom We (Allah) placed mercy from Us, and who received much knowledge from Us. *Surat Al Kahf (The Cave) 18:60-65*

Musa said to him, "Let me follow you so that you can teach me something about the truth you have learned." The man (whose name was **Al Khidr** الخضر) replied, "You certainly won't be able to have patience with me! And how can you have patience with things you don't fully understand?" He (Musa) said, "You will see, if Allah wills, that I will be patient. I won't disobey you at all." He (Al Khidr) replied, "If you want to follow me, then ask me no questions about anything until I myself tell you about it." *Surat Al Kahf (The Cave) 18:66-70*

So, they both moved ahead, until when they boarded a boat, he sliced it (by removing one of its planks). He (Musa) said, "Did you damage it in order to drown everyone on board? This is a strange thing you have done!"
He (Al Khidr) replied, "Didn't I tell you that you wouldn't have patience with me?" He (Musa) said, "Don't scold me for forgetting, and don't give me a hassle over this, please." Then they traveled on land until they met a young boy. But he (Al Khidr) killed him right away. He (Musa) cried, "Have you killed an innocent person who has killed no one? What a horrible thing you've done!" He (Al Khidr) answered, "Didn't I tell you that you wouldn't have any patience with me?" He (Musa) replied, "If I ever ask you about anything again, don't let me follow you anymore, and you would have full right to leave me." *Surat Al Kahf (The Cave) 18:71-76*

Then they traveled until they came to a small town. When they asked the townspeople for food, they refused to give them any. (Al Khidr and Musa) then saw an old wall that was crumbled and falling down. But he (Al Khidr) went and fixed it. He (Musa) commented, "If you wanted to, you could have asked the people here for payment for doing that work."

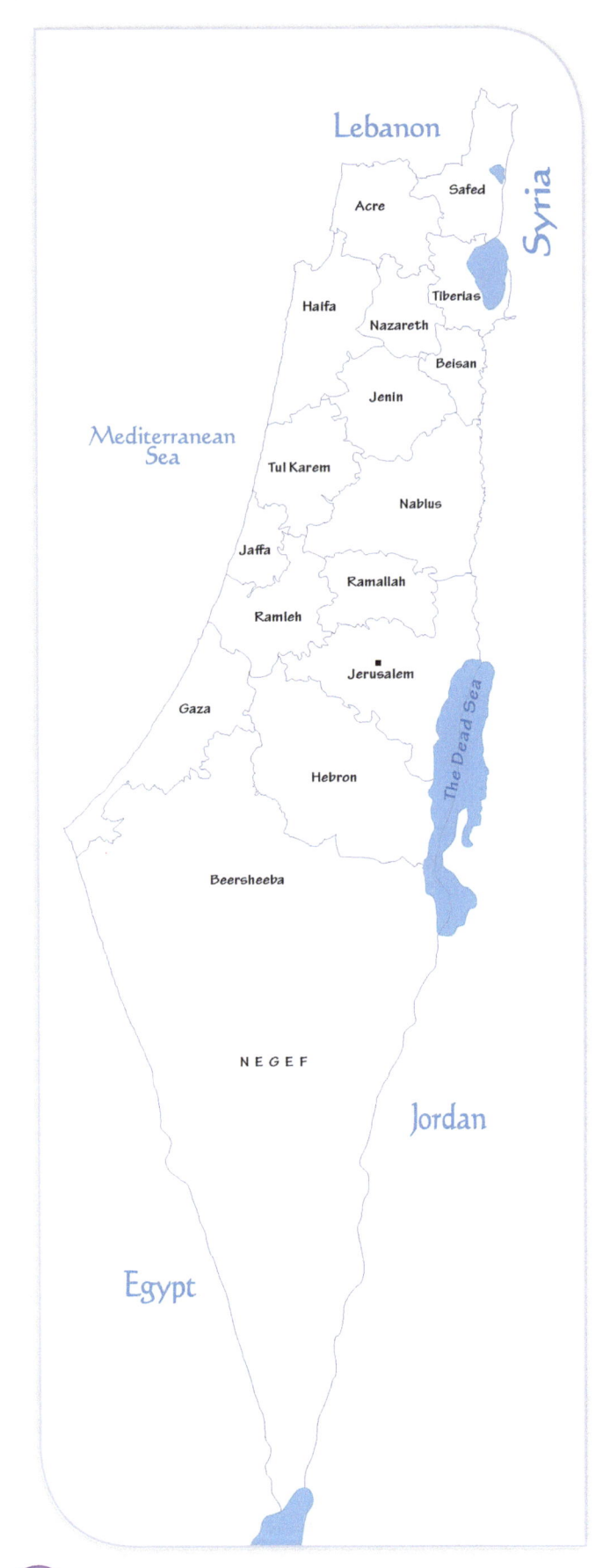

He (Al Khidr) answered, "This is where we separate. Now I'll tell you the meaning of all those things you couldn't be patient about. As for the boat, it belonged to some poor men who made their living by the sea. I only wanted to make it defective because there was a certain king coming their way who seized every boat by force. As for the young man, his parents were believers (in Allah), and we were afraid that he would sadden them with his rebellious and bad behavior. So we wanted their Lord to give them a better child in exchange who was more pure and loving. As for the wall, it belonged to two orphans in the town. Under it was a buried treasure that was meant for them. Their father was a good man, so your Lord wanted them to grow up and find their treasure, as a Mercy from your Lord. I didn't do it for me. This is the meaning of what you had no patience with." Surat Al Kahf (The Cave) 18:77-82

E. Prophet Musa's Legacy

The Blessed Prophet Musa led his people to the threshold of Palestine. There he commanded them to attack a mighty city of idol-worshippers whom Allah had decided to punish. Allah reminded them that he had sent them prophets in the past and that they were now living like kings since they were no longer slaves. Then he commanded them to enter the Holy Land promised to the descendants of Prophet Ibrahim.

But Banu Isra'il were afraid to fight, and they told him they would never go into battle unless the evil people left. Musa sent two scouts to look for weaknesses in the city's walls. Soon enough, they returned with news of a weak gate that would be easy to attack and lead to an easy victory.

They said, "O Musa, we shall never enter it, in any case, so long as they are there. So go, you and your Lord, and fight. As for us, we are sitting right here." He said, "O my Lord, I have no control except over myself and my brother. So, make a distinction between us and the sinning people." He (Allah) said, "This (land) is prohibited to them for forty years. They shall be wandering around the earth. So, do not grieve for the sinning people." Surat Al Ma'idah (The Table Spread) 5:24-25)

Allah ﷻ then declared that Banu Isra'il would be forbidden to enter the Holy Land of Palestine for 40 years. Prophet Musa ﷺ then led his people back into the desert.

For 40 years, he bore the brunt of their rebelliousness. But given their spiritual condition, they fell below Allah's ﷻ standards of being true servants. Wandering in the desert functioned as a training camp for them and as a crash course in obedience to the Truth.

Prophet Musa ﷺ recorded the **Tawrah** تَوْرَاة **Laws**, which consisted of Allah's ﷻ rules for them and for any prophets who would come later. By the time Prophet Musa ﷺ passed away, the leaders of Banu Isra'il were mature enough to call themselves an organized nation. They entered Palestine in about 1200 BCE and dwelled in a civilized fashion.

Masjid and tomb of Prophet Musa ﷺ, located on the side of the road from Jerusalem to Jericho.

People of the Book! (Jews and Christians). Now there has come to you Our Messenger (Muhammad), who is revealing to you a lot that you used to hide in the book (you had before) and passing over a lot (of things that are now unnecessary). There has come to you from Allah a (new) light and a clear book. Surat Al Ma'idah (The Table) 5:15

﴿يَٰٓأَهْلَ ٱلْكِتَٰبِ قَدْ جَآءَكُمْ رَسُولُنَا يُبَيِّنُ لَكُمْ كَثِيرًا مِّمَّا كُنتُمْ تُخْفُونَ مِنَ ٱلْكِتَٰبِ وَيَعْفُوا۟ عَن كَثِيرٍ ۚ قَدْ جَآءَكُم مِّنَ ٱللَّهِ نُورٌ وَكِتَٰبٌ مُّبِينٌ﴾ ﴿سُورَةُ المَائِدَة 5:15﴾

The mission of Banu Isra'il was to call surrounding nations to the worship of Allah ﷻ and to be an example to others. (5:12) Unfortunately, Banu Isra'il did not fulfill this responsibility. (2:75-77, 5:44-45)

Not only did they fail to fulfill their mission, but Banu Isra'il also rejected and killed other prophets sent to them from Allah ﷻ (5:70). They even started to write their own books and said that they were revelations from Allah ﷻ. (2:87-90) Their own tribal history, collected in the Bible, witnesses their wrong doing. (See in the Bible: Jeremiah 7:6-7 or Mathew 23:13-39, for example)

By about the year 900 BCE, Banu Isra'il began calling themselves 'Jews,' after one of their kingdoms, called 'Judah.' Today, many Jews claim to follow the legacy of the Prophet Musa ﷺ, but many of them fall far short of his example. (2:83-85) Many even claim that they are God's chosen people, and so they shy away from calling others to the Truth. (2:94-96) They also believe that God will not punish them in the afterlife. (7:169)

For following laws and practices that no prophet or messenger ever taught (2:91), and for not worshipping Allah ﷻ, Allah ﷻ says He will

punish them in the afterlife. (7:169) They earned the wrath of Allah ﷻ for their disobedience, Recall when your Lord declared that He would surely keep sending to them, till the Day of Judgement, those who inflict on them evil chastisement. Certainly, your Lord is swift in punishing, and certainly He is the Most-forgiving, Very Merciful.
Surat Al A'raf (The Heights) 7:167

Little of Prophet Musa's ﷺ original message survives today. Only a few of the descendants of Banu Isra'il have remained pure and followed the truth. (2:121) Those who are fortunate discover Islam and study it with an open heart. Then they become our Muslim brothers and sisters. Only then do they truly follow in the footsteps of the Blessed Prophet Musa ﷺ. (42:13, 4:153-155)

Questions to Answer

1. What custom did Banu Isra'il want to imitate after leaving Egypt and why?
2. Why did Prophet Musa ﷺ lead the people to Mount Tur?
3. What happened when Musa ﷺ asked to see Allah ﷻ?
4. What did Allah ﷻ give Prophet Musa ﷺ to take back to the people?
5. Who was the Samiri, and what did he do?
6. How did Banu Isra'il seek forgiveness from Allah ﷻ for what they had done?
7. Who was Al Khidr, and why did Musa ﷺ want to see him?
8. What were the three lessons which Al Khidr showed to Prophet Musa ﷺ?

Define: Tawrah.
Reflect: Sometimes Allah ﷻ teaches us meaningful life lessons through difficult experiences that we encounter as we grow up. What is one instance in which you learned a meaningful life lesson through your own difficult experience?
Act: Investigate at least five similarities and differences between Judaism and Islam using reliable sources.

IQ Builders:

1. Find one example from surat 2 that was not used in this chapter that highlights the shameful way Banu Isra'il treated Prophet Musa ﷺ as he led them in the desert. Explain the example and give the ayah references.
2. What does 5:70-71 say about the Jews in their conduct towards Allah ﷻ?
3. How does 61:5 describe what the Jews did to Musa ﷺ?

Literature Selection

Banu Isra'il and Musa ﷺ

From *Sahih Al Bukhari*

In the Name of Allah, The Most Gracious, The Most Merciful

The following story clearly illustrates the rebellious attitude of Banu Isra'il towards their Prophet ﷺ.

Abu Huraira ؓ narrated that the Prophet ﷺ said, "The (people of) Banu Isra'il used to take bath naked (all together) looking at each other. The Prophet Musa used to take a bath alone. They said, 'By Allah! Nothing prevents Musa from taking a bath with us except that he has a scrotal hernia.' So once Musa went out to take a bath and put his clothes over a stone and then that stone ran away with his clothes. Musa followed that stone saying, 'My clothes, O stone! My clothes, O stone!,' till the people of Banu Isra'il saw him and said, 'By Allah, Musa has got no defect in his body.' Musa took his clothes and began to beat the stone. Abu Huraira added, 'By Allah! There are still six or seven marks present on the stone from that excessive beating.'" (Al Bukhari)

عَنْ أَبِي هُرَيْرَةَ ؓ، عَنِ النَّبِيِّ ﷺ قَالَ: «كَانَتْ بَنُو إِسْرَائِيلَ يَغْتَسِلُونَ عُرَاةً، يَنْظُرُ بَعْضُهُمْ إِلَى بَعْضٍ، وَكَانَ مُوسَى يَغْتَسِلُ وَحْدَهُ، فَقَالُوا وَاللَّهِ مَا يَمْنَعُ مُوسَى أَنْ يَغْتَسِلَ مَعَنَا إِلَّا أَنَّهُ آدَرُ، فَذَهَبَ مَرَّةً يَغْتَسِلُ، فَوَضَعَ ثَوْبَهُ عَلَى حَجَرٍ، فَفَرَّ الْحَجَرُ بِثَوْبِهِ، فَخَرَجَ مُوسَى فِي إِثْرِهِ يَقُولُ ثَوْبِي يَا حَجَرُ. حَتَّى نَظَرَتْ بَنُو إِسْرَائِيلَ إِلَى مُوسَى، فَقَالُوا وَاللَّهِ مَا بِمُوسَى مِنْ بَأْسٍ. وَأَخَذَ ثَوْبَهُ، فَطَفِقَ بِالْحَجَرِ ضَرْبًا». فَقَالَ أَبُو هُرَيْرَةَ وَاللَّهِ إِنَّهُ لَنَدَبٌ بِالْحَجَرِ سِتَّةٌ أَوْ سَبْعَةٌ ضَرْبًا بِالْحَجَرِ." رَوَاهُ الْبُخَارِيُّ

26 Sulayman and Balqees

WHAT TO LEARN

When a person thinks they know the truth, they act in a certain way. If a person is unsure of what to believe, but still keeps an open mind, they may be able to find the right way.

VOCABULARY

Talut Saba'
Jalut Dawud

THINK ABOUT IT

How did Sulayman show Balqees that only Allah should be served?

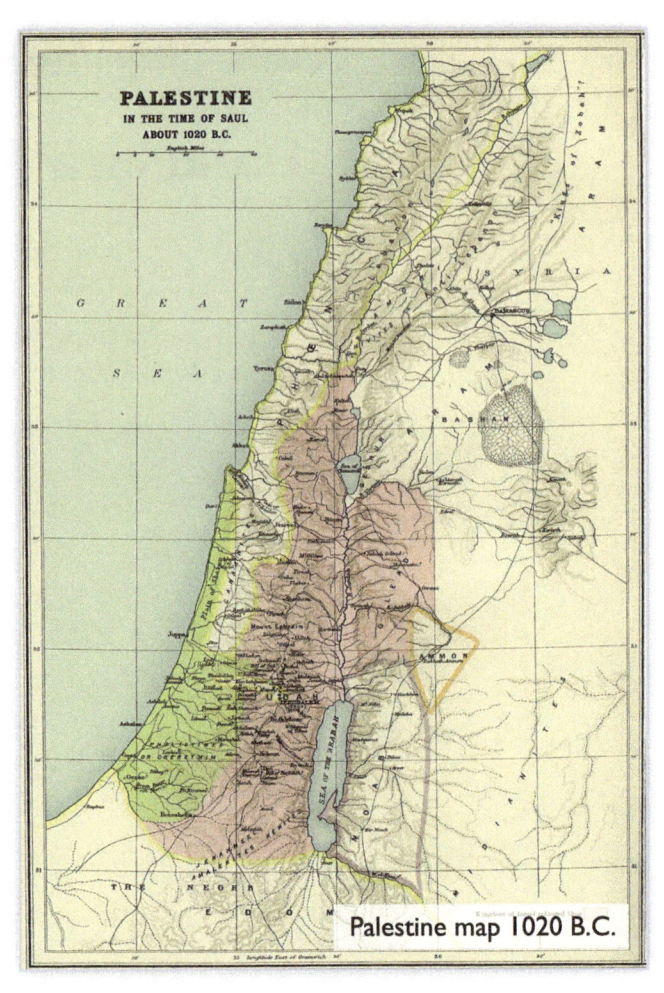

Palestine map 1020 B.C.

A. The Kingdom of Isra'il

Allah granted the descendants of Prophet Musa and Banu Isra'il a country of their own in ancient Palestine, which was then called Canaan. (10:93) They named it 'Isra'il.' Allah took the pledge of Banu Isra'il that they would obey His laws and be a light and guide to other nations, calling them to the truth.

In order to make their own nation, Banu Isra'il had to fight off many others. Allah sent them prophets to guide them, but they gave as much trouble to those prophets as their forefathers had given to Prophet Musa. (16:124)

Finally, in about the year 1020 BCE, a local prophet chose **Talut** طَالُوت, a poor young man, to be their king. It was not that Allah wanted them to have a king, rather they themselves demanded to have one because all the other surrounding nations had one too. (2:246) So Allah granted them one as a test.

When their prophet announced that Talut was to be king, they grumbled more, as he was poor and not influential. They agreed to follow him, however, after much argument. (2:247-248)

Talut proved to be an able leader and a military genius. He defeated the Canaanites in many battles and forged a powerful, though small, army.

In one decisive battle, the Canaanites brought out a man named **Jalut** جَالُوت who was tall, strong and fearless. (2:249-250)

He was able to easily defeat many soldiers from Banu Isra'il and caused Talut's army to lose hope.

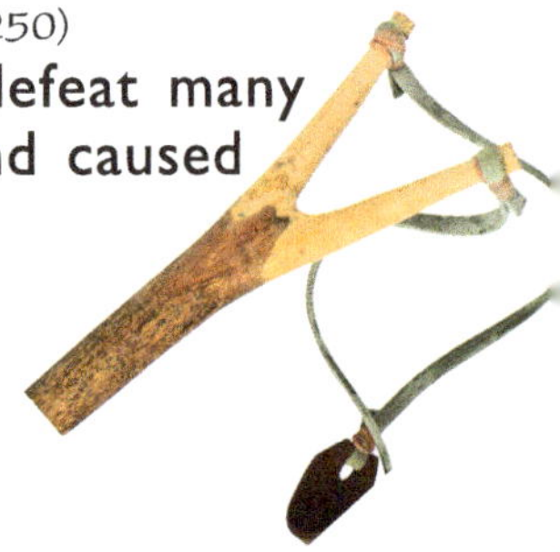

Finally, Allah ﷻ inspired **Dawud** داود ﷺ, a brave young man, to come forward and face the menacing warrior. With a slingshot, Dawud ﷺ knocked the giant warrior to the ground and then killed him with a sword. The army of Talut then defeated the enemy and carved out a secure country. (2:251)

After Talut passed away, Dawud ﷺ was made king. In addition, Allah ﷻ granted him the Zabur and made him a prophet. He proved to be fair and just and a brilliant general who drove his enemies further away. (21:80)

One interesting episode illustrates the wisdom of Dawud ﷺ and his young son, Sulayman ﷺ. Once, a man came and complained that his neighbor's sheep had come into his field and ruined some of the crops. At first, Dawud ﷺ ordered that the man could keep the sheep that wandered onto his land as compensation for the damages.

But Sulayman ﷺ, who, as the son of a ruler, usually attended the public forums, offered a solution that was more equitable. He suggested that the man keep the sheep only until he was compensated for his loss. So, after taking wool, milk, and baby lambs equal to his loss in crops, he would then return the original sheep to his neighbor. This way, both sides received their fair shares.

And (remember) Dawud (David) and Sulayman (Solomon), when they were adjudicating about the tillage in which the goats of other people wandered at night (and trampled it), and We were witness to their Judgement. So, We enabled Sulayman to understand it. And to each one of them We gave wisdom and knowledge. And with Dawud We subjugated the mountains that pronounced tasbeeh (Allah's purity) and the birds as well. And We were the One who did (it).
Surat Al Anbiya' (The Prophets) 21:78-79

B. Who Was Sulayman ﷺ?

After Prophet Dawud ﷺ passed away in 961 BCE, his son, Sulayman ﷺ, became king. He was to be the last righteous ruler of Banu Isra'il. Because of his piety and wisdom, Allah ﷻ was to make him a prophet as well.

During his reign, the nation of Banu Isra'il grew strong and powerful. Sulayman ﷺ called his people to obey Allah ﷻ, and he sent messages to other nations inviting them to the service of the One God.

After the end of his rule, at about 922 BCE, Banu Isra'il quickly fell into dispute and made divisions among themselves. They failed to keep their pledge to Allah ﷻ and sought worldly power over the rewards of the next life.

Within years, Banu Isra'il divided their nation into two different countries: Judah in the south, and Isra'il in the north. Their division made it easier for foreign enemies to attack them.

In 721 BCE, the Assyrians conquered Isra'il, and in 587 BCE, Judah fell to the Babylonians. Banu Isra'il lost their nation and their ways, and their set of beliefs evolved into what is modern-day Judaism. (4:51-55)

The Judaism of today has lost much of the real message that was given to the ancient prophets. One of the most powerful was Prophet Sulayman because of the gifts that Allah gave him.

C. The Power of Prophet Sulayman

Prophet Sulayman was given many special abilities from Allah. He was granted the power to understand the signals, or "speech," of birds and other animals, and he could even control the spirit-creatures known as jinn.

And Sulayman inherited (the traits of) Dawud and said, "O people we have been taught the speech of birds, and all sorts of things are given to us. Indeed, this is the evident grace (of Allah)." And mustered for Sulayman were his forces from among the jinns and the humans and the birds. So all of them were kept under (his) control. Surat An-Naml (The Ants) 27:16-17

Prophet Sulayman could understand the language of animals, including ants.

Once, while his army was marching, he passed through a valley with many ant-hills. Allah tells us that the ants warned each other to get in their holes so they wouldn't be stepped on by Prophet Sulayman's army! (27:18)

Sulayman heard the ants and laughed. Then he prayed to Allah, and thanked him for the power He gave him. He said, "My Lord! Direct me so that I may be thankful for Your favors, which You have given me and my parents, and that I may do the good things that please You. Admit me, by Your grace, to the ranks of Your righteous servants." Surat An-Naml (The Ants) (27:19)

D. The Hoopoe Bird Speaks

One day, Prophet Sulayman was inspecting his birds when he noticed one of them was missing. He asked for it and declared that the bird would be punished if it didn't offer a good excuse. (27:20-21)

The bird, called **Hudhud** هُدْهُد **Hoopoe**, eventually arrived with interesting news. It had found a country far to the south that was unknown to Sulayman, called **Saba'** سَبَأ. The land was ruled by a woman with a magnificent throne. The location of the Saba' kingdom is believed to have been in Ethiopia and Yemen.

The Hoopoe continued saying, "I found her and her people worshipping the sun besides Allah. Shaytan has made their deeds seem pleasing in their eyes, and has kept them away from the Path. Thus, they haven't received the guidance that they should serve only Allah. Who brings to light what is hidden in space and the Earth, and knows what you hide and what you reveal. Allah! There is no god but He! Lord of the Throne Supreme!" Prophet Sulayman said, "We shall see if you are telling the truth or a lie. You go with this letter of mine to them. Then wait for their reply." Surat An-Naml (The Ants) 27:22-28

E. The Queen of Saba'

The letter was tied to the bird's leg, and it flew south over the Arabian desert until it landed several days later in the palace of Queen Balqees, ruler of Saba'. She opened the letter and had someone translate it for her. When she heard its message, she immediately called for her advisors to be brought.

She announced to them, "My nobles! Here is a letter delivered to me that is worthy of considering. It is from Sulayman and says, 'In the Name of Allah, The Most Gracious, The Most Merciful. Don't be too proud towards me, but come to me in surrender (to Allah only).'"
Then she asked her advisors, "Nobles! Give me advice in this decision of mine. I never decide anything except in your presence."
They said, "We are a mighty nation and can wage terrible war. But the orders come from you, so think about what to command."
She said, "When kings enter a country, they ruin it and make the best of its people the worst. That's how they behave. But I'm going to send him a present, and then I'll wait and see what my ambassadors have to say when they return." Surat An-Naml (The Ants) 27:29-35

F. The Jinn and the Righteous Servant

Queen Balqees's ambassadors traveled north until they reached Jerusalem, the capital of Isra'il. When they approached Sulayman in his audience chamber, they laid gold and treasures at his feet.
But Sulayman was a Prophet of Allah, one not to be swayed by jewels or bought off with fancy rings. He told them, "Are you going to bring me a pile of wealth? What Allah

Balqees lived in the city of Saba', known today as the city of Marib.

already gave me is better than what He gave you. You are the ones who are happy with your gift." Surat An-Naml (The Ants) 27:36

Sulayman, thinking that those people were trying to buy him off, declared, "Go back to (your leaders), and be sure we will come to them with powerful forces they will never be able to match. We will expel them in disgrace, and they will feel humbled." Surat An-Naml (The Ants) 27:37

The ambassadors left in a hurry, and returned home with the news. When she received Sulayman's message, Queen Balqees knew drastic action was needed to save her land.
She decided to go personally to Jerusalem and meet with Sulayman and try to make a peace treaty with him. Perhaps, she realized, the biggest difference between herself and him was in spiritual beliefs. He worshipped Allah, while she worshipped the sun. She would meet him face to face.
When Sulayman was informed that the Queen of Saba' was coming herself for a visit, he knew he had to move carefully. He wanted her and her people to give up idol worship, so he needed some demonstration of the power of Allah.
Then he remembered something the Hoopoe told him. In his court, Sulayman called out, "O chieftains, which one of you will bring her throne to me before they

come to me submissively?" A stalwart of the jinn said, "I will bring it to you before you rise up from your place, and for this (task) I am powerful, reliable." Said the one who had the knowledge of the book, "I will bring it to you before your glance returns to you." So when he saw it (the throne) well placed before him, he said, "This is by the grace of my Lord, so that He may test me whether I am grateful or ungrateful. Whoever is grateful is grateful for his own benefit, and whoever is ungrateful, then my Lord is Need-Free, Bountiful." Surat An-Naml (The Ants) 27:38-40

G. The Meeting with Balqees

The throne was brought to Prophet Sulayman, all the way from Yemen, so quickly that it seemed like magic. The Queen knew nothing about it, as she was already on her journey northward.

Sulayman ordered his people to alter the throne and disguise it so it didn't look like her chair. He remarked that this would be her test to see if she could receive guidance.

A few weeks later, Queen Balqees arrived in Jerusalem with her caravan. She was brought to the audience chamber of Sulayman, and he asked her, "Is this your throne?"

She looked at it for a moment and said, "It was just like this!" Then she realized the power of Sulayman as Allah's prophet, and declared her submission to Allah.

She was given the great honor of entering the main palace of the city. When Sulayman brought her to the front gates and opened them up, Queen Balqees thought there was a shallow lake inside, for the floor was translucent and shimmered.

She tucked up her skirt in her hand, uncovering her legs, and was about to step in, when Sulayman told her, "This palace is paved with smooth glass."

At that moment, she fully realized the lesson of her disguised throne; namely, that things are not always as they seem. Her people saw the powerful sun in the sky and thought it was a god; she saw glass and thought it was water. In both cases, it was an error. She declared, "My Lord! I have wronged my soul. I surrender (to You) with Sulayman, to the Lord of the Universe." Surat An-Naml (The Ants) 27:42-44

H. The Legend of Sulayman

Prophet Sulayman was powerful and wise. He had great armies and extended his influence over many nations. He could ask Allah to calm stormy weather for him and it would be done. (21:81)

He built huge temples and palaces and other fortifications in his kingdom. He had the power to command the jinn to work for him, and they helped in the construction of arches, pillars, basins and giant cauldrons.

The Blessed Prophet Sulayman passed away while he was sitting on his throne, before the work was completed. But his body still sat upright and was balanced on his staff. The jinn thought he was still alive and completed their work.

A model of the temple of Prophet Sulayman in Jerusalem.

If they would have known that he had passed away, they would have stopped and fled, for they considered working for humans humiliating. What signalled to them his death was that a small worm had gnawed into his staff and unbalanced his body, causing it to topple over. (34:14) By this time, the work was already finished. The jinn did indeed feel humiliated and fled away.

One legend tells of a very mischievous jinn that Prophet Sulayman imprisoned in a lamp and set adrift in the ocean. From this legend comes the story of Aladdin and the Magic Lamp.

Another legend tells of secret treasure caves in East Africa where Sulayman hid piles of gold and silver. Many explorers have risked their lives searching for the lost mines of Sulayman.

Despite all the legends, one thing remains clear: Prophet Sulayman was one of the mightiest rulers the world has ever seen. Yet, people must look past his glory and treasures into the most valuable message of all: obtaining the pleasure of Allah. Submitting to His will is the only real treasure worth possessing.

Questions to Answer

1. How did Sulayman find out about the land of Saba'?
2. Who was Balqees, and how did she respond to Sulayman's letter?
3. What test did Sulayman give to Balqees when she arrived?
4. What made Balqees finally realize the truth of Allah's message?

Define: Jalut, Saba.

Reflect: When the jinn found out that Prophet Sulayman passed away, they stopped working. Think about the jinn's behavior and how it relates to the following questions: How do you behave when no one is watching? Do you do everything you are supposed to? Do you skimp and just do the surface duties? Do you leave everything because no one will catch you? How should you behave when no one is watching? Are you truly ever alone? Why or why not?

Act: Develop a plan for how you will monitor your progress towards an Islamic goal. Share this plan with a friend, and ask them for suggestions on how to improve it. Then begin implementing the plan from today onwards to help you achieve your goal.

IQ Builders:

1. What objections did Banu Isra'il raise over the selection of Talut as their king, according to 2:247?
2. What test did Talut give his army in 2:249?

27 Master of the Two Horns

WHAT TO LEARN

Sometimes Allah ﷻ tests rulers with some unique situations. History is full of rulers who were evil, but there were also rulers who were good. Can you think of any from your history lessons?

VOCABULARY

Dhul Qarnayn   **Cyrus the Great**

THINK ABOUT IT

How did Dhul Qarnayn react in each situation and why?

Can you see how Cyrus's empire formed two 'horns' with the Fertile Crescent and Persia in the middle?

A. Who Was Dhul Qarnayn?

The Holy Qur'an mentions the story of a very interesting ruler named **Dhul Qarnayn** ذو القَرْنَين **Master of the Two Horns** who is given as an example of a wise ruler. This title refers to the fact that his empire consisted of two great areas of territory that arched outwards in the shape of two horns.

Muslim scholars have long guessed at his true identity but no firm agreement has yet been made. Some say he was Alexander the Great, who lived from 356 BCE to 323 BCE. But that is highly unlikely, since Alexander was not a known believer.

This ruler, as he is mentioned in the Qur'an, is described as righteous and aware of Allah ﷻ. The only clues we have to his identity are that he controlled two large areas of land that formed the shape of a horn and that he built a wall to stop invading barbarian tribes.

Most scholars today are of the opinion that this mighty ruler was **Cyrus the Great** of Persia who ruled around 549 BCE. His first conquest was over the Lydians. Lydia was located in modern-day Turkey. Next, he defeated the Chaldeans in the Fertile Crescent and allowed all captive peoples, including the Jews, to return to their homelands.

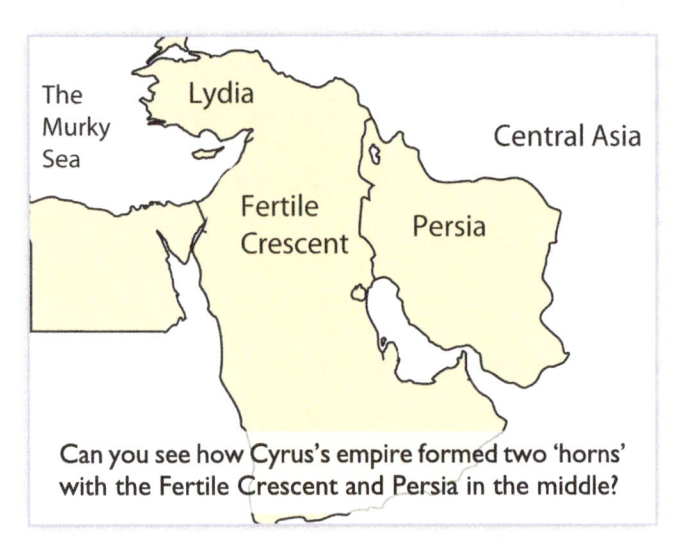

Finally, he conquered vast swaths of territory in Central Asia. Thus his empire formed the shape of two large 'horns.' Cyrus was killed in battle in 529 BCE by a fierce nomadic tribe in the east. During his reign, he proved to be a just man. In his story are lessons about how to fear Allah ﷻ and to deal with power and its responsibilities.

B. The Tests of Dhul Qarnayn

The Jews of Al Madinah often tried to trap the Blessed Prophet Muhammad ﷺ. In order to embarrass him, they would ask him about things that they felt he didn't know the answer to so that they could prove he was not a real Prophet of Allah ﷻ. But Allah ﷻ protected His Prophet and revealed the stories that the Jews asked about. One of these stories is about Dhul Qarnayn.

As Allah ﷻ said, (The Jews) ask you, (Muhammad) about Dhul Qarnayn. Tell them, "I will narrate to you something of his story." We (Allah) established his power on Earth and gave him the ability and knowledge to travel. He followed one direction (with his army) until he reached the setting of the sun. He found that it set behind a sea of murky water. Surat Al Kahf (The Cave) 18:83-86

The scholars have identified this dark sea as being most probably off the coast of Turkey, where the water is indeed colored with a dark hue. Another possible dark sea is a large lake named Ochrida in Asia Minor, which is fed by springs. The water is dark and murky in this 170 square mile lake.

Dhul Qarnayn saw the sun falling behind the western horizon of the dark water and made camp.

Near it, he found a community of people. We said, Dhul Qarnayn! (You can either) punish them or treat them with kindness. He decreed, "Whoever does wrong shall be punished. Then he will be sent back to his Lord; and He will punish him with a terrible punishment. But whoever believes and works righteousness, he shall have a goodly reward, and his work will be easy as we order it by our command." Surat Al Kahf (The Cave) 18: 86-88

Dhul Qarnayn's first test was in how he would treat these people who had no real laws.

These were, perhaps, the Lydians. He decided to give them laws and to fairly rule them by this code.

Then he followed (another) road, until he came to the rising of the sun. He found it rising on a people for whom We had provided no covering protection against the sun. (He left them) as they were. We completely understood what was before him. Surat Al Kahf (The Cave) 18:89-91

From Asia Minor (Turkey), he journeyed deep into Central Asia to the East, in the direction of the rising sun.

So his second test related to the treatment of people who were not educated or well civilized. They lived perhaps in the northern reaches of the Fertile Crescent, and because they did not know how to make shelters, they slept under trees and possibly in caves. Dhul Qarnayn could have easily enslaved them, but instead he chose to leave them alone.

C. The Yajuj and Majuj

Then he followed (another) way (north into Central Asia) until he reached (a valley) between two mountains. There he found beneath them a people who scarcely understood a word (of his own language). They (managed to get their message across) saying, "Dhul Qarnayn! The Yajuj and Majuj (people) cause chaos in the land. Can we pay you tribute in order that you might build a wall between us and them?" He said, "(The power) which my Lord has established me in is better (than tribute). Just help me with your strength (and labor). I will build a strong wall between you and them. Bring me blocks of iron." After a while passed, his men finished filling up the narrow pass between the two steep mountain-sides. Then he commanded, "Blow (with your bellows and melt the iron)." When it (became as red) as fire, he ordered, "Bring me molten lead so I can pour it over top." Surat Al Kahf (The Cave) 18:92-96

The wall was soon finished. The people in the valley were afraid of two barbarian tribes, the **Yajuj** يَأجُوج and **Majuj** مَأجُوج, who periodically invaded and plundered the land. They convinced Dhul Qarnayn to build a wall to keep the invaders out.

You can imagine the terror of the people when they saw the dust clouds of the approaching armies in the distance. Would Dhul Qarnayn's wall hold?

After repeated attacks, the barbarians were unsuccessful. Because this was the only pass through the mountains for many miles, the invaders were effectively sealed on the other side for good.

Thus the (Yajuj and Majuj invaders) were made powerless to scale it or to dig through it. Dhul Qarnayn said, "This is a mercy from my Lord. But when the promise of my Lord comes to pass, He will make it into dust, and the promise of My Lord is true." On that Day, We (Allah) will leave them (the barbarians) to surge like waves, one over another. The trumpet will be blown, and We shall collect all (humans) together. And We shall present Hell that Day for Unbelievers to see, all spread out. (Unbelievers) whose eyes had been under a veil from Remembrance of Me and who had been unable even to hear. Surat Al Kahf (The Cave) 18:97-101

D. The Sign of the Last Day

This famous wall does exist, and its ruins are located in northern Central Asia. There are many different walls there, strung throughout the Caucasus mountains, and any one of them could be the iron wall in question. One such wall, whose ruins lie in a valley about 150 miles southeast of the city of Bukhara, has long since lost much of its iron due to rust.

The seventh century Chinese traveler Hiouen Tsiang reports seeing this huge iron wall with a gate near a place called Derbend. In Arabic this walled valley was named **the Iron Door** بابُ الحَديد.

The Muslim khalifa Wathiq, who ruled from 842-846 CE, sent a team to Central Asia to report on this wall mentioned in the Qur'an. The explorers found it in a valley that was about 150 yards wide. It was supported by two huge jambs and was made of iron bricks welded together with lead. Two huge gates of iron were placed in the middle of the wall. This was reported in the year 985 CE by the famous Muslim geographer Muqaddasi.

One prophecy that Dhul Qarnayn made was that the wall would only last for so long, and then it would be gone. (18:98) When the barrier is no longer there, the invaders from the other side will surge over the land and cause great destruction.

Some scholars are of the opinion that the Russians and Chinese are the Yajuj and Majuj. This cannot be proven, but it does make for interesting discussion.

In any case, Dhul Qarnayn passed his third test by helping a people in need of protection against a terrible and cruel enemy. He didn't ask for any money from them except that they also help in the construction of the defensive wall.

With his example, we can see that a ruler must establish justice, not be a tyrant over weaker people and help those in need without forcing them to pay anything in gold and riches. How many of the rulers in our modern world could pass these tests?

Travel through the Earth and see how Allah began the creation. So, too, will Allah produce creation again because Allah has power over all things. Surat Al 'Ankabut (The Spider) 29:20

﴿قُلْ سِيرُوا فِي الْأَرْضِ فَانْظُرُوا كَيْفَ بَدَأَ الْخَلْقَ ثُمَّ اللَّهُ يُنْشِئُ النَّشْأَةَ الْآخِرَةَ إِنَّ اللَّهَ عَلَىٰ كُلِّ شَيْءٍ قَدِيرٌ﴾ سورة العنكبوت 29: 20

Questions to Answer

1. What does the term Bab al Hadid mean?
2. Summarize how explorers described the iron wall in their reports.
3. What were the three tests Dhul Qarnayn was given?
4. What is one of the signs of the Day of Judgement?
5. Where are the ruins of the iron wall located?
6. Who was Khalifa Wathiq?

Define: Dhul Qarnayn, Yajuj and Majuj.

Reflect: What are some lessons learned from this story?

Act: Dhul Qarnayn did not expect anything in return from the people he helped. Choose one injustice that you would like to do something about. Begin this quest by writing a letter to a representative from your local government, explaining the injustice and a possible solution to it. Remember to do this with a pure intention, seeking only the pleasure of Allah ﷻ. Find your state representatives' contact information on the web.

IQ Builder: Summarize the message of the following ayaat 6:19-20.

Unit 06 Review Exercise

VOCABULARY REVIEW

On a separate sheet of paper, write the definition of each word below.

1. Madyan
2. Asyah
3. Hebrews
4. Nile River
5. Pharaoh
6. Haman
7. Hieroglyphics
8. Banu Isra'il
9. Samiri
10. Khidr ﷺ
11. Talut
12. Balqees
13. Jalut
14. Dawud ﷺ

REMEMBERING WHAT YOU READ

On a separate sheet of paper, answer the following questions. Use complete sentences in your answers.

1. How did the descendants of Yusuf ﷺ and his people become slaves in Egypt?
2. What were some powers Allah ﷻ gave to Prophet Sulayman ﷺ?
3. Why did Musa ﷺ have to leave Egypt as a young man?
4. Describe how Musa ﷺ was made a Prophet of Allah ﷻ.
5. How did Musa ﷺ escape Egypt with his people and the other believers?
6. What happened to Pharaoh and the Egyptian army?
7. Why did Musa ﷺ have to follow Al Khidr?
8. Why did many of the Jews dislike Talut?
9. Who was the Samiri, and what did he do?
10. How did Balqees become a believer?

THINKING TO LEARN

On a separate sheet of paper, answer the questions below. Use complete sentences.

1. Summarize two ways in which the Prophet Musa ﷺ tried to guide Banu Isra'il and how they reacted to him in both situations.
2. Analyze the three tests that were given to Dhul Qurnayn. First, summarize each test. Then, describe what aspect of Dhul Qurnayn's character was being tested by it. Finally, using references from the Qur'an and the lessons in your book, describe how Dhul Qurnayn responded to each test.
3. Choose a story from one of the prophets described in this unit. Describe three ways in which the lessons from that prophet's time relate to your personal life?

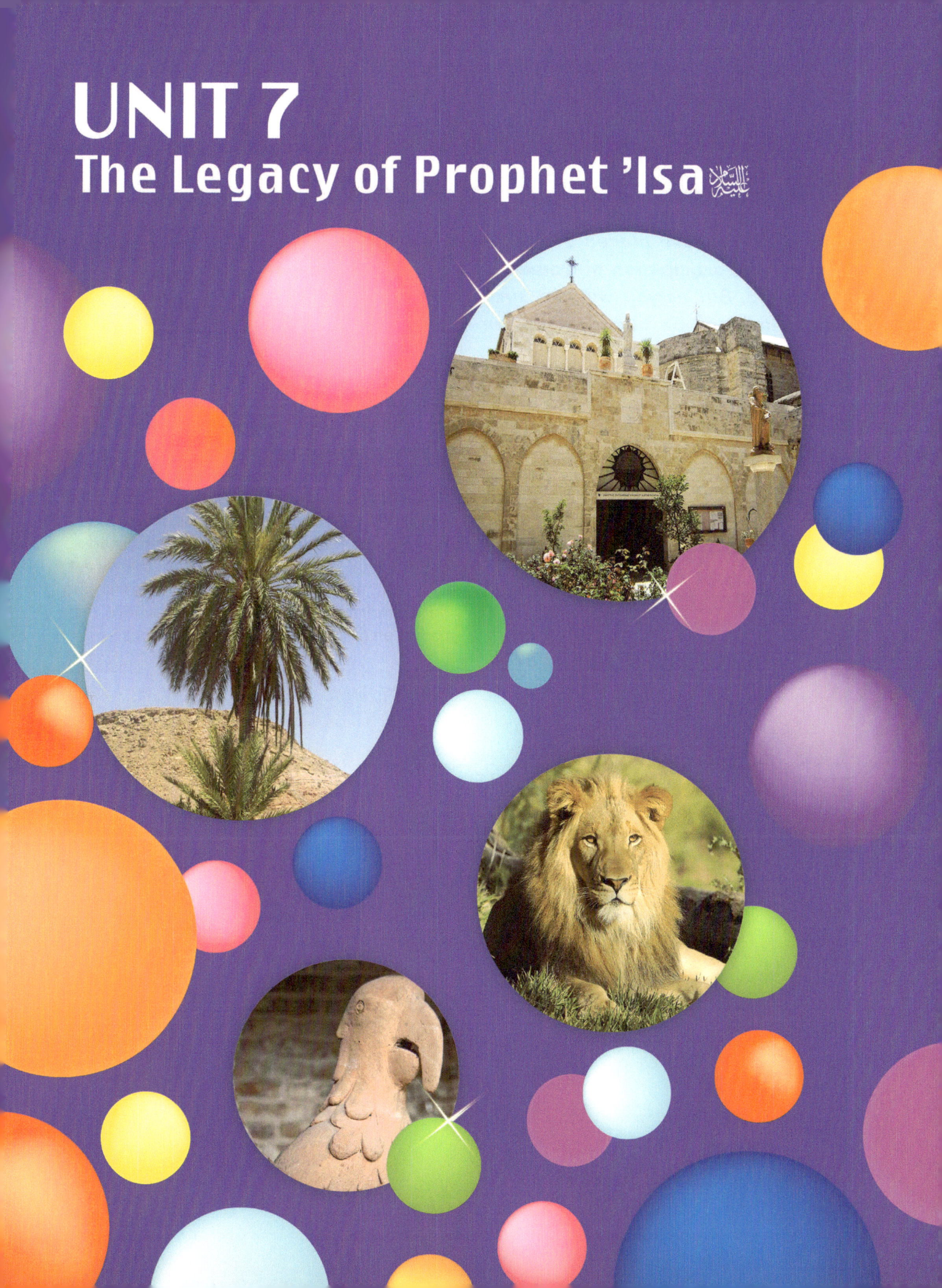

UNIT 7
The Legacy of Prophet 'Isa ﷺ

28 The Family of 'Imran

WHAT TO LEARN

Many societies have placed a smaller value on the participation of women in spiritual life. But as you will see, such faulty beliefs can be turned around in unimaginable ways.

VOCABULARY

Rabbi
Uzayr
Synagogues
'Imran

THINK ABOUT IT

How did Allah ﷻ bless two women with the most wonderful of gifts?

A. The Power of Rome

The year was 20 BCE in the Western calendar. One empire ruled supreme over all others in the Mediterranean region: Rome. At the height of its power, the Roman Empire controlled all of Egypt, North Africa, Western Europe and the Middle East up to Mesopotamia.

Each of the areas controlled by Rome was divided into provinces that were controlled by local governors who answered only to the Roman emperor, Augustus Caesar.

At that time, Palestine was a mosaic of different peoples and ethnic groups. There were Arabs, Jews, Syrians, Phoenicians, Romans and many other ethnicities. The Jews returned to Palestine in 540 BCE after Cyrus the Great, a Persian king, conquered Mesopotamia. He permitted them to leave Babylon, where they had been held prisoner for generations.

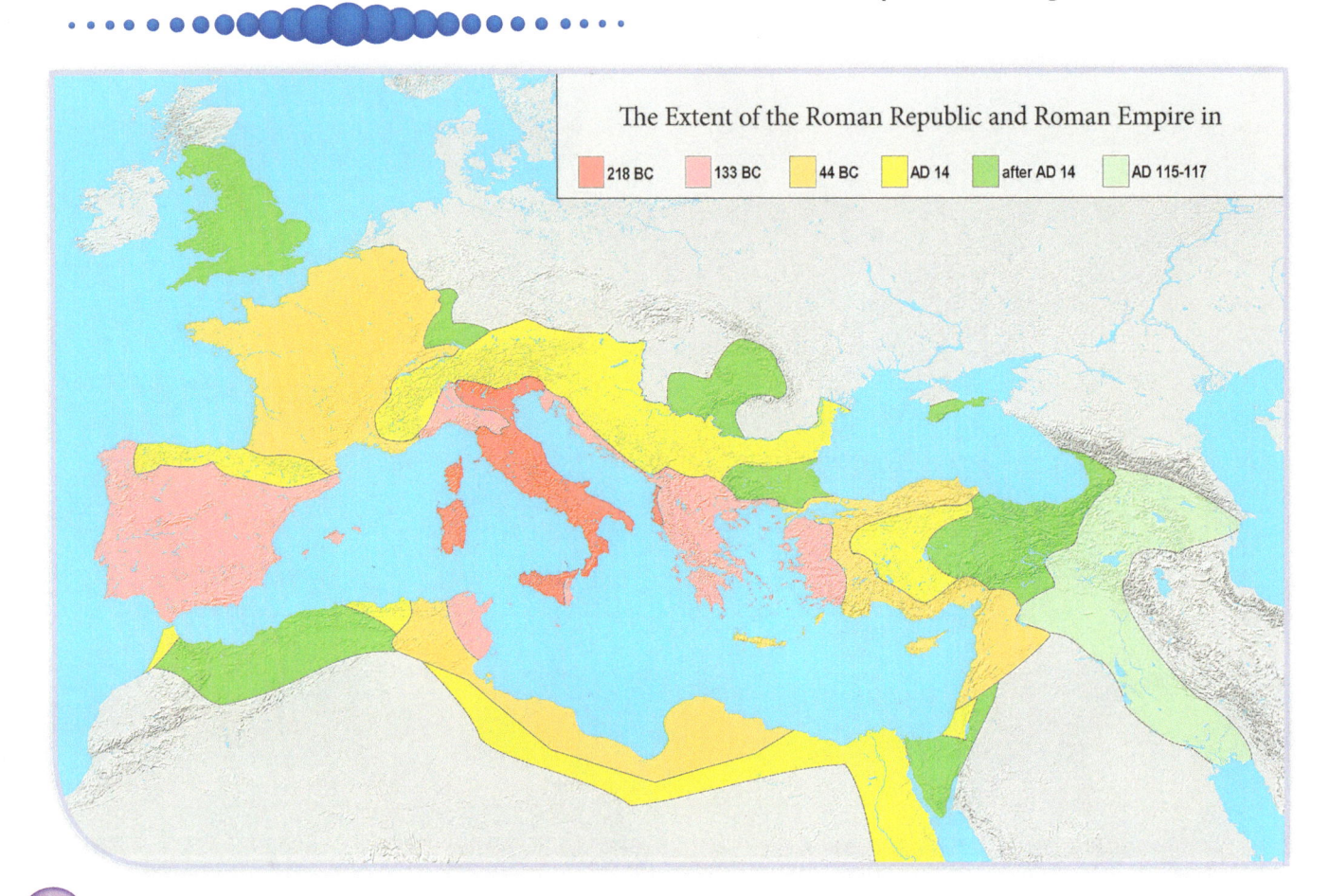

The Extent of the Roman Republic and Roman Empire in

| 218 BC | 133 BC | 44 BC | AD 14 | after AD 14 | AD 115-117 |

Although the Jews had lost their religious writings when their nations of Judah and Isra'il were crushed, a priest by the name of **Uzayr** عُزَيْر **Ezra** tried to recapture the original writings. He called this book the "Tawrah," which was the same name that Allah ﷻ had given to the book of Prophet Musa ﷺ. (3:78)

Of course, it wasn't an accurate book, nor was it the real Tawrah, for it contained only scattered fragments of the original writings. But Uzayr, who had the authority of the Persian kings behind him, ordered all Jews to follow it, which they did. (9:30)

The Jews governed themselves for the next few centuries, giving nominal allegiance to the Persian Empire. In about 200 BCE, however, the Jews fought Syrian invaders in a battle called the Revolt of the Maccabees. The Jews were brutal but successful and continued as a semi-independent nation.

But the invasion of the mighty Romans after 100 BCE was too much for any small nation to repel. Although the Jews tried to fight off the Roman invaders in several different battles, most notably at a hill-top fortress named Masada, they were eventually crushed and had to live as just another conquered people in the Roman empire.

In 70 BCE, as a punishment to the rebellious Jews, the Romans burned Jerusalem to the ground and destroyed the temple that was built by Prophet Sulayman ﷺ so many years before. The Jews would not occupy Jerusalem again until 2,018 years later.

B. The Importance of the Priesthood

Without the benefit of a temple to unite the Jews, the **Rabbis** الأحْبار **Scholars** assumed the local spiritual leadership. But the Jews disputed how to perform their religious duties. After all, they didn't even have their original revelations any longer, so it was easy to fall into disagreements. (3:19-20)

The two main groups who opposed each other were the Sadducees and the Pharisees. Each group had its own understanding and interpretation of the religion. But regardless of the differences, the priesthood became the most important institution in the life of the scattered Jewish communities. (62:5-6)

Synagogues مَعْبَدٌ يَهُودِيّ were set up as a gathering place for men to read their religious writings and to chant prayers. Because women were considered unclean, they were rarely ever allowed to go to the synagogue or even to touch religious scrolls.

The priests held such power over their people that they could make whatever laws they deemed fit. (5:78-79) As Allah ﷻ declared, They have taken their rabbis and their monks as gods beside Allah, and also (they have taken) Masih the son of Maryam (as god). And they were not commanded but to worship only One God. There is no god but He. Pure is He from what they associate with Him. Surat At-Tawbah (The Repentance) 9:31

﴿ اتَّخَذُوٓا۟ أَحْبَارَهُمْ وَرُهْبَٰنَهُمْ أَرْبَابًا مِّن دُونِ ٱللَّهِ وَٱلْمَسِيحَ ٱبْنَ مَرْيَمَ وَمَآ أُمِرُوٓا۟ إِلَّا لِيَعْبُدُوٓا۟ إِلَٰهًا وَٰحِدًا لَّآ إِلَٰهَ إِلَّا هُوَ سُبْحَٰنَهُۥ عَمَّا يُشْرِكُونَ ﴾ سُورَةُ التَّوْبَةِ 9: 31

Most of the revelations given to Prophets Ibrahim, Musa and Dawud were lost for good. Uzayr compiled a version from tradition and the collective cultural memory of his people.

C. A Mother's Prayer

Although many Jews had diverted from the straight path, the Qur'an clearly states that there were some who remained sincere to God. (2:250-251, 5:69) One of these spiritually sincere Jews was an expectant mother whose husband had recently passed away. In secret, she prayed to Allah with a very unique request.

She prayed: *"O my Lord, I have vowed that what is in my womb will be devoted exclusively for You. So, accept (it) from me. You, certainly You, are the All-Hearing, the All-Knowing."* Surat Al 'Imran (The Family of 'Imran) 3:35

She was a member of a very important household of the priestly class. Some of the most influential priests came from this family, including a high priest named **'Imran** عِمْران, a descendant of prophet Harun. (3:33-34) So naturally, this pious woman asked Allah to help make her child a priest as well.

Females could never be rabbis in Judaism, as that position was only reserved for men, so you can imagine her disappointment when she gave birth to a baby girl.

So, when she delivered her, she said, "O my Lord, I have delivered her, a female child." And Allah knew better what she had delivered, and the male was not like the female, "I have named her Maryam, and I place her and her progeny under Your shelter against Satan, the rejected." Surat Al 'Imran (The Family of 'Imran) 3:36

D. The Guardian

Because the new mother was a widow, a male relative had to, by custom, be appointed to provide her and the baby with financial support. Accordingly, the older men were assembled and they drew lots to see who would have to support the mother and baby, though none of them wanted the extra expense. (3:44)

The draw fell on Zakariyya, and thus, upon his shoulders came this responsibility. Yet, he was no ordinary relative. Zakariyya was a prophet of Allah—what better person to help raise the baby Maryam?

As time passed and Maryam grew older, she would spend more and more time in Zakariyya's home. He was tutoring her, giving her religious lessons that no one else would. Even though she was a girl, and was forbidden by Jewish custom to study such topics, Zakariyya was a true follower of Allah and didn't succumb to discrimination.

Zakariyya was old and had no children, but he was very poor. He didn't always have enough extra money to buy food for his wife and Maryam. Then a miraculous thing began to happen. Zakariyya would visit Maryam in her study chamber, and he would find that there was already food there!

Mihrab, Umayyad Masjid - Damascus.

So, her Lord accepted her, a good acceptance, and made her grow, a good growth, and made Zakariyya her guardian. Whenever Zakariyya visited her at the place of worship, he found food with her. He said, "Maryam, from where did you have this?" She said, "It is from Allah. Surely, Allah gives to whom He wills without measure." Surat Al 'Imran (The Family of 'Imran) 3:37

Zakariyya saw what a good and wholesome young girl Maryam was, and he began to long for a child of his own. What also pained him was the lack of faith of his relatives in Allah's teachings and commandments.

E. Yahya Is Born

Zakariyya prayed to Allah in secret. "My Lord!" he said, "My bones are weak and my hair is gray, but I am always blessed in my prayer to You. My Lord, now I'm afraid of what my relatives will do after me. But my wife is barren, so grant me an heir from Yourself. One that will truly represent me and the legacy of Ya'qub. Make him, My Lord, someone You will be pleased with." Surat Maryam (Mary) 19:3-6

So then, when he stood praying in the place of worship, the angels called out to him saying: "Allah gives you the good news of Yahya who shall come to confirm a word of Allah and shall be a chief, abstinent (from women), a prophet and one of the righteous." Surat Al 'Imran (The Family of 'Imran) 3: 38-39

He (Zakariyya) replied, "My Lord! How can I have a son when I am old and my wife is barren?" The angel replied, "So it will be that Allah does what He wishes." He answered, "My Lord! Give me a sign." The angel replied, "Your sign will be that you won't be able to speak to anyone for three days, except through hand motions. So celebrate the praises of your Lord over and over, and glorify Him at night and in the morning." Surat Al 'Imran (The Family of 'Imran) 3: 40-41

Then Zakariyya came out of his chamber and told the people, by hand gestures, to praise Allah in the night and in the morning. (19:11)

To everyone's astonishment, Zakariyya's wife soon gave birth to a healthy baby boy. He was named 'Yahya,' or 'life' because he was a life granted by Allah.

The boy grew up in wisdom and knowledge, under the careful guidance of his father Zakariyya. Later, when the young man began to receive revelation, Allah told him, Yahya! Take hold of the book (Allah's revelations) firmly! Surat Maryam (Mary) 19:12

As Allah tells us, He gave Yahya wisdom, even as a boy, and made him feel kindness towards all living things. He was pure, devout, kind to his parents and not arrogant. (19:13-14)

But the roads of Maryam and Yahya would not end there. Both would grow up as true believers and play a large role in the coming of the next major messenger from Allah.

Grave of Prophet Yahya, also known as John the Baptist, inside Omayyad Masjid.

IT'S ALL ABOUT ISLAM

سُبْحَانَ اللَّهِ وَبِحَمْدِهِ سُبْحَانَ اللَّهِ الْعَظِيمِ

Questions to Answer

1. How were the Jews able to leave Persia and return to Palestine?
2. Who was Uzayr (Ezra) and what did he do? What did some of the Jews of Al Madinah say about him according to 9:30?
3. Who were the Rabbis and what control did they have over their people?
4. Why was Maryam's mother surprised when she gave birth to a girl?
5. Why did Prophet Zakariyya want a son of his own?
6. Who was Yahiya and what kind of child was he while growing up?

Define: Synagogue, 'Imran.

Reflect: Think about a time when you really wanted something, but did not receive it. Reflecting on this, do you think there was any good that came out of the situation?

Act: Uzayr compiled a version of the Tawrah from his personal memory and the collective memory of his people. In order to understand how this approach can result in mistakes, even from a well-intentioned person, do the following exercise: In 10 minutes or less, write down a short story from your personal life, trying to include as many details as possible. Then, take turns reading your story to another student in your class. Afterwards, write down what you remember from your peer's story. Share what you have written with your peer, and see how much of it you accurately recorded. How many details did you remember correctly? How many details did you get wrong? How does this relate to the possible limitations of Uzayr's version of the Tawrah?

IQ Builders:

1. What call does Allah make to the Jews in 3:64?
2. How does Allah describe the parents of Yahya in 21:90?

29 The Struggle of Maryam

WHAT TO LEARN

Allah shows his power over all things in many miraculous ways. What are some of the ways Allah shows us his majesty with Maryam and 'Isa?

VOCABULARY

Prophet 'Isa   Masih

THINK ABOUT IT

How did Prophet 'Isa try to bring Bani Isra'il back into true faith in Allah?

A. Maryam's Quest

Maryam grew to be a very spiritual young woman. She knew her duty to Allah, and always tried to be sincere. When her guardian, Prophet Zakariyya, passed away, Maryam was left on her own.

Although Prophet Zakariyya had secretly taught her spiritual knowledge, she could never hope to be a priest or teacher, because she was a woman. In the corrupted religion that her people practiced, women were not allowed to even touch the holy books. Additionally, the people around her knew very little of the truth and instead practiced all kinds of superstitions and cultural practices. (2:102)

Seeing all the lies and hypocrisy from those around her, Maryam must have been in despair. The good teachings of Prophet Musa were being hopelessly twisted, and the priests were fighting over meaningless issues. Many of them didn't live like good examples themselves. (5:63, 66)

No Women! Keep Out!

I found one upright man among a thousand, but not one upright woman among them all. (Ecclesiastes 7:1)

A woman should learn in quietness and full submission. I do not permit a woman to teach or to assume authority over a man; she must be quiet. For Adam was formed first, then Eve. And Adam was not the one deceived; it was the woman who was deceived and became a sinner. (1 Timothy 2:11-14)

To the woman he said, "I will greatly increase your pains in childbearing; with pain you will give birth to children. Your desire will be for your husband, and he will rule over you." (Genesis 3:16)

Then the angel who was speaking to me came forward and said to me, "Look up and see what is appearing."
I asked, "What is it?"
He replied, "It is a basket." And he added, "This is the iniquity of the people throughout the land."
Then the cover of lead was raised, and there in the basket sat a woman! He said, "This is wickedness," and he pushed her back into the basket and pushed its lead cover down on it. (Zechariah 5:7)

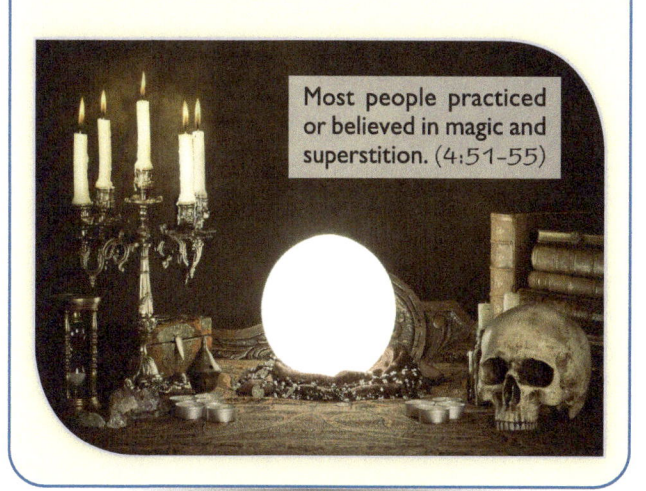

Most people practiced or believed in magic and superstition. (4:51-55)

As Allah ﷻ tells us, Maryam ؏ was a pure woman who avoided sin and bad behavior. (66:12) She left the area to worship Allah by herself. Her cousin, Yahya ؏, had already left and was trying to understand the purpose of his life. She, too, felt obliged to do the same.

And when the angels said, "O Maryam, Allah has chosen you and purified you and chosen you over the women of all the worlds. O Maryam, stand in devotion to your Lord and prostrate yourself and bow down in ruku' with those who bow." Surat Al 'Imran (The Family of 'Imran) 3:42-43

B. The Journey of Faith

Relate in the book (the story of) Maryam when she left her people and traveled to a place in the East. She built a lean-to (a half-tent) to screen herself from passing (people). Then, We (Allah) sent Our Angel to her, and he seemed to her like a man in all respects. She cried out, "I ask the protection of the Merciful from you. (Stay away) if you fear Allah." Surat Maryam (Mary) 19: 16-18

Maryam ؏ was alone, trying to meditate, when all of a sudden she saw a man approaching her tent. She called on Allah's ﷻ name to ward the stranger off. Little did she know, the stranger was sent from Allah himself.

Remember the time when the angels said, "O Maryam, Allah gives you the good news of a Word from Him whose name is Masih 'Isa, the son of Maryam a man of status in this world and in the Hereafter, and one of those who are near (to Allah). He shall speak to people while (he is still) in the cradle, and also later, when he is of mature age, and he shall be one of the righteous." She said, "O my Lord, how shall I have a son while no human has ever touched me?" Said He, "That is how Allah creates what He wills. When He decides a matter, He simply says to it 'Be,' and it comes to be." Surat Al 'Imran (The Family of 'Imran) 3:45-47

Imagine Maryam's ؏ surprise at this momentous news. Allah ﷻ chose her to have a son who would be a sign from Allah ﷻ! Before departing, the angel informed her that her son's mission would be to call Bani Isra'il back to true faith. (3:49) The very thing she had hoped for and dreamed of.

C. The Birth of 'Isa ؏

The angel "breathed" into her a ruh from Allah ﷻ, and soon she began to show signs of pregnancy. Before anyone could question her about it, she packed up her few belongings and retreated into a more remote and secluded place. (19:22 and 23:50)

And the pains of childbirth drove her to the trunk of a palm tree. She cried out (in her anguish), "Oh! If only I died before this! If only I was no more—gone!" But (a voice) cried out to her from beneath her, "Don't panic, for your Lord has provided a trickle of water below you.

Shake the trunk of the palm tree and fresh dates will fall on you. Eat and drink and cool your eyes. If you see any person, tell them, "I have promised a fast to the Merciful and won't talk to anyone today."
Surat Maryam (Mary) 19: 23-26

Maryam ﷺ gave birth to a healthy baby boy. She named him **'Isa** عِيسَى **Jesus**, just as the angel had told her before. He was to be the **Masih** مَسِيح **Anointed One**.

After resting and nursing the baby for a time, she realized that she couldn't raise him on her own. He had to grow up in a community and learn the knowledge of his faith and people.

She decided to return home, after being gone for nearly two years. But how would she be welcomed? How could she explain what had happened to her? Her relatives were decent people and members of the priestly class. Surely they would understand—after all, she grew up among them, and they knew her honesty well.

When she brought the baby to her people, carrying him, they shouted at her, "Maryam! What a strange thing you have brought! Sister of Harun! Your father wasn't a bad man, nor was your mother a loose woman." Surat Maryam (Mary) 19: 27-28

Her relatives were shocked, and immediately started to accuse her of committing a sin. They even reminded her that she was a descendant of the house of Harun and that she brought shame on the whole family. Maryam ﷺ stood mute. She was overwhelmed that they would turn on her, after she went through the most holy and wonderful experience. She was shocked and stunned. (4:156) She couldn't open her mouth to speak in the face of their accusations and insults.

So, she pointed towards him (the baby). They said, "How shall we speak to someone who is still a child in the cradle?" Surat Maryam (Mary) 19:29

Then something wondrous happened—the baby began to speak.

The infant 'Isa said loudly, "I am a servant of Allah! He has given me revelation and made me a prophet. He has made me blessed wherever I am, and has made prayer and charity my duty as long as I live. He has made me kind to my mother, and not defiant. Peace is on me the day I was born, the day that I die, and the day I will be raised to life again." Surat Maryam (Mary) 19:30-33

The people around Maryam ﷺ were speechless. No one would question Maryam ﷺ again, and no one would bother her. Allah ﷻ eased her transition back home.

IT'S ALL ABOUT ISLAM

$$رَبِّ إِنِّي ظَلَمْتُ نَفْسِي فَاغْفِرْ لِي$$

Questions to Answer

1. Why was Maryam﷦ perhaps a little dissatisfied with living in her village?
2. What two groups of priests were always having conflicts with each other?
3. Why did Maryam﷦ leave her home?
4. What did an angel announce to Maryam﷦ one day in her small camp?
5. How did Allahﷻ make her experience easier when she was in pain and afraid?
6. How did Maryam's﷦ people react to her when they saw the baby?
7. How did Allahﷻ protect Maryam's﷦ honor and make the people accept her again?

Define: Masih, 'Isa.

Reflect: There are many ways to find peace and tranquility when you are surrounded by chaos. What are some ways that you try to find peace?

Act: Maryam﷦ chose to retreat to a quiet place, away from the chaos of her town. Choose a quiet spot in your home, school, outdoors or a library. The place should have limited people and no distractions, including any technology. For at least 10 minutes, sit in the quiet and reflect on Allah'sﷻ signs and blessings all around you. Afterwards, write down some of the thoughts that came to you during this moment of peacefulness and the effect this had on you.

IQ Builder: How does Allahﷻ describe Maryam﷦ in 21:91?

30 The Message of the Injeel

WHAT TO LEARN

Prophet 'Isa ﷺ was sent to call the Jews back to true faith in Allah ﷻ. Most of his people rejected his message. Those who accepted it spread some of his teachings to non-Jews. In time, Prophet 'Isa's ﷺ message was changed and mixed with the beliefs of many idol-worshipping customs.

VOCABULARY

Injeel
Gospel
Disciple
Scripture

THINK ABOUT IT

How do Prophet 'Isa's ﷺ own teachings compare with what others claim about him?

A. The Early Years of 'Isa ﷺ

When 'Isa ﷺ was a child, he grew up under the care of his mother, Maryam ﷺ. He was good to her and always obeyed her wishes. He had a good teacher in his mother as she had been trained by Prophet Zakariyya ﷺ when she was young.

Christian tradition teaches that Maryam ﷺ married a man named Joseph before the baby was born and that 'Isa ﷺ grew up learning the carpentry trade. Yet this story is not supported by any Qur'anic or written historical evidence, so Muslims don't share the same version of 'Isa's ﷺ life.

We do know, from the Qur'an, that Prophet Yahya ﷺ was traveling throughout Palestine and announcing to people that a new messenger from Allah ﷻ was about to come. This unusual news made the Jewish king, Herod, suspicious. His power lay in keeping his Roman overlords pleased by maintaining order. Prophet 'Isa ﷺ had barely begun his mission when Herod ordered Yahya ﷺ to be arrested and killed.

B. The Message Begins

Allah ﷻ began sending revelations to Prophet 'Isa ﷺ when he was nearly 30 years old, instructing him to call the spiritually lost Jews back to a more godly way of life. (3:46) Prophet 'Isa ﷺ then began to travel from village to village, teaching his message of love, justice and true sincerity to God.

Because many of the people he met disbelieved in his call, Allah ﷻ granted him many miracles to impress them.

And (shall make him) a messenger to the Children of Isra'il (who will say to them), "I come to you with a sign from your Lord, that is, I create for you from clay something in the shape of a bird; then I blow in it, and it becomes a living bird by the will of Allah, and I cure the born-blind and the leper, and I cause the dead to become alive by the will of Allah, and I inform you of what you eat and what you store in your homes." Surat Al 'Imran (The Family of 'Imran) 3:49

He took some clay and shaped it into the form of a bird. Miraculously, the clay bird became real and flew away. (5:110)

Later, he was granted the ability to heal sick people and those who suffered from blindness. 'Isa ﷺ was even able to revive people who were thought to have just died. You would think that as he traveled performing these miracles that everyone would believe.

Quite the contrary occurred, though.

Most people dismissed 'Isa as nothing more than a magician. (5:110) Here is an example of one of his public statements:

"I have come to you to confirm the Tawrah, which came before me, and to make allowed some things that were forbidden to you before. I have come to you with a sign from your Lord, so fear Allah and obey me. It is Allah Who is my Lord and your Lord, so serve Him! This is the straight way." Surat Al 'Imran (The Family of 'Imran) 3:50-51

Everywhere he went, he preached using either sermons or parables, which were revealed to him through revelation. His message, which is called the **Injeel** الإنجيل **Gospel (A Proclamation of Good News)**, was meant for Bani Isra'il to listen to and accept. (5:46)

C. The Disciples of Prophet 'Isa

Soon it became very difficult for 'Isa to carry on his mission alone. He went from place to place, preaching. It was hard for him to handle the crowds of people who came to either learn from him or curse at him.

He prayed to Allah to send him help, because most people did not believe him or his teachings. Thereafter, he began to recruit people who would serve as his close **Disciples** حواريون those who would help him in his mission.

'Isa looked for disciples who would commit to spreading the truth about Allah among the people. When he had recruited a good number of them, he took their oath of service.

So, when 'Isa sensed disbelief in them, he said, "Who are my helpers in the way of Allah?" The disciples said, "We are helpers of Allah. We believe in Allah so be our witness that we are Muslims." Our Lord, we have believed in what You have revealed, and we have followed the messenger. So, record us with those who bear witness (to the Truth)." Surat Al 'Imran (The Family of 'Imran) 3:52-53

With the added help, Prophet 'Isa was able to organize better. He spread his disciples among crowds to answer everyone's questions. In time, many more people were won over to the persuasive message and truly surrendered their wills to their Lord.

Once, when the spiritual strength of the disciples was weak, they asked Prophet 'Isa for a special miracle.

When the disciples said, " 'Isa, son of Maryam! Can your Lord send to us a table spread (with food) from Paradise?" 'Isa replied, "Be aware of Allah if you are believers." They said, "We only want to eat from it and satisfy our hearts and to know that you have indeed told us the truth, and so that we may witness the miracles ourselves. So 'Isa, the son of Maryam, prayed, "Oh Allah our Lord! Send to us from Paradise a table spread (with food) so that there will be enough for all of us. A sign from You. Provide for us and You are the best of Providers." Surat Al Ma'idah (The Table) 5:112-114

We can well imagine that perhaps the disciples were tired from their traveling, and maybe had a lack of faith for a moment. But Allah revealed to 'Isa, I will send it to you, but if any of them reject (faith) after this, I will punish him with a penalty like I have never inflicted on anyone in the Universe. Surat Al Ma'idah (The Table) 5:115

D. The Plot Against Prophet 'Isa

Some of the leaders of the Jews were angry with Prophet 'Isa for teaching people that their religion had been corrupted. The rabbis held complete authority over their people in local matters. As long as they kept the peace and paid their taxes to the Roman governor, they could do as they wished.

The enemies of 'Isa met in Jerusalem to discuss the matter, and they decided to get rid of him. The Christians say that one of 'Isa's own disciples betrayed him for 30 pieces of silver, but we don't know for sure.

The involved rabbis brought 'Isa before the court and subjected him to intense questioning and torture. The following hadith is most likely referring to Prophet 'Isa.

'Abdallah bin Mas'ud narrated "As if I saw the Prophet talking about one of the prophets whose nation had beaten him and caused him to bleed, while he was cleaning the blood off his face and saying, 'O Allah! Forgive my nation, for they have no knowledge.'"

عَنْ عَبْدِاللهِ بْنِ مَسْعُودٍ قَالَ: «كَأَنِّي أَنْظُرُ إِلَى النَّبِيِّ يَحْكِي نَبِيًّا مِنَ الْأَنْبِيَاءِ ضَرَبَهُ قَوْمُهُ فَأَدْمَوْهُ، وَهُوَ يَمْسَحُ الدَّمَ عَنْ وَجْهِهِ، وَيَقُولُ: اللَّهُمَّ اغْفِرْ لِقَوْمِي فَإِنَّهُمْ لَا يَعْلَمُونَ». رَوَاهُ الْبُخَارِيُّ

The rabbis would have killed 'Isa themselves if they could have, but because they had to obey Roman laws, they were not allowed to execute anyone without the Roman governor's permission. They arranged a meeting with Pontius Pilate, the Roman governor for the province of Judea, and tried to convince him that Prophet 'Isa was planning a rebellion against Rome. The exact details of this informal trial are unknown to us, but we know that the rabbis successfully convinced Pontius Pilate and got an order for 'Isa's execution.

Prophet 'Isa prayed to Allah for protection, and later a wondrous thing happened. As the Roman soldiers were marching 'Isa through a crowd to be executed, some sort of confusion occurred, and the guards lost their grip on 'Isa. Muslim scholars say that the guards might have then grabbed the man who betrayed 'Isa instead, because they looked almost alike, and then went forward and executed this other man, thinking it was 'Isa.

The Qur'an states that the Jews did not kill 'Isa, nor did they have him nailed to a wooden cross. Allah states, however, that the Jews thought they did it.

And for their saying (The Jews), "We have certainly killed the Masih 'Isa the son of Maryam, the Messenger of Allah," while in fact they did neither kill him nor crucify him, but they were deluded by resemblance. Those who disputed in this matter are certainly in doubt about it. They have no knowledge of it, but they follow whims. It is absolutely certain that they did not kill him. Surat An-Nisa' (The Women) 4:157

> The Romans did not use small "t" crosses. Theirs were capital "T" style when they executed people. The very symbol of Christianity itself is incorrect!

The nickname 'Christ-killer' has haunted Jews throughout Europe, and many massacres of Jews have taken place because of it. Muslims have never blamed Jews for this crime, because Islam doesn't acknowledge a crime to have occurred in the first place. Additionally, it is forbidden in Islam to blame an entire people for a crime because of the acts of only one person.

So what happened to Prophet 'Isa? The Qur'an states, *But Allah lifted him towards Himself. Allah is All-Mighty, All-Wise.* Surat An-Nisa' (The Women) 4: 158

Most scholars believe that Prophet 'Isa was brought into Paradise, where he will remain until the end of times. (4:159) According to the sayings of Prophet Muhammad, 'Isa will return one day to fight an evil ruler called the Dajjal and will then die a natural death on Earth.

E. The Legacy of Prophet 'Isa

Within a few years of Prophet 'Isa's disappearance, his disciples fell into disputes among themselves. Some wanted to remain faithful to the message they were given, while others wanted to make it easier for non-Jews to enter the new way of life.

The second group became more powerful, and were strengthened even more when a Jewish leader named Paul entered the conflict on their side. Paul had never met 'Isa and had previously persecuted his followers.

Paul claimed a vision of 'Isa appeared to him compelling him to travel into the desert for a while to think. When he returned to Palestine, he introduced people to his new ideas. Many followed him, and those who wanted to remain faithful to 'Isa's original teachings were ostracized.

Paul slowly began to change the original message of 'Isa. For example, he taught that the laws given to previous prophets were no longer applicable. By about the year 60 CE, these new teachings became dominant. Paul also traveled all throughout the Roman world teaching his theories, refining his doctrines and winning many more converts from the Greeks and Romans.

A Roman governor began to notice this new movement. He called it Christianity. (The Greek word for 'Masih' is 'Christos.') Paul and his followers accepted this name and began to use it.

But, even more shocking is that Paul began writing letters to other groups of Christians, those who had beliefs that were different from his teachings. He started telling them that Prophet 'Isa was the real and only son of God.

Later, he would teach that God comprised three different entities and that 'Isa was one of them. This theory, called the Trinity, officially stated that 'Isa was the son of Allah and was also Allah at the same time.

To further please the Greeks and Romans and attract them to his ideas, Paul emphasized that no one needed to follow traditional Jewish religious rituals, despite the fact that Prophet 'Isa never said this himself.

He also taught that everyone was doomed to Hellfire due to the first or 'original' sin of Adam and his wife from long ago. The only way to be rid of this sin, Paul explained, was to believe that 'Isa died to take the punishment for us. In other words, Paul taught that only by killing Himself could God forgive our sins. Anyone who disagreed with Paul was called a disbeliever.

Paul's version of Christianity appealed to many in the Roman empire. Some even began worshipping Maryam, the mother of 'Isa. To this day, many Christians still call upon her for guidance and favors.

F. The Truth Is Known!

What does Allah say about the doctrines that Christianity teaches?

The likeness of 'Isa (Jesus) is the same as that of Adam: He (Allah) created him from dust and said, "Be" and he was. Surat Al 'Imran (The Family of 'Imran) 3:59

...The Christians label 'Isa, the Masih (the anointed one), the son of Maryam, as a son of God. But that is just a phrase from their tongues. They're only copying what unbelievers of old used to say (that God has children or was a human on Earth). Surat At-Tawbah (The Repentance) 9:30

People of the Book! Don't go to extremes in your religion, nor say anything about Allah but the truth. 'Isa, the Masih, the son of Maryam, was a Messenger from Allah and His word bestowed on Maryam and a spirit from Him. So believe in Allah and His Messengers. Don't say, "Trinity." Don't do it! It will be better for you because Allah is One God. Glory be to Him. He is far above having a child. Surat An-Nisa' (The Women) 4:171

They reject (faith) who say that Allah is 'Isa the Masih, son of Maryam. Declare, "Who could hold back Allah if it were His will to destroy the Masih, son of Maryam, his mother and everyone on Earth?" Surat Al Ma'idah (The Table) 5:17

They reject (faith) who say that Allah is the Masih, son of Maryam. The Masih, himself said, "Children of Isra'il! Serve Allah, my Lord and your Lord." Surat Al Ma'idah (The Table) 5:72

On the Day of Judgement, Allah will ask 'Isa if he ever taught people to worship him and his mother instead of Allah. Imagine the stunned look on the faces of most of the Christians when he replies, "Glory to You! I could never say what I had no right to say! If I said such a thing, You would have indeed known about it...I never said anything to them except what You commanded me to. Namely: To serve Allah, Who is my Lord and your Lord..." Surat Al Ma'idah (The Table) 5:116-117

'Isa's message, the Injeel, was never written down in his lifetime. His later followers wrote what they remembered or heard from others, but there was no way to check for accuracy. When the Christians finally did compile their **Holy Book (Scripture)** الكِتَابُ المُقَدَّس, they gathered together many different writings from many different sources, and voted on should be included in their book, or 'Bible.' A council was held in the year 325 CE (325 years after 'Isa left Earth). The place was a small Greek city called Nicea.

Why was the book made? A Roman leader, Emperor Constantine, wanted the Christians in his empire to stop fighting over their differing beliefs. They were divided into many groups,

Travel by ship enabled Paul to spread his version of Christianity faster than any other preachers.

each accusing the other of misunderstanding the true teachings of 'Isa.

Paul's teachings eventually came to dominate the Bible. (2:79) The men who were closer to the real teachings of 'Isa and against those of Paul were in the minority at that meeting. (3:113) Over the past 2,000 years, several other additions have been made to the religion, and there has been an increase in the divisions and groups. (9:30-31, 3:105)

Those who are true followers of 'Isa reject false ideas and eventually, as Allah wills, they may find their way into the light of Islam. Perhaps you will help guide them! (5:76-77)

Questions to Answer

1. What did 'Isa want to teach the Jews?
2. List three miracles that Allah gave 'Isa to convince the people to believe in him.
3. How did most people react to Prophet 'Isa's message?
4. Who were the Disciples?
5. How did Allah save Prophet 'Isa from being killed by the rabbis?
6. Who was Paul and what did he do?
7. What will 'Isa say on the Day of Judgement when asked about what he taught?

Define: Injeel, Gospel, Disciple, Scripture.

Reflect: Allah protected 'Isa's mother from slander when she returned to her village with baby 'Isa. Then, Allah protected 'Isa from those who doubted his status as a prophet by giving him miracles that could convince his people otherwise. Although you may not have been tested in the same manner as Maryam or Prophet 'Isa, can you think of how Allah has protected you from negative happenings in your life? Or, can you think of ways that Allah made others recognize you for who you truly are, especially when someone else may have doubted you?

Act: List two false ideas about 'Isa that Christians hold, and then list what Allah says about them.

IQ Builders

1. What does Allah say about 'Isa in 43:57-65?
2. How does ayah 2:79 apply to the Bible?
3. Describe the message of verses 19:35-40.
4. What is the message of verses 9:30-35?
5. Explain the meaning of verses 2:62.

Literature Selection

The Boy and the King

From *Sahih Muslim*

Suhaib reports that the Messenger of Allah ﷺ said, "There once lived a king who had a sorcerer. When the sorcerer started to grow very old, he told the king, 'I'm getting old now. So please send me a young man to whom I can teach my magic.'

The king granted the request and arranged for a young man to be the sorcerer's apprentice.

On his way to the sorcerer, the young man came across a monk sitting by the road. He stopped to speak with the monk and was impressed with his knowledge. It became his habit that whenever he went to the sorcerer, he would visit with the monk first.

Sometimes the visit to the monk would cause him to be late. As a punishment for being late, the sorcerer would beat the young man. One day, while he was sitting with the monk, the young man complained about this.

So the monk told him, 'When you're afraid of the magician, tell him, 'My family kept me.' And when you're afraid of your family tell them, 'The sorcerer delayed me.'

This pattern went on unchanged. Then one day the young man saw a great beast blocking the road. As he was dangerous to go near, the people couldn't go around it. The young man thought to himself, 'Now here is a way I can find out whether the knowledge of the sorcerer is better than the knowledge of the monk.'

So he grabbed a stone, and said, 'My Lord, if the way of the monk is more to Your liking than the way of the magician, then cause the death of this beast so people can pass again!' He then threw the rock at the beast's head, killing it immediately, and the people were able to travel freely once more.

When the young man told the monk about this, he replied, 'My son, today you have become better than me, but now I think you've come to a point where you might be tested. Should that happen, don't reveal my location.'

In time, the young man began to cure people from blindness, leprosy and all manner of diseases. News of his abilities finally reached a royal official who had become blind. So, he went to the young man with expensive gifts, and said, 'All this will be yours if you heal me.'

The young man replied, 'I, myself, do not heal anyone. It is Allah Who gives healing. If you will have faith in Allah, I will pray for you, and He may heal you.'

The royal official put total faith in Allah and Allah cured him of his blindness.

When he returned to the king, and sat with him as he always did, the surprised king asked him, 'Who has returned your sight?'

He answered, 'My Lord has.'

Then the king demanded, 'Do you have a lord besides me?!' The official replied, 'Allah is your Lord and mine.'

The enraged king ordered him arrested, and he was tortured until he spoke about the young man. The young man was promptly summoned to the court, where the king asked him, 'My son, have you become so skilled in magic that you can heal the blind, and the lepers and all manner of ailments?'

'I don't heal anyone,' he replied. 'It's only Allah Who heals.'

Then he was arrested and tortured until he disclosed the location of the monk, who, in turn was summoned. The king ordered him, 'Give up your belief.' When the monk refused, the king commanded a saw to be placed in the center of his head, and the monk was cut in half. Then the royal minister was sent for and commanded to give up his belief. He also refused and was cut as well.

Finally, the young apprentice was brought and ordered to give up his belief. When he also declined, the king handed him over to a company of his soldiers and told them, 'Take him to a high mountain, and when you get to the top, if he still refuses to give up his faith, throw him off.'

So they took him to the mountain and were bringing him to the highest point. Then he prayed, 'Oh Lord, deliver me from them in whatever way You will.'

Then the mountain shook and crumbled down. The young man then walked back into the presence of the king, who asked, 'What happened to the rest of your group?' He answered, 'Allah has saved me from them.'

He was then handed over to another group with orders to take him out to sea in a small boat. If he still persisted in his faith, he was to be thrown overboard. As they rowed out to sea, the young man prayed, 'Oh Lord, deliver me from them in whatever way You will.'

Then a wave overturned the boat and the men drowned, though the young man was able to swim to shore.

He then went back to the king, who asked, 'What happened to the rest of your group?'

He answered, 'Allah has saved me from them.' Then the young man continued, 'You will never be able to kill me unless you follow my instructions.'

So the king asked, 'What are your instructions?'

The young man replied, 'Gather your people in an open place. Next, tie me to the trunk of a tree. Then, take an arrow from my quiver, and while placing it in the middle of a bow, you must declare, 'In the name of Allah, the Lord of this young man,' then shoot the arrow at me. If you do this then you can kill me.'

So the king made the necessary arrangements. The people were gathered in an open place, the young man was tied to the trunk of a tree, and the king placed one of the young man's arrows in the middle of a bow. He then declared, 'In the name of Allah, the Lord of this young man!' and shot the arrow. It struck the young man on the side of his head. He raised his hand to the wound as he died. Upon seeing this, all the people began to cry out, 'We believe in the Lord of this young man!' Someone whispered to the king, 'Do you see? What you feared is now happening: the people are starting to believe in Allah.' Then, the king ordered great pits to be dug along the roads, and he had huge fires built. Whoever refused to give up their faith would be thrown in the fire or be made to jump in it. And so the believing people were brought to the pit. Then a woman came along with a small boy. She winced and hesitated to be thrown in the fire. Her son encouraged her saying, 'Be steady mother. You are in the right.' So she threw herself in the ditch along with her child, to be with the martyrs in Paradise."

Cursed were the People of the Trench, the (people of the) fire that was rich with fuel. When they were sitting by it and were watching what they were doing with the believers. They punished them for nothing but that they believed in Allah, the All-Mighty, the Worthy of All Praise, the One to whom belongs the Kingdom of the heavens and the earth. And Allah is witness over every thing. Surat Al Burooj (The Mansions of the Stars) 85:4-9

﴿قُتِلَ أَصْحَابُ الْأُخْدُودِ﴾ ﴿النَّارِ ذَاتِ الْوَقُودِ﴾ ﴿إِذْ هُمْ عَلَيْهَا قُعُودٌ﴾ ﴿وَهُمْ عَلَىٰ مَا يَفْعَلُونَ بِالْمُؤْمِنِينَ شُهُودٌ﴾ ﴿وَمَا نَقَمُوا مِنْهُمْ إِلَّا أَن يُؤْمِنُوا بِاللَّهِ الْعَزِيزِ الْحَمِيدِ﴾ ﴿الَّذِي لَهُ مُلْكُ السَّمَاوَاتِ وَالْأَرْضِ وَاللَّهُ عَلَىٰ كُلِّ شَيْءٍ شَهِيدٌ﴾

سُورَةُ الْبُرُوجِ 85: 4-9

Questions to Answer

1. Why do you think the boy liked the monk better?
2. Why was the evil king against the young man and his beliefs?
3. How did Allah prove to the king that only He is in control?

31. The Sleepers of the Cave

WHAT TO LEARN

What if you were living during a time when what you believed in could get you killed? How might you try to protect yourself from such a fate?

VOCABULARY

Unitarians   Trinitarians   Persecute

THINK ABOUT IT

What changes did the youths find in their new world?

Stone statues of emperors were erected throughout Roman lands.

A. The Christian World at a Glance

During Prophet 'Isa's life on Earth, the Jews of Palestine were against his message and teachings. They were afraid of losing their power, and many of them wanted to keep a steady hold on their religious traditions.

After 'Isa left the world, his followers spread his message far and wide. Some followers, like Barnabas and Thomas, who both left written records of 'Isa's life, wanted to maintain the message just as they had received it.

But some new converts, like Paul and Luke, sought to modify, or change, the message to make it easier for non-Jews to accept. They didn't consider that they had no right to make up their own teachings or to alter those of Prophet 'Isa.

From the years 40 CE to 150 CE, numerous new groups of Christians were formed in the many areas of the Roman world. Some followed Paul's teachings, while others followed different ones.

For example, the Christians who were most likely to follow the teachings of the Trinity, that of God having a son, were those who lived in lands influenced by the Greeks or in Italy. In these countries, there were well-established traditions of man-gods and sons of gods. If you have read of Zeus, Jupiter or Hercules, whose stories comprise Greek mythology, you'll understand why one more concept of 'son of God' could easily be accepted. Christians who uphold this belief are called **Trinitarians** المُؤْمِنينَ بِالتَّثْلِيثِ.

Those Christians who held closer to the true teachings of 'Isa and his faithful disciples were concentrated in North Africa, Palestine and Syria. These are known as **Unitarians** المُوَحِّدُون.

B. The Romans Lay a Heavy Hand

At first, the Romans were not interested in Christianity of any variety, as they ruled an empire with a thousand different kinds of religions. But as Christianity spread, in all its different versions, the rulers in Rome began to take note.

One of the problems that the Roman government faced with the new faith was that it taught people to worship an 'unseen god,' and not the very visible Roman emperor. One of the foundations of Roman society was based on the premise that the emperor was a 'god on Earth,' and all people had to worship him. As long as they continued to worship the emperor, then they could keep their own local religion as well.

The Christians, whether Unitarian or Trinitarian, refused to give offerings or bow to the statues of the emperors. This was a serious crime in the Roman world. Paul himself was arrested while in Rome, and he was brought for questioning before Caesar. He was later released.

In time, the Roman government started a campaign against the Christian religion. They began to **Persecute** يَضْطَهِد those who claimed to be Christians. Churches were closed, Christian leaders were arrested and property was seized. By the year 250 CE, Christians were being burned alive, and they were even fed to savage lions for the bizarre entertainment of the citizens of Rome in the arenas.

But due to the determined efforts of many underground Christian leaders, the movement kept spreading. Christian teachings appealed to many, particularly its emphasis on compassion, mercy and love.

C. The Hunt Begins

During the reign of Emperor Hadrian, who ruled from 117 CE to 138 CE, the order went out to all provinces in the empire to further persecute the Christians. In addition, local governors were charged with stamping out Christianity in their districts.

In the city of Ephesus, which is located in modern-day Turkey, a group of young converts to Christianity gathered secretly to plan their escape. The Roman governor was rounding up Christians in the city, and executing them if they refused to renounce, or give up, their faith.

These young converts publicly declared, "… *Our Lord is the Lord of the heavens and the earth. We shall never invoke any god other than Him; otherwise we would be*

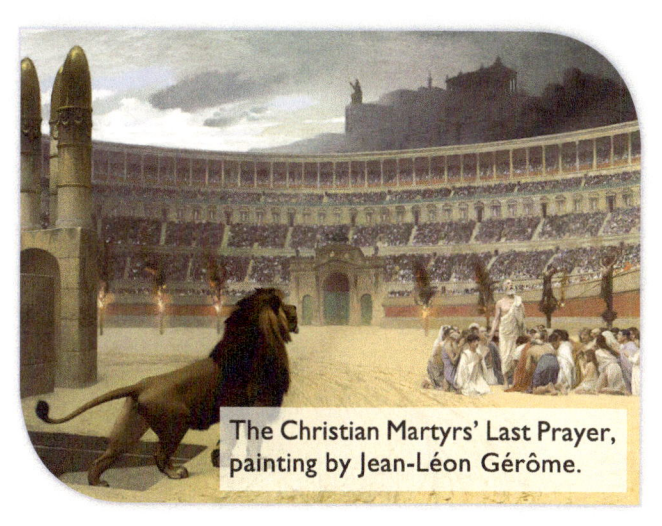

The Christian Martyrs' Last Prayer, painting by Jean-Léon Gérôme.

saying something far from the truth." Surat Al Kahf (The Cave) 18:14

When they found out that they were the next to be arrested, they ran, barely escaping the guards who came after them. They met at their secret place in the hills, knowing that they could never go home.

They talked among themselves, saying, *Our people here have taken to serving gods other than Him. Why don't they bring clear authority for what they do? Who does more wrong than one who invents a lie against Allah? When you turn away from them and the things they worship besides Allah, get to the cave. Your Lord will shower His mercy on you and take care of your problem.* Surat Al Kahf (The Cave) 18:15-16

One of them knew about a cave they could use as a hideout, so, they went there and set up a temporary base. One night they sat around their fire together and prayed to Allah, *Our Lord! Grant us mercy from You, and resolve our problem for us in a rightly guided way.* Surat Al Kahf (The Cave) 18:10

Then, as they lay down to sleep for the night, a miraculous thing occurred. Allah says, *We drew (an unconscious state) over them for a number of years in the cave.* Surat Al Kahf (The Cave) 18:11

If anyone stumbled upon the Sleepers in the Cave, they would have been filled with terror and run away.

Allah ﷻ put them in a state of hibernation, and they literally slept for decades! Allah ﷻ describes them in the cave like this, *You would see the sun when it rose, declining to the right from the cave, and when it set, turning away from them to the left, while they lay in the open space in the middle of the cave. You would (if you saw them) think they were awake, while they were asleep. We turned them on their right side and on their left. Their dog would stretch his legs at the entrance. If you would have come upon them, you would have run away in fright!* Surat Al Kahf (The Cave) 18:17-18

D. The Sleepers Awaken

Then We awakened them in order to test which of their two groups would be best at figuring out how many years they were there. Surat Al Kahf (The Cave) 18:12

They probably were amazed to find spider webs all over the place, and leaves and debris covering the entrance to their cave. When they awoke, they started asking each other a series of questions.

The young people knew they couldn't stay there forever. They also realized that something strange had happened, given the condition of their cave. But they were all right, and their dog Qitmir was also fine. They decided to send one of them back to the city to see what was going on.

In this way We raised them up until they asked each other. One of them said, "How long did you tarry?" They said, "A day or part of a day." They said, "Your Lord knows best how long you tarried." So, send one of you with this silver (coin) of yours to the city and let him look around which of the eatables are the purest and let him bring you some food from there. And he must act in polite manner and must not let anyone know about you. If they (the habitants of the city) will know about you, they will stone you or force you to revert to their faith, and in that case, you will never find success." Surat Al Kahf (The Cave) 18:19-20

So one of them went out to enter the city secretly. However, as soon as he entered the city, he found everyone staring at him. He was confused. What was wrong with him? What he didn't realize was that he and his companions had awakened during the reign of Emperor Theodosious II, who ruled from the years 408 CE to 450 CE.

The young man's clothes were in a style that had not been worn for centuries. To those around him, he appeared as if he just stepped out of a time machine. When he asked people for directions, because the city looked completely changed to him, he used old words and grammar from a time long past.

The young man must have attracted quite a crowd of curious people right away and realized he had failed miserably as a spy. He resolved to buy his food and get back to his friends as fast as he could. So he went to a food market and quickly picked out some breads and vegetables.

As he went to pay for his food, everyone watched in amazement as he pulled out his money from his bag. On the table he placed some coins that were minted in the reign of Emperor Hadrian, over 300 years before.

The people were struck with amazement. The local authorities were summoned, and the youths were brought from the cave for questioning. Everyone was stunned by their story. But none more so than the youths themselves.

When they entered the cave, they had been following a religion that would only result in their persecution. They had literally run for their lives because of their beliefs. But now, in this time, Christianity had become the official religion of Rome. They were safe now and could live by their convictions.

In time, the local government was flooded with requests by the people to build a memorial, or monument, over the cave where they had slept. (18:21) Instead, they built a religious center to commemorate this miracle of Allah.

The story of the Sleepers of the Cave is recorded in the history books of the Roman empire. The historian, James of Sarug, wrote down their story a few years after the last of the Sleepers had passed away. In the year 474 CE, he told the tale in his book entitled *Sermons*.

Because there were many stories and legends about the Sleepers, in time, people began to vary the stories about them. As Allah narrates, some people said the young people of the cave numbered four, five or as many as seven. But then Allah states that only He knows how many there were. (18:22)

On another issue, Allah recounts how people differ over the number of years they spent in the cave. He says, *(Some say) they stayed in the cave for three hundred years, (others) add nine more. Declare to them, "Allah knows best how long they stayed. With Him are the secrets of space and the Earth. He sees clearly and hears perfectly."* Surat Al Kahf (The Cave) 18:25-26

So only Allah knows for certain how long they remained there. The main lessons of the story, however, are important to know:
1. Never give in to falsehood, even if you have to escape from it to remain true.
2. Never despair of Allah's help.
3. Work together as a group and follow the plan that was agreed upon.
4. Things always change, and the future may be radically different from what you are experiencing now.

This last lesson was the most important one for the early Muslims of Makkah to hear. Allah revealed this story to the believers at a time when the idol-worshippers were persecuting Prophet Muhammad and those who believed with him.

The story gave them hope that despite their current suffering, their beliefs could become the dominant force in society if they held firm. And so it came to be.

But the believers didn't have to wait hundreds of years. In fact, the victory of Islam over idol-worship would happen in less than 30 years.

أستغفر الله

IT'S ALL ABOUT ISLAM

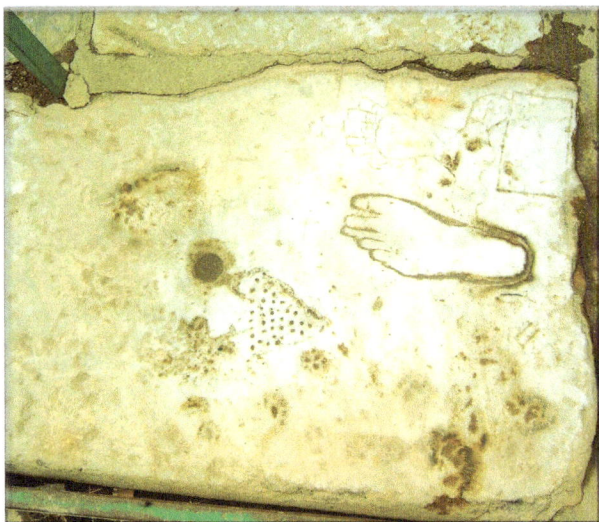

Monument to the Seven Sleepers - Ephesus, Turkey.

Questions to Answer

1. Why did some Christians want to modify or change the teachings of Prophet 'Isa ﷺ?
2. Why did the Roman government see Christianity as a threat at first?
3. Who was Emperor Hadrian, and what did he do?
4. What plan did a group of young people from Ephesus have to escape the persecution?
5. In what way did Allah ﷻ answer their prayer?
6. When the youths woke up, why was one of them sent out to the city?
7. How did the people react to the youth who went to the city and why?
8. What are four lessons we can learn from their story?

Define: Trinitarian, Unitarian, Persecute.

Reflect: The youth that are described in this story were probably close in age to you. They had the courage to remain firm in their beliefs, even when others were against them. What beliefs or ideas have you shown courage to stand for? Are there additional things you wish you had the courage to stand up for? How can you start to build that courage?

Act: The story about the Sleepers of the Cave gave the Muslims in Makkah hope that their difficult time would pass if they held firmly to their beliefs. There are many ayaat in the Qur'an that similarly provide people with hope when they face difficulties. Choose one ayah that gives you hope. Copy or print it on a piece of paper. Decorate and beautify the paper. Then, put it in a place, such as your mirror, that you look at every day.

IQ Builder: How did Allah ﷻ provide hope to the Sleepers of the Cave, as described in 18:15-16?

Unit 07 Review Exercise

VOCABULARY REVIEW

On a separate sheet of paper, write the definition of each word below.

1. Synagogue
2. Uzayr
3. Rabbi
4. Masih
5. Injeel
6. Disciple
7. Scripture
8. Tawrah
9. Persecute
10. Yahya
11. Christianity
12. Roman Empire
13. Qitmir
14. Trinitarians

REMEMBERING WHAT YOU READ

On a separate sheet of paper, answer the following questions. Use complete sentences in your answers.

1. Who was Uzayr, and what did he do?
2. What happened at a fortress called Masada?
3. Why was Maryam's mother disappointed when she saw she had a baby girl?
4. Why did Prophet Zakariyya want a child of his own?
5. Why did Maryam want to leave her home and go on a journey?
6. How did 'Isa defend his mother's honor?
7. When Prophet 'Isa began his mission, how did he start?
8. Describe what the true Injeel was.
9. What is one reason that the story of the Sleepers might have been revealed to the Muslims in Makkah by their Lord?
10. Why did the disciples of Prophet 'Isa ask for a special miracle, and what was it?

THINKING TO LEARN

On a separate sheet of paper, answer the questions below. Use complete sentences.

1. Compare the ways in which the holy texts revealed to Musa and 'Isa became changed over time.
2. Choose one person from the lessons in this unit that you feel is a positive role model for you. Describe the person and their characteristics. Then, explain how they motivate you to be a better person.
3. Summarize the story of the Sleepers of the Cave.

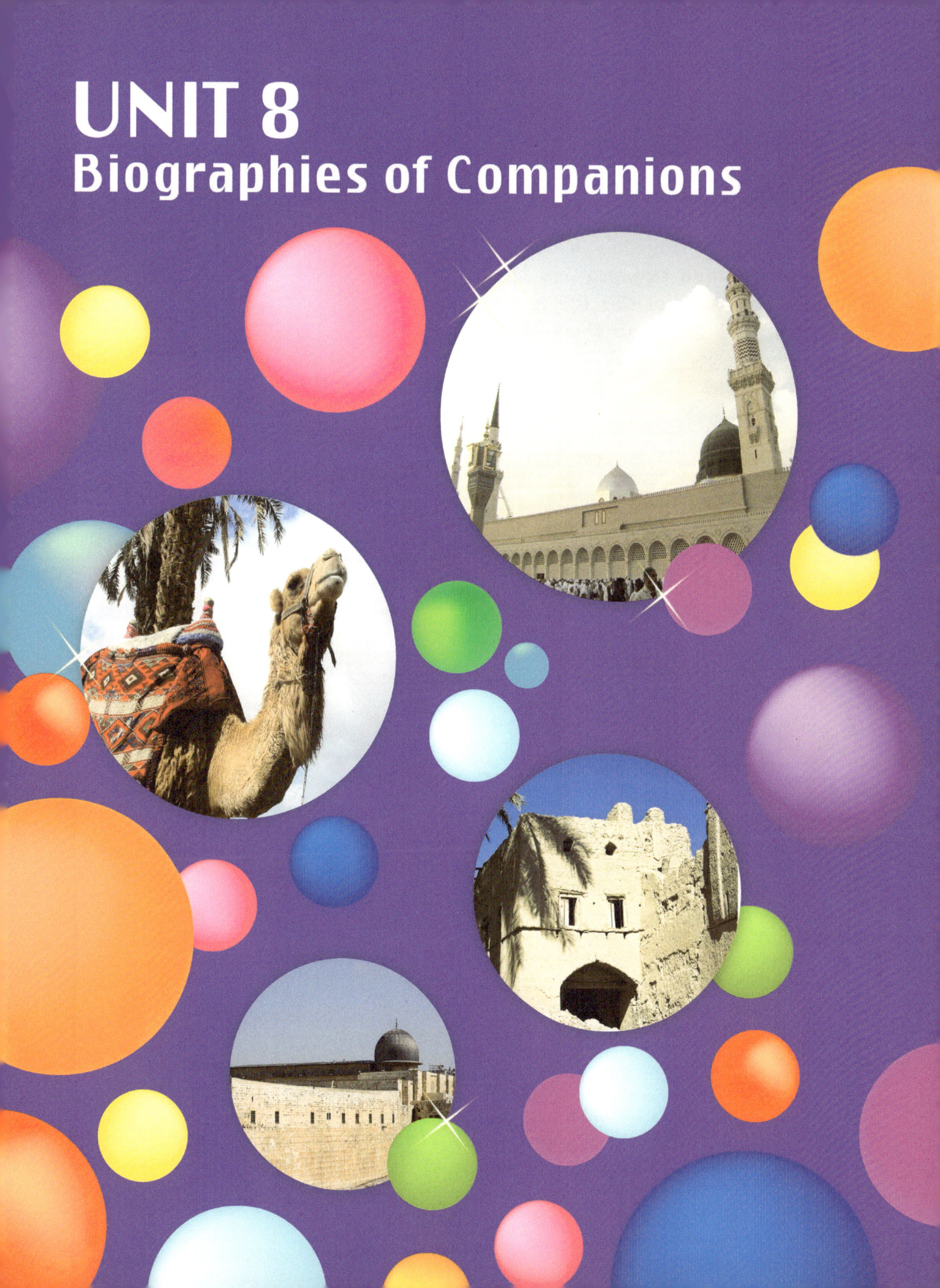

UNIT 8
Biographies of Companions

32 Who Was Um Salamah ﷺ?

WHAT TO LEARN

When we suffer tragedies in our life, many people find strength and hope in remembering that this life is only temporary. Why do you think this is comforting?

VOCABULARY

Sahabiyyat
Umuhat al Mu'mineen

THINK ABOUT IT

How did Um Salamah deal with her tragedies?

A. Who Was Um Salamah ﷺ?

One of the most interesting stories of the **Sahabiyyat** صَحابيّات **Female Companions** of Prophet Muḥammad ﷺ comes to us from the eventful life of Hind. She was also known as Um Salamah ﷺ.

She and her husband, 'Abdallah bin 'Abdul Asad ﷺ, were among the first to accept Islam in Makkah. When the leaders of the Quraysh heard about her and her husband's conversion, they began to antagonize and ridicule them. The Quraysh incited people to insult them in the streets. But the young couple remained firm in their faith.

Um Salamah ﷺ, her husband and her son ﷺ were among the people whom the Prophet ﷺ sent seeking refuge in Abyssinia at the peak of the Makkans' persecution. Um Salamah ﷺ left behind her nice home, relatives and her life of comfort. But she loved Allah ﷻ more and was willing to sacrifice in any way for His cause.

A short time later, false reports reached the Muslims in Abyssinia. They claimed that, due to the increased numbers of Muslims in Makkah, the Quraysh were not as confrontational with the believers as before.

Wishing to return home and to be near the Prophet ﷺ again, Um Salamah ﷺ and her family joined a group of Muslims that were making preparations to return.

No sooner had they arrived in Makkah, however, than they found out that the Makkans had started a new phase of vicious persecution and torture against the Muslim community. When the Prophet ﷺ ordered the Muslims to secretly immigrate to Al Madinah, Um Salamah ﷺ was among the first to try to leave.

It would be a hard and difficult journey. We will see what happened next, as she recounts in her own words, the most interesting part of her tale.

B. Um Salamah ﷺ - My Journey

When Abu Salamah (my husband) decided to leave for Al Madinah, he prepared a camel for me, helped me mount it, and placed our son, Salamah, up on my lap.

My husband took the lead and began moving without waiting for anything else. Before we were out of the city of Makkah, however, some people from my own clan stopped us and told my husband:

"Although you can do what you like with yourself, you have no authority over your wife. She is one of our daughters. Do you expect us to let you take her away from here?"

Then they overwhelmed him and carried me away. When my husband's clan, the Banu 'Abdul Asad, saw my clan taking both me and my child, they became angry.

"No! By God!" they shouted. "We will not abandon the child. He is our son and we have the first claim on him."

They grabbed him by the hand and pulled him away from me. Suddenly, I found myself alone and desperate. My husband had to head for Al Madinah by himself, and his clan had taken my son away from me. My own clan overpowered me and forced me to remain with them.

From that very moment, the day when my husband and son were separated from me, I made it my habit to go out at noon every day to that valley and sit in the very same spot where this tragedy occurred. I would recall those terrible moments and weep until night fell.

I continued doing this for a year or so, until one day, a man from the Banu Umayah passed by and saw my condition. He went back to my clan and said, "Why don't you free this poor woman? You caused her husband and her son to be separated from her." He continued to try and influence them by softening their hearts. Finally, they told me, "Go and join your husband if you want."

But how could I go to my husband in Al Madinah and leave my son, a piece of my own flesh, in Makkah among the Banu 'Abdul Asad? How could I be free from sorrow, and my eyes free from tears, if I went to the place of al hijrah not knowing anything more about my son, who I would be leaving behind in Makkah?

A few people realized what I was going through, and their sympathies went out to me. They asked the Banu 'Abdul Asad on my behalf and succeeded in convincing them to return my son. I didn't want to stay in Makkah waiting until I could find someone to travel with, because I was afraid that something else might happen that would delay or stop me from reaching my husband. So, I quickly got my camel ready, placed my son on my lap and left in the direction of Al Madinah. I had just reached Tanim (a point three miles out from Makkah) when I met a man named 'Uthman bin Talha.

"Where are you going, Daughter of Zad?" he asked.

"I am going to my husband in Al Madinah."

"And there's no one with you?"

"No, by Allah, except Allah and my son."

"By Allah, I won't abandon you until you reach Al Madinah," he promised.

He then took the harness of my camel and led us forward. I have, by Allah ﷻ, never met an Arab more generous and noble than he. When we stopped to rest, he would make my camel kneel down, wait until I dismounted, lead the camel to a tree and tie it. He would then go to the shade of another tree. When we were rested, he would get the camel ready and lead us forward again.

He did this every day until we reached the outskirts of Al Madinah. When we arrived at a village near Quba' belonging to the clan of Banu 'Amr bin 'Awf, he said, "Your husband is in this village. Enter it with the blessings of Allah." Then he turned back and headed for Makkah.

C. Tragedy and Good Fortune

The couple's paths finally came together after a long separation. Um Salamah ﷺ was happy to see her husband, and he was delighted to see his wife and child.

Important events soon followed in succession. First, there was the Battle of Badr in which 'Abdallah fought. Then the Battle of Uhud followed, in which the Muslims were

IT'S ALL ABOUT ISLAM

213

severely tested. 'Abdallah came out of that battle wounded very badly.

He appeared at first to respond well to treatment, but his wounds never healed completely, and he remained confined to his bed.

One day, while Um Salamah was attending to him, he said to her, "I heard the Messenger of Allah say, 'Whenever a hardship afflicts anyone, he should say, Surely from Allah we come and to Him we will certainly return.'"

Then 'Abdallah prayed, "My Lord, give me in return something good from this which only You, the Exalted and Mighty, can give."

'Abdallah remained sick in bed for several more days. His condition worsened. One morning the Prophet came to see him. While the Prophet was still at his bedside, 'Abdallah passed away. With his blessed hands, the Prophet closed the eyes of his dead Companion.

The Blessed Prophet said, "My Lord, grant forgiveness to Abu Salamah. Elevate him among those who are near to You. Take charge of his family at all times. Forgive us and him, Oh Lord of the Universe. Widen his grave and enlighten it for him." (Muslim)

قَالَ ﷺ: «اللَّهُمَّ اغْفِرْ لِأَبِي سَلَمَةَ وَارْفَعْ دَرَجَتَهُ فِي الْمَهْدِيِّينَ وَاخْلُفْهُ فِي عَقِبِهِ فِي الْغَابِرِينَ وَاغْفِرْ لَنَا وَلَهُ يَا رَبَّ الْعَالَمِينَ وَافْسَحْ لَهُ فِي قَبْرِهِ. وَنَوِّرْ لَهُ فِيهِ». رَوَاهُ مُسْلِمٌ

Um Salamah remembered the prayer her husband had quoted on his deathbed and began repeating it, "My Lord give me something good out of this."

The Muslims were greatly saddened by the plight of Um Salamah. She became known as 'The Widow.' She had no one in Al Madinah of her own except her small children. She was alone and had no source of income.

Both Al Muhajirun and Al Ansar felt they had a duty to Um Salamah. When she had completed the **'Iddah عدّه Waiting Period** before re-marriage is allowed (a total of four months and 10 days), Abu Bakr proposed marriage to her, but she refused.

Then 'Umar asked to marry her, but she also declined the proposal. The Blessed Prophet then approached her with a proposal of his own, and she replied with a very interesting answer.

She said, Messenger of Allah, "I have three characteristics. I am a woman who is extremely jealous, and I'm afraid that you'll see in me something that will anger you and cause Allah to punish me. Second, I am a woman who is already a bit old, and third, I am a woman who has a young family."

The Prophet ﷺ replied with an interesting answer of his own. He said, "Regarding the jealousy you mentioned, I pray to Allah, the Almighty, to let it go away from you. Regarding the question of age you have mentioned, I am afflicted with the same problem as you. Regarding the dependent family you have mentioned, your family is like my family."

They were then married, and in this way, Allah ﷻ answered her prayer of replacing a tragedy with something better. From that day on, Um Salamah ؓ became one of the **Umuhat al Mu'mineen** أُمَّهَاتُ الْمُؤْمِنِين **Mothers of Believers**, as the wives of the Prophet ﷺ were known.

She would soon became an important teacher and narrator of hadith, helping the early Muslims—in particular women—in understanding Islam. May Allah ﷻ bless Um Salamah ؓ with Jannah. Ameen!

Questions to Answer

1. Why did Um Salamah ؓ and her husband want to leave for Al Madinah?
2. What difficult situation did Um Salamah ؓ face on her first attempt to leave for Al Madinah?
3. How did her husband die?
4. What did the Prophet ﷺ ask of Allah ﷻ for 'Abdallah?
5. What were the three points Um Salamah ؓ brought up when the Prophet ﷺ proposed marriage to her?
6. How did the Blessed Prophet ﷺ answer each one of her objections?
7. What did she do in later life?

Define: 'Iddah, Um Salamah ؓ.

Reflect: Why do you think the wives of Prophet Muhammad ﷺ are called Umuhat al Mu'mineen?

Act: Learn more about one of the Prophet's ﷺ wives. Write a report that includes information about her family, status and contributions to Islam.

IQ Builder: Read 17:19-20. How might these ayaat provide comfort to those experiencing distress?

33. Mu'ath bin Jabal ﷺ

WHAT TO LEARN

Generally, when you need help with something, you look for the person who is the most skilled and knowledgeable on that subject. Why?

VOCABULARY

Amir

THINK ABOUT IT

How did Mu'ath's ﷺ love of learning make him well qualified for his tasks?

A. Who Was Mu'ath bin Jabal ﷺ?

Mu'ath bin Jabal ﷺ was a young man in Yathrib (Al Madinah) who accepted Islam at the hands of Mus'ab bin 'Umair ﷺ. If you will remember, Mu'sab ﷺ was the person that the Blessed Prophet ﷺ sent to Yathrib to help guide the new Muslims there.

Mu'ath ﷺ was one of the over 70 men and women who traveled to Makkah as part of the Second Pledge of 'Aqaba. In this pledge, the new believers promised to defend and follow Allah's Messenger ﷺ.

After he returned to Yathrib, he joined a group of Muslims who campaigned against idols in the city. They would go from house-to-house, trying to convince the people to smash their idols.

After the Prophet ﷺ made Hijrah to Al Madinah, Mu'ath ﷺ spent as much time as he could in his company. He memorized the entire Qur'an and learned all the teachings of Islam in great detail.

Once the Prophet ﷺ said of him, "Out of my entire Ummah, Mu'ath bin Jabal ﷺ is the most knowledgeable regarding permissible and prohibited things." (Ahmad)

قَالَ رَسُولُ اللهِ ﷺ : «أَعْلَمُ أُمَّتِي بِالْحَلَالِ وَالْحَرَامِ مُعَاذُ بْنُ جَبَلٍ».
رَوَاهُ أَحْمَد

After the liberation of Makkah, the Blessed Prophet ﷺ asked Mu'ath ﷺ to stay there and help instruct the Makkans in the knowledge of the Qur'an and in the teachings of the Islamic way of life.

B. The Mission to Yemen

Sometime after the Prophet ﷺ had returned to Al Madinah, delegates came from the land of Yemen announcing that many of the people there had accepted Islam. They asked for teachers who could come and instruct their nation in the ways of Islam.

The Blessed Prophet ﷺ organized a group of Sahaba to be sent and placed Mu'ath bin Jabal ﷺ in charge as their **Amir** أمير **Leader**.

Some Companions of Mu'ath bin Jabal ﷺ said, When the Messenger of Allah ﷺ intended to send Mu'ath bin Jabal to the Yemen, he asked, "How will you judge when the occasion of deciding a case arises?" He replied, "I shall judge in accordance with Allah's Book." He asked, "(What will you do) if you do not find any guidance in Allah's Book?" He replied: "(I shall act) in accordance with the Sunnah of the Messenger of Allah." He asked, "(What will you do) if you do not find any guidance in the Sunnah of the Messenger of Allah and in Allah's Book?" He replied, "I shall do my best to form an opinion and I shall spare no effort."

The Messenger of Allah then patted him on the breast and said, "Praise be to Allah Who has helped the messenger of the Messenger of Allah to find something which pleases the Messenger of Allah."
(Ahmad)

عَنْ أَصْحَابِ مُعَاذِ بْنِ جَبَلٍ ﷺ أَنَّ رَسُولَ اللهِ ﷺ لَمَّا أَرَادَ أَنْ يَبْعَثَ مُعَاذًا إِلَى الْيَمَنِ قَالَ: كَيْفَ تَقْضِي إِذَا عَرَضَ لَكَ قَضَاءٌ. قَالَ أَقْضِي بِكِتَابِ اللهِ. قَالَ: فَإِنْ لَمْ تَجِدْ فِي كِتَابِ اللهِ. قَالَ: فَبِسُنَّةِ رَسُولِ اللهِ. قَالَ: فَإِنْ لَمْ تَجِدْ فِي سُنَّةِ رَسُولِ اللهِ وَلَا فِي كِتَابِ اللهِ. قَالَ أَجْتَهِدُ رَأْيِي وَلَا آلُو. فَضَرَبَ رَسُولُ اللهِ صَدْرَهُ وَقَالَ: الْحَمْدُ لِلَّهِ الَّذِي وَفَّقَ رَسُولَ رَسُولِ اللهِ لِمَا يُرْضِي رَسُولَ اللهِ. رَوَاهُ أَحْمَد

When it came time to bid farewell, the Prophet ﷺ said to Mu'ath ﷺ, "O Mu'ath, perhaps you shall not meet me again after this year. Perhaps when you return you shall see only my mosque and my grave.' Mu'ath wept upon hearing this as he knew in his heart that he was never to meet the Prophet in this world again. A feeling of sadness and desolation overtook him as he parted from the Prophet ﷺ. The Prophet's ﷺ premonition was correct, the eyes of Mu'ath never beheld the Prophet ﷺ after that moment. The Prophet ﷺ died before Mu'ath returned from Yemen.

When Mu'ath ﷺ returned a few years later, the Blessed Messenger of Allah ﷺ had indeed passed away. Mu'ath ﷺ was surely overcome with grief when he visited his grave. However, Mu'ath ﷺ found relief in remembering the sayings of the Prophet ﷺ and in hoping to meet him one day in the next life. Mu'ath bin Jabal ﷺ loved the Prophet ﷺ dearly.

C. Later Life in the Service of Islam

Mu'ath ﷺ once said to his son, "My son, when you pray, do so as one who is bidding farewell to this world, and don't assume you will have another chance to pray again. My son, know that a believer dies in between two deeds: one he offers for today wherein he will attain immediate blessings, and the second in what he offers towards the Day of Resurrection, and in that he will gain the ultimate benefits."

In later years, a man named Al Khawlani entered the masjid in the city of Homs, Syria. He wrote, "I saw 30 elderly men who were Companions of the Blessed Prophet ﷺ. A slightly younger man with bright eyes and long, dark eyelashes sat among them. Whenever the elders needed an explanation about something, they went and asked him, and did so with great love and reverence. I asked someone who was sitting next to me, 'Who is that man?' He replied, 'That is Mu'ath bin Jabal, may Allah be pleased with him.' Instantly, I felt a sudden intense love and admiration for him. I stayed near their circle and listened closely to their discussion until they dispersed."

One Friday, Mu'ath bin Jabal ؓ was giving a khutbah in which he said, "Coming your way are awful trials where money will be plentiful, and the Qur'an will be read by a believer, as well as a hypocrite. The young, old, strong and weak from all nations will read the Qur'an. But a person will read the Qur'an in public and will be amazed and bewildered as he says to himself, 'How is it that I am reading the revealed Qur'an, and people seem neither to listen, nor do they follow its warnings?'"

During the rule of Khalifa 'Umar bin Al Khattab ؓ, Mu'ath ؓ was sent to Palestine to teach new Muslims the Qur'an. Mu'ath ؓ was old by then, and it wasn't long before he became ill.

When he was near his last days, he prayed, "Welcome death, welcome. A visitor has come after a long absence. Oh Lord, You know I did not desire the world or to lengthen my time in it. Oh Lord, accept my soul with goodness as You would accept a believing soul."

He then passed away as a life-long *da'i*, as well as a wise and intelligent servant of Islam.

وَزِنُوا بِالْقِسْطَاسِ الْمُسْتَقِيمِ

Questions to Answer

1. How did Mu'ath ﷺ learn about Islam?
2. After Mu'ath ﷺ returned to Yathrib, he joined a group of Muslims. What was the purpose of this group?
3. What was the special area of knowledge that he had?
4. What three things did Mu'ath ﷺ tell the Prophet ﷺ he would use to judge between people?
5. What prediction about the future did Mu'ath ﷺ make during one of his khutbahs?

Define: Ummah, Amir.
Reflect: Do you think the predictions that Mu'ath ﷺ made in his khutbah have come true?
Act: Consider the advice that the Mu'ath ﷺ gave to his son, mentioned in section C of this lesson. Try to apply it to your life.
IQ Builder: Find an ayah from the Qur'an that gives you inspiration to do good in this world. Share it with a friend.

What Is a Sahaba?

Once the Blessed Prophet ﷺ remarked, "I wish that I had seen our brothers!" The people with him said, "Messenger of Allah! Are we not your brothers?" "No," he said, "You are my Companions. Our brothers are those who have not yet come. And I will precede them to the Hawd." (The Hawd: the watering place of the Prophet, may Allah bless him and grant him peace, from which he will give to the people of his community on the day of rising.) They asked him, "Messenger of Allah! How will you recognize those of your community who come after you?" He said, "Doesn't a man who has horses with white legs and white blazes on their foreheads among totally black horses recognize which ones are his own?" They said, "Of course, Messenger of Allah." He went on, "Even so will they come on the day of rising with white marks on their foreheads, hands and feet from wudu', and I will precede them to the Hawd." (Malek)

قَالَ رَسُولُ اللهِ ﷺ: «وَدِدْتُ أَنَّا قَدْ رَأَيْنَا إِخْوَانَنَا. قَالُوا أَوَلَسْنَا إِخْوَانَكَ يَا رَسُولَ اللهِ؟ قَالَ أَنْتُمْ أَصْحَابِي وَإِخْوَانُنَا الَّذِينَ لَمْ يَأْتُوا بَعْدُ. فَقَالُوا كَيْفَ تَعْرِفُ مَنْ لَمْ يَأْتِ بَعْدُ مِنْ أُمَّتِكَ يَا رَسُولَ اللهِ؟ فَقَالَ: أَرَأَيْتَ لَوْ أَنَّ رَجُلًا لَهُ خَيْلٌ غُرٌّ مُحَجَّلَةٌ بَيْنَ ظَهْرَيْ خَيْلٍ دُهْمٍ بُهْمٍ، أَلَّا يَعْرِفُ خَيْلَهُ؟ قَالُوا: بَلَى يَا رَسُولَ اللهِ. قَالَ: فَإِنَّهُمْ يَأْتُونَ غُرًّا مُحَجَّلِينَ مِنَ الْوُضُوءِ وَأَنَا فَرَطُهُمْ عَلَى الْحَوْضِ». رَوَاهُ مَالِكٌ

A Sahaba, or Companion, of the Blessed Prophet ﷺ is anyone who heard, knew or spent time with him. These are the people who learned directly from him and passed their knowledge of Islam directly to their descendants. They were blessed in a way we can never be.

There were tens of thousands of Sahaba, each with their own unique story. Most were converts to Islam who had left idol-worship, Judaism or Christianity. A few were born into Muslim families whose parents were convert men and women.

Bilal, Anas, Abu Bakr, Um 'Amaarah, 'Uthman, Fatimah, Hussain, 'Aishah and 'Umar ﷺ are great examples for us even to this day. May Allah ﷻ help us learn from them.

Questions to Answer

1. According to a saying of the Blessed Prophet ﷺ, what is the difference between a Sahaba and a Muslim who lives at later point in history?
2. The Blessed Prophet ﷺ once said that the generation of the Sahaba was the best, and that after that, each generation will decline. Why do you think the Sahaba's generation could be described as the best?
3. Read 8:72 and explain how Allah ﷻ wants Muslims to treat each other.
4. The Blessed Prophet ﷺ had many Sahaba, both male and female. Select one of them not covered in this textbook and write a summary of their life and the major events in which he or she participated.

34 The Kitten Man ﷺ

WHAT TO LEARN

Part of learning is the ability to remember things. Some people have good memories, others forget things the moment you tell them. How can a person learn to remember things better?

VOCABULARY

Banu Daws Narrator
Abu Huraira ﷺ

THINK ABOUT IT

What was Abu Huraira's ﷺ great talent?

A. Who Was Abu Huraira ﷺ?

One of the most well-known of all the Prophet's ﷺ Companions was a man named Abu Huraira ﷺ. He belonged to the **Banu Daws Tribe** قبيلة بني دَوْس, which lived along the coast of the Red Sea. If you will remember, the Banu Daws were the ones who came to help the Muslims at the siege of Ta'if.

After the chief of the tribe, Al Tufayl bin 'Amr, had accepted Islam, Abu Huraira was curious about the religion. When he heard what Islam was all about from his chief, Abu Huraira ﷺ accepted Islam as well.

He was eager to meet the Prophet ﷺ and asked to accompany his chief on his next trip to Makkah. Thus, on his next journey, Al Tufayl took the young man along with him to see the Blessed Prophet ﷺ.

When Abu Huraira ﷺ came to Makkah, the Prophet ﷺ met with him and asked him his name.

"'Abdush-Shamms (Servant of the Sun)," he replied.

The Blessed Prophet ﷺ exclaimed, "Instead, let your name be 'Abdur Rahman, Servant of the Merciful." He immediately accepted the new name.

A few weeks passed, and then one day the Prophet ﷺ noticed that he liked to play with cats and kittens. The Blessed Prophet ﷺ called out to him, **Abu Huraira** أبو هُرَيْرَة, which means the **Kitten Man,** or literally, **Father of the Kitten.** The nickname remained and that's what everyone called him from then on.

After learning more about Islam from the Blessed Prophet ﷺ, Abu Huraira ﷺ returned to his village for a number of years to teach the religion to others. A few years after the Prophet's ﷺ Hijrah to Al Madinah, however, he and some other Muslims from his clan also went to live in Al Madinah.

Because he was poor and unmarried, he went to live in a room in the masjid called Bayt as-Saff with the other very poor Muslims.

B. The Mother of Abu Huraira ﷺ

Abu Huraira's ﷺ widowed mother had also come to Al Madinah although she was still an idol-worshipper. Her son always felt sad because she never accepted Islam even though he kept trying to convince her of the truth.

One time, when he tried to explain Islam to her again, she started yelling and saying terrible things against the Blessed Prophet ﷺ. Abu Huraira ﷺ came to the Prophet ﷺ with tears in his eyes. Upon seeing his sorrow, the Holy Prophet ﷺ asked him what happened.

Abu Huraira ﷺ replied, "I've never given up on inviting my mother to Islam, but she's always refused me. Today, I invited her again, and she said some words I couldn't stand. Please, make dua' to Allah ﷻ that my mother's heart will be moved towards Islam."

The Prophet ﷺ immediately prayed to Allah ﷻ for Abu Huraira's mother.

Later, he went home and found his door closed. He heard some water being splashed, and when he tried to enter the house, his mother said, "Stay out there, Abu Huraira."

Then she got dressed and finally said, "Come in!"

As soon as he entered and saw his mother, she announced smiling, "I declare that there is no god but Allah and that Muhammad is His servant and messenger."

Abu Huraira ﷺ hugged his mother joyfully, and then ran back to the Prophet ﷺ, crying tears of happiness. He announced, "I bring good news, Rasulullah. Allah has answered your prayer and guided my mother to Islam!"

C. The Long Memory

Abu Huraira ﷺ loved the Prophet ﷺ and wished to learn as much as he could. Once, when he was sitting in the masjid, the Prophet ﷺ heard him pray, "O Lord...I ask you for knowledge which will not be forgotten." The Prophet ﷺ himself said, *"Ameen."*

From then on, he spent a lot of time with the Blessed Prophet ﷺ. He memorized the entire Qur'an and many sayings of the Prophet ﷺ. He learned so many hadith that everyone became amazed with his knowledge.

Abu Huraira ﷺ later married Busrah bint Ghazwan and had many children of his own. He was also appointed the governor of Al Madinah, and later, of Bahrain.

But he never forgot his roots. He would often say, "I grew up as an orphan, and I immigrated as a poor person. I used to be given food by Busrah bint Ghazwan. I served people when they returned from journeys and led their camels when they set out. Then Allah caused me to marry Busrah. So praise be to Allah who strengthened his way of life and made Abu Huraira a leader."

Indeed, he became a leader in more ways than one. After the Prophet ﷺ had passed away, Abu Huraira ؓ dedicated his life to spreading his knowledge of the Prophet's ﷺ sayings to all.

A Muslim leader named Marwan bin al Hakim wanted to test Abu Huraira's ؓ memory of hadith one day. He invited Abu Huraira ؓ, who was then very old, to sit with him and tell him what the Prophet ﷺ had said. Secretly, Marwan had a scribe behind a curtain who was told to write down whatever Abu Huraira ؓ narrated. After many hours of speaking, he left. Marwan read the sheets of hadith.

After a year had passed, Marwan invited Abu Huraira ؓ again. He asked Abu Huraira ؓ to repeat the traditions he knew, and Marwan found that Abu Huraira ؓ had not forgotten a single word. Truly, Allah ﷻ answered his prayer, and gave him knowledge that would not be forgotten.

When you read sayings of the Blessed Prophet ﷺ, you will often see Abu Huraira ؓ listed as a **Narrator** رَاوِي, or teller of the hadith. We owe a debt of gratitude to Abu Huraira ؓ for his efforts in remembering and spreading the Prophet's ﷺ sayings.

Questions to Answer

1. Who taught Abu Huraira ؓ about Islam?
2. How did his mother come to accept Islam?
3. Where did he live when he first came to Al Madinah?
4. To which special dua' did the Prophet ﷺ say "ameen"?
5. How did he describe his humble origins and the blessings Allah ﷻ later gave him?
6. How was his memory tested?

Define: Narrator.
Reflect: How did Abu Huraira ؓ combine his dua' with 'action'?
Act: Look through the book to find a hadith that Abu Huraira ؓ narrated, and share it with a friend.
IQ Builder: Recite a portion of the Qur'an that you have memorized recently to a friend. Have them check to see how accurately you have memorized. Revise your memorization, if necessary.

35 Fatimah, Jewel of Islam

WHAT TO LEARN

Imagine seeing in one lifetime the rise of Islam from its early hard days to the end of the Prophet's mission! Fatimah saw it all! Throughout everything, she remained unwavering in her faith and dedication. She is one of the four most perfect women.

VOCABULARY

Nikah   Mahr

THINK ABOUT IT

How did Fatimah participate in the Islamic movement?

A. The Daughter of the Prophet

Fatimah was the fifth child of Muhammad and Khadijah. She was born in the year 606 CE, during the time before prophethood was bestowed on her father. While she was still an infant, Muhammad started the habit of going to the mountains around Makkah to meditate and think.

Her younger brother died soon after his birth, so she never knew him, and her three older sisters, Zaynab, Ruqaiyyah, and Umm Kulthum, were soon married and left home. This left Fatimah, along with Barakah, Zayd bin Harithah (the adopted son of Muhammad), 'Ali (the Prophet's cousin) and Khadijah, as part of the main household of the Prophet.

When Fatimah turned five years old, she learned that her father had been chosen by Allah to be His Prophet. Her mother, Khadijah, who was the first to believe in the message, explained to her daughter what her father had to do now.

Fatimah spent a lot of time with her father, and often went with him on his walks through the streets of Makkah. She even attended many of the secret gatherings that were held by the early Muslims when they were a persecuted minority.

One day, Fatimah was with her father when a group of idol-worshippers came and threw garbage on his back in the courtyard of the Ka'bah. With tears in her eyes, she cleaned the garbage off and yelled at the men.

When the Prophet finished his prayer, he made a dua' that Allah would punish those idol-worshippers. Later, at the Battle of Badr, those men would pay with their lives for what they had done to the Prophet.

The families into which Fatimah's three older sisters married all started persecuting them to retaliate against the Prophet for speaking out against idol-worship.

Ruqaiyyah and Umm Kulthum moved back into the Prophet's house after their husbands divorced them. Everyone was happy that they were now out of those bad families.

224

A short time later, the Makkans forced all the Muslims from their homes and made them live in a dusty, enclosed valley where there were only limited supplies of food. Fatimah was just 12 years old when she patiently endured the three long years of the boycott.

Even when it was finally over, Fatimah continued to face more trials and hardships. Her loving mother, Khadijah, passed away. Her death meant the loss of the one woman that everyone looked to for compassion. The Prophet's beloved uncle, Abu Talib, also passed away that year. Due to these events, this year came to be known as the Year of Sorrow.

B. A Loving Daughter

Fatimah soon realized that she had to give more comfort and support to her father. With great love and devotion, she dedicated herself to looking after him. She was so concerned with his health and welfare that she gained the nickname, **The Mother of Her Father** أُمُّ أبيها.

The Blessed Prophet had a special love for his daughter on account of her sincerity and good heart. He once said, "Fatimah is a part of me. Whoever pleased her, has pleased Allah, and whoever caused her to be angry, has angered Allah." (Al Bukhari)

قَالَ رَسُولُ اللهِ ﷺ: «فَاطِمَةُ بَضْعَةٌ مِنِّي، فَمَنْ أَغْضَبَهَا أَغْضَبَنِي».
رَوَاهُ الْبُخَارِيُّ

Fatimah earned the title, **Az-Zahra' The Shining Person** الزَّهْراء. That was because her beaming face seemed to radiate light. She preferred spending her time studying the Qur'an and serving Allah over such trivial things as gossiping and passing time in useless games.

Fatimah also had a close physical resemblance to her father. Once, 'Aishah remarked, "I've never seen anyone in Allah's creation resemble the Messenger of Allah more in speech, conversation and manners than Fatimah. When the Prophet saw her approaching, he would welcome her, stand up, kiss her, take her by the hand and then set her down in the same place he had been."

After Fatimah made the Hijrah from Makkah to Al Madinah, she stayed at first with her stepmother, Sauda, until her own home was ready. Soon, she started to receive marriage proposals which she promptly turned down. Then the young man 'Ali bin Abu Talib gained the courage to go to the Prophet and ask for Fatimah's hand in marriage.

When he approached the Prophet to ask, however, he became nervous and tongue-tied. He stared at the ground and said nothing. The Blessed Prophet then asked, "Why have you come? Do you need something?"

'Ali still couldn't bring himself to say what he wanted.

The Prophet then said, "Perhaps you came to propose marriage to Fatimah?"

"Yes," replied 'Ali.

The Prophet smiled and said, "Welcome to the family." Then he asked 'Ali what **Mahr Marriage Gift** مَهْر he had for Fatimah.

'Ali answered that he didn't have anything to give as a mahr. The Prophet then reminded him that he had a shield which could be sold. So, 'Ali sold the shield to 'Uthman for 400 dirhams (silver coins).

While 'Ali was rushing back to the masjid to see the Prophet, 'Uthman came after him and told him to wait a minute. Ali stopped, and 'Uthman told him, "I am returning your shield to you as a present from me on your marriage to Fatimah."

'Ali and Fatimah were married, and the Prophet himself performed the **Nikah Marriage** نكاح. The Blessed Prophet prayed, "Oh Lord, bless them both, bless their house and bless their children."

Life for the newlyweds was sweet yet difficult. To make their living, 'Ali worked as a water carrier, and Fatimah ground corn. One day, she said to her husband, "I've ground corn (so much so that) now my hands are blistered."

'Ali, who was also tired, replied, "I've

carried water until my chest hurts."

Then 'Ali ﷺ got an idea. "Allah has given your father some captives of war, so go and ask him to give you one as a servant."

After thinking about it, she went to the Prophet ﷺ to ask. But she felt shy and didn't say what she really wanted. Later, she and 'Ali ﷺ both went and asked together. The Prophet ﷺ replied that he had an obligation to help the poor Muslims first, so he couldn't grant their request.

Later that evening, the Prophet ﷺ came and visited them in their home and told them, "Shall I teach you something that is far better than what you asked me for? Words which Jibreel ﷺ taught me? You are highly recommended to say **SubhanAllah** سُبْحَانَ اللهِ 10 times after every salah, **Alhumdulillah** الْحَمْدُ لِلَّهِ also 10 times, and then **Allahu Akbar** اللهُ أَكْبَرُ 10 times. Then, before going to bed at night, you are highly recommended to say each one 33 times."

In later years, 'Ali ﷺ recalled that from that day forward, he never forgot to say those words.

C. A Blessed Lady

Life was hard for the Prophet's ﷺ family in Al Madinah, not because Islam was growing, but because the Prophet ﷺ lived a very simple lifestyle. He often went hungry and preferred to give food to others first before taking any himself. Once, Fatimah brought him a loaf of bread, and he replied that it was the first food he had eaten in three days.

On another occasion, the Prophet ﷺ returned to Al Madinah from a journey and immediately went to the masjid to perform two rak'as of prayer. Then he went to Fatimah's house to greet her. When she saw him, she began to cry. When the Prophet ﷺ asked her why she was crying, she replied, "I see you, Messenger of Allah, and your color is pale, and your clothes are worn out."

"Fatimah," he said, "don't cry. Allah has sent your father with a mission that He will make affect every house on the face of the Earth, whether it be in a town, village or tent. It will bring either glory or humiliation (on those who accept or reject it) until (Allah's) mission is finished, just as surely as nightfall always comes."

Fatimah ﷺ shared in the joys and sorrows of the Muslim community. She and 'Ali ﷺ were blessed with three beloved children, Hassan, Hussain and the little Zaynab. Although the duties of motherhood took up much of her time, she participated fully in the life and needs of the community.

In Al Madinah, she helped take care of the poor Muslims who lived in the masjid. After the Battle of Uhud, she acted as a doctor for the wounded. During the Battle of the Ditch, she recruited many other women to cook for the Muslim soldiers and led the prayer at her own prayer station. Today, there is a masjid called the Fatimah Masjid built in the place where her section of the defensive perimeter once stood.

Fatimah ﷺ also accompanied the Muslims when they made 'Umrah to Makkah, just before the Treaty of Hudaibiyah. She also marched, along with many other Muslim women, when the Muslim army finally took over Makkah from the idol-worshippers.

Imagine her happiness at being able to see her old neighborhood where she and her sisters grew up with their beloved mother, Khadijah ﷺ.

After a few more years, the Blessed Prophet ﷺ became ill. He told Fatimah ﷺ

that Angel Jibreel ﷺ had recited the entire Qur'an with him twice that year, whereas he had always done it once in previous years. This, the Prophet ﷺ explained, made him feel that perhaps his mission was coming to a close.

If you remember, as the Prophet ﷺ continued to grow weaker, he whispered to Fatimah ﷺ that he wasn't going to recover from his illness, so she cried. Then he told her that she would be the first of his family to join him in Paradise after he died, so she laughed.

Five months after the Blessed Prophet ﷺ died, Fatimah ﷺ woke up looking unusually happy. That afternoon, she called her friend Salma to help her take a bath and dress her in a new outfit. She asked Salma to help put her bed in the courtyard of her home, and then requested her to send for her husband, 'Ali ﷺ.

When 'Ali ﷺ came, he was shocked and full of worry when he saw her lying in the middle of the courtyard in bed. He rushed to her side and asked her what was wrong.

"I have an appointment today with the Messenger of Allah," she replied.

'Ali ﷺ cried tears of grief and she tried hard to comfort him. She told him to take good care of their children and asked that she be buried without any extra special ceremony.

She looked up at the sky, and then closed her eyes and entered an eternal sleep. She was less than 30 years old. May Allah ﷻ bless her and give her the best reward in Jannah! Ameen!

كل امرئ بما كسب رهين

Questions to Answer

1. List three examples of Fatimah's excellent character.
2. How did 'Uthman help his friend 'Ali bin Abu Talib?
3. What did Fatimah ask Salma to do?

Define: Nikah, Mahr.
Reflect: What, in your opinion, made Fatimah a great example for Muslims to learn from?
Act: Memorize the special thikr Prophet Muhammad ﷺ taught to Fatimah and 'Ali ﷺ.
IQ Builder: 'Ali and Fatimah lived life with little material wealth. Find ayaat in the Qur'an that discuss material wealth and its ultimate value.

36 Salman Al Faresi

WHAT TO LEARN

Allah guides Whom He wills to the truth. If a person shows they have a sincere desire to know what life is all about, then Allah will open his or her heart to Islam. A person who is on the trail of truth cannot be stopped by anyone except themselves.

VOCABULARY

Faresi
Ammuriyah

THINK ABOUT IT

How did Salman find Islam in the end?

A. The Story of Salman the Persian

If a person's heart is searching, no amount of material wealth or pleading can hold him down. This truth is spectacularly illustrated in the life of one of the most interesting of the Sahaba: Salman al Faresi. The word **Faresi** فارسيّ means **Persian**. He was from Persia, which refers to modern-day Iran.

He began life as a Zoroastrian, which is a follower of an ancient religion of Persia, and he later accepted Christianity. However, when he heard the message of Islam, he set out to search for its source.

This story inspire all to those who seek the truth all over the world. Salman's tale is told here in his own words, as he told it to others.

A map of Persia, which is modern-day Iran.

B. Salman Al Faresi - My Story

I grew up in the town of Jai in Persia, near the city of Asfahan. My father was the chief of the village. He was the richest person there and had the biggest home of all.

Ever since I was a boy, I remember my father loving me more than he did anyone else. And as time went by, his love for me became so strong that he developed an intense fear of losing me or of having something bad happen to me. So he made me stay at home, a virtual prisoner!

(Having nothing much else to do) I became devoted to the religion of Zoroaster and eventually became custodian of the household fire, which we worshipped daily. My duty was to make sure that the flame remained burning and that it did not go out for even a single hour, day or night.

My father had a huge estate which yielded many varieties of crops. He managed the estate himself and carefully calculated the harvest. One day, while he was occupied with his duties as chief of the village, he called to me and said, "My son, as you can tell, I'm too busy to go out to the estate just now. So you go and take care of matters there for me today."

The city walls of Bursa.

Off I went, but on my way back from the estate, I happened to pass by a Christian church. The sound of the people's voices inside attracted my attention. I didn't know anything about Christianity or about the followers of this or any other religion. This was because my father had always kept me in the house sheltered from people.

When I heard the melodic voices of the Christians, I stopped and entered the building to see what they were doing. I was impressed by the way they were praying and felt myself drawn to their faith.

"By God," I said, "this faith is better than what we have. I will stay here and not leave them until the sun sets." So I stayed and talked with the priest, who told me that the Christian religion originated in Syria.

There I remained the entire day and did not return to my father's home. When I finally did reach home later that night, my father met me and asked what had delayed me. I told him about my meeting with the Christians and how I was impressed by their faith. He became upset and said, "My son, there is nothing good in that religion. Your religion, and the religion of your forefathers, is better."

"No, their religion is better than ours," I insisted. My father became dismayed and feared that I would leave our ancestral faith. So he locked me up in the house and put a chain on my ankle. I managed, however, to send a message to the Christians, asking them to inform me of any caravan going to Syria that I might travel with.

C. The Escape to Syria

Before long, they contacted me and told me of a caravan that would soon be headed in that direction. I managed to unchain myself, and, concealing my true identity, accompanied the caravan to Syria.

When I arrived there, I asked who was the highest person in the Christian religion and was directed to the bishop of a local church. When I gained an audience with him, I explained my story and said, "I want to become a Christian, and I would like to become your servant so I can learn from you and pray with you."

The bishop agreed, and I entered the church in his service. I soon found out, however, that this man was corrupt. He would order his followers to give him money to use in charitable causes while holding out the promise of blessings for them. But when they gave money in the cause of God, he would take most of it for himself and give only a little to the poor and needy.

In this way he amassed a vast fortune. Then, when the bishop died and the Christians gathered to bury him, I told them of his corrupt doings. At their request, I showed them where he kept their stolen donations. When they saw the large jars filled with gold and silver, they cried, "By God, we will never bury him." Instead, they nailed his body on a cross and threw stones at it.

I stayed on, though, and continued to serve the person who replaced him. The new bishop was

IT'S ALL ABOUT ISLAM

D. From Slave to Sahaba

A group of Arabs from the tribe of Kalb were passing through the city. I asked them to take me with them to their land in return for whatever money I had. They agreed and I paid them.

When we reached Wadi al Qura (a place half-way between Al Madinah and Syria), they broke the deal and sold me into slavery. A Jewish trader bought me. I worked as a servant for him but eventually he sold me to a nephew of his who belonged to the tribe of Banu Quraytha.

This nephew took me with him to Yathrib, the city of palm groves, which is how the priest at Ammuriyah had described it. At that time, the Prophet ﷺ was inviting his people in Makkah to accept Islam, but I did not hear anything about him then because of the harsh duties that slavery brought upon me.

When the Prophet ﷺ reached Yathrib after his Hijrah from Makkah, I was working at the top of a date-palm tree belonging to my master, who was sitting under the tree. A nephew of his came up and said, "May Allah declare war on the Aws and the Khazraj (the two main Arab tribes of Yathrib). By Allah, they are even now gathering at Quba' to meet a man who has today come from Makkah and who claims he is a prophet. I passed by the crowd."

I felt hot flashes as soon as I heard those words, and I began to shiver so violently that I was afraid that I might fall on my master. I quickly climbed down from the tree and spoke to my master's nephew.

"What did you say?" I asked, "Repeat the news for me."

My master became very angry at my insolence, and he hit me hard. "What does it matter to you? Go back to what you were doing!" he shouted.

That night, I took some dates that I had gathered, and went to the place where the Prophet ﷺ was staying. I walked up to him and said, "I have heard that you are a righteous man and that you have Companions with you who are strangers and are in need. Here is something from me as charity. I see that you are more deserving of it than others."

The Prophet ﷺ asked his Companions to have them, but he himself didn't eat any of them. So a few days later, I gathered some more dates. When the

The Roman Orthodox Church of the Entrance of Theotokus - Hama, Syria.

a spiritual man who longed for the Hereafter. He would worship Allah day and night. I became greatly devoted to him and spent a long time in his company. But alas, he was very old and passed away, leaving me alone again.

So I set out to find a new priest I could serve and learn from. I traveled to Mosul, Nisibus and many other cities and served many important men. Some were good in character; others were less than virtuous. Finally, I came into the service of a wise priest in the city of **Ammuriyah** عَمُّورِيَّة, Palestine. He told me about a new prophet whom God was going to choose, and he would be in the land of the Arabs.

He gave me some signs by which I might recognize him. First, he would have a reputation for strict honesty. Next, he would accept charity but would never use it himself, he would give it away. But if given a gift for himself, he would take it. Also, he would have a birth mark between his shoulders.

He also added that the city where I would find him would be filled with date-palm groves. Hearing the news of a new prophet filled me with longing and delight. How I wished I could serve a man whom God Himself had given guidance to. With all haste, I gathered my meager supplies and looked for a way into the land of the Arabs.

Prophet ﷺ was leaving Quba' for Al Madinah, I went to him and said, "I noticed that you didn't eat any of the dates I gave in charity. These, however, are a gift for you especially." Of this gift of dates, both he and his Companions ate.

When I saw that he wouldn't take charity for himself, but only shared in the gift when I said it was for him, I became very excited. A few days later, I saw him attending a funeral. I came up behind him, and I saw the birthmark on his back where his shirt was parted.

All the signs were true! So I told the Prophet ﷺ my story and begged to be allowed to serve him and to follow his teachings. But I was a slave, I explained, and could not buy my freedom.

The Holy Prophet ﷺ then told me that he would buy my freedom from the Jew and that I was a seeker of truth. Elated, I returned to my master to await my promised freedom.

The next day, when the Prophet ﷺ came with some of his Companions, he offered to pay the Jew a sum of money to free me. The Jew agreed, but then added a condition that I had to plant a whole grove full of palm trees (300 trees in all) before the deal would go through.

I cried to the Messenger of Allah, "How can I pay this heavy price?" He merely told me, "Don't worry about it. Allah will manage things for you."

Imagine how my shock turned to joy! The following day, the Prophet ﷺ returned with a whole crowd of his Companions, who all worked together to plant an entire grove! The Prophet ﷺ placed each baby tree in the ground with his own hands, after his Companions dug the holes. My freedom was secured, and I became a Companion of Allah's Last Messenger on Earth.

From that day on, whenever I met anyone new, and they asked me whose son I was, I would always reply, "I am Salman, the son of Islam, from the children of Adam."

Questions to Answer

1. Why was Salman attracted to Christianity?
2. What bad deed did he see a priest doing?
3. What news was he given by the priest of Ammuriyah?
4. How was Salman betrayed by the Kalb tribe, and what happened to him?
5. How did Salman feel when he heard about Prophet Muhammad ﷺ?
6. What three tests did the Prophet ﷺ pass that satisfied Salman?

Define: Faresi, Asfahan.

Reflect: If you were Salman, how would you have answered your owner when he asked you why you had converted?

Act: Interview someone who has converted to Islam and summarize their story in your own words.

IQ Builder: Salman al Faresi's story illustrates some characteristics of Prophet Muhammad ﷺ. Find some other characteristics of the Prophet ﷺ described throughout the Qur'an, noting the ayaat numbers for each.

37 Julaybib ﷺ, the Unlikely Hero

WHAT TO LEARN

People often look down upon others if they are handicapped, short, less attractive or different in any way. But underneath the skin and the body, we're all the same, and Allah ﷻ only considers the soul of a person.

VOCABULARY

Julaybib

THINK ABOUT IT

Why did a girl decide to marry a deformed man?

A. The Lowest Man in Al Madinah

Julaybib was a poor man from Al Madinah. He had no family, no tribe and even worse, he was very unattractive. His very nick name, **Julaybib** جُلَيْبِيب, meant **Little Woman's Dress.** People used to make fun of him and tease him wherever he went. He truly had many challenges in his life.

When the Prophet ﷺ came to Al Madinah, Julaybib immediately accepted Islam, along with so many others. Because Islam taught the equality of all people, Julaybib ﷺ began to feel a little better about himself, and people teased him less.

Old habits and prejudices die hard in some people however. As you will see in the following story, sometimes a bad situation can turn itself around and become the best thing of all.

B. A Strange Proposal

The Blessed Prophet ﷺ decided to do something that should have been done long before. He went to the house of one of the Ansar and said, "I want your daughter to be married."

The man was overjoyed and replied, "How wonderful and blessed and what a great thing to see!"

"I don't want to marry her myself," the Prophet ﷺ remarked.

The man felt a little let down, and asked, "Then who will she marry?"

"Julaybib," he replied.

The man was shocked and horrified. After quickly calming himself down, however, he managed to say, "I will consult with her mother." Then he rushed to his wife.

"The Messenger of Allah wants to have your daughter married," he told her.

His wife was overjoyed and thrilled. "What a wonderful thing!" she cried with delight.

"He doesn't want to marry her himself," he lamented. "He wants her to marry Julaybib."

She was horrified and upset. She hated Julaybib ﷺ for his ugliness, just like most

An old Muslim cemetery.

everyone else did. She finally cried out, "To Julaybib! No, never to Julaybib! No, by Allah, we will never marry her to him!"

The man was about to go and tell the Prophet ﷺ what his wife decided when the daughter herself came into the room. "Who asked you if they could marry me?" she inquired.

Her mother told her about the Prophet's request that she marry Julaybib ﷺ. The daughter heard her mother complain and saw how she turned down the request. This bothered the daughter greatly.

"Do you refuse the request of the Messenger of Allah?" she finally asked her mother. "Send me to Julaybib, for he won't harm me."

The daughter then read a verse from the Qur'an to her parents that called believers to obey the Prophet ﷺ in all good things. Then she looked at them and said, "I am satisfied and submit myself to whatever the Messenger of Allah considers good for me."

When the Prophet ﷺ heard what she said, he prayed for her, "O Lord, grant her good in abundance and save her from a life of hard work and trouble."

Then, Julaybib ﷺ was wed to her. They lived together, though only for a short time.

C. The Unlikely Hero

Once, when he was traveling with the Prophet ﷺ on an expedition, a group of idol-worshippers ambushed them. After the battle was over, the Prophet ﷺ asked his Companions, "Have you lost anyone?"

The Companions gave the names of their relatives and friends that they had lost. Then the Prophet ﷺ asked another group of Sahaba nearby the same question. They also named the ones that they had lost in the battle. A third group reported that they had lost no one.

Then the Prophet ﷺ said, "But I have lost Julaybib. Look for him on the battlefield."

They searched for him and finally located his body lying next to seven dead idol-worshippers. The Prophet ﷺ rushed to the scene, and when he saw Julaybib, he said sadly, "He killed seven and then was killed? This (man) is of me, and I am of him."

He repeated these words a couple more times. Then, he bent down and held Julaybib ﷺ in his arms. The Prophet ﷺ dug a grave for him with his own hands and placed him in it. He did not wash his body because martyrs are not washed before burial.

When Julaybib's ﷺ wife was told of her husband's death, she must have been filled with sorrow. But she was a woman who knew what this life was really about, as demonstrated by her willingness to marry him in the first place for the sake of Allah ﷻ.

She probably remembered another ayah of the Qur'an that speaks about those who are killed in the Cause of Allah ﷻ. She might have repeated that ayah that night before drifting off to sleep.

Don't say those who are killed in the Cause of Allah are dead. No, they are alive even though you don't understand how. Surat Al Baqarah (The Cow) 2:154

﴿وَلَا تَقُولُوا لِمَن يُقْتَلُ فِي سَبِيلِ اللَّهِ أَمْوَاتٌ ۚ بَلْ أَحْيَاءٌ وَلَٰكِن لَّا تَشْعُرُونَ﴾ سُورَةُ البَقَرَة 2: 154

Questions to Answer

1. Why was Julaybib not accepted in his society?
2. When the Prophet ﷺ asked the family to marry their daughter to Julaybib, how did the parents react?
3. The Blessed Prophet ﷺ once said, "Allah ﷻ does not care about your looks or your money; rather, He cares about your taqwa and actions." How does this hadith relate to the story of Julaybib?

Define: Julaybib

Reflect: How would you answer someone who, because of their own prejudices, advised you not to marry someone?

Act: The Blessed Prophet ﷺ once said, "The example of a believer is like a fresh plant; the wind tilts it this way and that way; so is a believer; he continues to be subjected to afflictions. The likeness of a hypocrite is of a firm cedar tree; it does not shake—until it is uprooted all at once." (Al Bukhari and Muslim) Write or print this hadith and pair it with an illustration. Frame it and place it where you can see it whenever you are troubled.

IQ Builder: Look up the ayah that the future bride read to her parents, copy it down in English or Arabic and then explain how knowing that ayah affected her decision. (See 33:36)

38. Abu Dharr Al Ghifari ﷺ

WHAT TO LEARN

There have always been people so brave that they would do something they believed in even if it got them into trouble. Have you ever stood up for something even though you knew it might get you hurt?

VOCABULARY

Ghifar

THINK ABOUT IT

What were Abu Dharr's ﷺ experiences while giving da'wah?

A. Abu Dharr ﷺ from the Tribe of Ghifar

Islam teaches that the truth must be spread to all. The Qur'an offers the best advice on how to give da'wah, and the Blessed Prophet ﷺ explained how it should be done.

The story of **Abu Dharr** أبو ذر ﷺ, from the tribe of **Ghifar** غفار, is one of the many real-life examples of how an everyday person put this into effect. Though he was just a young man from a poor family in a place called the Waddan Valley, Abu Dharr ﷺ lived a very full life.

Known for his great courage, he practical nature and had already decided from an early age that idol-worship was foolish.

When he heard that there was a prophet in the distant city of Makkah, he wasted no time in asking his brother Anis to go and gather more information about him. He said, "Go to Makkah and get whatever news you can about this man. He claims to be a prophet and to receive revelation that comes to him from heaven. Listen to some of his words and come back and repeat them to me."

Anis went to Makkah and met the Prophet ﷺ as instructed. He listened to what he had to say. Then he returned to Abu Dharr ﷺ, who met him and anxiously asked for news of the Prophet ﷺ.

"I have seen a man," reported Anis, "who calls people to noble qualities, and there is no mere poetry in what he says."

"What do people say about him?" asked Abu Dharr ﷺ.

"They say he is a magician, a fortune-teller or a poet."

"My curiosity isn't satisfied. I'm not finished with this matter. Will you look after my family while I go out and examine this Prophet's mission myself?"

"Yes. But beware of the Makkans."

B. The Encounter with 'Ali

On his arrival in Makkah, Abu Dharr ﷺ immediately felt very apprehensive and decided to exercise great caution. The Quraysh were noticeably angry over the Muslim's verbal attacks on their idols.

Abu Dharr ﷺ heard of the terrible violence they were inflicting on the followers of the Prophet ﷺ, though he wasn't surprised. He therefore refrained from asking anyone about Muhammad ﷺ, not knowing whether that person might be a friend or an enemy.

At nightfall, he lay down in the courtyard of the Ka'bah. 'Ali bin Abu Talib ﷺ passed by him and, realizing that he was a stranger, asked him to come to his house. Abu Dharr ﷺ spent the night with him and returned to the courtyard in the morning. He took his water pouch and bag containing provisions. He had asked no questions, and no questions were asked of him.

Abu Dharr ﷺ spent the following day without getting to meet the Prophet ﷺ. In the evening, he went to the courtyard of the Ka'bah to sleep, and 'Ali ﷺ again passed by him and said, "Isn't it time that a man knows his house?"

Abu Dharr ﷺ accompanied him and stayed at his house a second night. Again, no one asked the other about anything.

On the third night, however, 'Ali ﷺ asked him, "Aren't you going to tell me why you came to Makkah?"

"Only if you will take it upon yourself to guide me to what I seek." 'Ali ﷺ agreed and Abu Dharr ﷺ said, "I came to Makkah from a distant place seeking a meeting with the new prophet and to listen to what he has to say."

'Ali's face filled with happiness as he said, "By Allah, he is really the Messenger of Allah." Then he went on telling Abu Dharr ﷺ more about the Prophet ﷺ and his teachings.

Finally, he said, "When we get up in the morning, follow me wherever I go. If I see anything that I'm afraid of for your sake, I will stop as if to pass water. If I continue, follow me until you enter where I enter."

Abu Dharr ﷺ hardly slept a wink the rest of the night because of his intense longing to see the Prophet ﷺ and listen to the words of revelation. In the morning, he followed closely in 'Ali's footsteps until they were in the presence of the Prophet ﷺ.

"Assalamu 'alayka yaa Rasulullah," said Abu Dharr ﷺ, greeting him with the words 'Peace be upon you, O Messenger of Allah.'

"Wa 'alayka assalamullahi wa rahmatuhu wa barakaatuhu," replied the Prophet ﷺ, telling him 'And on you be the peace of Allah, His mercy and His blessing.'

Abu Dharr ﷺ was, thus, the first person to greet the Prophet ﷺ with the greeting of peace. After that, the greeting spread and came into general use.

The Prophet, peace be on him, welcomed Abu Dharr ﷺ and invited him to Islam. He recited some of the Qur'an for him. Before long, Abu Dharr ﷺ declared the shahadah, and entered the new faith. He was among the first people to accept Islam.

Now Abu Dharr ﷺ will continue the story of what happened in his own words.

C. My Adventure in Da'wah— Abu Dharr al Ghifari ﷺ

After (accepting Islam), I stayed with the Prophet ﷺ in Makkah, and he taught me Islam and how to recite the Qur'an. Then he said to me, "Don't tell anyone in Makkah about your acceptance of Islam. I'm afraid they might kill you."

"By Him in whose hands is my soul, I shall not leave Makkah until I go to the courtyard of the Ka'bah and proclaim the call of Truth in the midst of the Quraysh," I said.

The Prophet ﷺ remained silent. I went to the courtyard of the Ka'bah. The leaders of the Quraysh were sitting and talking. I went in their midst and called out at the top of my voice, "O people of Quraysh, I declare that there is no god but Allah and that Muhammad is the Messenger of Allah."

My words had an immediate affect on them. They jumped up and said, "Get this one who has left his religion!"

They pounced on me and began to beat me mercilessly. They clearly meant to kill me. But 'Abbas bin 'Abdul Muttalib, the uncle of the Prophet ﷺ, recognized me. He rushed into the middle of the angry men and bent over me to protect me from them. He told them,

"Ruin to you! Would you kill a man from the Ghifar tribe, and this while your caravans must pass through their territory?" They then released me.

I went back to the Prophet ﷺ, upon whom be peace, and when he saw my condition, he said, "Didn't I tell you not to announce your acceptance of Islam?"

"Messenger of Allah," I said. "It was a need I felt in my soul, and I fulfilled it."

"Go to your people," he commanded, "and tell them what you have seen and heard. Invite them to Allah. Maybe Allah will bring them good through you and reward you through them. And when you

hear that I have come out in the open, then return to me."

I left and went back to my people. My brother came up to me and asked, "What have you done?" I told him that I had become a Muslim and that I believed in the truth of Muhammad's teachings.

"I'm not against your faith. In fact, I'm now a Muslim and a believer too," he announced.

Then we both went to our mother and invited her to Islam.

"I do not have any dislike towards your religion. I accept Islam also," she said.

D. The Great Wisdom

From that day onward, this family of believers went out tirelessly, inviting the Ghifar to Allah ﷻ and did not flinch from their purpose. Eventually, a large number became Muslims, and the Salat Al Jum'uah was instituted among them.

Abu Dharr ﷺ remained in his country home, and then returned to Makkah when the persecution of the idol-worshippers was at its peak. He remained in Makkah for a little while until after the Prophet ﷺ had gone to Al Madinah.

When he arrived in Al Madinah at last, he asked the Prophet ﷺ if he could be in his personal service. The Prophet ﷺ agreed and was pleased with his companionship and service. He sometimes showed preference to Abu Dharr ﷺ above others, and whenever he met him, he would pat him and smile.

When the Prophet ﷺ led the Muslim army on the expedition to Tabuk, everyone except the hypocrites came along. One evening, while the army was making camp on the road, the Prophet ﷺ and the Sahaba saw a single man walking towards them from out of the desert.

Some people asked, "Who could that man be coming on foot alone?" The Blessed Prophet ﷺ answered, "It must be Abu Dharr."

When the man came within close sight, the Prophet ﷺ remarked, "May Allah have mercy on Abu Dharr. He is a loner. He walks alone. He will die alone and be raised up alone on the Day of Judgement."
(Al Hakem)

فقال النبي ﷺ: ((رَحِمَ اللهُ أبا ذَرٍّ، يَمْشي وَحْدَهُ ويَموتُ وَحْدَهُ ويُبْعَثُ وَحْدَهُ)). رواه الحاكم

When he reached the camp, Abu Dharr ﷺ explained that he was running late because his camel refused to move and had to resume his journey on foot. The Prophet ﷺ told him, "You are one of those I miss very much. For every step you have walked, Allah has forgiven one of your sins."

One day many years later, a man visited Abu Dharr ﷺ and began looking at the contents of his house. After searching for a while, he found it quite bare and empty. He asked Abu Dharr ﷺ, "Where are your possessions?"

"We have a house over there in the next life," said Abu Dharr ﷺ, "to which we send the best of our possessions."

The man understood what he meant and said, "But you must have some possessions as long as you are living in this world."

"The owner of this world will not leave us in it," replied Abu Dharr ﷺ.

During the rule of Khalifa 'Uthman ﷺ, Abu Dharr ﷺ became critical of how so many people were gathering wealth and living a life of luxury. He lived out his last days in a small village, in a simple house. His last dying wish to his wife and her maid was to be prepared in the sheets of burial when he passed away and to be taken to the side of the road.

There, his wife was to ask the first person who passed by to help her bury his body. She was to announce, "This is the body of Abu Dharr, the Companion of the Messenger of Allah. Help us bury him."

When he passed away a few days later, his wife carried out his request and took his wrapped body to the roadside. A short time later, a group of riders passed by led by a famous Sahaba named 'Abdallah bin Mas'ud ﷺ. Abu Dharr's wife declared her message to them, and the announcement brought tears to the eyes of the men.

'Abdallah bin Mas'ud ﷺ said, "The Messenger of Allah was right when he remarked, 'He walks alone, will die alone and will be raised alone on the Day of Judgement.'" The group of men then buried him in silent sorrow. Then they moved on.

Questions to Answer

1. Why do you think Abu Dharr ﷺ was curious about the news his brother told him?
2. Why do you think Abu Dharr ﷺ did not go to see the Prophet ﷺ right away in Makkah?
3. How did Abu Dharr ﷺ wind up staying in the house of 'Ali bin Abu Talib ﷺ?
4. How did his family react to him becoming a Muslim?
5. How did Abu Dharr ﷺ explain to his friend why he didn't collect a lot of things in his house?

Define: Ghifar.

Reflect: If you were Abu Dharr ﷺ, would you have gone and declared your Islam to the Makkans? Why or why not?

Act: Choose one thing that impresses you the most about Abu Dharr ﷺ and share it with a peer.

IQ Builder: Abu Dharr ﷺ invited his entire family to Islam. What are some ways that Allah ﷻ advises us in the Qur'an to invite others to Islam? Use an index to find such ayaat.

39 Asma' ﷺ bint Abu Bakr

WHAT TO LEARN

Asma' ﷺ saw the rise of Islam from its humble beginnings all the way to its final triumph. Then she saw how her son, the first child born to a free Muslim community, died in the cause of Islam. She could have remained sad, but she understood that Allah ﷻ had His own plan. She lived her life with dignity and hope in Allah ﷻ.

VOCABULARY

The Woman with the Two Belts

THINK ABOUT IT

What were the good qualities of Asma's character?

A. A Very Clever Woman

Asma' ﷺ, the daughter of Abu Bakr, is one of the most celebrated women in Islamic history. She was among the earliest people to accept Islam, and she devoted herself to the success of the Islamic cause with all her strength and ability.

Asma' ﷺ was one of the few people who knew about the Prophet's ﷺ plan to migrate to Al Madinah. She packed a food bag and a water jug for the Prophet ﷺ and her father, but could find nothing to tie it with. She decided to use the extra cloth of her dress-belt, and her father suggested she tear it into two strips. She earned the nickname, **Woman with the Two Belts** ذاتُ النِّطاقَيْن.

After most of the other Muslims had left Makkah for Al Madinah, she remained behind for a little while longer.

Asma's ﷺ quick-thinking in difficult situations was remarkable. When her father left Makkah, he took all his wealth, amounting to some 6,000 gold coins and did not leave any for his family. Abu Quhafah, Abu Bakr's old, blind and unbelieving father, heard of his departure. He went to Asma's ﷺ house and said to her, "I hear that he left you without money and has all but abandoned you."

"No, grandfather," replied Asma' ﷺ. "Actually, he left us a lot of money."

239

Then she took some pebbles and put them on a small shelf in the wall where they used to put money. She threw a cloth over the heap and took the hand of her grandfather and said, "See how much money he left us?"

In so doing, Asma' aimed to calm the fears of the old man and keep him from giving them anything of his own small resources. This was because she didn't want to receive any help from an idol-worshipper even if it was her own grandfather.

When the final emigration from Makkah to Al Madinah took place, Asma' was pregnant. She did not let her pregnancy, or the prospect of a long and difficult journey, delay her from leaving.

As soon as she reached Quba', on the outskirts of Al Madinah, she gave birth to a son. She named him 'Abdallah. The Muslims shouted, "Allahu Akbar" and "La ilaha ill Allah," in happiness, because he was the first child to be born to the Muhajirun in Al Madinah.

B. Asma's Nobility

Asma' became known for her fine and noble qualities and for the keenness of her intelligence. She was also an extremely generous person.

Her son, 'Abdallah, once said of her, "I have never seen two women more generous than my aunt, 'Aishah, and my mother, Asma'. But their generosity was expressed in different ways. My aunt would accumulate one thing after another until she had gathered what she felt was sufficient and then distributed it all to those in need. My mother, on the other hand, would not keep anything even for the next day."

Asma's mother, Qutaylah, once came to visit her in Al Madinah. She was not a Muslim yet, and was divorced from her father. Her mother brought her gifts of raisins and seeds. Asma' at first refused to admit her into her house or accept the gifts. She sent someone to ask 'Aishah and the Prophet of the legitimacy in her attitude towards her mother. 'Aishah, as advised by the Prophet, replied that she should certainly admit her to her house and accept the gifts. On this occasion, the following revelation came to the Prophet:

Allah does not forbid you (to have contact with), those who don't fight you because of your faith, nor drive you out of your homes. (You may) deal kindly and justly with them. Allah loves those who are just. Allah only forbids you (to have contact with) those who fight you for your faith, and drive you from your homes, and support others in driving you out. (Do not) turn to them (for friendship and protection). It is those who turn to them (in these circumstances) that do wrong. Surat Al Mumtahana (The Woman to be Examined) 60: 8-9

﴿لَا يَنْهَىٰكُمُ ٱللَّهُ عَنِ ٱلَّذِينَ لَمْ يُقَٰتِلُوكُمْ فِى ٱلدِّينِ وَلَمْ يُخْرِجُوكُم مِّن دِيَٰرِكُمْ أَن تَبَرُّوهُمْ وَتُقْسِطُوٓا۟ إِلَيْهِمْ ۚ إِنَّ ٱللَّهَ يُحِبُّ ٱلْمُقْسِطِينَ﴾ ﴿إِنَّمَا يَنْهَىٰكُمُ ٱللَّهُ عَنِ ٱلَّذِينَ قَٰتَلُوكُمْ فِى ٱلدِّينِ وَأَخْرَجُوكُم مِّن دِيَٰرِكُمْ وَظَٰهَرُوا۟ عَلَىٰٓ إِخْرَاجِكُمْ أَن تَوَلَّوْهُمْ ۚ وَمَن يَتَوَلَّهُمْ فَأُو۟لَٰٓئِكَ هُمُ ٱلظَّٰلِمُونَ﴾ سورة الممتحنة 60: 8 – 9

Omayyad Mosque (Grand Mosque of Damascus).

C. Courage in Tough Times

Asma' ﷺ lived to be about 100 years old, and survived through the terrible time of civil wars in the Muslim world. Her son, 'Abdallah, would later become a martyr during the Ummayid period. These were the days when Muslims were fighting each other for control of the Ummah.

Many Muslims supported 'Abdallah as the most fit for the job of khalifa. But the Ummayids were rival Muslims who were based in Syria. They had more powerful armies and wanted 'Abdul Malik bin Marwan to be the khalifa. In addition, they were willing to shed Muslim blood to get their man in power.

When 'Abdallah went to his old and blind mother for advice, the following conversation took place:

"Assalaamu alaikum, Mother."

"Wa 'alaikum salaam, 'Abdallah," she replied. "What is it that brings you here at this hour, while boulders from General Hajjaj's catapults are raining down on your soldiers in the masjid of the Ka'bah and shaking the houses of Makkah?"

"I came to seek your advice," he said.

"To seek my advice?" she asked in astonishment. "About what?"

"The people have deserted me out of fear of Hajjaj or are being tempted by what he has to offer. Even my own children and family have left me. There is only a small group of men with me now, and however strong and steadfast they are, they can only resist for an hour or two more. Messengers of the Banu Umayah are even now negotiating with me, offering to give me whatever worldly possessions I want if I just put down my arms and swear allegiance to 'Abdul Malik. What do you think?"

She replied, "It's your decision, 'Abdallah, and you know yourself better. If you think you're right and that you're standing up for the truth, then persevere and fight on as your companions who were killed under your flag showed perseverance. But if you desire the world, what a miserable soul you are. You would destroy yourself and you would destroy your men."

"But I'll probably be killed today, there's no doubt about that."

"That's better for you than surrendering yourself to Hajjaj voluntarily and letting some slaves of the Ummayid's play with your head."

"I'm not afraid of death. I'm only afraid that they'll mutilate my body."

"There's nothing after death that a man should fear. Skinning does not cause any pain to the slaughtered sheep."

'Abdallah's face brightened as he said, "What a blessed mother! Blessed be your noble qualities! I have come to you at this hour to hear what I have heard. Allah knows that I haven't weakened or given up. He is witness over me that I haven't stood up for what I have out of love for this world and its attractions, but only out of anger for the sake of Allah. His limits have been breached. Here am I, going to what is pleasing to you. So if I'm killed, don't feel bad for me but commend me to Allah."

"I will feel bad for you," spoke the aging but determined Asma' ﷺ, "only if you are killed in a useless and unjust cause."

"Be assured that your son has not supported an unjust cause nor committed any bad deed, nor done any injustice to a Muslim or a non-Muslim and that there is nothing better in his sight than the pleasure of Allah The Greatest. I do not say this to cover myself. Allah knows that I've only said it to make your heart firm."

"Alhumdulillah that Allah has made you act according to what He likes and according to what I like. Come close to me, my son, so I can smell and feel your body, for this might be my last meeting with you."

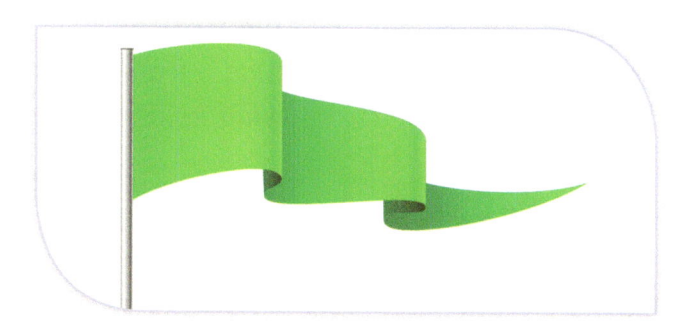

'Abdallah knelt before her. She hugged him and kissed him. Her hands began to squeeze his body when suddenly she withdrew them and asked, "What is this that you're wearing?"

"This is my armor."

"This, my son, is not the dress of one who desires martyrdom. Take it off. That will make your movements lighter and quicker. Wear a long robe instead, so that if you are killed, your body will not be exposed."

'Abdallah took off his armor and put on the robe. As he left for the center of town to join the fighting, he said, "Mother, don't deprive me of your dua'."

Raising her hands in supplication, she prayed, "My Lord, have mercy on him for his staying up for long hours and his loud crying in the darkness of the night while other people slept. My Lord, have mercy on his hunger and his thirst, on his travels from Al Madinah and Makkah while he fasted. My Lord, bless his good conduct to his mother and his father."

"My Lord, I give him to Your cause and am pleased with whatever You decide for him. Grant me, for his sake, the reward of those who are patient."

At the end of the day, 'Abdallah lay dead. 'Abdallah was a victim of *fitna*, or 'a tragic conflict,' between Muslims. Just over 10 days later, his mother joined him.

May Allah have mercy on her soul, and grant her the finest rewards for her emaan and strength of character. Ameen.

Questions to Answer

1. What happy event occurred when Asma' arrived in Quba'?
2. How did her son describe Asma's generous nature?
3. Who was Qutaylah, and why did Asma' feel strange about seeing her?
4. What is the main idea in the ayah that was revealed to cover the situation between Asma' and Qutaylah?
5. Why did her son come to her for advice many years later?
6. Who was Hajjaj?

Define: The Woman with the Two Belts.

Reflect: What is your attitude towards your mother or caregiver? Do you seek her advice on a regular basis? What kinds of things might your mother have more insight into than you do?

Act: Write down the advice you would you give to your son, if you had one, if he was fighting a large enemy.

IQ Builder: How does 3:139-142 explain what happened to the cause of Asma's son?

40 Other Sahaba ﷺ of Note

WHAT TO LEARN

The example of those who accomplished great things can inspire us to have courage during our own struggles. Has there ever been anyone you knew who overcame negative odds and went on to do something admirable?

VOCABULARY

As-Siddiq   Ahadun Ahad

THINK ABOUT IT

How did each of the Sahaba confront the ignorance of their people, and how did they overcome it?

A. Abu Bakr As-Siddiq ﷺ

Abu Bakr ﷺ, whose real name was 'Abdallah, was one of Muhammad's ﷺ closest friends, even before prophethood. After the Blessed Messenger ﷺ announced his mission to the world, Abu Bakr ﷺ was one of the first to accept it and become a Muslim.

Throughout the early days in Makkah, Abu Bakr ﷺ proved a faithful and solid believer. He stood up for the truth and never once wavered in his faith. It was Abu Bakr ﷺ who traveled with the Prophet ﷺ when they were on the run from the idol-worshippers during the Hijrah to Al Madinah. Abu Bakr ﷺ hid with the Prophet ﷺ in the famous cave of Thawr, which was protected with the miracle of a spider's web and a bird's nest.

In Al Madinah, Abu Bakr ﷺ was part of the Prophet's ﷺ advisory council and routinely donated large sums of money whenever the Muslims were in need.

He freed countless slaves, including Bilal ﷺ, who became pillars of the Muslim community. Before the expedition to Tabuk to fight the mighty Byzantine Romans, Abu Bakr ﷺ donated everything he owned except the clothes on his back.

When the Blessed Prophet ﷺ fell ill near the end of his life, he gave Abu Bakr ﷺ the responsibility of leading the salah for him in the main masjid. Once, when the Prophet ﷺ was well enough to attend the salah, he came out and went to join the rows of people praying. When Abu Bakr ﷺ saw the Prophet ﷺ out of the corner of his eyes he started to step back to let the Prophet ﷺ lead the salah. Amazingly, the Prophet ﷺ nudged Abu Bakr ﷺ back in the imam's position and prayed behind him.

After the Prophet ﷺ passed away, the Muslims elected Abu Bakr ﷺ as the first Khalifa. They knew that a critical phase in the life of the Muslim Ummah had come and that Abu Bakr ﷺ could provide that special leadership.

Abu Bakr ﷺ had a lot to deal with. First, he had to suppress rebellious tribes that wanted to change Islam. He then had to confront false prophets that arose in every corner of Arabia. Finally, he had to organize a system of administration from scratch.

With the help of Allah ﷻ, he succeeded on all fronts, and the Islamic state was established on a solid footing. He gained the nickname of **As-Siddiq** الصِّدِّيق **The Truth-Affirmer**. Indeed, he lived up to that title until the end of his life.

B. Bilal bin Rabaah ﷺ

Among the most well-known Companions of the Blessed Prophet ﷺ was Bilal bin Rabaah ﷺ. His example set forth the shining truth of the equality of all people. He lived in

243

IT'S ALL ABOUT ISLAM

a place where racism dominated and where a man was judged by the color of his skin.

Bilal ﷺ was the child of an African slave named Rabaah. People of African ancestry were often looked down upon by the idol-worshipping Arabs. Although skin color doesn't make one human different from another, this lesson wasn't known by the people of the world at that time.

Allah ﷻ made all human beings with the same inner components: a soul, feelings and the capacity for good and evil. When Bilal ﷺ, who was also a slave, heard about Islam, he saw it as humanity's chance to be released from the bonds of ignorance.

Because of his choice to accept Islam, he was endured horrible torture. After Bilal ﷺ declared that he was a Muslim, the man who owned him, Umayya bin Khalaf, was furious. He believed a slave had no right to worship anything except what his master told him. He ordered Bilal ﷺ to be whipped and to be pressed under heavy stones.

Once he asked some local teenage boys to take Bilal ﷺ out and beat him. They drove Bilal ﷺ out onto the hot plains and tormented him. Through all his suffering, Bilal ﷺ kept repeating over and over, the following phrase, **Ahadun Ahad!** أَحَدٌ أَحَدٌ **Only One! Only One!** His emaan never faltered, and the idol-worshippers could not break his hold on Islam. When Abu Bakr ﷺ heard about what was happening to Bilal ﷺ, he offered to buy him from his master. The disgusted Umayya sold him, and Abu Bakr ﷺ promptly freed his Muslim brother. Bilal ﷺ later killed Umayya in the Battle of Badr. He went on to become a great warrior, scholar and teacher. He even had the honor of being the first man to call Muslims to prayer.

The Blessed Prophet ﷺ even named Bilal ﷺ as one of his special compassionate Companions, whom Allah ﷻ granted to be with him in his mission.

Abu Buraidah ﷺ narrated, "the Messenger of Allah ﷺ awoke in the morning and called for Bilal, then said: 'O Bilal! By what have you preceded me to Paradise? I have not entered Paradise at all, except that I heard your footsteps before me. I entered Paradise last night, and I heard your footsteps before me, and I came upon a square palace having balconies made of gold. So I said: 'Whose palace is this?' They said: 'A man among the Arabs.' So I said: 'I am an Arab, whose palace is this?' They said: 'A man among the Quraysh.' So I said: 'I am from the Quraysh, whose palace is this?' They said: 'A man from the Ummah of Muhammad.' So I said: 'I am Muhammad, whose palace is this?' They said: ' 'Umar bin Al Khattab's.' So Bilal said: 'O Allah's Messenger! I have never called the Adhan except that I prayed two rak'ah, and I never committed Hadath except that I performed wudu' upon that, and I considered that I owed Allah two Rak'ah.' So the Messenger of Allah said: 'For those two.'" (At-Tirmidhi)

حَدَّثَنِي عَبْدُ اللهِ بْنُ بُرَيْدَةَ، قَالَ حَدَّثَنِي أَبِي بُرَيْدَةَ، قَالَ أَصْبَحَ رَسُولُ اللهِ ﷺ: «فَدَعَا بِلَالًا فَقَالَ: يَا بِلَالُ بِمَ سَبَقْتَنِي إِلَى الْجَنَّةِ مَا دَخَلْتُ الْجَنَّةَ قَطُّ إِلَّا سَمِعْتُ خَشْخَشَتَكَ أَمَامِي دَخَلْتُ الْبَارِحَةَ الْجَنَّةَ فَسَمِعْتُ خَشْخَشَتَكَ أَمَامِي فَأَتَيْتُ عَلَى قَصْرٍ مُرَبَّعٍ مُشْرِفٍ مِنْ ذَهَبٍ فَقُلْتُ لِمَنْ هَذَا الْقَصْرُ فَقَالُوا لِرَجُلٍ مِنَ الْعَرَبِ فَقُلْتُ أَنَا عَرَبِيٌّ لِمَنْ هَذَا الْقَصْرُ قَالُوا لِرَجُلٍ مِنْ قُرَيْشٍ قُلْتُ أَنَا قُرَشِيٌّ لِمَنْ هَذَا الْقَصْرُ قَالُوا لِرَجُلٍ مِنْ أُمَّةِ مُحَمَّدٍ قُلْتُ أَنَا مُحَمَّدٌ لِمَنْ هَذَا الْقَصْرُ قَالُوا لِعُمَرَ بْنِ الْخَطَّابِ. فَقَالَ بِلَالٌ يَا رَسُولَ اللهِ مَا أَذَّنْتُ قَطُّ إِلَّا صَلَّيْتُ رَكْعَتَيْنِ وَمَا أَصَابَنِي حَدَثٌ قَطُّ إِلَّا تَوَضَّأْتُ عِنْدَهَا وَرَأَيْتُ أَنَّ لِلَّهِ عَلَيَّ رَكْعَتَيْنِ. فَقَالَ رَسُولُ اللهِ: بِهِمَا». رَوَاهُ التِّرْمَذِيُّ

Bilal ﷺ was also one of the first seven people to publicly accept Islam. As you have learned before, after the Blessed Prophet ﷺ passed away, Bilal ﷺ vowed to never say the athan again. In later years, he dedicated his entire life to jihad and marched with the Muslim armies in Syria.

Bilal ﷺ was there when the victorious Muslims captured Jerusalem. 'Umar bin Al Khattab ﷺ traveled from Al Madinah to Jerusalem to capture the city himself, upon the request of the city leaders.

After establishing the peace treaty with the leaders of the city, 'Umar ﷺ asked to see the site of the ancient temple of Prophet Sulayman ﷺ. The temple had been destroyed by the Romans more than 600 years earlier. When 'Umar was taken to the location, he asked Bilal ﷺ to say the athan, given that they were standing in a holy place.

Bilal ﷺ agreed. When his powerful and full voice rang out over the city, all the Muslims who hadn't heard his sweet call for years stood in silence. When Bilal ﷺ returned to 'Umar ﷺ and the Sahaba around him, he found them in tears.

The only other time he said the athan again was when he was visiting Al Madinah, about five years later. He went to the grave of the Prophet ﷺ, and then sat down in tears, remembering all the times he had with his beloved guide and friend.

Suddenly, he felt a pat on his shoulders. He turned around to find Hassan and Hussain, the grandsons of the Blessed Prophet ﷺ, looking at him eagerly. A smile spread across his face, and he stood up and hugged them warmly.

Bilal ﷺ stayed with them through the night, talking about and remembering the old times. They finally asked him if he would say the athan for them at Fajr, which was fast approaching. For the sake of the grandsons of the Prophet ﷺ, he immediately agreed and accompanied them to the masjid.

When the people heard Bilal's ﷺ voice carry over the morning sky, they were stunned. Everyone recognized the voice they hadn't heard for many years. Throngs of people rushed to the masjid to see him. Many cried as a flood of memories of the Blessed Prophet ﷺ returned.

The Prophet ﷺ once remarked about Bilal ﷺ, "How worthy is Bilal! Only good believers try to follow his steps. Bilal ﷺ is the chief of all mu'athins, and mu'athins will be the most fortunate people on the Day of Judgement."

Let us learn from his lesson and make our emaan as strong as steel!

C. The Advice of Abu Darda' ﷺ

The Blessed Prophet ﷺ once observed that Islam is about giving good advice to each other. Some of the best advice for how we are to live our lives comes from people who learned their Islam from the Prophet ﷺ himself.

One of the most thoughtful Companions of the Blessed Prophet ﷺ was Abu Darda ﷺ. He accepted Islam after his best friend smashed his idol to bits showing him that idols were false. Although Abu Darda ﷺ was mad at first, he quickly saw that a god made of wood was no god at all.

Once he was a Muslim, he began to get restless in his quest for knowledge. He studied the Qur'an and thought about its meaning. After a while, he stopped opening up his store regularly.

A friend asked him why he wasn't doing much business lately, and Abu Darda ﷺ replied, "I was a merchant before my pledge to the Messenger of Allah. When I became a Muslim, I wanted to combine my business with my 'ibadah, but I didn't achieve what I wanted. So I left off business and have moved more towards 'ibadah."

"By the One Who holds my soul," he went on, "I want to open a shop near the door of the masjid so I won't miss any salah. Then, I can buy and sell and make a little profit every day."

In later years, Abu Darda ﷺ was asked to marry his daughter to Yazid, the son of Mu'awiyah, who was very rich. Instead, Abu Darda ﷺ married his daughter to a poor Muslim who had very good morals. When people asked him why he didn't marry his daughter to the rich Yazid, Abu Darda ﷺ replied, "What would you think of my daughter if she had servants, and lived in the glamour of a palace? What would happen to her (Islamic) lifestyle then?"

His wisdom was perhaps best demonstrated when he went walking one day, as was his usual practice. Along the way, he noticed a crowd of people beating and insulting a man. When he asked someone why the man was being beaten, someone replied that the man had committed a big sin.

Abu Darda stopped the people and said, "If you were walking and saw the man trapped in the bottom of a well, what would you do?"

They answered that they would probably help him out. So Abu Darda said, "Then don't insult and beat him. Instead, admonish him and help him understand that what he did was wrong. Then, praise Allah Who has saved you from committing the same sin."

One person asked, "But don't you hate him?"

Abu Darda answered, "I only hate what he has done, and if he stops doing it, then he is my brother."

Upon hearing this, the man who had been beaten began to cry, and he announced to everyone that he was truly sorry to Allah for what he did.

Questions to Answer

1. What cruelties did Bilal have to endure from his master?
2. What did Bilal say to the Prophet ﷺ when he was asked about how he got into Paradise?
3. Why do you think that Abu Darda lost interest in his trading business?
4. What was Abu Darda's philosophy about the punishing of wrong-doers?

Define: Ahadun Ahad.

Reflect: Why do you think the Blessed Prophet ﷺ appointed Abu Bakr to lead the salah during prayer times?

Act: Think about a Sahaba whose story resonates most with you. Choose one thing you have learned from that Sahaba and determine to apply it to your life from today onwards.

IQ Builder: How does the ayah 49:13 play a role in the way that people of different backgrounds are treated in Islam?

Unit 08 Review Exercise

VOCABULARY REVIEW

On a separate sheet of paper, write the definition of each word below.

1. Nikah
2. The Mother of Her Father
3. Mahr
4. Ahadun Ahad
5. Masjid
6. Amir
7. The Woman with the Two Belts
8. Banu Daws
9. Abu Huraira
10. 'Iddah
11. Ummah
12. Sahaba
13. Emaan

REMEMBERING WHAT YOU READ

On a separate sheet of paper, answer the following questions. Use complete sentences in your answers.

1. What terrible situation befell Umm Salamah ﷺ when she was escaping Makkah?
2. How did Mu'ath bin Jabal ﷺ say he was going to decide matters in Yemen?
3. What problem did Abu Huraira ﷺ have with his mother, and how was it resolved?
4. Describe three noble qualities of Fatimah's ﷺ character.
5. How did Salman al Faresi ﷺ go from being a Zoroastrian in Persia to a Muslim in Al Madinah?
6. What are two lessons from the story of Julaybib ﷺ?
7. Why did Abu Dharr ﷺ want to declare Islam publicly at the Ka'bah?

THINKING TO LEARN

On a separate sheet of paper, answer the questions below. Use complete sentences.

The Sahaba continued to teach Islam long after the Prophet ﷺ passed away. The people who learned Islam from the Sahaba are called the 'Tabi'een,' or 'followers.' Once the Prophet ﷺ mentioned that there would come a time when learning would vanish. A man named Ziyad asked, "Oh Messenger of Allah ﷺ, how will learning vanish while we have been reading the Qur'an and teaching our children to read it, and their children will teach it to their children, until the Day of Resurrection?" The Prophet ﷺ answered, "Oh Ziyad...Don't the Jews and Christians say they read the Tawrah and the Injeel, and they don't even know what is in them?" Explain what you think this statement means.

UNIT 9
Timeless Teachings: Fiqh and Shari'ah

41 Fiqh for Life: Islamic Law

WHAT TO LEARN

If there was a society without laws or norms of behavior, then it would be in chaos. Have you ever heard about a city or country in the news that collapsed into chaos?

VOCABULARY

Shari'ah   Fatwa   Haram
Fiqh   'Olama'a   Makruh
Hudood   Halal

THINK ABOUT IT

How do we know the best way to live?

A. Shari'ah: The Islamic Way

The word **Shari'ah** شَرِيعَة Islamic Law literally means a straight path or 'an endless supply of water.'

Then We have put you (O Muhammad) on a (plain) way of (Our) commandment [like the one which We commanded Our Messengers before you (i.e. legal ways and laws of the Islamic Monotheism)]. So follow you that (Islamic Monotheism and its laws), and follow not the desires of those who know not. Surat Al Jaathiyah (The Crouching) 45: 18

﴿ثُمَّ جَعَلْنَاكَ عَلَىٰ شَرِيعَةٍ مِنَ الْأَمْرِ فَاتَّبِعْهَا وَلَا تَتَّبِعْ أَهْوَاءَ الَّذِينَ لَا يَعْلَمُونَ﴾ سُورَةُ الجَاثِيَة 45: 18

It is the term used to describe the rules of the deen ordained for us by Allah. When you live your life the Islamic way, you are following the Shari'ah.

In more practical terms, the Shari'ah includes all the limits of Islam. What is allowed is called **Halal** حَلَال, and what is forbidden is called **Haram** حَرَام. What is allowed, but not recommended to do, is called **Makruh** مَكْرُوه.

The Shari'ah is meant for our own protection. For example, drinking alcohol, which is very common in non-Muslim societies, is in fact bad for people. Although a sip of red wine may be good for your heart, no one stops at just a sip. Instead, many people get drunk. That is because alcohol is a mind-numbing and addictive substance. Therefore, Allah has forbidden it.

They ask you about wine and gambling. Say, "In both there is great sin, and some benefits for people. And their sin is greater than their benefit." Surat Al Baqarah (The Cow) 2: 219

﴿يَسْأَلُونَكَ عَنِ الْخَمْرِ وَالْمَيْسِرِ قُلْ فِيهِمَا إِثْمٌ كَبِيرٌ وَمَنَافِعُ لِلنَّاسِ وَإِثْمُهُمَا أَكْبَرُ مِنْ نَفْعِهِمَا﴾

سُورَةُ البَقَرَة 2: 219

The word **Hudood** حُدُود limits of Allah means the edge of the border between acceptable actions and bad deeds, which we do not want to stray into.

These are the limits set by Allah. Whoever obeys Allah and His Messenger, He will

Allah's Limits

Halal	Makruh	Haram
Any object or action that is permissible to use or engage in or that is approved of by the Qur'an or by the expressed or silent approval of the Prophet.	Any action not forbidden but that seems to push the limits of the Halal standard.	Any action forbidden by the Qur'an or the Prophet. Any action that goes against the spirit of Islam.

249

admit him to gardens beneath which rivers flow, where he will live forever. That is a great success. Whoever disobeys Allah and His Messenger and transgresses the limits set by Him, He shall admit him to the Fire, where he will remain forever. For him there is a humiliating punishment.
Surat An-Nisa (The Women) 4:13-14

﴿ تِلْكَ حُدُودُ ٱللَّهِ وَمَن يُطِعِ ٱللَّهَ وَرَسُولَهُ يُدْخِلْهُ جَنَّٰتٍ تَجْرِى مِن تَحْتِهَا ٱلْأَنْهَٰرُ خَٰلِدِينَ فِيهَا وَذَٰلِكَ ٱلْفَوْزُ ٱلْعَظِيمُ ۝ وَمَن يَعْصِ ٱللَّهَ وَرَسُولَهُ وَيَتَعَدَّ حُدُودَهُ يُدْخِلْهُ نَارًا خَٰلِدًا فِيهَا وَلَهُۥ عَذَابٌ مُّهِينٌ ﴾ سُورَةُ النِّسَاءِ 4: 13-14

The operating principle of Islam is pretty simple: everything is allowed unless it is forbidden by the standards of the Qur'an or Sunnah. (59:7 & 7:157)

The Blessed Prophet Muhammad ﷺ said once, "Allah has given you certain duties to perform, so don't neglect them. He has defined certain limits, so don't go beyond them. He has forbidden some things, so don't do them. And He has kept silent about some things, out of mercy for you, and not because of forgetfulness, so don't ask questions about them." (Al-Daraqutni)

عَنْ رَسُولِ اللهِ ﷺ: «إِنَّ اللهَ فَرَضَ فَرَائِضَ فَلَا تُضَيِّعُوهَا، وَحَدَّ حُدُودًا فَلَا تَعْتَدُوهَا، وَحَرَّمَ أَشْيَاءَ فَلَا تَنْتَهِكُوهَا، وَسَكَتَ عَنْ أَشْيَاءَ رَحْمَةً لَكُمْ غَيْرَ نِسْيَانٍ، فَلَا تَبْحَثُوا عَنْهَا». حَدِيثٌ حَسَنٌ، رَوَاهُ الدَّارَقُطْنِيُّ وَغَيْرُهُ

B. Understanding the Way

The Shari'ah is the ideal path for us to follow. We learn what the Shari'ah contains from two primary sources: the Qur'an and the Sunnah. The Prophet ﷺ told us in his Farewell Sermon to hold on to these two sources.

All the major issues regarding our beliefs, others' rights, and what is good and bad to do, are covered in these two primary sources. Sometimes, however, people have different interpretations about what an ayah or a hadith means. Other times, there are situations where we need to find a clear-cut answer to a new issue facing us. What is the Islamic position on cloning, for example?

HARAM OR HALAL?

To help us overcome these hurdles, Muslims have developed a very detailed legal system in which complex issues can be studied, compared with known Islamic teachings and then evaluated. This science is known as **Fiqh** فقه **the science of understanding legal positions in Islam**. In the famous answer Mu'ath bin Jabal ؓ gave to the Prophet ﷺ before leaving for Yemen, he listed three things he would use to conduct legal affairs: Qur'an, Sunnah and Reason.

Thus, we can say that the Shari'ah is the path of living Islam, and Fiqh is the explanation of how to live Islam better. Even then, there will still be disagreements. But generally, most opinions fall under the four main schools of thought. Each school has its own particular methods of research and interpretation. This is not a problem, though, because it is the active pursuit of reason and knowledge that the Blessed Prophet ﷺ encouraged.

C. The Tools of Fiqh

The main tool developed by the **'Olama'a** عُلَماء, or **Scholars** of Islamic knowledge utilizes an important principle called **Ijtehad** اجتهاد **Independent Reasoning**. For example, if we wanted to determine the direction of the Qiblah while on the moon (a possibility of the future), a scholar would first look in the Qur'an and Sunnah to find an answer.

It is not for a believer, man or woman, when Allah and His Messenger have decreed a matter that they should have any option in their decision. And whoever disobeys Allah and His Messenger, he has indeed strayed in to a plain error.
Surat Al Ahzab (The Confederates) 33:36

﴿وَمَا كَانَ لِمُؤْمِنٍ وَلَا مُؤْمِنَةٍ إِذَا قَضَى ٱللَّهُ وَرَسُولُهُۥٓ أَمْرًا أَن يَكُونَ لَهُمُ ٱلْخِيَرَةُ مِنْ أَمْرِهِمْ وَمَن يَعْصِ ٱللَّهَ وَرَسُولَهُۥ فَقَدْ ضَلَّ ضَلَـٰلًا مُّبِينًا﴾ سُورَةُ الأحزاب 33: 36

If he or she doesn't find the answer there, then the next source would be the rulings and writings of the Sahaba. This is because the Sahaba learned directly from the Blessed Prophet ﷺ and dealt with many new issues. Their **Ijmaa'** إجماع **Agreement** on the subject would weigh heavily.

If there was still no answer, the scholar would then think about the issue. Then, guided by Islamic principles, he or she will arrive at a solution. This is called **Qiyas** قياس **Analogy**.

When a decision is made by a prominent scholar or other responsible scholars, a **Fatwa** فتوى **Official Legal Proclamation** is announced. Their verdicts are the scholars' best attempts at answering a difficult issue.

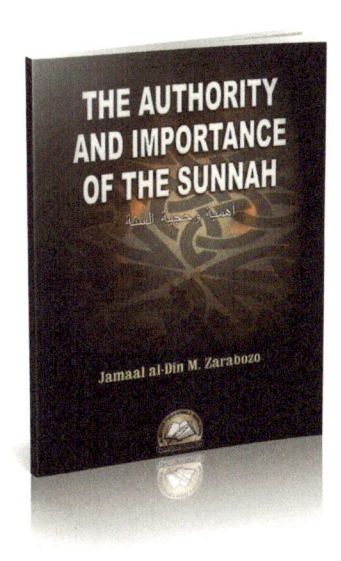

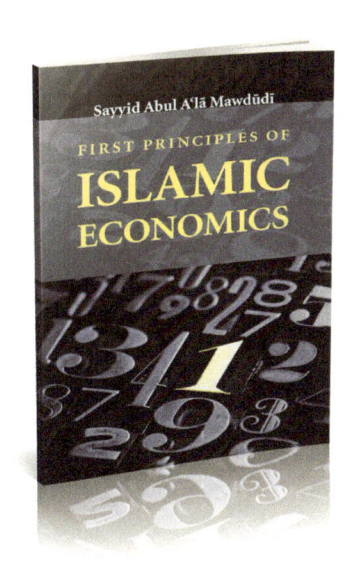

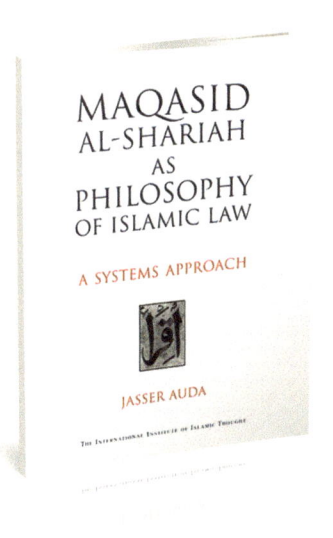

Books available at www.noorarat.com

A fatwa is not to be considered as binding for all time, however. This is because later scholars may understand an issue better as more facts come to light. In that case, new fatwas can be issued. It is strongly recommended for Muslims to listen to fatwas, and to take them seriously, because Islam teaches us to consult and follow people of knowledge. (16:43)

Have there been scholars who made mistakes and issued wrong fatwas? Of course, because they are only human. The Blessed Prophet ﷺ once mentioned that a scholar who tries their best, but makes a mistake, still gets a reward from Allah ﷻ for at least trying. If there is a fatwa that was issued that seems a little weak, it is the duty of Muslims in general to challenge it and arrive at the best answer possible.

The Islamic legal sciences are able to meet any new issue they come up against, because Islam is a way of life that can be lived in any time, any place, and any reality. Islamic Fiqh is a growing, transforming, and adaptive institution.

Whether we are stuck on our changing planet, colonize the stars or go back into a more primitive mode of civilization, Muslims will never be confused as to how to relate our way of life to the environment we live in. This is because Islam is based on the eternal principles of Allah ﷻ.

Questions to Answer

1. What are the four sources for ijtehad?
2. Are fatwas to be considered equal to the Qur'an and the Sunnah? Explain your answer.

Define: Makruh, Fatwa, Hudood.

Reflect: The Blessed Prophet Muhammad ﷺ said, "Whoever goes out seeking knowledge, then he is in Allah's cause until he returns." (At-Tirmidhi)

قَالَ رَسُولُ اللهِ ﷺ : ((مَنْ خَرَجَ فِي طَلَبِ الْعِلْمِ فَهُوَ فِي سَبِيلِ اللهِ حَتَّى يَرْجِعَ)). رَوَاهُ التِّرْمَذِيّ

What does this hadith mean to you?

Act: Create a display of the relationship between Shari'ah and Fiqh.

IQ Builder: What is the role of the Blessed Prophet ﷺ for the world, according to 33:45-47?

42. What Are 'Schools of Thought'?

WHAT TO LEARN

The Qur'an and the Sunnah of the Blessed Prophet ﷺ are pretty clear about how to live a good, dedicated life. However, there is room for interpretation and differences of opinion on some of the finer points and particular details.

VOCABULARY

Madhab   Al Furqan

THINK ABOUT IT

What is the purpose of a madhab?

A. Following the Shari'ah in Daily Life

Islam is a way of life that can be adapted to any time or place. This is proven everyday when millions of Muslims from every race, ethnic group and country, arise from their beds and live as believers in Allah ﷻ.

The path we follow, the 'Shari'ah,' contains the commandments of Allah ﷻ and His Messenger ﷺ about the best way to live our everyday lives. The source for this information is the Qur'an and the Sunnah.

If we face an issue that requires more help to answer, a scholar can do 'ijtehad,' or 'independent reasoning,' to arrive at an Islamically acceptable solution. The tools of ijtehad are: Qur'an, Sunnah, 'ijma and qiyas.

In the early days of Islam, some concerned Muslims wanted to make the Shari'ah easier for the common people to follow. Not everyone had the time to study the Qur'an and the Sunnah, nor were most people qualified to do ijtehad. In addition, new Muslims needed a simplified list of the do's and dont's of Islam.

So the 'Olama'a made it their mission in life to study the Shari'ah in detail and explain it to the people. There were many people engaged in this activity, both men and women. They worked tirelessly and wrote many books explaining the laws of Islam, the duties of people, halal and haram issues and much more. Some of these scholars were persecuted by evil rulers and spent time in jail for speaking out against tyrants. Most, however, were able to travel freely and spread their knowledge of Shari'ah far and wide.

Al-Hasan Al-Basri said, "The ink of a scholar is more noble than the blood of a martyr." This was a powerful incentive for people to study and promote learning.

Name of Scholar	Fact Sheet
Imam Ja'far As Sadeq	Lived: 699-765. Born in Al Madinah, Arabia. Renowned scholar and alchemist. Studied in Al Madinah and elsewhere. He is revered as an imam by the adherents of Shi'a Islam and as a renowned Islamic scholar and personality by Sunni Muslims.
Imam Abu Hanifa	Lived: 703-767. Born in Iraq. Studied in Al Madinah.
Imam Malik bin Anas	Lived: 717-801. Born in Al Madinah. Wrote the famous book Al Muwatta at the request of Khalifa Harun ar-Rasheed.
Imam Muhammad Ash-Shafi'i	Lived: 769-820. Born in Palestine. Studied in Al Madinah under Imam Malik bin Anas. Developed the basics of the methodology of Fiqh.
Imam Ahmad bin Hanbal	Lived: 778-855. Born in Baghdad. Studied in Al Madinah under Imam Ash-Shafi'i.

B. The Five Major Scholars

The five scholars that most Muslims recognize and follow today are: Imam Abu Hanifa, Imam Anas bin Malik, Imam Ash-Shafi'i, Imam Ahmad bin Hanbal and Imam Ja'far As Sadeq. Each of them gained many students who continued their work and developed fiqh into highly organized bodies of knowledge that are still consulted to this day.

It must be remembered that these scholars were trying to gain a better understanding of Islam. They were not inventing anything new in the deen. For example, Imam Malik did not want people to follow him, or any other person, in place of following the Qur'an and the Sunnah. He is quoted as saying, "The word of any person other than the Prophet ﷺ is sometimes accepted and sometimes rejected."

Each of these scholars also knew they were not perfect. Imam Ash-Shafi'i once said, "My opinion is correct, with the possibility of it being wrong. An opinion different from mine is wrong, with the possibility that it is correct."

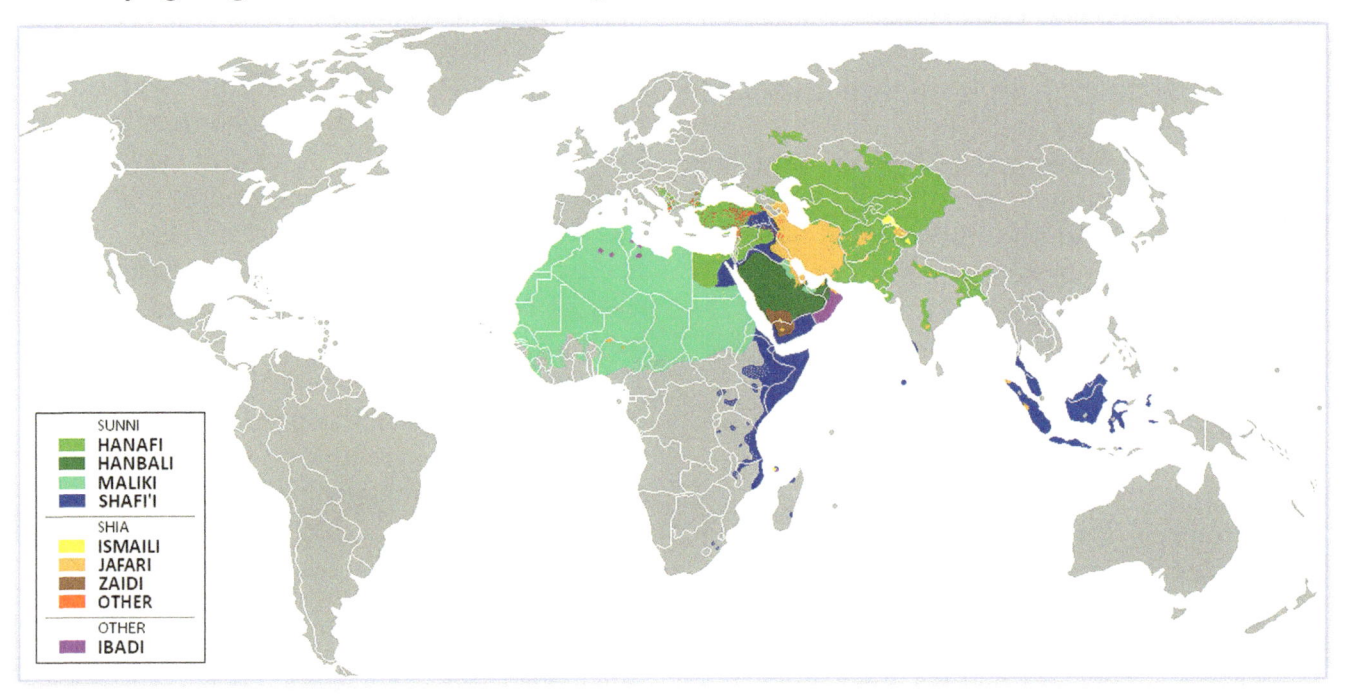

By stating this, the imam recognized that others may understand things better than him.

Each of the scholars were teachers and instructors. Although there were many other scholars working in the field of fiqh and Shari'ah, these five gained the most popularity.

The students of these scholars continued and expanded their work after they passed away. They formed what we might call 'intellectual clubs,' where the spirit of the founding scholar was used as the inspiration for the techniques, reasoning or methods of Islamic study that were developed.

In other words, the founding scholar taught his students whatever he knew. Then those students became teachers and passed on what they had learned to students after them. All along the way, new knowledge was added, and the people involved in that particular association of teachers and students became known as a **Madhab** مَذْهَب **School of Thought**.

C. Schools of Thought Today

Presently there are five main *madhahib* (plural of madhab) in the world: *Maliki, Hanifi, Shafi'i, Hanbali* and *Ja'fari*. Each is named after the founder of that madhab.

Each madhab is based on the Qur'an and the Sunnah. They employ the tools of ijtehad to find solutions to new issues that arise. Though there are differences of opinion between them on some things, they all agree on the major issues.

In fact, the madhahib agree on about 85% of all issues. The differences are usually regarding concerns that are not foundational to the practice of Islam. For example, let's say a woman's husband disappears while traveling without a trace and is never heard from again. When can the woman safely remarry? When can the long lost man be safely declared deceased? There's no ayah or hadith covering such a situation.

One madhab says you must wait one year, while another says you must wait for 99 years. The scholars use ijtehad arrive at an answer, and scholars can come up with very different responses. Thus, we can understand the nature of the differences between the various madhahib.

Unfortunately, some Muslims believe that the madhab they follow is the only way to live Islam. They look down on people who follow other madhahib and criticize them. This attitude is against Islam. Muslims should follow whatever methodology they choose, as long as it is in accordance with the Qur'an and the Sunnah.

Abu Huraira narrated that the Messenger of Allah said, "The Qur'an was revealed with five categories: Things lawful, things unlawful, clear and positive teachings, allegories, and stories. So hold lawful what is lawful for you and hold forbidden things forbidden.
Act according to the clear and positive teachings, affirm your faith in the allegories and draw lessons from the stories." (Al Baihaqi)

عَنْ أَبِي هُرَيْرَةَ قَالَ: قَالَ رَسُولُ اللهِ: «إِنَّ الْقُرْآنَ نَزَلَ عَلَى خَمْسَةِ أَوْجُهٍ: حَلَالٌ، وَحَرَامٌ، وَمُحْكَمٌ، وَمُتَشَابِهٌ، وَأَمْثَالٌ، فَاعْمَلُوا بِالْحَلَالِ، وَاجْتَنِبُوا الْحَرَامَ، وَاتَّبِعُوا الْمُحْكَمَ، وَآمِنُوا بِالْمُتَشَابِهِ، وَاعْتَبِرُوا بِالْأَمْثَالِ».

رَوَاهُ الْبَيْهَقِيُّ

The founding scholars of these schools of thought did not think they were teaching a new outlook on Islam. They simply wanted to know more, and make it easier for Muslims to practice Islam. In fact, most of these scholars studied together to begin with.

You can choose to follow a madhab if you wish, but you don't need to subscribe to one at all. It is helpful, however, to have some kind of fiqh books in your home to help guide you in your daily affairs.

The Blessed Prophet ﷺ oftentimes taught us many ways to do the same thing. This was a mercy for us. It gives us some choice in customizing our ''Ibadah,' or 'service to Allah ﷻ.'

For example, At-Tahiyat and At-Tashahud can be said in at least three different ways in the salah, all of them similar and traceable to the Prophet ﷺ. Each madhab prefers one over the other, but some followers argue that there's only way to say it.

There are many such instances, and Muslims must be aware that Islam is a faith with many allowable methods. If it can be traced to the Qur'an and the Sunnah, then you are welcome to follow it.

May Allah ﷻ help us recognize the madhahib for what they are: useful tools for understanding how to live the Shari'ah. May He help us not to fall into the ignorance of believing that the madhahib are different religions unto themselves that must be followed. Ameen.

D. How Do We Deal With Differences?

"Islam teaches that wudu' is done this way," the man said confidently.

"But you're wrong," the younger man replied. "That's totally against the laws of Islam."

"But it says in a hadith that—" the older man started saying.

"That's a weak hadith!" the younger man interrupted.

"Oh yeah! What's your proof? I read in a book that the Blessed Prophet ﷺ said to—"

By this time, both men were fuming. The young man screamed, "I read in a book, too, that—"

But before he could finish his sentence, the older brother pushed him, and he pushed back. A fight would have ensued if some quick-thinking men nearby hadn't broken it up.

The two brothers eyed each other angrily and left in opposite directions. Those who remained just shook their heads in silence. Here were two brothers ready to fight over a minor difference of opinion.

And obey Allah and His Messenger, and do not dispute (with one another) lest you lose courage and your strength departs, and be patient. Surely, Allah is with those who are As-Sabirun (the patient). Surat Al Anfaal (The Spoils of War) 8: 46

﴿وَأَطِيعُوا۟ ٱللَّهَ وَرَسُولَهُۥ وَلَا تَنَـٰزَعُوا۟ فَتَفْشَلُوا۟ وَتَذْهَبَ رِيحُكُمْ ۖ وَٱصْبِرُوٓا۟ ۚ إِنَّ ٱللَّهَ مَعَ ٱلصَّـٰبِرِينَ﴾ سُورَة الأنفال 8: 46

The funny thing was they both could have been right. They just didn't know how to handle a difference of understanding.

The Blessed Prophet ﷺ often remarked that Muslims are those who remain brothers even when they have a disagreement. He didn't mean that Muslims should argue about everything. Instead, he pointed out that if Muslims disagreed over something, then they must consult the Qur'an, Sunnah and the righteous scholars. This will prevent them from fighting amongst themselves and from disliking each other.

On many occasions, Muslims have disagreed over what something means or what to do. The key is to follow the Islamic manners of how to deal with differences. We don't have to agree all the time, but we shouldn't fight over disagreements either.

For example, before the Battle of Uhud, the Muslims had to decide what to do. Some wanted to go out and fight, while others wanted to stay in the city and defend it from there. The Prophet ﷺ listened to both sides. In the end, he accepted the will of the majority, who wanted to go out and fight. People disagreed over the issue, but they united after a majority decision was taken.

Allah ﷻ gave us a formula for dealing with differences. He told us that the Qur'an is **Al Furqan** الفُرْقَان, which means **the Standard**. A standard is something that we use to guide us towards the best beliefs, behaviors and actions. Further, Allah ﷻ instructed us to follow the example of the Blessed Prophet ﷺ.

If we have a disagreement, especially between one madhab and another, we must respect each other's opinions and present our evidence. In the end, even if neither side persuades the other, we must be courteous and respectful. If we find our position is wrong, then we should not stick with something that is not true. Simply say, "Alhumdulillah," and thank the brother or sister for helping you to understand the Shari'ah better.

'Umar bin Al Khattab ﷺ was once quoted as saying, "Allah ﷻ bless the person who makes me a gift of my own faults." The 'gift' is being able to realize and learn from one's mistakes. An arrogant person refuses to accept logic and never likes to listen to Allah's ﷻ guidance. In contrast, the Qur'an prefers those who are humble. It states: Those are the people whom Allah has blessed with bounties, the prophets from the progeny of Adam,

---

The Blessed Prophet ﷺ said, "Allah is gentle and loves gentleness in all things." (Muslim)

عَنِ النَّبِيِّ ﷺ: «إِنَّ اللهَ جَمِيلٌ يُحِبُّ الْجَمَالَ». رَوَاهُ مُسْلِم

The Blessed Prophet ﷺ said, "A rude and ill-tempered person shall not enter Paradise." (Abu Dawud)

قَالَ رَسُولُ اللهِ ﷺ: «لَا يدخُلُ الجنَّةَ الجوَّاظُ ولا الجعظريُّ». رَوَاهُ أبو داود

The Blessed Prophet ﷺ said, "Fear Allah wherever you may be. Follow an evil deed with a good one, and you will erase it. Deal with people on the basis of good conduct." (At-Tirmidhi)

عَنْ رَسُولِ اللهِ ﷺ قَالَ: «اتَّقِ اللهَ حَيْثُمَا كُنْتَ وَأَتْبِعِ السَّيِّئَةَ الْحَسَنَةَ تَمْحُهَا وَخَالِقِ النَّاسَ بِخُلُقٍ حَسَنٍ». رَوَاهُ التِّرْمَذِيّ

The Blessed Prophet ﷺ said, "A strong man is not someone who knocks other people out in a fight. A strong man is someone who controls himself when he is angry." (Al Bukhari)

قَالَ رَسُولُ اللهِ ﷺ: «لَيْسَ الشَّدِيدُ بِالصُّرَعَةِ إِنَّمَا الشَّدِيدُ الَّذِي يَمْلِكُ نَفْسَهُ عِنْدَ الْغَضَبِ». رَوَاهُ الْبُخَارِيّ

Anas bin Malik ﷺ narrated that the Blessed Prophet ﷺ said, "Don't be hostile to each other, or jealous or indifferent. Instead, be brothers as Allah's servants. No Muslim should avoid his brother for more than three days." (Al Bukhari)

عَنْ أَنَسِ بْنِ مَالِكٍ ﷺ، أَنَّ رَسُولَ اللهِ ﷺ قَالَ: «لَا تَبَاغَضُوا، وَلَا تَحَاسَدُوا، وَلَا تَدَابَرُوا، وَكُونُوا عِبَادَ اللهِ إِخْوَانًا، وَلَا يَحِلُّ لِمُسْلِمٍ أَنْ يَهْجُرَ أَخَاهُ فَوْقَ ثَلَاثِ لَيَالٍ». رَوَاهُ الْبُخَارِيّ

and of those whom We caused to board (the Ark) along with Nuh, and from the progeny of Ibrahim and Isra'il (Jacob), and from those whom We guided and selected. When the verses of The Rahman (The All-Merciful) were recited before them, they used to fall down in Sajdah (prostration), while they were weeping.

Surat Maryam (Mary) 19:58

﴿أُولَٰئِكَ ٱلَّذِينَ أَنْعَمَ ٱللَّهُ عَلَيْهِم مِّنَ ٱلنَّبِيِّۦنَ مِن ذُرِّيَّةِ ءَادَمَ وَمِمَّنْ حَمَلْنَا مَعَ نُوحٍ وَمِن ذُرِّيَّةِ إِبْرَٰهِيمَ وَإِسْرَٰٓءِيلَ وَمِمَّنْ هَدَيْنَا وَٱجْتَبَيْنَآ إِذَا تُتْلَىٰ عَلَيْهِمْ ءَايَٰتُ ٱلرَّحْمَٰنِ خَرُّوا۟ سُجَّدًا وَبُكِيًّا﴾ سُورَةُ مَرْيَمَ 19: 58

'Umar bin Al Khattab went up to a person he disliked one day and told him to his face, "I don't like you."

The person merely replied, "Are you going to take away my rights?"

'Umar answered, "I don't like you, but I will respect your rights."

On another occasion, Khalid bin Walid and Saad bin Waqqas were having a heated argument. After Khalid left, a friend of Saad's started saying bad things about Khalid. Saad immediately stopped the man, and told him, "The disagreement between us does not affect the bond of our faith."

Clearly, that is the best example for us to follow, in regards to dealing with differences among us.

Questions to Answer

1. Why was the science of fiqh developed?
2. What goal drove the scholars to research and travel far and wide?
3. What was the opinion of the scholars about the value of what they were doing, compared with the Qur'an and Sunnah?
4. What are the five main madhahib today?
5. What can we say about the differences between the madhahib on various issues?

Define: Madhab, 'Olama'a, Al Furqan.

Reflect: How do you deal with the differences of opinion over Islamic teachings? Is it in a manner that reflects the teachings of the Prophet?

Act: Create a visual aid that helps explain the relationship between a Muslim and a madhab.

IQ Builder: How does 30:31-32 and 6:159 relate to this lesson?

43. What Is Halal & Haram Food?

WHAT TO LEARN

We have to eat every day to survive. But the mere act of eating brings no benefit unless the food is good for our bodies.

VOCABULARY

Processed
Halal Foods
Dhabiha
Haram Foods

THINK ABOUT IT

Why are some foods haram?

A. The Food Issue

"That's haram!" she shouted to the little boy as he opened up his lunch box.

Inside there were two marshmallow-filled candy bars. The girl snatched them up and looked at the ingredients. Sure enough, there was gelatin and lard in them.

The little boy, who realized he was losing his tasty treats, frowned and looked down at his now-empty lunch box.

He didn't know why he couldn't eat them. After all, his own mom bought those candy bars for him all the time. How could something his mother got him be bad? He wouldn't understand for many years.

Does this situation sound familiar? I'm sure it does, and you may wonder sometimes why certain foods are called 'haram' and others 'halal.'

To put it simply, haram foods are forbidden foods because they contain ingredients that Allah ﷻ has told people not to consume.

Allah ﷻ said, *People, eat from the world what is lawful and good. But don't follow in the ways of the Shaytan, because he is your declared enemy.* Surat Al Baqarah (The Cow) 2:168

﴿يَٰٓأَيُّهَا ٱلنَّاسُ كُلُوا۟ مِمَّا فِى ٱلْأَرْضِ حَلَٰلًا طَيِّبًا وَلَا تَتَّبِعُوا۟ خُطُوَٰتِ ٱلشَّيْطَٰنِ ۚ إِنَّهُۥ لَكُمْ عَدُوٌّ مُّبِينٌ﴾ سُورَةُ البَقَرَة 2: 168

Halal Foods الأَطْعِمَةُ الحَلال are those that Allah ﷻ has said are acceptable for people to eat. The basic rule is that something is halal, unless it has been deemed otherwise. Therefore, there are more foods that are halal than haram, even in our modern society.

There are four specific types of **Haram Foods** الأَطْعِمَةُ الحَرام, or those that are forbidden by Allah ﷻ. Allah ﷻ tells us about these in the Qur'an: *He has only forbidden you to eat dead meat, blood, pork, and food dedicated to idols in place of Allah. But if someone is forced to eat those things—without willfully disobeying nor going overboard—then there is no blame on them because Allah is the Forgiving and Merciful.* Surat Al Baqarah (The Cow) 2:173

﴿إِنَّمَا حَرَّمَ عَلَيْكُمُ ٱلْمَيْتَةَ وَٱلدَّمَ وَلَحْمَ ٱلْخِنزِيرِ وَمَآ أُهِلَّ بِهِۦ لِغَيْرِ ٱللَّهِ ۖ فَمَنِ ٱضْطُرَّ غَيْرَ بَاغٍ وَلَا عَادٍ فَلَآ إِثْمَ عَلَيْهِ ۚ إِنَّ ٱللَّهَ غَفُورٌ رَّحِيمٌ﴾ سُورَةُ البَقَرَة 2: 173

The Blessed Prophet ﷺ always used to ask the name of a food before eating it. If it was a haram food, he wouldn't eat of it.

IT'S ALL ABOUT ISLAM

The trouble we have, living in our day and age, is that so many foods in the supermarket are **Processed** foods. A food is called 'processed' when many ingredients are brought together, and then mixed and pre-cooked so that it is ready to eat.

These processed foods are filled with chemicals and strange ingredients. Many are then radiated to make them resistant to spoilage while they sit on the store shelves for weeks, months or even years.

That candy bar you're eating could be a year old or more! The source for many of these unusual ingredients is often from animals, in particular cows and pigs. For example, enzymes, a main ingredient for almost all cheeses and dairy products, are usually scraped out of dead cow or pig stomachs. Some cheeses may use plant-based or lab-created enzymes, however.

Many brands of flavored gelatins and marshmallows are made from collagen that is extracted from the skin and bones of animals—mostly cows and pigs. Dough conditioners and emulsifiers are often-times taken from pig and cow intestines, stomachs and other animal parts. If most people traced back the source of their foods, they might reconsider their diet.

B. The Best Foods

The best things for a Muslim to consume are fresh halal meats, fruits, grains, vegetables and fresh-baked breads and pastries. If you want to buy processed foods, then check the ingredients carefully. Don't buy things with lard (pig and cow grease), enzymes (unless it says vegetable enzymes), mono- and di-glycerides (unless it says vegetable mono- and di-glycerides), or other strange ingredients.

As Muslims, we place our trust in Allahﷻ. If He has told us not to eat certain things, then it's for a good reason. Remember this phrase, "Allahﷻ said it, the Prophet ﷺ lived it, and I will follow it."

If you have a favorite food, write to the company and ask for a complete list of ingredients and their sources. It is your right as a consumer to know these ingredients, thus, you will find that the companies will reply to your concerns. You can also look in a halal/haram food guide. However, these lists are being constantly revised, so contacting the company is usually a more accurate method.

Sample Ingredients List: Underlined items are most likely from haram sources.

Ingredients: Wheat, wheat flour, barley malt, beef fat, canola oil, <u>dough conditioners</u>, salt, <u>lard</u>, <u>mono and di-glycerides</u>, sodium benzoate, BHT, citric acid, <u>sherry</u>, <u>brandy</u> and <u>red wine</u>.

Seafood is halal.

Remember, if you stay away from something in this life for Allah's ﷻ sake, He will reward you more than you can ever imagine.

C. The Meat of Ahl Al Kitab

Islam does teach that the meat slaughtered by the Ahl Al Kitab (People of the Book: Jews and Christians) is halal for us. (5:5) However, unless the meat at the supermarket is specifically labeled as such, there is no guarantee that it was slaughtered in accordance with the standards of those religions.

Currently, only animals killed according to kosher guidelines by observant Jews is similar to the standards in Islamic texts. Others, whether religious groups or federal organizations, have few guidelines that are humane, clean or sanitary.

However, in Islam, there are guidelines that protect animals from cruelty and that ensure a clean, safe and sanitary method of slaughter. In contrast, the meat-packing industry today does not ensure the same protections and end results.

For example, blood is not always fully drained from slaughtered cows and chickens. Carcasses may lay around for hours before they are even processed, allowing ample time for germs and diseases to spread throughout the meat. In some cases, the bladder may become ruptured in the slaughtering process, causing urine to spill onto the meat. Slaughterhouse workers don't even make sure the animal dies a quick and painless death, as is required by Islam. Animals may be shocked or electrocuted to death, shot in the head with bullets or cut to pieces before they are even dead!

Modern-day slaughterhouse workers don't even mention Allah's ﷻ name when the animals are slaughtered. It becomes questionable, therefore, that modern-day slaughtering techniques qualify as halal. To be safe, it is better for a Muslim to preserve his or her health and way of life and only buy halal or kosher meat.

D. Dhabiha Meat

The method of slaughtering an animal according to Islam is called **Dhabiha** ذَبِيحَة. 'Dhabiha' is a category that falls under 'halal,'

How to Stay on the Straight Path

An-Nu'man bin Bashir said, I heard Allah's Messenger ﷺ saying, "Both legal and illegal things are evident but in between them there are doubtful (suspicious) things and most of the people have no knowledge about them. So whoever saves himself from these suspicious things saves his religion and his honor. And whoever indulges in these suspicious things is like a shepherd who grazes (his animals) near the Hima (private pasture) of someone else and at any moment he is liable to get in it. (O people!) Beware! Every king has a Hima and the Hima of Allah on the earth is His illegal (forbidden) things. Beware! There is a piece of flesh in the body if it becomes good (reformed) the whole body becomes good but if it gets spoilt the whole body gets spoilt and that is the heart." (Al Bukhari)

عَنْ النُّعْمَانَ بْنَ بَشِيرٍ، يَقُولُ سَمِعْتُ رَسُولَ اللَّهِ ﷺ يَقُولُ: «الْحَلَالُ بَيِّنٌ وَالْحَرَامُ بَيِّنٌ، وَبَيْنَهُمَا مُشَبَّهَاتٌ لَا يَعْلَمُهَا كَثِيرٌ مِنَ النَّاسِ، فَمَنِ اتَّقَى الْمُشَبَّهَاتِ اسْتَبْرَأَ لِدِينِهِ وَعِرْضِهِ، وَمَنْ وَقَعَ فِي الشُّبُهَاتِ كَرَاعٍ يَرْعَى حَوْلَ الْحِمَى، يُوشِكُ أَنْ يُوَاقِعَهُ. أَلَا وَإِنَّ لِكُلِّ مَلِكٍ حِمًى، أَلَا إِنَّ حِمَى اللَّهِ فِي أَرْضِهِ مَحَارِمُهُ، أَلَا وَإِنَّ فِي الْجَسَدِ مُضْغَةً إِذَا صَلَحَتْ صَلَحَ الْجَسَدُ كُلُّهُ، وَإِذَا فَسَدَتْ فَسَدَ الْجَسَدُ كُلُّهُ، أَلَا وَهِيَ الْقَلْبُ». رَوَاهُ الْبُخَارِيُّ

and is preferred for Muslims. Dhabiha meat is slaughtered by a sharp knife, and the animals die with minimal pain. A worker is not allowed to slaughter one animal in front of another, nor starve them beforehand. They may not pack them cruelly in cages. Allah's name must be mentioned at the time of slaughter, and the disease-ridden blood is drained out, making the meat more healthy and safe.

The Blessed Prophet ﷺ once said that whoever believes in Allah, practices Islam and eats halal food is a Muslim. Let's keep our tables pure, as we try to keep our hearts pure, too.

Remember that buying halal meat is the best way to prevent cruelty to animals and inhumane treatment of Allah's creatures. May Allah help us to eat only halal foods, and to teach others that even animals used for food must be treated well and with kindness, all the way. Ameen.

Questions to Answer

1. What are two reasons to avoid haram foods?
2. What two things can you do if you are unsure about the ingredients in a food product you buy?

Define: Halal Foods, Dhabiha.

Reflect: How can the following hadith apply to avoiding haram foods for Allah's sake? *Whoever practices self-denial in the world, Allah will cause wisdom to grow in his heart; He will make his tongue say wise things; He will help him see the imperfection of the world, its disease, and its cure; and He will bring him safely from it to the abode of peace.* (Al Baihaqi)

قَالَ رَسُولُ اللهِ ﷺ: «مَا زَهِدَ عَبْدٌ فِي الدُّنْيَا إِلَّا أَنْبَتَ اللهُ الْحِكْمَةَ فِي قَلْبِهِ، وَأَنْطَقَ بِهَا لِسَانَهُ، وَبَصَّرَهُ عَيْبَ الدُّنْيَا وَدَاءَهَا وَدَوَاءَهَا، وَأَخْرَجَهُ مِنْهَا سَالِمًا إِلَى دَارِ السَّلَامِ». رَوَاهُ البَيْهَقِي

Act: Conduct a research study on one aspect of the meat-packing industry. Compare it to what you have learned about the standards for halal foods in this lesson. Present three of the most interesting facts you find to your peers in a visual format.

IQ Builder: What four things are haram according to 5:90?

44 Muslims & Making Money

WHAT TO LEARN

The Blessed Prophet ﷺ once remarked that it would be better to take an ax and cut firewood in the forest than to go around begging. In Islam, there is great blessing and respect for work. Why is work important?

VOCABULARY

Riba

THINK ABOUT IT

What is halal earning?

A. The Need for Work

When Captain John Smith took over the Jamestown colony in Virginia in 1608, he found no one working and everyone hungry. He declared, "He that will not work shall not eat."

Working is a fact of life. In fact, one of the most important activities of any human being is the gathering of resources. In ancient days, this may have consisted of collecting nuts and berries or putting aside supplies for the long winter ahead.

We are no longer in the Stone Age, but the hunt for resources lives on. Instead of gathering food directly from the land, we often go to places of work, where we can make money that we then exchange for supplies in stores.

Because this is the most time-consuming of all our pursuits, the potential exists for people to want to gain their money by less-than-fair means. Therefore, money and business transactions are the subject of a special section of the Shari'ah.

B. Truth in Business

We must make our money in an honest and fair fashion. If we do, Allah ﷻ rewards our earnings with still more rewards and blessings. If we lie, cheat, steal or trick others, then our money can be the source of our ruin, in both this life and in the next.

You who believe! Don't consume other's property among yourselves by deception, but let there be among you trade and business with mutual good will. And don't destroy yourselves, for indeed Allah has been merciful to you. If anyone does injustice, We will soon throw them into the fire. That is easy for Allah. If you reject the worst sins you were forbidden to do, We will take out of you all your lowly deeds, and admit you to a gate of great honor. *Surat An-Nisa' (The Women) 4:29-31*

﴿يَٰٓأَيُّهَا ٱلَّذِينَ ءَامَنُوا۟ لَا تَأْكُلُوٓا۟ أَمْوَٰلَكُم بَيْنَكُم بِٱلْبَٰطِلِ إِلَّآ أَن تَكُونَ تِجَٰرَةً عَن تَرَاضٍ مِّنكُمْ وَلَا تَقْتُلُوٓا۟ أَنفُسَكُمْ إِنَّ ٱللَّهَ كَانَ بِكُمْ رَحِيمًا﴾ ﴿وَمَن يَفْعَلْ ذَٰلِكَ عُدْوَٰنًا وَظُلْمًا فَسَوْفَ نُصْلِيهِ نَارًا وَكَانَ ذَٰلِكَ عَلَى ٱللَّهِ يَسِيرًا﴾ ﴿إِن تَجْتَنِبُوا۟ كَبَآئِرَ مَا تُنْهَوْنَ عَنْهُ نُكَفِّرْ عَنكُمْ سَيِّـَٔاتِكُمْ وَنُدْخِلْكُم مُّدْخَلًا كَرِيمًا﴾ سُورَةُ النِّسَاءِ 4: 29 – 31

Business must be conducted in a spirit of friendliness, and with fairness. We must not indulge in deceit, and we must use our profits wisely and not wastefully.

The Blessed Prophet ﷺ once said, "The truthful and trustworthy business person will be in the company of the prophets, righteous people, and martyrs, on the Day of Judgement." (At-Tirmidhi)

عَنِ النَّبِيِّ ﷺ: «التَّاجِرُ الصَّدُوقُ الأَمِينُ مَعَ النَّبِيِّينَ وَالصِّدِّيقِينَ وَالشُّهَدَاءِ». رَوَاهُ التِّرْمِذِيُّ

The Blessed Prophet ﷺ once said, "The flesh and body that is fed on unlawful earnings shall not enter Paradise. Hellfire is more fitting for flesh that grows on the body out of haram earnings." (Ahmad)

قَالَ رَسُولُ اللهِ ﷺ: «لَا يَدْخُلُ الْجَنَّةَ لَحْمٌ نَبَتَ مِنْ سُحْتٍ، النَّارُ أَوْلَى بِهِ». رَوَاهُ أَحْمَدُ

There are several ways of making money that Allah ﷻ has forbidden. They include working with haram substances (such as alcohol or pork), taking **Riba** ربا Interest-money, unfair money-exchanging, gambling and using any dishonesty. The list also includes a type of stock transaction called 'futures-trading,' where you pay for the delivery of an item in the future, not knowing if you will gain or lose money on the deal.

Dealing in riba is practiced almost everywhere in the world today. Banks pay interest to account holders to get people to deposit money in their banks. The bank then turns around and lends the money it collects to others, and charges them interest, until the person or business pays the money back in full.

The person receiving money from interest didn't work for it, and the one paying off a loan has to pay extra money back. If a person takes a loan, they were often poor to begin with, so it's a worse hardship to ask them to pay more.

Jabir ؓ said that, "The Prophet ﷺ cursed the one who accepted riba, the one who paid it, the one who recorded it, and the one who witnessed it, saying they were all alike." (Muslim)

عَنْ جَابِرٍ ؓ قَالَ: «لَعَنَ رَسُولُ اللهِ ﷺ آكِلَ الرِّبَا وَمُوكِلَهُ وَكَاتِبَهُ وَشَاهِدَيْهِ وَقَالَ هُمْ سَوَاءٌ». رَوَاهُ مُسْلِمٌ

Almost any type of trade or business is a halal way to make money. The Blessed Prophet ﷺ personally showed us, by his own example, how we can be the best business person. He was always fair, honest, and trustworthy.

The Blessed Prophet ﷺ once said, "May Allah show mercy to the person who is kind when he sells, when he buys and when he makes a claim." (Al Bukhari)

قَالَ رَسُولُ اللهِ ﷺ: «رَحِمَ اللهُ رَجُلًا سَمْحًا إِذَا بَاعَ، وَإِذَا اشْتَرَى، وَإِذَا اقْتَضَى». رَوَاهُ الْبُخَارِيُّ

C. Islamic Business Ethics

1. **Halal Enterprises:** A Muslim may only participate in a venture or occupation that does not engage in any haram practices or pursuits. Any business involving intoxicants, dealing with riba, dishonesty, swine products, futures speculation (futures markets), injustice or environmental abuse is strictly off-limits. The Prophet ﷺ said, "To earn a clean living is also a duty next to the main duties of emaan." (Al Baihaqi)

قَالَ رَسُولُ اللهِ ﷺ: «كَسْبُ الْحَلَالِ فَرِيضَةٌ بَعْدَ الْفَرِيضَةِ». رَوَاهُ الْبَيْهَقِيُّ

2. **Ready Compensation:** Timely payment of employees or contractors must be made. Wages cannot be held for more than a reasonable time.

It was narrated from 'Abdallah bin 'Umar ﷺ that the Messenger of Allah ﷺ said, "Give the worker his wages before his sweat dries." (Ibn Majah)

عَنْ عَبْدِ اللهِ بْنِ عُمَرَ، قَالَ: قَالَ رَسُولُ اللهِ ﷺ: ((أَعْطُوا الْأَجِيرَ أَجْرَهُ قَبْلَ أَنْ يَجِفَّ عَرَقُهُ)). رَوَاهُ ابْنُ مَاجَهْ

3. Fair Dealing: A Muslim cannot seek to cheat partners, employees, contractors or others in the pursuit of his or her profits. Unfair burdens result in injustice. All important business dealings must have a written contract and witnesses. (2:282)

Abu Huraira ﷺ narrated that the Prophet ﷺ said, "(There are) three (types of persons to whom) Allah will neither speak to them on the Day of Resurrections, nor look at them (They are): (1) a man who takes a false oath that he has been offered for a commodity a price greater than what he has actually been offered; (2) and a man who takes a false oath after the 'Asr (prayer) in order to grab the property of a Muslim through it; (3) and a man who forbids others to use the remaining superfluous water. To such a man Allah will say on the Day of Resurrection, 'Today I withhold My Blessings from you as you withheld the superfluous part of that (water) which your hands did not create.'" (Al Bukhari)

عَنْ أَبِي هُرَيْرَةَ ﷺ، عَنِ النَّبِيِّ ﷺ قَالَ: ((ثَلَاثَةٌ لَا يُكَلِّمُهُمُ اللهُ يَوْمَ الْقِيَامَةِ وَلَا يَنْظُرُ إِلَيْهِمْ رَجُلٌ حَلَفَ عَلَى سِلْعَةٍ لَقَدْ أَعْطَى بِهَا أَكْثَرَ مِمَّا أَعْطَى وَهُوَ كَاذِبٌ، وَرَجُلٌ حَلَفَ عَلَى يَمِينٍ كَاذِبَةٍ بَعْدَ الْعَصْرِ لِيَقْتَطِعَ بِهَا مَالَ امْرِئٍ مُسْلِمٍ، وَرَجُلٌ مَنَعَ فَضْلَ مَاءٍ فَيَقُولُ اللهُ يَوْمَ الْقِيَامَةِ، الْيَوْمَ أَمْنَعُكَ فَضْلِي، كَمَا مَنَعْتَ فَضْلَ مَا لَمْ تَعْمَلْ يَدَاكَ)). رَوَاهُ الْبُخَارِيُّ

4. Generosity: Kindness, graciousness, and a general sense of good-heartedness must prevail in business or work relations.

5. Continuous Improvement: Muslim workers and entrepreneurs must seek to reach new levels of excellence.

The Blessed Prophet ﷺ said, "Allah loves those who, when they do a thing, they do their best." (At-Tabarani)

قَالَ رَسُولُ اللهِ ﷺ: ((إِنَّ اللهَ يُحِبُّ إِذَا عَمِلَ أَحَدُكُمْ عَمَلًا أَنْ يُتْقِنَهُ)). رَوَاهُ الطَّبَرَانِيُّ

6. Open Dealing: In any transaction of goods, services, or information, the seller must provide complete details of any and all defects, or potential defects, to the buyer. One day, while in the market, the Blessed Prophet ﷺ caught a grain merchant who tried to hide the poor quality of his product, and he admonished him.

7. Personal Responsibility: When money or position is entrusted to the Muslim

265

worker or business owner, he or she must not seek to enrich himself at the expense of either his employer or stockholders while at the same time doing poorly in their service. Debts which lead to a bankruptcy must be answered equitably.

8. **Efficient Use:** Waste is strictly forbidden. Recycling, full exploitation of materials at hand and a strict process of accountability is a must. Pollution is also forbidden, as it corrupts the Earth.

Questions to Answer

1. What did the Blessed Prophet ﷺ say about 'truth and business'?
2. What does Islam say about riba?
3. How should a Muslim business person conduct business dealings?
4. What did the Blessed Prophet ﷺ say about the best kind of business person?
5. List three things a Muslim must be aware of when having financial dealings?

Define: Riba.

Reflect: What are some guiding principles for Muslims for ethical business transactions, according to what you read in this lesson?

Act: Compare the restrictions placed on interest for Muslims, Christians and Jews. Look at the way in which each of their three respective books talk about 'interest.' In the Bible, refer to the books Exodus 22:25, Leviticus 25:36, Ezekiel 3:18 and 18:5 and Deuteronomy 23:20.

IQ Builders:

1. Copy down and explain the meaning of ayaat 26:181-183.
2. What does Allah ﷻ say about trade, in 17:35?

45 Who Makes the Best Friend?

WHAT TO LEARN

We often come into contact with people and find that we like their personality enough to want to become friends with them. Everyone has their own preferences in a friend.

VOCABULARY

Awlia'a

THINK ABOUT IT

What points must a Muslim remember if they have a non-Muslim friend?

A. The Big Question

Many people wonder if they are allowed to have non-Muslim friends. Sometimes it is hard to find a clear answer from those around you. Thankfully, the Qur'an and Hadith are clear.

To begin with, Islam teaches that you can have non-Muslim friends, but there are a few conditions. When you consider what a real friend is, you will understand the wise guidance. Becoming friends with someone means making a personal commitment to share some of your time and to share fulfilling experiences.

The Holy Qur'an declares that a believer should never prefer a non-Muslim over a Muslim. If a person did so, then they would put themselves in danger of harming their faith. Therefore, we must realize that it is better to be with those who believe as we do.

If you do choose to have some non-Muslim friends, you should make sure you have some Muslim friends also. As Allah ﷻ said, Keep your soul content with those who call on their Lord, morning and evening, seeking His face. Don't let your eyes go away from them, seeking the glittery things of this life, nor obey anyone whose heart We have allowed to forget Our remembrance. One who follows his own desires has gone beyond all bounds. *Surat Al Kahf (The Cave) 18:28*

﴿وَاصْبِرْ نَفْسَكَ مَعَ الَّذِينَ يَدْعُونَ رَبَّهُم بِالْغَدَوٰةِ وَالْعَشِيِّ يُرِيدُونَ وَجْهَهُۥ ۖ وَلَا تَعْدُ عَيْنَاكَ عَنْهُمْ تُرِيدُ زِينَةَ الْحَيَوٰةِ الدُّنْيَا ۖ وَلَا تُطِعْ مَنْ أَغْفَلْنَا قَلْبَهُۥ عَن ذِكْرِنَا وَاتَّبَعَ هَوَىٰهُ وَكَانَ أَمْرُهُۥ فُرُطًا﴾ سُورَةُ الْكَهْفِ 18 : 28

Thus, we see it's better to be around those who are more like us in their spiritual orientation. However, if we do choose to have non-Muslim friends, there are certain conditions which Islam places upon us.

The first condition is that you do not become dependent on a non-Muslim. In other words, they should never hold power or authority over you. (60:1-2)

Don't let the believers take for protectors an unbeliever over a believer. If anyone does that, then there will be no help from Allah. (The only exception is) if it's a matter of safety. You must guard yourselves from them. Allah, Himself, cautions you and (remember that) the final end is with

267

IT'S ALL ABOUT ISLAM

Allah. Surat Al 'Imran (The Family of 'Imran) 3:28

﴿لَا يَتَّخِذِ ٱلْمُؤْمِنُونَ ٱلْكَٰفِرِينَ أَوْلِيَآءَ مِن دُونِ ٱلْمُؤْمِنِينَ وَمَن يَفْعَلْ ذَٰلِكَ فَلَيْسَ مِنَ ٱللَّهِ فِى شَىْءٍ إِلَّآ أَن تَتَّقُوا۟ مِنْهُمْ تُقَىٰةً وَيُحَذِّرُكُمُ ٱللَّهُ نَفْسَهُۥ وَإِلَى ٱللَّهِ ٱلْمَصِيرُ﴾

سُورَةُ آلِ عِمْرَانَ 3: 28

The word used in the Arabic text is **Awlia'a** أَوْلِيَاء which comes from the word **Wali** وَلِيّ **Protector**. Allah ﷻ says in this ayah to not take non-Muslims as protectors. Only reliable Muslims should have authority or power over you. (3:118-120) This is because, in the end, non-Muslims have their own way of life and it is natural for them to want their friends to follow their style. Therefore, they may not always respect your beliefs and may sometimes work against them, even if they don't mean to. (2:109)

The Jews and Christians will never be satisfied with you, unless you follow their ways. Tell them, "The guidance of Allah is the only guidance." If you followed their desires after the knowledge (of Islam) came to you, then you would find no protector or helper against Allah. Surat Al Baqarah (The Cow) 2:120

﴿وَلَن تَرْضَىٰ عَنكَ ٱلْيَهُودُ وَلَا ٱلنَّصَٰرَىٰ حَتَّىٰ تَتَّبِعَ مِلَّتَهُمْ قُلْ إِنَّ هُدَى ٱللَّهِ هُوَ ٱلْهُدَىٰ وَلَئِنِ ٱتَّبَعْتَ أَهْوَآءَهُم بَعْدَ ٱلَّذِى جَآءَكَ مِنَ ٱلْعِلْمِ مَا لَكَ مِنَ ٱللَّهِ مِن وَلِىٍّ وَلَا نَصِيرٍ﴾

سُورَةُ الْبَقَرَةِ 2: 120

The second condition is also very important, in that your non-Muslim friends should not ridicule or disrespect Islam. If they do, what kind of friend would they be to you? Can you imagine insulting their most cherished beliefs? (5:57)

You have already been given the command in the Book, that when you hear the signs of Allah being insulted or joked with, you are not to sit with them unless they start talking about something else. If you stayed with them while they were insulting Allah, then you would be like them. Allah will gather all the hypocrites and the unbelievers in Hell. Surat An-Nisa' 4: 140

﴿وَقَدْ نَزَّلَ عَلَيْكُمْ فِى ٱلْكِتَٰبِ أَنْ إِذَا سَمِعْتُمْ ءَايَٰتِ ٱللَّهِ يُكْفَرُ بِهَا وَيُسْتَهْزَأُ بِهَا فَلَا تَقْعُدُوا۟ مَعَهُمْ حَتَّىٰ يَخُوضُوا۟ فِى حَدِيثٍ غَيْرِهِۦٓ إِنَّكُمْ إِذًا مِّثْلُهُمْ إِنَّ ٱللَّهَ جَامِعُ ٱلْمُنَٰفِقِينَ وَٱلْكَٰفِرِينَ فِى جَهَنَّمَ جَمِيعًا﴾

سُورَةُ النِّسَاءِ 4: 140

> Abu Huraira ؓ narrated that the Prophet ﷺ said, "A person molds his way of life according to his friend. So you should be careful about who you make your friend." (Ahmad)
>
> عَنْ أَبِي هُرَيْرَةَ ؓ، قَالَ: أَنَّ النَّبِيَّ ﷺ قَالَ: «الرَّجُلُ عَلَى دِينِ خَلِيلِهِ فَلْيَنْظُرْ أَحَدُكُمْ مَنْ يُخَالِلُ». رَوَاهُ أَحْمَدُ
>
> Abu Sa'id narrated that the Messenger of Allah ﷺ said, "Keep company only with the believers, and let your food be eaten only by the righteous." (At-Tirmidhi)
>
> عَنْ أَبِي سَعِيدٍ، - أَنَّهُ سَمِعَ رَسُولَ اللَّهِ ﷺ يَقُولُ: «لَا تُصَاحِبْ إِلَّا مُؤْمِنًا وَلَا يَأْكُلْ طَعَامَكَ إِلَّا تَقِىٌّ». رَوَاهُ التِّرْمِذِيُّ

The third condition is that you must try your best to give them Islamic da'wah whenever the opportunity arises. (3:104) According to Islamic teachings, your intention when establishing new friendships should be to set an example of a good Muslim. Another reason should be to help them to discover the benefit and beauty of Islam. That's really being a true friend on your part! Think how much stronger your friendship could be if you brought your non-Muslim friend to the best way of life!

The fourth and final requirement is that you should prefer to have nice, believing Muslims as close friends, whenever possible. (4:144)

You want to constantly surround yourself with people who practice Islam the right way. People who may be nice, but live a lifestyle that clashes with Islamic teachings, such as drinking or dating, are not the best choice. Whether Muslim or not, choose your friends wisely, and not just because the person is popular.

To those who take unbelievers for protectors rather than believers, are they looking for honor or greatness from them? But all honor is with Allah. *Surat An-Nisa' (The Women) 4: 139*

﴿ ٱلَّذِينَ يَتَّخِذُونَ ٱلْكَافِرِينَ أَوْلِيَآءَ مِن دُونِ ٱلْمُؤْمِنِينَ أَيَبْتَغُونَ عِندَهُمُ ٱلْعِزَّةَ فَإِنَّ ٱلْعِزَّةَ لِلَّهِ جَمِيعًا ﴾ سُورَةُ النِّسَاء 4: 139

كل امرئ بما كسب رهين

Questions to Answer

1. Can a Muslim have non-Muslim friends?
2. What are the four things we must keep in mind when having non-Muslim friends?
3. Why is there a danger in getting too close with non-Muslims?
4. What is the best way to strengthen your friendship with a non-Muslim?

Define: Awlia'a

Reflect: Based on this lesson, what is the purpose of friendship?

Act: Brainstorm activities that you can do with your Muslim and non-Muslim friends that can raise your level of emaan higher. Then, choose one of those activities, and—with your parents' permission—plan to do one of them on an upcoming weekend.

IQ Builders:

1. What does Allah say about those who just don't care about goodness and right in 6:70?
2. What is the message in ayaat 5:55-56?

46. How Is a Marriage Contract Made?

WHAT TO LEARN

Every society has its rules and rituals surrounding marriage. After all, it's the most important step two people can take. The ceremony of marriage is a way to show society that the new couple promises to live together as one. Why is marriage important?

VOCABULARY

Nikah Mahr
Walimah Wali

THINK ABOUT IT

What is the ceremony of marriage like?

A. What to Look for in a Mate

The Islamic term for the wedding ceremony is **Nikah** نكاح. It is a very important event in the life of a young man and woman, and it affects the life of two different families.

And among His Signs is this, that He created for you wives from among yourselves, that you may find repose in them, and He has put between you affection and mercy. Verily, in that are indeed signs for a people who reflect.
Surat Ar-Rum (The Romans) 30:21

﴿ وَمِنْ ءَايَٰتِهِۦٓ أَنْ خَلَقَ لَكُم مِّنْ أَنفُسِكُمْ أَزْوَٰجًا لِّتَسْكُنُوٓا۟ إِلَيْهَا وَجَعَلَ بَيْنَكُم مَّوَدَّةً وَرَحْمَةً إِنَّ فِى ذَٰلِكَ لَءَايَٰتٍ لِّقَوْمٍ يَتَفَكَّرُونَ ﴾ سُورَةُ الرُّومِ 30: 21

The Prophet ﷺ said, "A woman is married for four things, her wealth, her family status, her beauty and her religion. So you should marry the religious woman, otherwise you will be a loser." (Al Bukhari)

عَنِ النَّبِيِّ ﷺ قَالَ: «تُنْكَحُ الْمَرْأَةُ لِأَرْبَعٍ لِمَالِهَا وَلِحَسَبِهَا وَجَمَالِهَا وَلِدِينِهَا، فَاظْفَرْ بِذَاتِ الدِّينِ تَرِبَتْ يَدَاكَ». رَوَاهُ الْبُخَارِيُّ

Unfortunately, some Muslims skip the inner beauty of taqwa and emaan that the Prophet ﷺ suggested to look for in a mate. Instead, people tend to focus on the outer beauty, wealth or status. Consequently, these people may end up in bad marriages in which greed and envy prevail. While there are many reasons that may cause a couple to divorce—many of which may be outside of the individual's control—sometimes it can be traced to these misplaced priorities.

In addition, using a person's race or ethnicity as the only factor in the selection of a spouse is undesirable. Islam counsels against it. Besides, any Muslim, regardless of their skin color or ethnic group, is equal in the Ummah of the Blessed Prophet Muhammad ﷺ.

The Blessed Prophet ﷺ said, "There is no superiority of an Arab over a non-Arab or a non-Arab over an Arab. And there is no superiority of a white over a black or a black over a white, except with God-consciousness." (Ahmad)

قَالَ رَسُولُ الله ﷺ: «لَا فَضْلَ لِعَرَبِيٍّ عَلَى عَجَمِيٍّ، وَلَا لِعَجَمِيٍّ عَلَى عَرَبِيٍّ، وَلَا لِأَبْيَضَ عَلَى أَسْوَدَ، وَلَا لِأَسْوَدَ عَلَى أَبْيَضَ: إِلَّا بِالتَّقْوَى». رَوَاهُ أَحْمَد

Therefore, it is best to look for taqwa, or genuine awareness of Allah ﷻ, before looking for wealth or anything else. After these priorities have been established and clearly agreed upon by everyone involved, the search for the spouse begins.

B. The Setting of the Agreement

Once a prospective spouse has been identified, usually there are a lot of behind-the-scenes meetings and discussions. The parents contact each other and discuss the matter, then the young man and woman are approached with the idea of meeting each other. If they both agree to meet, then a formal affair is arranged, such as a dinner, where they can meet without being the center of attention.

Abu Huraira ؓ reported that the Blessed Prophet ﷺ said, "The worst food is from a Walimah in which only the rich are invited and not the poor." (Agreed upon)

عَنْ أَبِي هُرَيْرَةَ ؓ، قَالَ: قَالَ رَسُولُ الله ﷺ: «بِئْسَ الطَّعَامُ طَعَامُ الْوَلِيمَةِ يُدْعَى إِلَيْهَا الْأَغْنِيَاءُ، وَيُتْرَكُ الْفُقَرَاءُ». مُتَّفَقٌ عَلَيْهِ

The prospective bride and groom can see each other, talk together and get to know each other for days, weeks, even months. There should be a chaperone nearby, however, to keep things properly within the limits of Allah ﷻ.

The Blessed Prophet ﷺ said, "When an (unmarried) man and woman are together, the third with them is Shaytan." (At-Tirmidhi)

عَنِ النَّبِيِّ ﷺ: «لَا يَخْلُوَنَّ رَجُلٌ بِامْرَأَةٍ إِلَّا كَانَ ثَالِثَهُمَا الشَّيْطَانُ». رَوَاهُ التِّرْمَذِيّ

If the man and woman agree to marry, then there is a formal engagement announced, and a wedding date is set. According to the Prophet ﷺ, no one can be forced to marry someone they are not interested in. The Prophet ﷺ specifically mentioned the importance of obtaining the female's decision in the matter. This was overlooked in the culture at that time and continues to be ignored in many cultures, even today. It must be a free choice for both parties. Only then can the wedding be performed.

The nikah should be a simple one. According to the hadith of the Prophet ﷺ, "The best wedding is the one with the least amount of burden." (Al Baihaqi)

عَنْ عَائِشَةَ ؓ، قَالَ النَّبِيُّ ﷺ: «إِنَّ أَعْظَمَ النِّكَاحِ بَرَكَةً، أَيْسَرُهُ مَئُونَةً». رَوَاهُ البَيْهَقِي

Islam does not support the practice of having extravagant and expensive affairs. An imam, or an equally knowledgeable Muslim, typically performs the ceremony. The bride is represented by her **Wali** وَلِيّ **Protective Guardian**. Usually this is her father, brother or uncle. The groom also has someone who acts on his behalf, much like a best man.

A marriage contract is written beforehand, both by the bride and the groom. In the wedding contract, each side lists what they expect from the marriage. For example, the details of how the bride expects to be treated in the marriage, wedding vows or even a prenuptial agreement clause can be included, along with any other stipulations that she chooses.

In Islam, the groom is obligated to present his bride with a **Mahr** مَهْر **Dowry** to the wife. It is not the other way around. An example of where Muslims mix up this Islamic requirement is through a custom practiced in Southeast Asia, where the bride's family offers a dowry to the family of the husband; yet, this is not the Islamic way at all.

The mahr can consist of anything the bride desires, whether it's some amount of money, jewelry, a house or other item. The husband is not allowed to ever take her mahr away, but the wife can allow the husband to pay it to her over time. Some men need time to pay the mahr, if it's very high, or if the groom is not well-off.

And give women their mahr as a free gift, but if they forgive any of it of their own good pleasure, accept it and enjoy it with gladness. Surat An-Nisa' (The Women) 4:4

﴿وَءَاتُوا۟ ٱلنِّسَآءَ صَدُقَٰتِهِنَّ نِحْلَةً ۚ فَإِن طِبْنَ لَكُمْ عَن شَىْءٍ مِّنْهُ نَفْسًا فَكُلُوهُ هَنِيٓـًٔا مَّرِيٓـًٔا﴾ سُورَةُ النِّسَاء 4:4

Both parties will sign the contract, and then the actual nikah starts. The imam begins by confirming publicly that both sides have agreed to marry, and then the amount of the mahr is announced.

Next, the imam reads the nikah khutbah. This describes the purpose of marriage and how Allah made it to be the trust of men and women to abide faithfully in love and fairness to each other. One of the beautiful ayaat that is often read is:

O men, fear your Lord who created you from a single soul, and from it created its match, and spread many men and women from the two. Fear Allah in whose name you ask each other (for your rights), and fear (the violation of the rights of) the womb-relations. Surely, Allah is watchful over you. Surat An-Nisa' (The Women) 4:1

﴿يَٰٓأَيُّهَا ٱلنَّاسُ ٱتَّقُوا۟ رَبَّكُمُ ٱلَّذِى خَلَقَكُم مِّن نَّفْسٍ وَٰحِدَةٍ وَخَلَقَ مِنْهَا زَوْجَهَا وَبَثَّ مِنْهُمَا رِجَالًا كَثِيرًا وَنِسَآءً ۚ وَٱتَّقُوا۟ ٱللَّهَ ٱلَّذِى تَسَآءَلُونَ بِهِۦ وَٱلْأَرْحَامَ ۚ إِنَّ ٱللَّهَ كَانَ عَلَيْكُمْ رَقِيبًا﴾ سُورَةُ النِّسَاء 4:1

Following the nikah is a joyous celebration called a **Walimah** وَلِيمَة **Reception**, where friends and family celebrate the birth of the new marriage.

Questions to Answer

1. What is the best quality to look for in a mate, according to the Blessed Prophet ﷺ?
2. What does Islam say about the role that racism can play in looking for a spouse?
3. What is a marriage contract, and what's in it?
4. Describe the nikah ceremony's main details.
5. What is a walimah?

Define: Nikah, Wali, Mahr.

Reflect: Consider the Islamic boundaries placed on Muslims for interacting with the opposite sex. Using these boundaries, what are some halal methods by which Muslim youth can get to know one another for marriage, in today's age?

Act: We say, "Amantobillah" (Let it be so, by Allah's ﷻ will) to newlyweds. Memorize this phrase.

IQ Builder: What does 24:30-31 advise us to do if we are around people of the opposite sex that we are not married or related to?

Literature Selection

The Best Marriage Gift

Adapted from *Companions of the Prophet*
Compiled by 'Abdul Wahid Hamid

Rumaysa bint Milhan was one of the first women in Al Madinah to accept Islam. Her husband, who was an idol-worshipper, was on a trip at the time and didn't know about his wife's decision. When he returned home, he noticed that his wife seemed invigorated and full of excitement. When he asked her why, she answered that she accepted the Message of Prophet Muhammad ﷺ and gave up idol-worshipping.

Her husband didn't like what she did and he became angry. When he found out she was teaching their young son, Anas, how to say the Shahadah, his rage peaked and he became abusive.

One day, her husband left the house on some errand but was ambushed by an enemy that he had a feud with. He was killed in the attack. Everyone was upset, but Rumaysa was not terribly upset. She vowed to never marry again unless her son approved.

A few months later, a local man named Abu Talha wanted to marry her. He knew she was a Muslim while he wasn't, but he didn't care if they had different beliefs. He went to her house and asked to marry her.

She refused on the grounds that he was an unbeliever. Abu Talha was shocked! He couldn't believe that any woman would turn him down, because he was very rich. So Abu Talha asked her if she wanted some gold and silver as gifts first.

She shook her head, "No" and said, "I swear to Allah that if you accept Islam, I would be pleased to have you as my husband, without giving me any gold or silver. I'll consider your acceptance of Islam as my wedding gift."

Abu Talha, who had an expensive and beautiful idol made of wood, became worried about leaving his old ways. While he was thinking, Rumaysa asked him, "Don't you know that the idol you worship grew from the ground?"

Abu Talha nodded, "Yes."

Then she continued, "Don't you feel stupid worshipping part of a tree, while you use the rest of it for fuel to bake your bread or to warm yourself? Accept Islam and I'll be pleased to take you as my husband."

Abu Talha thought about it and asked, "Who will teach me about Islam?"

Rumaysa replied, "I will. Say that there is no god but Allah and that Muhammad is His Messenger. Then, go to your house and break your idol and throw it away."

Abu Talha left and reflected upon what she had told him. When he realized his idol was something stupid to worship, he broke it. Then rushed back to her smiling and declared himself a Muslim. Anas approved, and they were married.

Muslims would later say that there was no better marriage gift than that of Rumaysa, because she had given Islam as her marriage gift.

Unit 09 Review Exercise

VOCABULARY REVIEW

On a separate sheet of paper, write the definition of each word below.

1. Hudood
2. 'Olama'a
3. Fatwa
4. Shari'ah
5. Madhab
6. Fiqh
7. Makruh
8. Mahr
9. Nikah
10. Haram
11. Ahl Al Kitab
12. Halal
13. Awlia'a
14. Walimah

REMEMBERING WHAT YOU READ

On a separate sheet of paper, answer the following questions. Use complete sentences in your answers.

1. What is the relationship between the Shari'ah and fiqh?
2. What is the process of arriving at an answer, using ijtehad?
3. Who were the five main scholars of fiqh? What are the madhahib named after?
4. What kind of a business person should a Muslim be? Explain in detail.
5. When differences arrive between people, how does Islam teach us to deal with these tough issues?
6. List five important points for people to know about haram and halal food.

THINKING TO LEARN

On a separate sheet of paper, answer the questions below. Use complete sentences.

1. Is a madhab like a sect, like a division in Islam or like something else? Explain your answer.
2. Explain the process of getting married in an Islamic manner, from the beginning (searching for a spouse) to the end (the marriage ceremony).

UNIT 10
Islam in Society

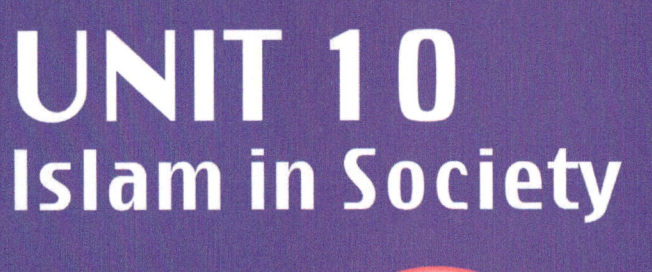

47 Building Islamic Character: The Essentials

WHAT TO LEARN

Manners make it easy to know what to expect from others. In Japan, when two people meet, they bow to each other. In some Muslim countries, they shake hands. If we lacked these traditions, it would be a confusing world.

VOCABULARY

Adab   Akhlaq

THINK ABOUT IT

How should a Muslim behave?

A. The Best Habits

One quality that makes humans different from all other living creatures is our ability to modify our behavior. A person can be taught to eat with his fingers or with a fork, just as a person can learn to stay up all night and sleep during the day.

The best habits are those that are the most beneficial to us as humans. Obviously, it wouldn't be good to hit yourself in the head with a stick when you meet someone. Similarly it would probably be a bad idea to always pour swamp water in your bathtub.

Many societies have tried to set standards for behaviors and manners at the personal and social level. The Chinese bow slightly to each other when they meet; some South American Indian tribes have the custom of washing each other's hair, and Americans are taught not to put their elbows on the dinner table.

For Muslims, our **Adab** آداب **Good Manners** relate directly to our character, or **Akhlaq** أخْلاق. The adab that we follow was not developed over many centuries. Rather, one man taught us everything about how to be good to others and good to ourselves.

It was none other than Prophet Muhammad ﷺ who taught us the finest mode of civilization that ever existed. By following his great example, our akhlaq becomes refined and full of social graces.

The challenge now is to learn what adab entails and then to put it into practice. Nearly every Muslim knows that they should say "السَّلامُ عَلَيْكُم" (Peace be to you) when they meet each other. But this is just one small part of the many manners we should make a part of our daily life. The Blessed Prophet ﷺ is our model, and his path is the best to follow.

You have indeed in the Messenger of Allah, a beautiful pattern (of conduct), for any whose hope is in Allah and the Last Day and who remember Allah much. *Surat Al Ahzab (The Confederates) 33:21*

﴿ لَقَدْ كَانَ لَكُمْ فِي رَسُولِ اللَّهِ أُسْوَةٌ حَسَنَةٌ لِّمَن كَانَ يَرْجُو اللَّهَ وَالْيَوْمَ الْآخِرَ وَذَكَرَ اللَّهَ كَثِيرًا ﴾ سُورَةُ الأَحْزَاب 33: 21

The Blessed Prophet ﷺ once remarked that he was sent to perfect manners. Read the following two sayings of the Blessed Prophet ﷺ and then memorize them in Arabic and English.

1. "The believers who show the best character are the best in faith." (At-Tirmidhi)

قَالَ رَسُولُ اللهِ ﷺ: «أَكْمَلُ الْمُؤْمِنِينَ إِيمَانًا أَحْسَنُهُمْ خُلُقًا».
رَوَاهُ التِّرْمِذِيُّ

2. "The best of you are those with the best character." (Al Bukhari)

قَالَ رَسُولُ اللهِ ﷺ: «إِنَّ خِيَارَكُمْ أَحَاسِنُكُمْ أَخْلَاقًا».
رَوَاهُ الْبُخَارِيُّ

IT'S ALL ABOUT ISLAM

The great lady 'Aishah was once asked what the Blessed Prophet's manners were like. She gave a very interesting reply. She said, "His manners were the Qur'an."

B. Manners for Greeting

Our adab comes from the Qur'an and Sunnah. Any cultural practices that one follows must not go against these two sources. Islamic teachings must come first if we are to be true believers.

When two Muslims meet each other, after exchanging the greetings of peace, they should shake hands. The Blessed Prophet said the better one is the one who lets his hand go last.

The Prophet also said, "Those who are nearest to Allah are those who are the first to give a greeting." (Abu Dawud)

قَالَ رَسُولُ اللهِ ﷺ: «إِنَّ أَوْلَى النَّاسِ بِاللهِ مَنْ بَدَأَهُمْ بِالسَّلَامِ».

رَوَاهُ أَبُو دَاوُدَ

The greeting of Islam, **Peace be to you** السلام عليكم, has a special significance for us. The word 'peace' is the highest and most honored term. Allah says about it: 'Peace!' is a word from a Merciful Lord. Surat Ya-sin 36:58

﴿سَلَامٌ قَوْلًا مِّن رَّبٍّ رَّحِيمٍ﴾ سُورَةُ يس 36: 58

Therefore it is the best word for people to use between each other. If a small group comes to a larger group, the rule is that the smaller group should greet the larger one first. If some people are sitting down, they should not stand up if someone comes to join them. The Blessed Prophet didn't even like people to get up for him!

A younger person should greet an older person first. When a greeting is given, the reply should be something equal to or better than that. For example, if someone says, "السَّلَامُ عَلَيْكُمْ," you can reply with **And you have peace** وَعَلَيْكُمُ السَّلَامُ, which is an equal greeting.

Or you can improve upon it by saying **Peace be upon you and Allah's mercy** السَّلَامُ عَلَيْكُمْ وَرَحْمَةُ اللهِ, or **Peace be upon you and Allah's mercy and blessings** السَّلَامُ عَلَيْكُمْ وَرَحْمَةُ اللهِ وَبَرَكَاتُهُ.

C. Respect for People

Islam teaches us to have regard for others. If we don't treat all people with respect, then we lack adab.

The Blessed Prophet said, "Nothing is heavier in the scales of good deeds than good behavior." (At-Tirmidhi)

عَنِ النَّبِيِّ ﷺ قَالَ: «مَا شَيْءٌ أَثْقَلُ فِي مِيزَانِ الْمُؤْمِنِ يَوْمَ الْقِيَامَةِ مِنْ خُلُقٍ حَسَنٍ وَإِنَّ اللهَ لَيُبْغِضُ الْفَاحِشَ الْبَذِيءَ». رَوَاهُ التِّرْمِذِيُّ

With regards to elderly people, we are supposed to treat them with kindness and respect. Think about it, they have lived much longer than you, and they've already gone through trials and struggles you have yet to experience. And in the case of your parents, they spent a lot of time and effort raising you.

The Blessed Prophet declared, "Whenever a young person honors an old

person because of their age, then Allah will give him or her somebody to honor them when they are old themselves."
(At-Tirmidhi)

قَالَ رَسُولُ اللهِ ﷺ: «مَا أَكْرَمَ شَابٌّ شَيْخًا لِسِنِّهِ إِلَّا قَيَّضَ اللهُ لَهُ مَنْ يُكْرِمُهُ عِنْدَ سِنِّهِ». رَوَاهُ التِّرْمَذِيّ

Allah commands us to address our parents in kindness and not to lose patience with them or insult them if they frustrate us. He said, *Your Lord has decreed that you worship none but Him, and do good to parents. If any one of them or both of them reach old age, do not say to them: uff (a word or expression of anger or contempt) and do not scold them, and address them with respectful words, And submit yourself before them in humility out of compassion, and say, "My Lord, be merciful to them as they have brought me up in my childhood."*
Surat Al Isra' (The Journey by Night) 17:23-24

﴿ وَقَضَىٰ رَبُّكَ أَلَّا تَعْبُدُوٓا۟ إِلَّآ إِيَّاهُ وَبِٱلْوَٰلِدَيْنِ إِحْسَٰنًا ۚ إِمَّا يَبْلُغَنَّ عِندَكَ ٱلْكِبَرَ أَحَدُهُمَآ أَوْ كِلَاهُمَا فَلَا تَقُل لَّهُمَآ أُفٍّ وَلَا تَنْهَرْهُمَا وَقُل لَّهُمَا قَوْلًا كَرِيمًا ﴾ ﴿ وَٱخْفِضْ لَهُمَا جَنَاحَ ٱلذُّلِّ مِنَ ٱلرَّحْمَةِ وَقُل رَّبِّ ٱرْحَمْهُمَا كَمَا رَبَّيَانِى صَغِيرًا ﴾ سُورَةُ الإِسْرَاء: 23-24

Guests are also to be treated well. When a person invites another to their house, food should be served, and the guest should be made to feel welcome and at home.

Abu Huraira narrated that Allah's Messenger said, "Let him who believes in Allah and the Last Day speak good, or keep silent; and let him who believes in Allah and the Last Day be generous to his neighbour; and let him who believes in Allah and the Last Day be generous to his guest." (Al Bukhari and Muslim)

IT'S ALL ABOUT ISLAM

عَنْ أَبِي هُرَيْرَةَ ﷺ أَنَّ رَسُولَ اللهِ ﷺ قَالَ: «مَنْ كَانَ يُؤْمِنُ بِاللهِ وَالْيَوْمِ الْآخِرِ فَلْيَقُلْ خَيْرًا أَوْ لِيَصْمُتْ، وَمَنْ كَانَ يُؤْمِنُ بِاللهِ وَالْيَوْمِ الْآخِرِ فَلْيُكْرِمْ جَارَهُ، وَمَنْ كَانَ يُؤْمِنُ بِاللهِ وَالْيَوْمِ الْآخِرِ فَلْيُكْرِمْ ضَيْفَهُ». رَوَاهُ الْبُخَارِيُّ وَمُسْلِمٌ

For their part, the guest should not try to take advantage of his or her host. The Blessed Prophet ﷺ advised us, in another saying, that the guest should not overstay his welcome. Guests should respect the privacy, home and family of the host.

D. Basic Respect

Islam teaches that there are some types of behavior that are not good. A Muslim is not allowed to spy on another Muslim, for example. And if we hear gossiping, we should refrain from joining the conversation and walk away. (49:12)

Finally, we are not allowed to tease each other or call each other hurtful names. Allah said, *O you who believe, no men should ever scoff at other men. Maybe, the latter are better than the former. Nor should women (ever scoff) at other women. Maybe, the latter women are better than the former ones. And do not find fault with one another, nor call one another with bad nicknames. Bad is the name of sinfulness after embracing Faith. If anyone does not repent, then such people are the wrongdoers.* Surat Al Hujrat (The Rooms) 49:11

279

﴿يَٰٓأَيُّهَا ٱلَّذِينَ ءَامَنُوا۟ لَا يَسْخَرْ قَوْمٌ مِّن قَوْمٍ عَسَىٰٓ أَن يَكُونُوا۟ خَيْرًا مِّنْهُمْ وَلَا نِسَآءٌ مِّن نِّسَآءٍ عَسَىٰٓ أَن يَكُنَّ خَيْرًا مِّنْهُنَّ وَلَا تَلْمِزُوٓا۟ أَنفُسَكُمْ وَلَا تَنَابَزُوا۟ بِٱلْأَلْقَٰبِ بِئْسَ ٱلِٱسْمُ ٱلْفُسُوقُ بَعْدَ ٱلْإِيمَٰنِ وَمَن لَّمْ يَتُبْ فَأُو۟لَٰٓئِكَ هُمُ ٱلظَّٰلِمُونَ﴾

سُورَةُ الْحُجُرَاتِ 49: 11

If two Muslims fall to fighting, we must break it up and solve the problem. (49:9-10) No cursing or foul language should be used, and we must all present ourselves as dignified, refined and decent human beings. (33:58) These are examples of akhlaq in a Muslim.

سُبْحَانَ اللهِ وَبِحَمْدِهِ سُبْحَانَ اللهِ الْعَظِيمِ

Questions to Answer

1. How should guests be treated?
2. How does adab affect our akhlaq?

Define: Adab, Akhlaq.

Reflect: The Prophet ﷺ said, "The best gifts that a father can give to his children are a good education and manners." (At-Tirmidhi) Can you think of ways that you can implement the meaning of this saying in your own life?

عَنِ النَّبِيِّ ﷺ قَالَ: «مَا نَحَلَ وَالِدٌ وَلَدًا مِنْ نَحْلٍ أَفْضَلَ مِنْ أَدَبٍ حَسَنٍ». رَوَاهُ التِّرْمِذِيُّ

Act: Choose three examples of Islamic adab that you currently do not implement in your own life. Plan to implement these in the coming two days, on a consistent basis. Record the ways in which you feel afterwards. Also, record the ways that others reacted to you.

IQ Builders:

1. What does Allah ﷻ tell us about teasing in 49:11?
2. What is backbiting equal to, as explained in 49:12?
3. What does 4:80 tell us about the Sunnah?

48 The Muslim Family

WHAT TO LEARN

Every society has a way of organizing its social and family structures. Where families are strong, societies are safe and prosperous. Where families are weak and disunited, there is crime, chaos and fear.

VOCABULARY

Shura

THINK ABOUT IT

What are the rights and duties of every member of a Muslim family?

A. Islam in the Family

O you who believe! Save yourselves and your families from a fire whose fuel is men and the stone (of idols). Surat At-Tahrim (The Prohibition) 66:6

﴿ يَٰٓأَيُّهَا ٱلَّذِينَ ءَامَنُوا۟ قُوٓا۟ أَنفُسَكُمْ وَأَهْلِيكُمْ نَارًا وَقُودُهَا ٱلنَّاسُ وَٱلْحِجَارَةُ ﴾ سورة التحريم 66: 6

Islam is the way of life—guidance from the Creator to us. It is concerned with our personal life, our social life as well as our family life. If Islam teaches that it is wrong to steal, shouldn't it also teach us how family members should behave with each other and shouldn't it explain their rights? In the Islamic family structure, both the father and mother are considered equal partners.

The structure of the Muslim family can best be summed up in the following hadith: 'Abdallah bin 'Umar ؓ reported that the Blessed Prophet ﷺ once said, "Every one of you is a shepherd and is responsible for his flock. The leader of the people is a guardian and is responsible for his subjects: a man is the guardian of his family and is responsible for his subjects, a woman is the guardian of her husband's home and of his children and is responsible for them, and the slave of a man is a guardian of his master's property and is responsible for it. Surely, everyone of you is a shepherd and responsible for his flock." (Muslim)

عَنِ ابْنِ عُمَرَ ؓ، عَنِ النَّبِيِّ ﷺ قَالَ: « أَلاَ كُلُّكُمْ رَاعٍ وَكُلُّكُمْ مَسْئُولٌ عَنْ رَعِيَّتِهِ فَالأَمِيرُ الَّذِي عَلَى النَّاسِ رَاعٍ وَهُوَ مَسْئُولٌ عَنْ رَعِيَّتِهِ وَالرَّجُلُ رَاعٍ عَلَى أَهْلِ بَيْتِهِ وَهُوَ مَسْئُولٌ عَنْهُمْ وَالْمَرْأَةُ رَاعِيَةٌ عَلَى بَيْتِ بَعْلِهَا وَوَلَدِهِ وَهِيَ مَسْئُولَةٌ عَنْهُمْ وَالْعَبْدُ رَاعٍ عَلَى مَالِ سَيِّدِهِ وَهُوَ مَسْئُولٌ عَنْهُ أَلاَ فَكُلُّكُمْ رَاعٍ وَكُلُّكُمْ مَسْئُولٌ عَنْ رَعِيَّتِهِ ». رَوَاهُ مُسْلِمٌ

B. The Duties of the Husband

The husband is considered the protector and leader of the home, but at the same time, Islam says he is not a dictator. (4:34) The wife's opinions should carry as much weight as his own. They must decide things together by **Shura** شورى **Mutual Consultation**.

The husband is expected to provide the financial resources of the family. Although the wife can have a career of her own, she doesn't have to spend a dime of her own money on the family if she doesn't want to. However, if the husband makes very little money, it is noble on her part to help in the paying of the bills.

The husband also has the responsibility of maintaining the safety of the family. He must protect them from danger and ensure that the wife and children can live without fear and poverty to the best of his ability.

'Abdallah bin 'Amr narrated that, the Blessed Prophet once said, "The Lord's pleasure is in the parent's pleasure, and the Lord's anger is in the parent's anger." (At-Tirmidhi)

عَنْ عَبْدِاللَّهِ بْنِ عَمْرٍو ، عَنِ النَّبِيِّ ﷺ قَالَ: «رِضَا اَللَّهِ فِي رِضَا الْوَالِدَيْنِ، وَسَخَطُ اَللَّهِ فِي سَخَطِ الْوَالِدَيْنِ». رَوَاهُ التِّرْمِذِيُّ

Again, this is assuming that the father is following Islam sincerely and teaching it to his children with some wisdom.

C. Duties of the Wife

The wife is the major caregiver in the home. She must nurture the children, with the husband's help, so that they become good Muslims and well-mannered people. The wife can work and have a career if she chooses, as long as she understands that raising her children is her priority.

If there are no relatives to help raise the children right, it is best for her to stay home for at least a few years to put them on the right path of Islam.

A man came to the prophet and said, "O Messenger of Allah! I intend to go on a military expedition, but I have come to ask your advice." He said, "Is your mother alive?" He said, "Yes." He said, "Then stay with her, for the garden is under her feet." (An-Nasa'i)

أَنَّ جَاهِمَةَ السُّلَمِيَّ جَاءَ إِلَى النَّبِيِّ ﷺ فَقَالَ: «يَا رَسُولَ اللَّهِ أَرَدْتُ أَنْ أَغْزُوَ وَقَدْ جِئْتُ أَسْتَشِيرُكَ. فَقَالَ: هَلْ لَكَ مِنْ أُمٍّ. قَالَ نَعَمْ. قَالَ: فَالْزَمْهَا فَإِنَّ الْجَنَّةَ تَحْتَ رِجْلَيْهَا». رَوَاهُ النَّسَائِيُّ

The mother is the most loved person in the home, even three times more than the father, according to a hadith of the Blessed Prophet.

Abu Huraira reported that a person came to Allah's Messenger and said, "Who among the people is most deserving of a fine treatment from my hand?" He said, "Your mother." He again said, "Then who (is the next one)?" He said, "Again it is your mother (who deserves the best treatment from you)." He said, "Then who (is the next one)?" He (the Holy Prophet) said, "Again, it is your mother." He (again) said, "Then who?" Thereupon he said, "Then it is your father." (Muslim)

عَنْ أَبِي هُرَيْرَةَ، قَالَ: «جَاءَ رَجُلٌ إِلَى رَسُولِ اللَّهِ ﷺ فَقَالَ مَنْ أَحَقُّ النَّاسِ بِحُسْنِ صَحَابَتِي قَالَ: أُمُّكَ. قَالَ ثُمَّ مَنْ قَالَ: ثُمَّ أُمُّكَ. قَالَ ثُمَّ مَنْ قَالَ: ثُمَّ أُمُّكَ. قَالَ ثُمَّ مَنْ قَالَ: ثُمَّ أَبُوكَ». رَوَاهُ مُسْلِمٌ

Children, according to another hadith, are even forbidden to disobey their mothers.

The Blessed Prophet said, "Allah has indeed forbidden you to disobey your Mothers." (Al Bukhari)

عَنِ النَّبِيِّ ﷺ قَالَ: «إِنَّ اللَّهَ حَرَّمَ عَلَيْكُمْ عُقُوقَ الْأُمَّهَاتِ». رَوَاهُ الْبُخَارِيُّ

Islam teaches the equality of men and women. Both are equal in the sight of Allah and one is not more valuable to Allah than the other. Although Allah did give men the position of 'head of the family,' it doesn't mean that men get more attention from Allah.

Allah said, For Muslim men and Muslim women, for believing men and believing women, for devout men and devout women, for patient men and patient women, for humble men and humble women, for charitable men and charitable women, for fasting men and fasting women, for chaste men and chaste women, and for men and women who engage in the praise of Allah—for them Allah has prepared forgiveness and a great reward. Surat Al Ahzab (The Confederates) 33:35

﴿إِنَّ ٱلْمُسْلِمِينَ وَٱلْمُسْلِمَٰتِ وَٱلْمُؤْمِنِينَ وَٱلْمُؤْمِنَٰتِ وَٱلْقَٰنِتِينَ وَٱلْقَٰنِتَٰتِ وَٱلصَّٰدِقِينَ وَٱلصَّٰدِقَٰتِ وَٱلصَّٰبِرِينَ وَٱلصَّٰبِرَٰتِ وَٱلْخَٰشِعِينَ وَٱلْخَٰشِعَٰتِ وَٱلْمُتَصَدِّقِينَ وَٱلْمُتَصَدِّقَٰتِ وَٱلصَّٰٓئِمِينَ وَٱلصَّٰٓئِمَٰتِ وَٱلْحَٰفِظِينَ فُرُوجَهُمْ وَٱلْحَٰفِظَٰتِ وَٱلذَّٰكِرِينَ ٱللَّهَ كَثِيرًا وَٱلذَّٰكِرَٰتِ أَعَدَّ ٱللَّهُ لَهُم مَّغْفِرَةً وَأَجْرًا عَظِيمًا﴾

سُورَةُ الأَحْزَابِ 33:35

D. The Rights and Duties of Children

Children have rights and duties in Islam. It is their right to be raised as Muslims, with good manners and to be educated. It is their duty to obey their parents in everything they can, as long as it isn't haram.

The Blessed Prophet once advised children, "Obey your parents and treat them kindly, for if you do, then your own children will be obedient and kindly to you." (At-Tabarani)

قَالَ رَسُولُ اللهِ ﷺ: «بَرُّوا آبَاءَكُمْ تَبَرَّكُمْ أَبْنَاؤُكُمْ، وَعِفُّوا تَعِفَّ نِسَاؤُكُمْ». رَوَاهُ الطَّبَرَانِيُّ

On another occasion he remarked, "Allah will forgive whatever wrong actions He wills until the Day of Judgement except disobedience of parents, because Allah Most High punishes the person who is disobedient to his (or her) parents before death right in this world." (Al Baihaqi)

قَالَ رَسُولُ اللهِ ﷺ: «كُلُّ الذُّنُوبِ يَغْفِرُ اللهُ مِنْهَا مَا يَشَاءُ إِلَّا عُقُوقَ الْوَالِدَيْنِ، فَإِنَّهُ يُعَجِّلُ لِصَاحِبِهِ فِي الْحَيَاةِ قَبْلَ الْمَمَاتِ». رَوَاهُ البَيْهَقِيُّ

The Blessed Prophet spelled out the rights of children and stressed their rights often, as the following sayings confirm:

- "There is no one who has three daughters, or three sisters, and he treats them well, except that he enters paradise." (At-Tirmidhi)

قَالَ رَسُولُ اللهِ ﷺ: «لَا يَكُونُ لِأَحَدِكُمْ ثَلَاثُ بَنَاتٍ أَوْ ثَلَاثُ أَخَوَاتٍ فَيُحْسِنُ إِلَيْهِنَّ إِلَّا دَخَلَ الْجَنَّةَ». رَوَاهُ التِّرْمِذِيُّ

- "There is no gift that a father gives his son more virtuous than good manners." (At-Tirmidhi)

قَالَ رَسُولُ اللهِ ﷺ: «مَا نَحَلَ وَالِدٌ وَلَدًا مِنْ نَحْلٍ أَفْضَلَ مِنْ أَدَبٍ حَسَنٍ». رَوَاهُ التِّرْمِذِيُّ

- "He is not one of us who is not kind to children." (Al Bukhari)

قَالَ رَسُولُ اللهِ ﷺ: «إِنَّهُ مَنْ لَا يَرْحَمْ لَا يُرْحَمْ». رَوَاهُ الْبُخَارِيُّ

E. Extended Family

While it is not always possible to live this way, ideally, Muslim families would have extended family members living nearby. A home where the parents, grandparents and children live together, or at least in the same neighborhood, is the most valued in many Muslim cultures. If possible, it helps to have aunts, uncles and cousins nearby to create a strong support network in times of difficulty and happiness.

'Aishah narrated that the Messenger of Allah said, "The best of you are those who are best to their families, and I am best to my family." (At-Tirmidhi)

عَنْ أُمِّ الْمُؤْمِنينَ عَائِشَةَ قَالَتْ قَالَ رَسُولُ اللهِ ﷺ: «خَيْرُكُمْ خَيْرُكُمْ لِأَهْلِهِ وَأَنَا خَيْرُكُمْ لِأَهْلِي». رَوَاهُ التِّرْمِذِيّ

Therefore, we must study how he interacted with his family and try to do the same ourselves.

There is indeed a good model for you in the Messenger of Allah – for the one who has hope in Allah and the Last Day, and remembers Allah profusely. Surat Al Ahzab (The Confederates) 33:21

﴿لَقَدْ كَانَ لَكُمْ فِي رَسُولِ اللَّهِ أُسْوَةٌ حَسَنَةٌ لِّمَن كَانَ يَرْجُو اللَّهَ وَالْيَوْمَ الْآخِرَ وَذَكَرَ اللَّهَ كَثِيرًا﴾ سُورَةُ الأَحْزَابِ 33: 21

Abu Usayd Malik bin Rabi'ah As-Sa'idi narrated, "While we were with the Messenger of Allah! a man of Banu Salmah came to Him and said: 'Messenger of Allah is there any kindness left that I can do to my parents after their death?' He replied: 'Yes, you can invoke blessings on them, forgiveness for them, carry out their final instructions after their death, join ties of relationship which are dependent on them, and honour their friends.'" (Abu Dawud)

عَنْ أَبِي أُسَيْدٍ، مَالِكِ بْنِ رَبِيعَةَ السَّاعِدِيِّ قَالَ بَيْنَا نَحْنُ عِنْدَ رَسُولِ اللهِ ﷺ إِذْ جَاءَهُ رَجُلٌ مِنْ بَنِي سَلَمَةَ فَقَالَ: «يَا رَسُولَ اللهِ هَلْ بَقِيَ مِنْ بِرِّ أَبَوَيَّ شَيْءٌ أَبَرُّهُمَا بِهِ بَعْدَ مَوْتِهِمَا؟ قَالَ: نَعَمْ الصَّلَاةُ عَلَيْهِمَا وَالِاسْتِغْفَارُ لَهُمَا وَإِنْفَاذُ عَهْدِهِمَا مِنْ بَعْدِهِمَا وَصِلَةُ الرَّحِمِ الَّتِي لَا تُوصَلُ إِلَّا بِهِمَا وَإِكْرَامُ صَدِيقِهِمَا». رَوَاهُ أَبُو دَاوُد

Grandparents and the elderly are also highly respected. They are to be looked upon with love and affection and cared for when they become weaker with age. It is better to take care of your elderly parents and grandparents in your home, instead of sending them to a retirement home. Sometimes, though, they may need professional care that requires such housing situations.

Abu Huraira reported that the Blessed Prophet said, "May his nose be rubbed in dust," then he repeated it twice more, the companions asked, "who is that Prophet

of Allah?" The Prophet said, "Who found one or both of his parents approaching old age, but failed to enter Paradise (for not serving them)." (Muslim)

عَنْ أَبِي هُرَيْرَةَ ﷺ، قَالَ قَالَ رَسُولُ اللهِ ﷺ: «رَغِمَ أَنْفُهُ ثُمَّ رَغِمَ أَنْفُهُ ثُمَّ رَغِمَ أَنْفُهُ. قِيلَ مَنْ يَا رَسُولَ اللهِ قَالَ: مَنْ أَدْرَكَ وَالِدَيْهِ عِنْدَ الْكِبَرِ أَحَدَهُمَا أَوْ كِلَيْهِمَا ثُمَّ لَمْ يَدْخُلِ الْجَنَّةَ». رَوَاهُ مُسْلِمٌ

وَقُل رَّبِّ ارْحَمْهُمَا كَمَا رَبَّيَانِي صَغِيرًا

Questions to Answer

1. What is the ideal living arrangement for a Muslim family?
2. What are two rights that children have?
3. What is one duty that they have to their parents?

Define: Elderly, Shura.

Reflect: Explain the following hadith: Mu'awiyah al-Qushayri narrated that "Mu'awiyah asked: 'Messenger of Allah, what is the right of the wife of one of us over him?' He replied: 'That you should give her food when you eat, clothe her when you clothe yourself, do not strike her on the face, do not revile her or separate yourself from her except in the house.'" (Abu Dawud)

عَنْ حَكِيمِ بْنِ مُعَاوِيَةَ الْقُشَيْرِيِّ، عَنْ أَبِيهِ، قَالَ قُلْتُ يَا رَسُولَ اللهِ مَا حَقُّ زَوْجَةِ أَحَدِنَا عَلَيْهِ قَالَ: «أَنْ تُطْعِمَهَا إِذَا طَعِمْتَ وَتَكْسُوَهَا إِذَا اكْتَسَيْتَ - أَوِ اكْتَسَبْتَ - وَلاَ تَضْرِبِ الْوَجْهَ وَلاَ تُقَبِّحْ وَلاَ تَهْجُرْ إِلاَّ فِي الْبَيْتِ». رَوَاهُ أَبُو دَاوُدَ

Act: Memorize the dua' in 17:23-24 and say it everyday.

IQ Builders:
1. If someone dies, when it comes time to divide the shares of the inheritance, what are we advised in 4:9 about our poor relatives who are present?
2. What does 2:83 tell us about who deserves to be treated well?

49 Islamic Society: Ideals and Realities

WHAT TO LEARN

We are extremely fortunate that we have all the information we need about how to create a model Islamic society. All we must do now is implement what we know.

VOCABULARY

Dar As-Salaam

THINK ABOUT IT

What would it be like to live as a Muslim in a pure Islamic society?

A. Societies Out of Control

Everyone talks about how Muslims form one *Ummah*, or community, but what does that mean? What does it mean to have an Islamic society and social system?

Do Muslim countries have an Islamic social system? Sadly, this is not the case in most Muslim-majority countries. Just because you have 10, 10,000, 1,000,000 Muslims living in a place, doesn't mean they are living according to Islam. In fact, many so-called Muslim countries provide us with few role models. So, how can we define what our Islamic society should look like? You know the answer. All we have to do is learn about Muslims who lived true to their beliefs in former times and then put their values into practice.

You could look at the model of Al Madinah during the Prophet's time and gain the most valuable insight. Then you could look at the growth and vitality of the Muslim Ummah for the next thousand years and get a pretty good idea of what an Islamic society entails.

B. Characteristics of an Islamic Society

To begin with, the law of the land is the Shari'ah of Allah. The leader, or khalifa of the Islamic nation, implements the Shari'ah in society. The people try to follow it as best they can in order to save their souls in the Hereafter.

All people are equal before the law and no one gets any special treatment. People greet each other with the greetings of peace and do their best to avoid committing haram acts. People would feel ashamed to litter and reluctant to pick a fight or harm others.

When someone is in need, people help him or her. When it's prayer time, the shops and businesses close for a little while. During Ramadan, the streets are filled with people going to Tarawih Salah. During the 'Eid holidays, people are celebrating with great fun and fanfare.

Al Masjid An-Nabawi.

Hospitals are affordable, and schools are available for everyone to learn how to read and write. Criminals are punished as they deserve. The army protects the people from attacks by outside enemies rather than oppressing the people like so many armies do today. No one goes hungry. Widows and orphans are supported by the community with fairness and compassion. (4:36) Hajj time is treated as a solemn occasion, and the Hujjaj are congratulated and asked about their wonderful journey when they return.

Children are taught to love Allah and the Messenger and to respect their elders with due deference. Men are taught to respect women, and women are taught to guard their modesty. Abusing one's wife or child is rare, and those guilty of it are punished severely. Women are allowed to hold any jobs they wish and also hold to leadership positions in such roles as judges, administrators, teachers, doctors and scholars. People do not fear that if they lose their jobs they will be ruined, because zakah money is available for the unemployed.

All these things may sound like a tall order, but if you read your Qur'an, hadith and history books, you'll see that they are the foundation of an Islamic society. They were all implemented, in one form or another, in various Muslim communities throughout history. If something can be done once, it can be done again. Muslims lost their way as the Blessed Prophet predicted they would.

The Blessed Prophet Muhammad said, "By Allah, I don't fear poverty for you, but that worldly possessions may be given to you as lavishly as they were to your predecessors. You may incline towards the delights of the world as they did, and it may destroy you as it destroyed them." (Al Bukhari and Muslim)

عَنِ النَّبِيِّ ﷺ قَالَ: «وَاللهِ مَا الفَقْرَ أَخْشَى عَلَيْكُمْ، وَلَكِنِّي أَخْشَى أَنْ تُبْسَطَ عَلَيْكُمُ الدُّنْيَا كَمَا بُسِطَتْ عَلَى مَنْ قَبْلَكُمْ، فَتَنَافَسُوهَا كَمَا تَنَافَسُوهَا، وَتُهْلِكَكُمْ كَمَا أَهْلَكَتْهُمْ» رَوَاهُ البُخَارِيُّ وَمُسْلِمٌ

C. How Do We Become Great Again?

Muslims dream of establishing the power of Islam in the world. Muslims of all backgrounds agree that the Islamic system is the best for humanity in this life. Even non-Muslim writers, such as Bertrand Russel and Napoleon, have recognized that the Islamic system is the best for the ordering of human affairs. But how do we regain what our ancestors lost so long ago? How do we once again build our Ummah into a shining example for all people to follow?

Some people believe it will only happen if we become secular, or non-religious, and adopt so-called 'modern' values. Others think we must build up current Muslim countries or have revolutions there. Still others say it will only happen when the non-Muslim world destroys itself from the inside, like the Roman empire did.

Who has the answer? Everyone has an opinion, so what should you and I do to contribute to the rebirth of the Islamic World?

For all their talk, most political thinkers have forgotten the most important truth of all. (3:186) In all their secret meetings, shouting matches and plans for sweeping Muslim glory, they failed to start from square one. That is, victory comes from Allah and not from our wishes. (61:8-9)

When we look at the model of the Blessed Prophet Muhammad, we find that the first 13 years of his mission were devoted to building a core of dedicated followers. After this training period, they would go through anything they had to for Allah and the Prophet. (5:105)

People were approached with the call of Islam in the street, in the marketplace, in homes, at parties, on hills and in the city center. Those who embraced the message were taught to respect and love each other as brothers and sisters, and they formed one spiritual block.

Then, when the dominant society could no longer stand the existence of righteous people in their midst, the Muslim community relocated to a more friendly environment where Islam was the governing system. There, Islam flowered into a civilization with traditions, laws, customs, holidays, manners and substance. Islam became a nation. Importantly, all this could have only happened with strong, dedicated followers.

The first phase was known as the Makkan Period. During this period, the people delivering the message of Islam were persecuted, but proclaimed it to any who would listen.

The second time period is known as the Madinan Period. After the Muslims migrated to Al Madinah, Islam grew in strength and then was able to become a self-sustaining force. The reason it was so strong was because it had strong people behind it. That was the key.

We can't just look at past Muslim civilizations either and think that's what we need to re-create. When it comes down to it, many of the leaders in later Muslim history were not practicing Muslims. Do we want to remake the same old corrupt empire-model in the coming centuries? Of course not.

We want the ideal of Al Madinah for the next generations. But we will never get it without the struggle of the Makkan period. To illustrate this truth, look at the Muslim countries. They are full of Muslims, but the countries are far from Islamic. (3:179)

If all we needed was a lot of Muslims living together, then those countries would be the **Dar As-Salaam** دَارُ السَّلَام **Land of Peace**. But they're not. According to the Qur'an, not every Muslim is a believer. We need believers, whose faith is unwavering under any circumstance.

We cannot hope to build an Islamic nation on the backs of people who are hypocrites, weak in their emaan or just plain lazy. Allah even mentions that some people only serve Him if times are good, but then run away if things get tough. In fact, there are some Muslim countries where the people actually oppose the implementation of Shari'ah-based laws because they love their alcohol and illicit relations too much. You can't build a solid wall with bricks made of soft mud.

There was an interesting remark made by a scholar some time ago. He said, "The only thing that can reform Muslims today is the same thing that made them great before (following the Qur'an)."

In other words, we must build our character, build our emaan, build our *taqwa* and then truly surrender to Allah completely. Why shouldn't we do that? Our lives are shorter than the blinking of an eye. We have so little time to understand why we're here. What's wrong with insuring the eternal happiness of our soul? Like Allah says, *Do not lose heart and do not grieve, and you are the uppermost if you are believers.* Surat Al 'Imran (The Family of 'Imran) 3:139

﴿وَلَا تَهِنُوا وَلَا تَحْزَنُوا وَأَنتُمُ الْأَعْلَوْنَ إِن كُنتُم مُّؤْمِنِينَ﴾ سُورَةُ آلِ عِمْرَان 3: 139

Indeed, only when we produce a generation of people who actually fear the Day of Judgement, and love to be closer to the Prophet's example, will we be able to make Islam dominant on Earth. This means we have to sweep away the old ideas from our minds. No longer can we view Qur'anic education as a punishment with a stick. No longer can we consider the masjid a place to hang out with people of the same ethnic group. No longer can we hold backward regional cultures as more important than Islamic culture.

Allah has said He will not change our condition until we change our hearts. (13:11) If we wish to change our condition and to receive the aid of Allah, then we must become true believers again. *O you who believe, be patient, compete with each other in patience, and guard your frontiers, and fear Allah, so that you may be successful.* Surat Al 'Imran (The Family of 'Imran) 3:200

﴿يَا أَيُّهَا الَّذِينَ ءَامَنُوا اصْبِرُوا وَصَابِرُوا وَرَابِطُوا وَاتَّقُوا اللَّهَ لَعَلَّكُمْ تُفْلِحُونَ﴾ سُورَةُ آلِ عِمْرَان 3: 200

IT'S ALL ABOUT ISLAM

Islam only lives when there are people who believe in it and who practice it. Surely, in the creation of the heavens and the earth, and in the alternation of night and day, there are signs for the people of wisdom, Who remember Allah standing and sitting, and (lying) on their sides, and ponder on the creation of the heavens and the earth (and say) "Our Lord, You have not created all this in vain. We proclaim Your purity. So, save us from the punishment of Fire. Our Lord, whomsoever You admit into the Fire, he is disgraced by You indeed, and for the unjust there are no supporters. Our Lord, We heard a herald calling towards Faith: 'Believe in your Lord.' So we believed. Our Lord, forgive us, then, our sins, and write off our evil deeds, and make us die only when we have joined the righteous. Our Lord, give us what You have promised us through Your messengers, and do not put us to disgrace on the Day of Judgement. Surely you do not go back on Your promise." Surat Al 'Imran (The Family of 'Imran) 3:190-194

﴿إِنَّ فِى خَلْقِ ٱلسَّمَـٰوَٰتِ وَٱلْأَرْضِ وَٱخْتِلَـٰفِ ٱلَّيْلِ وَٱلنَّهَارِ لَـَٔايَـٰتٍ لِّأُو۟لِى ٱلْأَلْبَـٰبِ ۝ ٱلَّذِينَ يَذْكُرُونَ ٱللَّهَ قِيَـٰمًا وَقُعُودًا وَعَلَىٰ جُنُوبِهِمْ وَيَتَفَكَّرُونَ فِى خَلْقِ ٱلسَّمَـٰوَٰتِ وَٱلْأَرْضِ رَبَّنَا مَا خَلَقْتَ هَـٰذَا بَـٰطِلًا سُبْحَـٰنَكَ فَقِنَا عَذَابَ ٱلنَّارِ ۝ رَبَّنَآ إِنَّكَ مَن تُدْخِلِ ٱلنَّارَ فَقَدْ أَخْزَيْتَهُۥ وَمَا لِلظَّـٰلِمِينَ مِنْ أَنصَارٍ ۝ رَّبَّنَآ إِنَّنَا سَمِعْنَا مُنَادِيًا يُنَادِى لِلْإِيمَـٰنِ أَنْ ءَامِنُوا۟ بِرَبِّكُمْ فَـَٔامَنَّا رَبَّنَا فَٱغْفِرْ لَنَا ذُنُوبَنَا وَكَفِّرْ عَنَّا سَيِّـَٔاتِنَا وَتَوَفَّنَا مَعَ ٱلْأَبْرَارِ ۝ رَبَّنَا وَءَاتِنَا مَا وَعَدتَّنَا عَلَىٰ رُسُلِكَ وَلَا تُخْزِنَا يَوْمَ ٱلْقِيَـٰمَةِ إِنَّكَ لَا تُخْلِفُ ٱلْمِيعَادَ﴾ سورة آل عمران 3: 190-194

IT'S ALL ABOUT ISLAM

إِنِ الْحُكْمُ إِلَّا لِلَّهِ

Questions to Answer

1. Describe what a real Islamic society would look like.
2. **What is your understanding of the following hadith and how it applies to Muslims in the world today?** The Prophet ﷺ said, "There will come a time upon humanity when nothing will remain of Islam except its name only, and nothing will remain of the Qur'an except its ritual. The masaajid will be full, but will be lacking in guidance. The learned people will be the worst under the sky, and trouble will come from them and go back to them." (Al Baihaqi)

عَنِ النَّبِيِّ ﷺ قَالَ: ((يُوشِكُ أَنْ يَأْتِيَ عَلَى النَّاسِ زَمَانٌ لَا يَبْقَى مِنَ الْإِسْلَامِ إِلَّا اسْمُهُ، وَلَا يَبْقَى مِنَ الْقُرْآنِ إِلَّا رَسْمُهُ، مَسَاجِدُهُمْ عَامِرَةٌ وَهِيَ خَرَابٌ مِنَ الْهُدَى، عُلَمَاؤُهُمْ شَرُّ مَنْ تَحْتَ أَدِيمِ السَّمَاءِ، مِنْ عِنْدِهِمْ تَخْرُجُ الْفِتْنَةُ وَفِيهِمْ تَعُودُ)). رواه البيهقي

Define: Dar As-Salaam.
Reflect: Are Muslim countries today a good role model for us? Why or why not?
Act: Look through previous lessons and write down three rules that were in effect when Islam was the ruling force in Al Madinah. Then, write a sentence or two describing how those rules could be applied today.

IQ Builders:
1. What does 3:176-177 teach us? How does this relate to the state of Muslim affairs today?
2. Read the translation of 6:53. What does this mean to you?

Literature Selection

Father, May I Have a Ring?

Adapted from *God-Oriented Life*
Compiled by Wahiduddin Khan

Once, 'Umar bin Al Khattab, who was the second khalifa, was notified of some valuables that had come into the treasury from the tax collections. When he was asked what should be done with them, 'Umar replied, "I'm busy right now, remind me about this in a few days when you see that I'm free."

A few days later, 'Umar was reminded again, so he went to the treasury and had the gold and silver plates and ornaments brought out for counting.

When he saw all the sparkling things, he recited the following ayah of the Qur'an: *Men are tempted by the love of women and children, of piled up treasures of gold and silver, and of fine horses, cattle and lands.* Surat Al 'Imran (The Family of 'Imran) 3:14

﴿ زُيِّنَ لِلنَّاسِ حُبُّ الشَّهَوَاتِ مِنَ النِّسَاءِ وَالْبَنِينَ وَالْقَنَاطِيرِ الْمُقَنطَرَةِ مِنَ الذَّهَبِ وَالْفِضَّةِ وَالْخَيْلِ الْمُسَوَّمَةِ وَالْأَنْعَامِ وَالْحَرْثِ ۗ ذَٰلِكَ مَتَاعُ الْحَيَاةِ الدُّنْيَا ۖ وَاللَّهُ عِندَهُ حُسْنُ الْمَآبِ ﴾ سورة آل عمران 3: 14

Then 'Umar said, "We can't help rejoicing in something that tempts us. O Lord, may we spend it rightly. So protect us from its evil."

Just then, one of 'Umar's own sons, 'Abdul Rahman, came along and asked his father if he could have a ring out of the treasures there.

'Umar remembered what he had just said, and addressed his son saying, "Go to your mother. She will feed you barley soup."

It was thus that 'Umar gave him nothing. *(It was reported by Ahmad.)*

Questions to Answer

1. Why didn't 'Umar want to go over the tax revenues right away?
2. What was his reaction when he saw all the wealth?
3. Why do you think he denied giving his son a ring?

50 An Islamic State: The Past and the Future

WHAT TO LEARN

Imagine a land where there were no laws, and everyone did exactly as they pleased, with no regard for others. What would happen? Also, how does Islam ensure that these injustices don't happen in society?

VOCABULARY

Majlis Ash-Shura   Qadi
Colonialism

THINK ABOUT IT

What is the political system of Islam like?

A. Religious and Political Systems

How would you describe the political system of Islam? Is it a democracy, a theocracy, a plutocracy or a monarchy? If you try to use one of these man-made labels, you will always fall short of the answer.

In many countries today, the governments are usually secular democracies—that is, a government where the people make all their own laws and elect leaders with no relation to any revealed wisdom or Divine Guidance. Some countries are constitutional monarchies, which means a democratic country with a king or queen. However, monarchs have only a fraction of the power they once held hundreds of years ago. England is a good example because its queen is just a figure head. She is a symbol and has no real power. The elected members of Parliament make all the laws.

In most Western countries, religion is supposed to be kept separate from the government. In the United States, this practice is called 'the separation of church and state.' This principle means that the government will not be influenced by any religious teachings, nor will it support any religion at all. At the same time, it will not try to suppress any religion either.

B. Christianity and Politics

Because early Christians disputed among themselves, their faith never held together as a unified system. Every Christian country has its own kind of Christianity that is distinct from the other. (3:187-188) The biggest three sects of Christianity are the Catholic, Protestant and Orthodox churches. They have been disagreeing for centuries over religious issues.

Historically, whenever a country has tried to mix its local brand of Christianity with politics, disaster has soon followed. The officially-sanctioned priests have hunted down and persecuted all those Christians who belonged to other religious sects. For example, you may have studied the Spanish Inquisition, the French Huguenot Struggle or the Salem Witch Trials. Even scientists were sometimes arrested, such as Galileo, and books were burned. The masses were kept uneducated and ignorant, easily controlled by The Church for most of Western history.

Because of this corruption, by the middle of the 1700's, nearly every Christian country had pushed the power of their churches out of the government. They chose to have all their laws created by the public, or by their representatives, and to not let religion play any further role in the affairs of state. Consequently, science was able to grow, the people were better educated and the leaders of the countries could get down to the business of building states without interference from religious fanatics.

C. Colonial Impact on Muslim Countries

But what about Islam? Did the same results occur when Muslims intertwined Islam with politics? Was Islam ever against education or science or freedom of religion? The answer to all these questions is a big "**No**." Here are the facts:

The way of life known as Islam is a complete system. It was revealed by the Creator of the Universe as a guide for people to live by. This being the case, Islam provides answers for individuals, families, societies and governments. There is no separation of masjid and state, because the goal of the Islamic state is the establishment of the Deen of Allah.

By contrast, the goal of many Western countries, guided by a mix of secularism and ethno-religious nationalism, is the dominance of their nations over others and the gathering of riches. "Survival of the fittest" and "might makes right" are their implicit mottoes.

Muslims know that Allah is the Supreme Being in the Universe; therefore, His laws and commandments must form the basis for all human affairs. If we don't follow Allah's commandments, but still call ourselves Muslims, then we are hypocrites, like the followers of many other religions today. Surely, there are many hypocrites among Muslims today, and most Muslim countries are governed by people who try to suppress the free practice of Islam.

Some of this can be attributed to the history of many Muslim countries, in which Western nations invaded and occupied Muslim lands about 300 years ago. During the era of **Colonialism** استعمار, European countries took over the Muslim world and divided it up. Muslims were forced to follow un-Islamic political systems.

To reinforce the permanence of this change, the colonialists raised a group of local people in every land who would be their loyal servants. The money and power tempted these Muslims away from practicing Islam, and instead they started 'loving' many of the non-Islamic practices. Then, when the colonialists were finally forced to leave the Muslim lands, these now-corrupt Muslims assumed control and continued the same political system that the outsiders brought.

Although Muslim lands may have been freed of direct control from colonialist powers, they have never been truly free. This is because the men trained by the colonialists simply moved into power and maintained the same un-Islamic system. Thus, we see that the Muslim countries have not yet returned to being Islamic nations.

D. Islam and Politics

What would a real Islamic system look like today? In an Islamic political system, the leader or khalifa, is the head of the whole Ummah, not

Basics of an Islamic Government

Judicial Branch

Title: Qadi System.
Qualifications: Muslim, male or female, well grounded in the principles of Fiqh and Shari'ah.
Selected: Appointed by the khalifa in consultation with the Majlis Ash-Shura.
Job: To dispense justice, to make decisions about legal issues and to rule on the actions of the khalifa and the Majlis Ash-Shura. A council of Fiqh scholars may advise here.

Executive Branch

Title: Khalifa and Amir ul Mu'mineen.
Qualifications: Muslim, male, over 40 years old, of good standing and recognized knowledge and ability.
Selected: Chosen by vote of either the people directly or by their representatives.
Job: To implement the Shari'ah, manage the affairs of government and lead the Ummah in all its political affairs.
Term: Can be for life or a set period. Majlis Ash-Shura determines this time period. Un-Islamic behavior is grounds for removal or impeachment.

Representative Branch

Title: Majlis Ash-Shura.
Qualifications: A body of elected representatives chosen by the community. Can be male or female, must be Muslim and of recognized knowledge and ability.
Selected: By vote.
Job: To advise the khalifa, represent the people, approve or disapprove of the leader's decisions and remove him from office if he deviates from the Shari'ah.

---

just of one country or another. He should be elected by the community and is in charge of establishing Islam and justice on the Earth. (2:30) He must not ask for the position, nor can it be given to someone merely because their father was a khalifa before them. Hereditary rule of the Islamic state is haram in Islam.

The Blessed Prophet ﷺ declared, "Do not ask for the position of leader, for if you are given it after asking for it, you will be left to carry it out for yourself. But if you are given leadership without asking for it, you will be helped (by Allah) to carry out its duties." (An-Nasa'i)

The khalifa, however, is not a dictator and must consult with the representatives of the community. This **body of representatives** is known as the **Majlis Ash-Shura** مَجْلِسُ الشُّورى. The members of the Shura should also get elected and confirmed by the community. This is the Sunnah of the Blessed Prophet ﷺ.

قَالَ رَسُولُ اللهِ ﷺ: «لَا تَسْأَلِ الإِمَارَةَ فَإِنَّكَ إِنْ أُعْطِيتَهَا عَنْ مَسْأَلَةٍ وُكِلْتَ إِلَيْهَا وَإِنْ أُعْطِيتَهَا عَنْ غَيْرِ مَسْأَلَةٍ أُعِنْتَ عَلَيْهَا». رَوَاهُ النَّسَائِي

Next, the Muslim community will have a judicial system in which a highly educated judge, known as **Qadi** قاضي, will administer justice. Scholars of Fiqh and Shari'ah assist in the application of the law.

The basis of the legal and political system is the Shari'ah of Allahﷻ. Its main sources are the Qur'an and Sunnah. While the Shura is free to make laws for everyday life, there will be certain things that are eternal Islamic principles that must remain unchanged. On those things that have no apparent answer in the Qur'an and Sunnah, people deliberate over the issues and come up with laws (ijtehad) that reflect the spirit of Islam.

For example, Allahﷻ gave us the law that zakah must be paid to help the needy. The government can't change this law, because Allahﷻ made it. However, Allahﷻ didn't say anything about speed limits on the roads or immigration laws. In those instances, Muslim scholars would work out laws that are fair and safe. The Majlis Ash-Shura and khalifa could then approve it.

The duty of Muslim citizens is to be loyal to the Islamic State, to live as good Muslims, to approve of good and oppose wrong-doing and to answer the call of their leader if he needs them. (4:59)

The Blessed Prophet ﷺ said, "A Muslim must hear and obey, both in what he likes and in what he dislikes, so long as he is not commanded to perform an act of disobedience to Allah, in which case he must neither hear nor obey." (Al Bukhari & Muslim)

قَالَ رَسُولُ اللهِ ﷺ: «عَلَى الْمَرْءِ الْمُسْلِمِ السَّمْعُ وَالطَّاعَةُ فِيمَا أَحَبَّ وَكَرِهَ إِلاَّ أَنْ يُؤْمَرَ بِمَعْصِيَةٍ فَإِنْ أُمِرَ بِمَعْصِيَةٍ فَلَا سَمْعَ وَلَا طَاعَةَ». رَوَاهُ الْبُخَارِيُّ وَمُسْلِمٌ

Non-Muslims who are living in an Islamic state and are loyal citizens of the country and pay their **Jizyah** جِزْيَة **Taxes** have equal rights with Muslims and have the right to practice

The Blessed Prophet ﷺ said, "Whoever obeys me, obeys Allah. Whoever disobeys me, disobeys Allah. Whoever obeys my amir, obeys me. Whoever disobeys my amir, disobeys me." (Al Bukhari)

قَالَ رَسُولُ اللهِ ﷺ: «مَنْ أَطَاعَنِي فَقَدْ أَطَاعَ اللهَ، وَمَنْ عَصَانِي فَقَدْ عَصَى اللهَ، وَمَنْ أَطَاعَ أَمِيرِي فَقَدْ أَطَاعَنِي، وَمَنْ عَصَى أَمِيرِي فَقَدْ عَصَانِي». رَوَاهُ الْبُخَارِيُّ

Ibn Mas'ud﷠ narrated that the Prophet ﷺ said, "What should you do with the orders of leaders who do not follow the sunnah and delay prayer on its permissible time?" I said, "What do you order me Prophet?" The Prophet replied, "There is no obedience to one who does not obey Allah." (Ahmad)

عَنِ ابْنِ مَسْعُودٍ﷠، أَنَّ النَّبِيَّ ﷺ، قَالَ: «كَيْفَ بِكَ يَا عَبْدَ اللهِ، إِذَا كَانَ عَلَيْكُمْ أُمَرَاءُ يُضَيِّعُونَ السُّنَّةَ، وَيُؤَخِّرُونَ الصَّلَاةَ عَنْ مِيقَاتِهَا؟ قَالَ: كَيْفَ تَأْمُرُنِي يَا رَسُولَ اللهِ؟ قَالَ: تَسْأَلُنِي ابْنَ أُمِّ عَبْدٍ، كَيْفَ تَفْعَلُ؟ لَا طَاعَةَ لِمَخْلُوقٍ فِي مَعْصِيَةِ اللهِ عَزَّ وَجَلَّ». رَوَاهُ أَحْمَدُ

'Abdallah bin Mas'ud narrated that the Prophet ﷺ said, "Among those in charge of you, after I am gone, will be men who extinguish the Sunnah and follow innovation. They will delay the prayer from its proper time." I said: "O Messenger of Allah, if I live to see them, what should I do?" He said: "You ask me, O Ibn 'Abd, what you should do? There is no obedience to one who disobeys Allah." (Ibn Majah)

عَنْ عَبْدِ اللهِ بْنِ مَسْعُودٍ، أَنَّ النَّبِيَّ ﷺ قَالَ: «سَيَلِي أُمُورَكُمْ بَعْدِي رِجَالٌ يُطْفِئُونَ السُّنَّةَ وَيَعْمَلُونَ بِالْبِدْعَةِ وَيُؤَخِّرُونَ الصَّلَاةَ عَنْ مَوَاقِيتِهَا، فَقُلْتُ: يَا رَسُولَ اللهِ إِنْ أَدْرَكْتُهُمْ كَيْفَ أَفْعَلُ؟ قَالَ: تَسْأَلُنِي يَا ابْنَ أُمِّ عَبْدٍ كَيْفَ تَفْعَلُ لَا طَاعَةَ لِمَنْ عَصَى اللهَ». رَوَاهُ ابْنُ مَاجَهْ

their religion. No one can be persecuted, and no one can be forced to change their beliefs. They are called أَهْلُ الذِّمَّة. (2:256)

In fact, the historians of the world recognize that Islamic civilizations have been the most tolerant and fair out of all the world's civilizations. There has never been anything like the Inquisition, the Holocaust or the Soviet collectivization famine, in all of Muslim history.

The principles of the Islamic legal and political system are well developed. They have been studied and implemented for centuries. Even when some traditional Muslim empires and territories were ruled by kings and princes who falsely called themselves khulafa', the Islamic Shari'ah was still used to one degree or another to oppose their abuses of power.

Examples of how this system was implemented throughout Muslim history are many. Once we become educated in the authentic system of Islam, we must try to establish it somewhere. This is our mission. Some Muslims say they want to establish it, but then they commit haram and violent acts in the process. We must not follow their example.

The best example to follow is that of the Messenger of Allah ﷺ, the Sahaba and those righteous people throughout Muslim history who followed Islam sincerely.

E. Our Role in Creating a Real Islamic State

The Blessed Prophet ﷺ once said that when we see a wrong being committed, we must try to change it with our own hands. If we can't do that, then we must at least speak out against it. And if we can't do that, then we should at least feel bad about it in our hearts. The Prophet ﷺ then added that the third option was the weakest level of emaan.

If we want to establish a real Islamic state based on justice and equality for all people, then we must first build our emaan to the level of being so motivated that we have no choice but to take action. Otherwise, we will continue to flounder, and our communities will move aimlessly.

Blessed is the One Who sent down the Standard (the Qur'an) to His servant, so it can be a warning to all creatures. The control of space and the Earth belongs to Him. He has not given birth to any son, nor does He have any partner in His control. He is the One Who created all things and made them properly measured. Surat Al Furqan (The Criterion) 25:1-2

﴿تَبَارَكَ ٱلَّذِى نَزَّلَ ٱلۡفُرۡقَانَ عَلَىٰ عَبۡدِهِۦ لِيَكُونَ لِلۡعَٰلَمِينَ نَذِيرًا ۞ ٱلَّذِى لَهُۥ مُلۡكُ ٱلسَّمَٰوَٰتِ وَٱلۡأَرۡضِ وَلَمۡ يَتَّخِذۡ وَلَدًا وَلَمۡ يَكُن لَّهُۥ شَرِيكٌ فِى ٱلۡمُلۡكِ وَخَلَقَ كُلَّ شَىۡءٍ فَقَدَّرَهُۥ تَقۡدِيرًا﴾ سُورَةُ الفُرۡقَان 25: 1 – 2

Questions to Answer

1. What has been the experience of Muslims and Islam in politics?
2. What are the rights and responsibilities of non-Muslims in an Islamic State?
3. What was colonialism?

Define: Qadi.
Reflect: Why are Muslim countries still not functioning in the way that Islam has guided?
Act: With a partner, work together to describe how an Islamic government would function. Include points you have learned from this chapter, as well as lessons you learned from the Prophet's leadership in Al Madinah. Your description can be in the form of an illustration, diagram or essay.

IQ Builders:

1. Explain what ayah 5:8 is trying to teach us.
2. Copy down ayaat 14:42-52. Explain in 2-4 paragraphs how these ayaat can be applied towards the people who do wrong and think they can get away with it.

Skill Builder

How Do I Live Islam Today?

The Blessed Prophet Muhammad ﷺ once said that there will come a time when the struggle to live like a good Muslim will be so hard that it will be like holding a hot coal in your hand. It's not always easy to live in the full spirit of Islam when the world is dominated by people who follow their every whim, right or wrong, and who call you towards sinful living.

Indeed, whenever someone makes a stand for truth, justice, morality and an honest, clean living, the people in the society around them attack them mentally, verbally and sometimes physically. The problem has become so difficult that even in traditionally Muslim countries, the true followers of Islam are often discriminated against by un-Islamic governments, simply because they assert that Islam is the true path to follow for success in both worlds.

But it cannot be said that we are the only people who have lived in difficult times. In every age, and in every society, there have been temptations, worries, social problems and people who would try to steer us from the straight way of submission to Allah's ﷻ will. Shaytan has never rested, and he has ways of getting at the best of us through our weaknesses.

One famous Muslim writer, Imam Abu Hamid Muhammad Al Ghazzali, also knew what it was like to live in a world full of temptations and stumbling blocks on the road to true and sincere taqwa (awareness of Allah ﷻ). He was born in the year 1058 in the city of Tus in the Middle East. At that time, the Muslim world was expanding and growing. Muslim lands were not under the control of non-Muslims, nor were the leaders particularly bad.

Imam Al Ghazzali should have had an easy time being a good Muslim in such a situation. But, because of human shortcomings found within us all, he saw that his own society was filled with un-Islamic temptations and that men were motivated more by the delights of the world than by the delights of faith. Even Imam Al Ghazzali had a crisis of faith trying to understand how a person could be a sincere believer in such a situation.

After withdrawing from society for a while to think, he returned with the answers he had sought. He successfully identified the thorny path that the sincere believer must follow, and wrote a book entitled *Ihya 'Uloom Ad-Deen* إحياء عُلوم الدِّين (*The Reawakening of Knowledge of the Deen*) and helped millions of Muslims, even up to our present day, see how to live as a true Muslim in a world full of temptation and distraction.

The following reading selection is Imam Al Ghazzali's analysis of the difficult path towards true peace that everyone who wants to submit to Allah ﷻ must pass through. Pay close attention to the stages and the features of each. Then write a response essay of 2-3 pages exploring the issues raised and how they relate to our own lives.

Skill Builder

The Allegory of the Seven Valleys

by Imam Abu Hamid Al Ghazzali

Know, my brothers and sisters, that 'ibadah, or 'service for Allah,' is the fruit of knowledge, the benefit of life and the currency of the righteous. It's the aim and object of people of noble aspirations having sharp inward understanding. It's their reason for being and their everlasting paradise. "I am your Creator," says Allah in the Qur'an. "Serve Me. You will have your payback and your efforts will be rewarded."

'Ibadah, then, is essential for people, but at the same time it is filled with difficulties and hardships. It has stumbling blocks and pitfalls in its tortuous path, which is haunted by cut-throats and goblins, while helpers are scarce and friends are few. But this path of 'ibadah must be dangerous, for as the Blessed Prophet says, "Paradise is surrounded by sufferings and covered by trials, while Hell is surrounded by easy things and unlimited enjoyment of passions."

The poor human! He is weak; his responsibilities are heavy; times are hard, and life is short. But because the journey from here to the hereafter is unavoidable, if he neglects taking the necessary supplies for the trip, he will be sure to perish. Think over the importance of the situation and the seriousness of our condition. By Allah, our condition is sorry indeed, for many are called, but few are chosen.

When I realized that the path of 'ibadah was so difficult and dangerous, I wrote certain books. Chiefly among them, *Ihya Uloom-id Deen*, in which I pointed out the ways and means of getting over those difficulties, facing the dangers boldly and crossing the path with success. But certain people, who didn't see what I was trying to do in my writings, failed to understand the meaning and purpose of it. They not only rejected the book, but treated it in a manner unbecoming of a Muslim.

But I was not discouraged. These were the same types of people who used to ridicule the Holy Qur'an, calling it, 'The Stories of the Ancients.' Nor was I offended by them. I felt pity on them because they didn't know what they were doing to themselves. I hate conflicts even now, but I feel I must do something for them. So out of compassion for my brothers and sisters, I prayed to Allah to enlighten me on the subject (of difficulty in living the *deen*) in a new manner.

Listen, then, and know that the first thing which awakens a person from the sleep of forgetfulness, and turns him towards the straight path, is Allah's grace, which stirs the mind to think the following thoughts:

"I am the receiver of so many gifts—life, power, reason, speech—and I find myself mysteriously protected from so many troubles and disasters. Who is my benefactor? Who is my savior? I must be grateful to Him in a fitting manner; otherwise, the gifts might be taken away, and I will be finished off forever! These gifts reveal their purpose, like tools in the hands of an artist, and the world appears to me like a beautiful picture leading my thoughts towards the painter."

These thoughts take the awakened person into the Valley of Knowledge where the Messenger of Allah ﷺ leads the way and tells him:

"The Benefactor is the One Who has no partner with Him. He is your Creator Who is everywhere, though you can't see Him, Whose commandments must be obeyed both inwardly and outwardly. He has decided that good will be rewarded and evil will be punished. The choice is now yours, because you are held responsible for your actions. Seek knowledge from teachers who fear Allah ﷻ with an unshakable conviction."

When the Valley of Knowledge is crossed, a person then prepares for 'ibadah but his guilty conscience assaults him, saying, "How can you knock at the door of Heaven (when you are so filled with bad ways and behavior)? Away with the immorality and bad deeds first!"

The poor sinner then falls down into the Valley of Repentance, when suddenly a voice is heard crying, "Repent, repent! For your Lord is forgiving!"

He asks for repentance sincerely and cries to His Lord for mercy. He now takes heart and rises up with joy and proceeds further on the path. Then he enters into a Valley Full of Stumbling Blocks, chief of which are four in number:
1) The tempting world,
2) The attractive people,
3) The old enemy Shaytan, and finally,
4) The weak inner-self.

So let him have four weapons he can use to defeat the four main enemies. These four are:
1) Choosing a simple lifestyle.
2) Avoiding mixing with all sorts of people.
3) Fighting the old enemy, Shaytan, with increased learning.
4) Controlling the inner-self with the overseer of taqwa.

Let it be remembered that these four weapons, themselves, have to face four other psychological troubles. They are:
1) Worrying over money due to living a simple lifestyle.
2) Doubts and anxieties about our private affairs disturbing our peace of mind.
3) Worry, hardship and embarrassment, because of not meeting new people all the time. Indeed, when a person wishes to serve Allah ﷻ, Shaytan attacks him openly and secretly from all sides!
4) Unpleasant happenings and unexpected suffering come out of nowhere.

These psychological worries throw the poor traveler into the Valley of Trials and Troubles. In this plight, let a person protect himself by:
1) Dependence on Allah in the matter of his earnings.
2) Calling for His help when he finds himself helpless.
3) Patience in suffering.
4) Joyous submission to His Will.

Crossing this fearful Valley of Trials and Troubles makes a person think that the path will not be easy, but to his amazement, he finds that 'ibadah is boring, prayers are mechanical and contemplation has no pleasure. He is lazy, depressed, gloomy and stupid. Puzzled and perplexed, he now enters into the Thundering Valley. The lightning flash of Hope dazzles his sight, and he falls down trembling when he hears the deafening sound of the Thunder of Fear.

His eyes, brimming with tears, imitate the clouds; his pure thoughts flash with the lightning. In a moment, the mystery of Human Responsibility, with its rewards for good actions and punishment for wicked deeds, was solved. Afterwards, his 'ibadah will not be just lip service, and his daily work will not be just drudgery. Soaring on high, he will go forward on the wings of Hope and Fear.

With a light heart and in a happy mood, he now proceeds further until suddenly the Abysmal Valley presents its dreadful sight. Looking deep into why he does things, he finds that people who do good are motivated, either by the desire to show off to their fellow people, or they are simply trying to impress themselves.

On one side of the Abysmal Valley he sees the ten-headed monster of hypocrisy lurking, and on the other side he sees the bewitching Pandora of Conceit with her box open. In despair, he doesn't know what to do, when suddenly, the Angel of Sincerity emerges from the depths of his heart and takes him by the hand and carries him through the valley.

While expressing his thanks for the mercy of Allah, he proceeds further until the thought of Allah's numerous favors to his unworthy self, and his inability to do full justice in giving thanks, overwhelms him.

And thus he enters into the Valley of Hymns where, mortal as he is, he tries his best to sing the songs of praise to the ever lasting Allah. The Invisible Hand of Divine Mercy then opens the door to the Garden of Love. He is ushered inside with his body and soul, because both had played their part directly or indirectly. Here ends the journey. The servant of Allah now lives among his fellow travelers, but his heart lives in contemplation of Allah, waiting to carry out the last order, *O soul at peace! Return to your Creator well-pleased and well pleasing. Then enter among My Servants, and enter into My Paradise.* Surat Al Fajr (The Dawn) 89:27-30

﴿يَا أَيَّتُهَا النَّفْسُ الْمُطْمَئِنَّةُ﴾ ﴿ارْجِعِي إِلَى رَبِّكِ رَاضِيَةً مَرْضِيَّةً﴾ ﴿فَادْخُلِي فِي عِبَادِي﴾ ﴿وَادْخُلِي جَنَّتِي﴾ سُورَةُ الْفَجْرِ 89: 27 – 30

Unit 10 Review Exercise

VOCABULARY REVIEW

On a separate sheet of paper, write the definition of each word below.

1. Adab
2. Akhlaq
3. Shura
4. Elderly
5. Majlis Ash-Shura
6. Dar As-Salaam
7. Imam
8. Deen
9. Qadi
10. Khalifa
11. 'Ibadah
12. Sunnah
13. Islamic State
14. Representative

REMEMBERING WHAT YOU READ

On a separate sheet of paper, answer the following questions. Use complete sentences in your answers.

1. Write down one hadith about good manners.
2. List two points about how to greet another Muslim properly.
3. What are three hurtful things we are not allowed to do to another person?
4. What are two duties of a wife in a Muslim family?
5. What are two duties of a husband in a Muslim family?
6. What are four rights of parents?
7. List three characteristics of a true Islamic society.
8. How did colonialism affect much of the Muslim world?
9. Describe the different parts of an Islamic government and the role of each.

THINKING TO LEARN

On a separate sheet of paper, answer the questions below. Use complete sentences.

1. Identify and explain three things that could improve the state of the Muslims in the world today.
2. How can we build our community into an Islamic one that follows Islamic guidelines?
3. What are some of the duties of a khalifa in an Islamic government?

Reference Section

World Muslim Population

Resources & Reference

Glossary

Where Do Muslims Live?

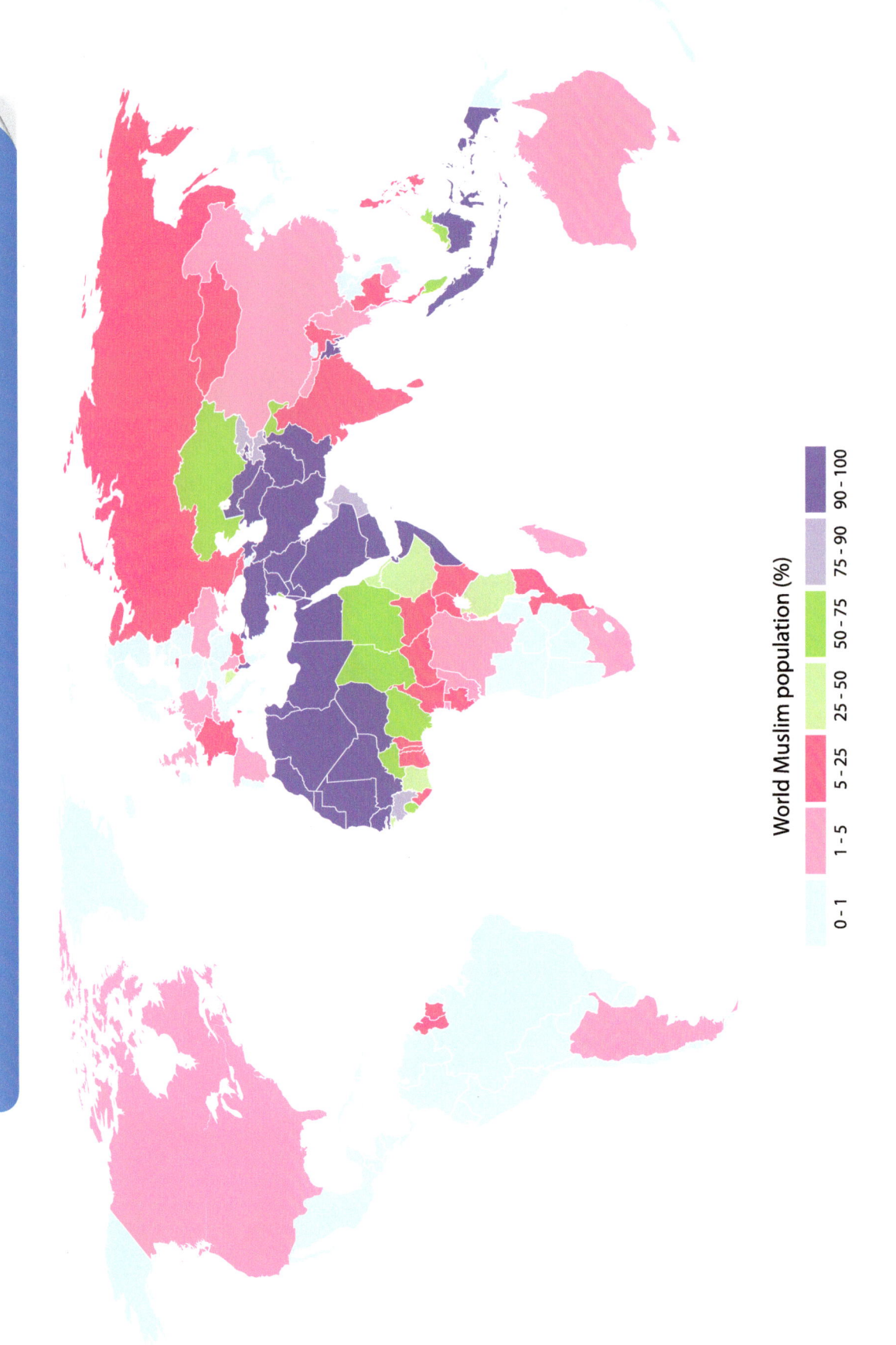

World Muslim population (%)

- 0 - 1
- 1 - 5
- 5 - 25
- 25 - 50
- 50 - 75
- 75 - 90
- 90 - 100

Suggested Enrichment Literature

Islam in General
- Minhaj Al-Muslim (The Muslim's Path): Abu Bakr Jabir Al-Jaza'iry
- The Beautiful Commands of Allah: Ruqaiyyah Waris Maqsood
- Al Tawhid: Ismail Raji Al-Faruqi
- Islamic Creed Series (Set of 8 Books): 'Umar S. al-Ashqar
- What Everyone Needs to Know about Islam: John L. Esposito
- Understanding Islam: Jerald F. Dirks
- Let Us Be Muslims: Sayyid Abul Ala Mawdudi
- Islam Today: Akbar S. Ahmed
- What Everyone Should Know About Islam and Muslims: Suzanne Haneef
- Islam The Straight Path Author: John L. Esposito
- The Everything Understanding Islam Book-A complete guide to Muslim beliefs, practices, and culture Author: Christine Huda Dodge
- Essential Message of Islam: Muhammad Yunus and Ashfaque Ullah
- Islam in Focus Author: Hammudah 'Abd al 'Ali
- A Basic Dictionary of Islam Author: Ruqaiyyah Waris Maqsood
- Islam Author: Ismail Raji Al-Faruqi
- Islam its Meaning and Message: Author: Khurshid Ahmad
- The Complete Idiot's Guide to Understanding Islam: Yahiya Emerick
- The Most Beautiful Names of Allah: Samira Fayyad Khawaldeh

Comparative Religion and Current Issues:
- What You Weren't Taught In Sunday School: Jerald F. Dirks
- The Cross and the Crescent: Jerald F. Dirks
- Problems Muslims Face in Today's World: Isa M. Tofte
- Struggling to Surrender: Some Impressions of an American Convert to Islam: Jeffrey Lang
- What I Believe: Tariq Ramadan
- Losing My Religion: A Call for Help: Jeffrey Lang
- Living Islam Treading the Path of Ideal: Ruqaiyyah Waris Maqsood
- A Young Muslim's Guide to the Modern World: Seyyed Hossein Nasr
- Why Islam? لماذا الإسلام؟: K. Sherman
- From MTV to Mecca: How Islam Inspired My Life Author: Kristiane Backer
- Islam - A Thousand Years of Faith and Power Author: Jonathan Bloom and Sheila Blair

Adab - Manners
- Muslim Character : An American-English Translation of Muhammad al-Ghazali's Khuluq al-Muslim
- The Ideal Muslim Society As defined in the Qur'an and Sunnah Living Islam: Muhammad Ali Al-Hashimi
- Treading the Path of Ideal: Ruqaiyyah Waris Maqsood
- Reclaim Your Heart: Yasmin Mogahed
- Morals and Manners in Islam (A Guide To Islamic Adab): Marwan Ibrahim Al-Kaysi

Learn Arabic:
http://www.noorart.com/shop_by_age/learn_arabic_adults_books_2

Suggested Enrichment Literature

Pillars of Islam
- Salat Guide Made Simple: Mohammad Thompson
- Salaat the Islamic Prayer from A to Z: Mamdouh N. Mohamed
- The Muslim Prayer Encyclopedia: Ruqaiyyah Waris Maqsood
- A Simple Guide to Muslim Prayer: Muhammad Mahmud Al-Sawwat
- Zakat Calculation: Mushfiqur Rahman

Prophet Muhammad
- When the Moon Split: Safi Ar-Rahman Al-Mubarakfoury
- The Prophet Muhammad - A Role Model for Muslim Minorities
- Daily Wisdom - Sayings of the Prophet Muhammad: Abdur Raheem Kidwai
- Who Is Muhammad: Khurram Murad
- Remembrance and Prayer The Way Of Prophet Muhammad: Muhammad Al-Ghazali
- In the Footsteps of the Prophet: Tariq Ramadan
- Muhammad(ﷺ) His Life Based on the Earliest Sources: Martin Lings
- The Sealed Nectar: Safi Ar-Rahman Al-Mubarakfour
- The Life of the Last Prophet: Yusuf Islam
- Critical Lives: Muhammad(ﷺ): Yahiya Emerick
- Muhammad Man and Prophet: Adil Salahi
- Muhammad: His Character and Conduct: Adil Salahi
- A Day with the Prophet: Ahmad Von Deffner
- The Prophet Muhammad: The Best of All Husbands: Dr. Ghazi aShammari

The Holy Qur'an
http://www.noorart.com/shop_by_age/holy_quran_adults_books

Prophets
- Stories of the Prophets: Ismaeel Ibn Katheer
- Prophets Models for Humanity: Alia N. Athar

Du'a - Supplication
- The Accepted Whispers (English Translation of Munajaat-e-Maqbul): Maulana Ashraf Ali Thanvi
- Daily Wisdom: Islamic Prayers & Supplications: Abdur Raheem Kidwai
- Don't be Sad: Aaidh ibn Abdullah al-Qarni
- Living in Allah's Presence: Aspects of Islamic Spirituality: Abdur Rashid Siddiqui

Women in Islam
- Great Women of Islam: Mahmood Ahmad Ghadanfar
- Woman In Islam: Aisha Lemu and Fatima Heeren
- Tajweed Made Easy: Ruqaiyyah Islam

Suggested Enrichment Literature

Family and Marriage
- The Muslim Marriage Guide: Ruqaiyyah Waris Maqsood
- Marriage and Family Building in Islam: Muhammad Abdul Bari
- Family Leadership (Qawamah): Dr. Mohamed Rida Beshir
- Before the Wedding: Munira Lekovic Ezzeldine

Ahadith
- Authentication of Hadith - Redefining the Criteria: Israr Ahmad Khan
- Summarized Sahih Al-Bukhari: Imam Bukhari
- English Translation of Sahih Muslim (7 Books): Imam Abul-Husain Muslim
- Riyad-us-Saliheen (2 Books): Imam Al-Nawawi
- Forty Hadith: Assad Nimer Busool
- The Hadith for Beginners: Dr. Muhammad Zubayr Siddiqi
- An-Nawawi's Forty Hadith

Islamic History and Civilization
- Islamic Civilization : It's Foundational Beliefs and Principles: Sayyid Abul Ala Mawdudi
- A Journey Through Islamic History: Yasminah Hashim & Dr M A J Beg
- Muslim Contributions to World Civilization: M. Basheer Ahmed & Syed A. Ahsani & Dilnawaz A. Siddiqui
- The House of Wisdom: How the Arabs Transformed Western Civilization Author: Jonathan Lyons
- Lost History: The Enduring Legacy of Muslim Scientists, Thinkers, and Artists Author: Michael Hamilton Morgan
- A Vanished World: Muslims, Christians, and Jews in Medieval Spain Author: Chris Lowney
- How Islam Created The Modern World Author: Mark Graham
- Winning the Hearts & Souls Author: Hafiz Ibn Kathir
- Studies in Islamic Civilization: The Muslim Contribution to the Renaissance Author: Ahmed Essa and Othman Ali
- 1001 Inventions: The Enduring Legacy of Muslim Civilization Author: Professor Salim T.S. Al-Hassani
- Stories from Islamic History: Sayyed Abul Hasan Ali Nadwi The History of Islam: 3 Volumes: Akbar Shah Najeebabadi
- Companions of the Prophet: 2 Books Author: Abdul Wahid Hamid
- Heroes of Islam Author: Prof. Mahmoud Esma'il Sieny
- A History of the Prophets of Islam: 2 Volumes Author: Suzanne Haneef
- Lost Islamic History - Reclaiming Muslim Civilisation from the Past: Firas Alkhateeb
- The Stories of the Sahaba (5 books): Noura Durkee
- Men & Women around the Messenger (ﷺ): Sa'd Yusuf Abu Aziz

Resources & Reference

The following main sources for reference were used in this book:

Main General Islamic Sources
- The Holy Qur'an In Arabic
- The Holy Qur'an: Abdullah Yusuf Ali
- The Message of the Qur'an: Muhammad Asad
- The Meaning of the Holy Qur'an in Today's English: Yahiya Emerick
- The Holy Qur'an for School Children: Juz 30: Yahiya Emerick
- Hadith Sahih Al Bukhari
- Hadith Sahih Muslim

Islamic Beliefs
- Islam: A Comprehensive Guidebook: Altaf Kherie
- What Islam is All About: Yahiya Emerick
- Thinking about God: Ruqaiyyah W. Maqsood
- I am a Muslim (Vols 1 & 2): Sheikh Abubaker Najaar

History of the Blessed Prophet
- The Life of Muhammad: M.H. Haykal
- Muhammad the Last Prophet: Vehbi Ismail
- The Life of Muhammad: Tahia Ismail
- Muhammad: Yahiya Emerick
- Muhammad: Martin Lings
- In the Footsteps of the Prophet: Tariq Ramadan

Fiqh, Shari'ah, Islam in Society
- The Lawful and Prohibited in Islam: Yusuf al Qaradawi
- Fiqh Us-Sunnah: Sayyid Sabiq
- Everyday Fiqh: Yusuf Islahi
- The Islamic ruling on Music and Singing: Mustafa al Kanadi
- Manners and Morals in Islam: Ibrahim Kaysi

Islamic History
- Concise History of the Muslim World Vols. 1-3: Rafai A. Fidai
- The Illustrated History of Islam: M. Abdul Rauf
- Studies in Islamic History: Dr. Ali
- The Encyclopedia of Islam: Cyril Glase
- The Atlas of Islamic History since 1500: Francis Robinson

Selected Index

A
'Aad, 123, 125, 126
'Abbas bin 'Abdul Muttalib, 236
'Abdallah bin 'Abdul Asad, 212
'Abdallah bin Mas'ud, 197, 238, 295
'Abdul Malik bin Marwan, 241
'Abdul Wahid Hamid, 274
'Abdush-Shamms, 222
Abu Bakr As-Siddiq, 243
Abu Darda', 245
Abu Dharr, 235, 236, 237, 238
Abu Dharr al Ghifari, 235, 236
Abu Huraira, 67, 80, 221, 222, 223, 255
Abu Talib, 225
Adab, 277, 278, 305
Adam, 92, 93, 94, 95, 112, 113
Advocate, 87, 141
Ahadith, 23, 307
Ahadun Ahad, 244
'Aishah, 26, 60, 220, 225, 240, 278
Ahl Al Kitab, 261
Akhlaq, 277, 280
Al Ansar, 214, 309
Al Bukhari, 26, 59, 61, 69, 70, 80
Al Furqan, 257,
Al hamdulillah, 22
Al Huruf Al Muqatta'h, 52
Al Khidr, 168, 169, 170
Al Madinah, 36, 44, 180, 212, 213, 214
Al Tufayl bin 'Amr, 221
Aladdin, 179
Alhumdulillah, 226, 241, 257
'Ali bin Abu Talib, 105, 225, 235
Allah, 15, 16, 17, 20, 21, 22
Allahu Akbar, 37, 226, 240
Allahu Akbar and La ilaha ill Allah, 240
Ameen, 17, 66, 215, 222, 227, 242
Amir, 216, 295
Ammuriyah, 230
Angel, 26, 29, 34, 35, 41, 52
Anonymous, 139,
'Aqaba, 216
Archaeology, 128, 129
Arkan Al Emaan, 60
Arkan Al Islam, 61
Asfahan, 228
Ash-Shafi'i, 254, 255
Asma' bint Abu Bakr, 239
Assalamu 'alayka yaa Rasulullah, 236
As-Siddeeq, 243
Asyah, 155, 156, 160, 163
At-Tirmidhi, 28, 244, 252, 264, 268, 271
Augustus Caesar, 186
Authentic, 58, 139, 296
Awlia'a, 268
Aws, 230
ayaat, 19, 21, 23, 36, 40, 44
Azar, 130, 132
'Aziz Misr, 144, 145, 146, 147
Az-Zahra', 225

B
Badr, 213, 224, 244
Balqees, 174, 177, 178
Banu 'Abdul Asad, 213
Banu 'Amr bin 'Awf, 213
Banu Daws, 221
Banu Isra'il, 154, 162, 166, 167, 168, 170
Banu Quraytha, 230
Banu Umayah, 213, 241
Bayt As-Saff, 222
Benjamin, 142, 143, 147, 148, 150
Big Bang Theory, 79, 82, 83
Bilal bin Rabaah, 243
Bukhara, 182
Busrah bint Ghazwan, 222

C
Cahokia, 139
Cave of Thawr, 243
Chaldeans, 180
Christos, 198
Colonialism, 293
Creationism, 87
Cyrus the Great, 180, 186

D
Da'wah, 61, 66, 73, 154, 235, 268
Damascus, 188, 240
Dar As-Salaam, 288
Dawud, 175, 176, 187
Deen, 249, 254, 293, 299
Dhabiha, 261, 262
Dhul Qarnayn, 180, 181, 182, 183
Disciple, 196, 197, 198, 204
Druze, 58
Dua', 23, 136, 222, 224, 242

E
'Eid, 286
Elderly, 163, 218, 278, 284
Emaan, 68, 104, 106, 107, 242, 244
Encouraging good while forbidding evil, 61
Ephesus, 205, 208
Ethnicities people, 186
Etiquette, 25
Evolution, 86, 87, 88

F
Faith, 15, 16, 17, 29, 41, 48
Faresi, 288
Fatimah, 220, 224, 225, 226, 227
Fatimah bint al Khattab, 37
Fatwa, 251
Fiqh, 249, 250, 251, 254, 255, 256
Fir'aun, 163
Fitrah, 59, 67, 95
Fus-ha, 23, 39

G
Ghifar, 235, 236, 237
Ghusl, 27
Gospel, 196

H
Habeel, 113, 114
hadith, 24, 40, 61, 117, 197, 215
Hadrian, 205, 207
Hafith, 40
Hafsah, 21, 40, 41
Hajar, 134, 135
Hajjaj bin Yusuf, 41
Halal, 249, 253, 259, 260, 261, 262
Haman, 155, 162
Hanbali, 255
Hanifi, 255
Haram, 249, 253, 259, 260, 264, 283
Harun, 156, 158, 159, 160, 161, 162
Hassan, 226, 245
Hawd, 220
Hawwa, 93, 94, 95, 112, 113
Hebrews, 154, 155, 156, 160, 161, 163
Herod, 195
Hieroglyphics, 160
Hijrah, 36, 213, 216, 222, 225, 230
Homs, 218
Hoopoe, 176, 177

Selected Index

Hud, 122, 124, 125, 126
Hudaibiyah, 227
Hudhayfahd, 40
Hudhud, 176
Hudood, 249
Huffath, 40
Human, 16, 33, 34, 39, 44, 47
Hussain, 220, 226, 245
Hyksos, 146, 154

I

'Ibadah, 245, 256, 299, 300, 301
Ibadis, 58
Iblis, 92, 93, 112, 113, 117
Ibn Majah, 58, 265, 295
Ibrahim, 17, 60, 130, 131, 132, 133
'Iddah, 214
Ihya 'Uloom Ad-Deen, 298
Ijmaa', 251
Ijtehad, 251, 253, 255, 295
Imam Abu Hanifa, 254
Imam Ahmad bin Hanbal, 254
Imam Al Ghazzali, 298
Imam Anas bin Malik, 254
Imam Ash-Shafi'i, 254
Imam Ja'far As Sadeq, 254
'Imran, 186, 188
Injeel, 195, 196, 199, 247
insha'Allah, 48
Iqra, 33
Iram, 122, 123
'Isa, 17, 60, 75, 136, 192, 193
Ishaq, 134, 135, 142, 145
Islam, 15, 17, 20, 26, 36, 37
Islamic State, 20, 243, 292, 293, 294, 295
Isma'il, 134, 135, 136
Isma'ilis, 58

J

Ja'fari, 255
Jahannam, 93, 109
Jalut, 174
Jericho, 171
Jibreel, 34, 35, 36, 39, 40, 226
Jihad, 61, 244,
Jinn, 91, 92, 102, 112, 113, 176
Jizyah, 295
Judah, 171, 175, 176, 187
Julaybib, 232, 233, 234

K

Ka'bah, 61, 136, 224, 235, 236, 241
Kafara, 68
Kafir, 68, 69
Khabbab, 37
Khadijah, 34, 224, 225, 227
Khalid bin Walid, 258
Khalifa, 40, 41, 103, 112, 182, 218
Khalifa Wathiq, 182
Khazraj, 230
Khulafa', 296
Khutbah, 218, 272
King, 133, 134, 146, 147, 154, 170
Kuffar, 68

L

Lut, 133, 134, 135
Lydians, 180, 181

M

Ma'rib, 140
Madhab, 255, 256, 257
Madhahib, 255, 256
Madinan, 44, 288
Madinan Period, 288
Madyan, 157, 159
Mahr, 225, 272
Majlis Ash-Shura, 294, 295
Majuj, 181, 182
Makkah, 27, 34, 36, 44, 52, 61, 98
Makkan, 44, 212, 216, 225, 235, 288
Makkan Period, 288
Makruh, 249
Malik bin Marwan, 41, 241
Maliki, 255
Marwan bin al Hakim, 223
Maryam, 188, 189, 191, 192, 193, 195
Masada, 187
Masih, 187, 192, 193, 197, 198, 199
Masjid, 66, 218, 222, 225, 226, 241, 243
Meroe, 139
Mihrab, 188
Modernists, 58
Mount Judi, 120, 121
Mu'ath bin Jabal, 216, 217, 218, 250
Mu'min, 294
Muhajirun, 214, 240
Muhkamat, 44
Munaafiqoon, 69

Munir, 49
Muqaddasi, 182
Mus'ab bin 'Umair, 216
Musa, 17, 26, 136, 146, 155, 156, 158
Mushriks, 60
Muslim, 15, 17, 20, 21, 33, 41
Mutashabihat, 44

N

Namrud, 133, 134
Narrator, 215, 223
Nasra, 117
Nicea, 199
Nifaaq, 70
Nikah, 225, 270, 271, 272
Nile River, 154, 156
Nuh, 116, 117, 118, 119, 120, 122, 136

O

Ochrida, 181
'Olama'a, 251, 253
Ozone Layer, 83, 84

P

Palestine, 123, 134, 135, 142, 154, 163
Peace be upon you and Allah's mercy and blessings, 178
Persecute, 198, 205, 224, 253, 288, 293
Pharaoh, 99, 146, 154, 155, 156, 158
Philosopher, 91
Photosynthesis, 86, 87
Pontius Pilate, 197
Prehistoric, 116, 117
Processed, 260, 261
Prophet, 15, 16, 17, 20, 21, 23
prophethood, 158, 160, 224, 243

Q

Qabeel, 113, 114
Qadi, 292, 294, 295
Qitmir, 206
Qiyas, 251, 253
Quba', 213, 230, 231, 240
Qur'an, 17, 18, 20, 21, 22, 23, 25
Qur'anic, 21, 47, 80, 81, 195, 288
Quraysh, 212, 235, 236, 244
Qurayshi, 41
Qutaylah, 240

Selected Index

R
Rabbi, 187, 188, 197
Rahman, 80, 140, 222, 258, 291
Rasulullah, 222, 236
Repentance, 104, 300
Representative, 168, 293, 294
Revelation, 20, 21, 29, 33, 35, 36, 37
Riba, 264
Ruh, 95, 106, 192
Ruku', 192
Rumaysa bint Milhan, 274
Ruqaiyyah, 224

S
Saad bin Waqqas, 258
Saba', 176, 177
sahaba, 40, 41, 216, 220, 228, 230
sahabi, 41
Sahabiyyat, 212
Sahih Al Bukhari, 173
Salafis, 58
Salah, 61, 66, 105, 226, 243, 245
Salat Al Jum'uah, 237
Salat Al Jumu'ah, 66
Salih, 17
Salman Al Faresi, 163, 228
Samiri, 167, 168
Saqar, 29
Scribe, 36, 40, 223
Scripture, 53, 61, 73, 98, 199
scrotal, 173
Sect, 53, 58, 75, 100, 292, 293
Sentient, 86
Shahadah, 67, 236, 274
shaheed, 163
Shari'ah, 249, 250, 253, 255, 256, 263
Shaytan, 75, 93, 95, 102, 103, 113
Shi'a, 58, 254
Shu'aib, 19, 157
Shu'ayb, 157
Shura, 52, 243, 281, 294, 295
Signs, 29, 47, 54, 69, 81, 93
Sira, 49
step-temples, 130
SubhanAllah, 226
Sufis, 58
Suhaib, 201
Suhuf, 133
Sulayman, 48, 174, 175, 176, 177, 178

Sunnah, 15, 17, 59, 60, 62, 250
Sunni, 58, 254
Surat, 19, 23, 29, 40, 52, 66
Suwa', 117
suwar, 19, 23, 44, 52
Synagogues, 187

T
Ta'if, 221
Tadabbur, 27
Tafseer, 40
Talut, 174, 175, 179
Taqwa, 74, 270, 271, 288, 298, 300
Tasbeeh, 175
Tawbah, 104
Tawrah, 171, 187, 196
Test, 15, 29, 52, 86, 93, 94
The Iron Door, 182
The Mother of Her Father, 225
The Prehistoric, 116
The Twelve Imams, 58
The Woman with the Two Belts, 239
Tilawah, 27
Timeline, 90
Traditionalists, 58
Transliteration, 23, 24
Trinitarians, 204
Tuwa, 37, 166

U
Ubar, 123
Uhud, 213, 226, 256
Um Al Qurah, 52
Um Salamah, 212, 213, 214, 215
'Umar bin Al Khattab, 21, 26, 36, 37, 218, 244
Umayyad Masjid, 188
Umm Al Kitab, 97
Umm Kulthum, 224
Ummah, 241, 243, 244, 271, 286, 287
Umuhat al Mu'mineen, 215
Unitarians, 204
'Uthman, 21, 26, 39, 40, 41, 225
'Uthman bin Talha, 213,
Uzayr, 187

W
Wa 'alayka assalamullahi wa rahmatuhu wa barakaatuhu, 236

Wahhabis, 58
Wali, 268, 272
Walimah, 271, 272
Wife of 'Aziz Misr, 144, 145, 146
Wudu', 27, 220, 244, 256

Y
Ya'qub, 142, 143, 145, 148, 149, 150
Ya'uq, 117, 119
Yaghuth, 117, 119
Yahya, 189, 192, 195
Yajuj, 181, 182
Yamamah, 40
Yathrib, 216, 230
Yusha', 169
Yusuf, 142, 143, 144, 145, 146, 147

Z
Zabur, 175
Zaidis, 58,
Zakah, 61, 105, 287, 295
Zakariyya, 188, 189, 191, 195
Zamzam, 135
Zayd bin Harithah, 224
Zayd bin Thabit, 21, 36, 40, 41
Zaynab, 224, 226
Ziggurats, 130

Glossary

	Vocabulary Word	Arabic Script	Definition	Page
1	'Aad people	عاد	The powerful people of Prophet Hud, known for their structures, who were destroyed by Allah.	121
2	Abu Dharr	أبو ذَرّ	One of the first Sahabah of Prophet Muhammad.	234
3	Abu Huraira	أبو هُرَيرَة	One of the Companions of Prophet Muhammad, literally "Father of the Kitten."	220
4	Adab	آداب	Manners.	276
5	Adam	آدَم	First created man.	110
6	Advocate	مؤيد	A person who upholds or defends a cause; supporter.	138
7	Ahadun Ahad	أَحَدٌ أَحَد	Only One! Only One!	242
8	Akhlaq	أخلاق	Virtue, morality and manners.	276
9	Al Furqan	الفُرْقان	The standard or criterion by which things are judged. A name of the Qur'an.	251
10	Al hamdulillah	اَلحَمْدُ لله	Praise be to Allah.	18
11	Al Huruf Al Muqatt'ah	الحُروف المُقَطَّعَة	Unique letters that appear in the beginning of twenty-nine suwar of the Qur'an, literally from disjointed or unconnected letters.	50
12	Al Khidr	الخِضْر	A man given extraordinary wisdom by Allah.	165
13	Al Rub' al Khali	الرُّبْعُ الخالي	The Empty Quarter. A region of southeastern Arabia.	121
14	Alhumdulillah	الحَمْدُ لله	Thanks and Praise to Allah.	225
15	Allah	الله	The name of God used by all Muslims and Arab regardless of their religious affiliation.	13
16	Allahu Akbar	الله أكبَر	God is the Greatest.	225
17	Amir	أمير	Leader.	215
18	Ammuriyah	عَمُّوريّة	A city in Palestine.	227
19	And to you peace.	وَعَلَيْكُم السَّلام	Response to Islamic greeting.	277
20	Angel Jibreel	جِبْريل	Angel of Revelation.	31
21	Angels	مَلائِكَة	Unseen creatures made from the elements of light and created for carrying out the commands of Allah.	89
22	Anonymous	مَجْهول	Unknown author or source.	138

Glossary

	Vocabulary Word	Arabic Script	Definition	Page
23	Arabic	اللُغَةُ العَرَبِيَّة	An advanced and comprehensive Semitic language in which the Qur'an was revealed and is spoken by Arab peoples and Muslims throughout the world.	18
24	Arkan al Emaan	أرْكانُ الإيمَان	Pillars of Belief.	56
25	Arkan al Islam	أرْكانُ الإسْلام	Pillars of Islam.	56
26	As-Salat al Ibrahimiyya	الصَّلاةُ الإبراهيْميَّة	The ending supplication of the Muslim prayer.	129
27	As-Siddeeq	الصِّدِّيق	The literally, "the Truth-Affirmer." The title of Abu Bakr ﷺ companion and close ally of Prophet Muhammad ﷺ.	242
28	Asyah	آسْيا	Wife of Pharaoh at the time of Prophet Musa (as).	153
29	Authentic	حَقيقيّ	Genuine.	138
30	Awlia'a	أوْلِياء	Protectors.	265
31	Ayaat	آيَات	Verses, literally 'signs,' of the Qur'an.	18
32	Azar	آزَر	Idol worshipper and father of Prophet Ibrahim ﷺ.	129
33	'Aziz Misr	عَزيزُ مِصْر	Minister of Egypt in story of Prophet Yusuf.	141
34	Az-Zahra'	الزَّهْراء	The title for Fatimah, daughter of Prophet Muhammad ﷺ, literally, The Shining Person.	224
35	Banu Daws Tribe	قَبيلَةُ بَني دَوْس	Arab tribe in the time of Prophet Muhammad ﷺ who lived along the coast of the Red Sea.	220
36	Banu Isra'il	بَنو إسْرائيل	Descendants of Prophet Ya'qub ﷺ.	153
37	Benjamin	بِنْيامين	Youngest brother of Prophet Yusuf ﷺ.	141
38	Big Bang Theory	الانْفِجارُ الكَبير	A theory of the creation of the Universe.	77
39	Colonialism	اسْتِعْمار	The act of dividing nations and establishing governments by Western powers.	291
40	Creationism	الخَلْق	A theory that God created the Universe in one step and at one moment.	84
41	Cyrus the Great	كورش الكبير	King of Persia 549 BCE.	179
42	Da'wah	الدَّعْوَة	Inviting others to Islam.	59
43	Dar As-Salam	دارُ السَّلام	Land of Peace.	285
44	Dawud	داود	Prophet who defeated Jalut and his army and carved out a secure country in Israel then became king. Father of Prophet Sulayman ﷺ.	173

Glossary

	Vocabulary Word	Arabic Script	Definition	Page
45	Dhabiha	ذَبِيحَة	Meat that is slaughtered according to Islamic regulations.	257
46	Dhul Qarnayn	ذُو القَرنَين	Literally, Master of the Two Horns. A pious and wise world explorer.	179
47	Disciple	حَوارِيّون	Companions or helpers of Prophet 'Isa.	194
48	Dua'	دُعاء	Personal supplication.	21
49	Emaan	إيْمان	Belief.	100
50	Etiquette	آداب	Manners.	23
51	Evolution	تَطَوُّر	A theory that all life happened and evolved by chance without divine intervention.	84
52	Faresi	فارِسيّ	Language or person of Persia.	227
53	Fatwa	فَتوى	Official, legal proclamation.	248
54	Fiqh	فِقه	The science of understanding legal positions in Islam.	248
55	Fitrah	فِطرَة	Basic natural way or instinct.	56, 57
56	Fus-ha	فُصحى	Standard, classical Arabic language.	37
57	Ghifar	غِفار	Tribe of Abu Dharr.	234
58	Ghusl	غُسل	Purifying wash necessary before prayer in specific circumstances.	23
59	Gospel	الإنجيل	Gospel, or proclamation of good news.	194
60	Habeel	هابيل	Abel, son of Adam.	110
61	Hafith (Hafiz)	حافِظ	One who has memorized the entire Qur'an.	37
62	Halal	حَلال	That which is allowed.	248
63	Halal Foods	الأطعِمَةُ الحَلال	Food that is allowable.	257
64	Haman	هامان	Pharaoh's second-in-command.	159
65	Haram	حَرام	That which is forbidden.	248
66	Haram Foods	الأطعِمَةُ الحَرام	Food that is forbidden.	257
67	Hawwa	حَوّاء	Frist created women and wife of Adam.	110
68	Hebrews	العِبرانِيّين	People of Prophet Musa who believed in one God and were enslaved by Pharaoh.	153

Glossary

	Vocabulary Word	Arabic Script	Definition	Page
69	Hieroglyphics	الهيروغليفيّة	Ancient Egyptian writing.	159
70	Hijrah	هِجْرَة	The migration or journey of Prophet Muhammad ﷺ and his followers from Makkah to Madinah.	34
71	Hud	هُود	Arabic prophet sent to the 'Aad people.	121
72	Hudhud	هُدْهُد	Hoopoe bird.	175
73	Hudood	حُدود	The limits or boundaries.	248
74	Human	بَشَر	Creature made from the earth with choices to do good or bad.	89
75	Ibrahim	إِبْراهيم	Great Prophet of Allah ﷻ through whom descended Prophets Musa ﷺ, 'Isa ﷺ and Muhammad ﷺ among others.	129
76	'Iddah	عِدّه	Waiting period for a woman following the death of her spouse.	213
77	Ihya 'Uloom Ad-Deen	إِحْياء عُلوم الدّين	The Reawakening of Knowledge of the Deen of Islam.	297
78	Ijma'a	إِجْماع	Agreement or consensus in numbers.	250
79	Ijtehad	اِجْتِهاد	Independent reasoning.	249
80	'Imran	عِمْران	Family name of Mary, mother of 'Isa ﷺ.	185
81	Injeel	الإِنْجيل	Revelation by Allah ﷻ to Prophet 'Isa ﷺ.	194
82	Iram	إِرَمَ ذاتِ العِمادِ	A lost city of tall structures destroyed by Allah ﷻ for its sins.	121
83	Ishaq	اسحاق	2nd born son of Prophet Ibrahim.	129
84	Islam	إِسْلام	1. A monotheistic religion based on revelations received by Prophet Muhammad ﷺ. 2. Derived from the Arabic word meaning peace and surrender.	13
85	Jalut	جالُوت	A soldier of great size and strength sent to fight Bani Isra'il.	173
86	Jihad	الجهاد	Striving.	59
87	Jinn	جن	Unseen creatures made of fireless smoke.	89
88	Jizyah	جِزْيَة	Taxes levied on non-Muslim citizens of Muslim lands.	294
89	Julaybib	جُلَيْبيب	Literally, "Little Woman's Dress." A martyr and lesser known companion of Prophet Muhammad ﷺ.	231

Glossary

	Vocabulary Word	Arabic Script	Definition	Page
90	Kafara	كَفَرَ	To cover up or hide something.	66
91	Kafir	كافِر	Disbeliever. Literally a person who denies or 'covers' the truth.	65
92	Khadijah	خَدِيْجَة	First wife of Prophet Muhammad and first to accept Islam.	31
93	Khalifa	خَلِيفة	Leader of the Muslim nation.	37
94	King	مَلِك	Ruler of a nation, usually inherited.	145
95	Kuffar	كُفَّار	Plural of kafir كافِر, or disbelievers.	65
96	Madhab	مَذْهَب	School of thought.	251
97	Madinan	مَدَنِيّ	Qur'anic revelations made while the Prophet resided in Madinah.	42
98	Madyan	مَدْين	Land located in the northern tip of the Arabian peninsula to whom Allah sent Prophet Salih.	153
99	Mahr	مَهْر	Marriage gift given by groom to bride.	223
100	Mahr	مَهْر	Dowry.	268
101	Majlis Ash-Shura	مَجْلِس الشُّورى	Body of representatives of consultation.	291
102	Majuj	مَأْجُوج	Disbelievers who caused great mischief.	181
103	Makkan	مَكِّيّ	Qur'anic revelations made while the Prophet resided in Makkah.	42
104	Makruh	مَكْرُوه	Not recommended.	248
105	Ma'roof and Munkar	الأمْرُ بِالمَعْرُوفِ والنَّهْيُ عَنِ المُنكَر	Encouraging good while forbidding evil.	59
106	Masih	مَسِيح	The Anointed, a title of Prophet Isa'.	190
107	Mount Judi	جَبَلُ الجُودِيّ	Location where the ark of Nuh came to land.	115
108	Muhkamat	مُحْكَمات	Clear in meaning.	41
109	Munaafiqoon	مُنافِقُون	Hypocrites.	65
110	Munir	مُنِير	Reflection of light.	45
111	Mus-haf	مُصْحَف	The original revealed Qur'an in Arabic only without explanation or transliteration.	18
112	Muslim	مُسْلِم	A person who submits to God by following the guidance of the Qur'an and the Sunnah of Prophet Muhammad thereby finding inner peace.	13

Glossary

	Vocabulary Word	Arabic Script	Definition	Page
113	Mutashabihat	مُتَشابهات	Mystical or allegorical in meaning.	41
114	Namrud	نَمْرُود	King of Ur, birthplace of Prophet Ibrahim.	129
115	Narrator	رَاوي	One who transmits Hadith.	220
116	Nasra	نَسْرا	Idol adopted by the ancestors of Nuh.	116
117	Nifaaq	نفاق	Hypocrisy.	65
118	Nikah	نكاح	Marriage or wedding ceremony.	223
119	Nikah	نِكاح	The Islamic term for the wedding ceremony	268
120	Nuh	نُوح	Prophet Noah who preached to his people for 950 years.	115
121	Ozone Layer	طَبَقَةُ الأُوزون	A protective layer above the earth.	77
122	Palestine	فِلَسْطين	An ancient land once promised to the descendants of Prophet Musa.	129
123	Peace be to you.	السَّلامُ عَلَيْكُم	The Islamic greeting between Muslims.	277
124	Peace be upon you and Allah's mercy and blessings.	السَّلامُ عَلَيْكُم وَرَحْمَةُ اللهِ وبَرَكاتُه	Response to Islamic greeting.	277
125	Peace be upon you and Allah's mercy.	السَّلامُ عَلَيْكُم ورحمة الله	The Islamic greeting between Muslims.	277
126	Persecute	يَضْطَهِد	To treat harshly or oppress.	203
127	Pharaoh	فِرْعون	Title of ruler of Egypt in ancient times.	145
128	Philosopher	فَيْلَسوف	A person engaged or learned in philosophy, esp. as an academic discipline.	89
129	Philosophers	الفَلاسِفَة	Those who study the rational investigation of the truths and principles of being, knowledge, or conduct.	89
130	Photosynthesis	التَّرْكيبُ الضَّوْئِيّ	The process by which green plants and some other organisms use sunlight to synthesize foods from carbon dioxide and water.	84
131	Prehistoric	ما قَبْلَ التَّاريخ	A period that existed previous to historical documentation.	115
132	Processed	طَعَام مُعالج	Many ingredients mixed together, often pre-cooked and ready to eat.	257
133	Prophet	رَسول	One who is chosen by God to speak, guide or warn his society.	31
134	Prophet 'Isa	عيسَى	Prophet of Allah sent to Bani Isra'il.	190

Glossary

	Vocabulary Word	Arabic Script	Definition	Page
135	Qabeel	قابيل	Cain, son of Adam.	110
136	Qadi	قَاضي	A judge.	291
137	Qiyaas	قِياس	Islamic jurisprudence.	250
138	Qur'an	قُرْآن	The Islamic Holy Book and last revelation of God to mankind, addressing all of humanity, revealed to Prophet Muhammad ﷺ.	13
139	Rabb Al 'Alameen	رَبُّ العالَمين	Lord of all the Universe.	86
140	Rabbi	الأخْبار	Jewish scholar or leader of congregation.	185
141	Revelation	وَحي	The primary way of communication from Allah ﷻ to mankind.	31
142	Riba	رِبا	Money accumulated through interest, usually on a loan in which the debtor owes more than the amount borrowed.	261
143	Ruh	رُوح	The spirit.	89
144	Saba'	سَبَأ	Tribes of ancient Yemen in the story of Prophet Sulayman ﷺ.	173
145	Sahaba	صَحابَة	Companion(s) of Prophet Muhammad ﷺ.	37
146	Sahabiyyat	صَحابِيّات	Female Companions of Prophet Muhammad ﷺ.	211
147	Samiri	سامِرِيّ	A man from the tribe of Banu Isra'il who fashioned an idol out of gold.	165
148	Scribe	كاتِب	One who writes what is dictated.	37
149	Scripture	الكِتابُ المُقَدَّس	Revealed word of God.	194
150	Sect	طائِفَة	A group adhering to a particular religious faith or denomination.	56
151	Sentient	واعٍ	Self-aware.	84
152	Shahadah	شَهادَة	The declaration that there is no god but Allah ﷻ, and Muhammad is His Messenger.	65
153	Shaheed	شَهيد	Martyr.	159
154	Shari'ah	شَريعَة	Islamic Law.	248
155	Shaytan	شَيْطان	Devil or Satan.	89
156	Shura	شُورى	Advisory council.	242

Glossary

	Vocabulary Word	Arabic Script	Definition	Page
157	Shura	شُورى	Mutual consultation.	280
158	Signs	آيات	Another word for ayaat or verses of the Qur'an.	45
159	Siraj	سِراج	Producer of light.	45
160	SubhanAllah	سُبْحانَ الله	Exalted or praised is Allah.	225
161	Suhuf	صُحُف	Scrolls of revelation given to Prophet Ibrahim.	129
162	Sunnah	سُنَّة	The example of Prophet Muhammad, including his actions and words.	13
163	Surat	سُورَة	Chapter of the Qur'an.	21
164	Suwa'	سَواع	Idol adopted by the ancestors of Prophet Nuh.	116
165	Synagogues	مَعْبَدٌ يَهودِيّ	Jewish places of communal worship.	185
166	Tadabbur	تَدَبُّر	Reflection.	23
167	Tafseer	تَفْسير	Commentary and explanation.	37
168	Talut	طالوت	Young man chosen to be the king of Bani Isra'il.	173
169	Taqwa	تَقْوى	God consciousness. Literally, that someone acts knowing that Allah sees him at all times.	70
170	Tawbah	تَوْبَة	Repentance.	100
171	Tawrah	تَوْراة	The Holy Book revealed by Allah to Prophet Musa.	165
172	The Iron Door	بابُ الحَديد	Iron wall that prevents Yajuj and Majuj from exiting and creating havoc.	181
173	The Mother of Her Father	أُمُّ أبيها	Nickname of Fatimah, daughter of Prophet Muhammad.	224
174	The Woman with the Two Belts	ذاتُ النِّطاقَين	Nickname of Asma bint Abu Bakr, sister of Ayesha.	238
175	Tilawah	تِلاوَه	Recitation of the Holy Qur'an.	23
176	Transliteration	التَّرجَمَةُ الصَّوتيَّة	The representation of letters or words in the corresponding characters in the alphabet of another language.	21
177	Trinitarians	المُؤمِنينَ بالتَّثليث	Christians who believe that God is comprised of three separate and distinct beings: Father, Son and Holy Spirit.	203
178	Ubar	أوبار	An ancient destroyed by Allah for its sins.	121

Glossary

	Vocabulary Word	Arabic Script	Definition	Page
179	'Ulama'	عُلَماء	Scholars of Islam.	248
180	'Umar Bin Al Khattab	عُمَرُ بْنُ الخَطَّاب	Fierce enemy of Islam who became one of greatest Sahaba of Prophet Muhammad ﷺ and 2nd khalifa.	34
181	Umuhat al Mu'mineen	أُمَّهاتُ المُؤْمِنين	Mothers of the Believers (wives of Prophet Muhammad ﷺ).	211
182	Unitarians	المُوَحِّدُون	Christians believing in the oneness of God.	203
183	Uzayr	عُزَيْر	Prophet of Allah ﷻ whom some of the Bani Israel take as 'son' of God.	185
184	Wali	وَلِيّ	Protective guardian for a young woman who is persuing marriage.	266
185	Walimah	وَليمَة	Public reception or party announcing a marriage.	268
186	Wife of 'Aziz Misr	زَوْجَةُ العَزيز	Wife of the Minister of Egypt in the story of Prophet Yusuf ﷺ.	141
187	Wud	ود	Idol adopted by the ancestors of Prophet Nuh ﷺ.	116
188	Wudu'	وُضوء	An obligatory washing of specific body parts prior to making Salah (the prayer).	23
189	Ya'uq	يَعوق	Idol adopted by the ancestors of Prophet Nuh ﷺ.	116
190	Yaghuth	يَغوث	Idol adopted by the ancestors of Prophet Nuh ﷺ.	116
191	Yajuj	يَأْجوج	Disbelievers who caused great mischief.	181
192	Yaqui	يَعْقوب	Prophet of Allah ﷻ and father of Prophet Yusuf ﷺ.	141
193	Zamzam	زَمْ زَمْ	Miraculous well in the desert revealed to Hajar, the wife of Prophet Ibrahim ﷺ that continues to flow today.	129